Under the Crescent Moon with the XI Corps in the Civil War

Volume 2: From Gettysburg to Victory, 1863-1865

James S. Pula

Savas Beatie
California

Library of Congress Cataloging-in-Publication Data

Names: Pula, James S., 1946- author.
Title: Under the Crescent Moon with the XI Corps in the Civil War / by James S. Pula.
Description: First edition. | El Dorado Hills, California: Savas Beatie, 2017. |
Includes bibliographical references and index. Contents: v. 1.
From the Defenses of Washington to Chancellorsville, 1862-1863
v. 2. From Gettysburg to victory, 1863-1865.
Identifiers: LCCN 2017017368 | ISBN 9781611213379 (vol. 1: alk. paper) |
ISBN 9781611213386 (vol. 1: ebk.) | ISBN 978-1-61121-390-4 - hardcover
(vol. 2: alk paper) |
ISBN 9781611213911 (vol. 2: ebk.)
Subjects: LCSH: United States. Army of the Potomac. Corps, 11th. | United
States--History--Civil War, 1861-1865--Regimental histories. | United
States--History--Civil War, 1861-1865--Campaigns.
Classification: LCC E493.1 11th .P85 2017 | DDC 973.7/3--dc23
LC record available at https://lccn.loc.gov/2017017368

First Edition, First Printing

SB

Published by
Savas Beatie LLC
989 Governor Drive, Suite 102
El Dorado Hills, CA 95762

Phone: 916-941-6896
(web) www.savasbeatie.com
(E-mail) sales@savasbeatie.com

FSC
www.fsc.org
MIX
Paper from
responsible sources
FSC® C011935

Savas Beatie titles are available at special discounts for bulk purchases in the United States by corporations, institutions, and other organizations. For more details, please contact Savas Beatie, P.O. Box 4527, El Dorado Hills, CA 95762, or you may e-mail us at sales@savasbeatie.com, or visit our website at www.savasbeatie.com for additional information.

Proudly printed in the United States of America

Für Silvia mit Liebe und Bewunderung

Table of Contents

Table of Contents (continued)

Photos and Illustrations have been placed throughout the book for the convenience of the reader.

Introduction

THE XI CORPS WAS FORMED in the dark days following the lengthy series of Federal defeats in the Shenandoah Valley, on the Peninsula, and at Second Bull Run in the spring and summer of 1862. With the consolidation of the Army of the Potomac with Gen. John Pope's short-lived Army of Virginia, the new corps was organized around 17 regiments from Gen. Franz Sigel's corps that had served under Pope. It was supplemented with eleven newly-recruited regiments raised in response to President Abraham Lincoln's summer call for 300,000 new troops. Even with these additions, it was under strength compared to the other corps in the Army of the Potomac and would remain so throughout its existence.

By the end of 1862 the corps contained twelve infantry regiments from New York, seven from Ohio, five from Pennsylvania, and one each from Connecticut, Illinois, Massachusetts, and Wisconsin. Its six batteries of light artillery included three from New York and three from Ohio. Nearly two-thirds of the units were "veterans," the balance being new recruits. Sigel's original command had been built around Gen. Ludwig Blenker's "German" division that served under Gen. John Frémont in the Shenandoah Valley against Stonewall Jackson. Most of its senior German officers had served in the revolutions of the European "Springtime of Nations" and were staunchly anti-slavery. The new additions to the corps diluted the German character to less than half of the troops—although it nevertheless continued to be known throughout the Army of the Potomac as the "German" corps—but they did not weaken the support for emancipation. Among the newcomers were the German abolitionists Friedrich Hecker, Bernhard Domschcke, and Elias Peissner, along with noted inventor Elias Howe and his son, Harriet Beecher Stowe's son Frederick, and Augustus C. Hamlin, the nephew of Vice President Hannibal Hamlin.

Gen. Ambrose Burnside held the XI Corps in reserve at Fredericksburg. Although some of its officers observed that bloodbath from afar, the men were fortunately spared the slaughter. After participating in Burnside's abortive "Mud March," the corps settled into winter camp while the army underwent a change of command. Its new leader, Gen. Joseph Hooker, undertook the difficult task of restoring morale following months of successive defeats. He did this by attending to the troops' needs—arranging for back pay to be distributed, providing better food, issuing new uniforms and equipment, and boosting unit pride through new corps insignia and the listing of engagements on regimental colors. To facilitate command, Hooker reorganized the army, eliminating the former "Grand Divisions" so that corps leaders reported directly to the commanding general. In the process, Sigel protested what appeared to him to be a demotion from Grand Division to corps leadership, with his corps being the smallest despite his relative seniority. The resulting quarrel led to the German's resignation.

Maj. Gen. Oliver Otis Howard arrived from outside the corps to assume command from Sigel, but the troops did not take to him nor he to them. A very devout New Englander, his excessive religiosity distanced some from him while his replacement of the popular Sigel, at the expense, many believed, of another popular German, Gen. Carl Schurz, aggravated the internal divide between "German" and "native American" troops. The corps carried this lack of harmony into its first major campaign, still the smallest unit of that level in the army.

The Chancellorsville Campaign began with high hopes. Hooker led part of his army, including the XI Corps, on a wide flanking move that placed his force behind Gen. Robert E. Lee's army at Fredericksburg, seemingly trapped between Hooker and the balance of the Federal army facing Lee's position. Although he had the initiative, Hooker called a halt to his advance, giving Lee an opportunity to respond. The rebel leader did so by sending forces to hold Hooker's attention while dispatching Stonewall Jackson with most of his available men on an enveloping movement of his own to come in behind the right flank of the Federal position, the location held by the XI Corps.

In the early morning of May 2, 1863, Hooker inspected Howard's dispositions and suggested some changes, following up his verbal recommendations with specific written orders to guard against a possible attack from the right flank. Throughout the day, repeated warnings arrived at Howard's headquarters from the nearby III Corps and from officers in the XI Corps informing him that large numbers of Confederate troops were marching across the corps front toward the exposed flank. Howard not only ignored them, taking no action whatever to attend to the weakness of his dispositions, but absented himself from his own command for some two hours during the late afternoon. While he did so, Jackson formed 33,000 men in position to assault less than one-third their number placed in completely untenable positions.

The Confederate storm rolled forward about 5:30 pm, smashing into the outnumbered Federals end-on, perpendicular to the XI Corps line, so that the rebels could envelop individual regiments and brigades with their greatly superior numbers.

The Federals fought back desperately, withdrawing from successive positions only when in danger of being surrounded, maintaining as best they could the unequal contest. By nightfall, the corps suffered over 2,400 casualties, nearly a quarter of those engaged. Despite their sacrifice, in the wake of the eventual Federal defeat the men of the XI Corps were cruelly chastised as cowards by the press and the rest of the army. The brunt of the condemnation fell unjustly on the German element in the corps, leading in some cases to internal dissension as well.

Rather than support his men, Howard appeared to blame them for his own failures. To make matters worse, he brought in some officers from outside the corps and promoted Brig. Gen. Francis Barlow, who was known to despise the Germans, to division command. These moves only served to exacerbate the troops' injured morale and the ethnic divisions within the corps. It was under the weight of this emotional baggage that the XI Corps began its march north toward Gettysburg, the burden increasing as Barlow's attempts to enforce rigid discipline further distanced him from his men.

Lee's army was already scores of miles ahead in the race north by the time the corps received orders to pursue. Through blazing sun, along Virginia's parched roads with clouds of smothering dust they trudged, occasionally swept by drenching rain that turned the dried powder into instant mud. Heckled along the way when they met troops from other corps, the men nevertheless marched well, perhaps intent upon redeeming their reputation after the Chancellorsville disaster. On they went, crossing the Potomac into Maryland where for once they received warm greetings from the inhabitants. Through Jefferson and Poolesville, Middletown and Frederick, on they marched to Emmitsburg where they camped amid the rolling grounds and religious serenity of the Sisters of Charity at St. Mary's and St. Joseph's Colleges on the night of June 30.

Tired from their exertions, some of the men took time to go to Communion, some wrote letters home, others simply went to sleep. While they slept that night couriers rushed to and fro with orders for the morrow. Confederate infantry had been reported on the outskirts of the soon-to-be-famous town of Gettysburg some thirteen miles distant and Maj. Gen. George Gordon Meade, the Army of the Potomac's newly appointed commander, was busy ordering the various corps into position to meet the threat. July 1 would no doubt be the last day on earth for many of those enjoying their sleep that night.

In addition to those acknowledged at the beginning of Volume 1 of *Under the Crescent Moon*, I would like to offer my thanks to the following who provided material for this volume after the previous one was already in print: Clay Feeter, Rex D. Hovey, and Jeffrey Stocker.

James S. Pula
Purdue University Northwest

Chapter 10

"Every Pulse Beats Louder"

Morning, July 1, 1863

IT WAS JUST GETTING DARK when an aide knocked on the door of Maj. Gen. Oliver Otis Howard's room at Rev. J. Francis Burlando's residence. Wearily, he rose to see what had interrupted his sleep. It was a message from Maj. Gen. John Reynolds commanding the I Corps requesting that Howard meet him at his headquarters some six miles north near Marsh Run. Howard quickly set off with his brother Charles, Lt. F. W. Gilbreth and an orderly. When he arrived, Reynolds showed him an order from Maj. Gen. George Gordon Meade giving Reynolds command of the I, III, and XI Corps and "handed me the confidential appeal which General Meade had just made to his army commanders. The purport of these papers was that a general engagement was imminent, the issues involved immense, and all commanders urged to extraordinary exertions." Then, "we next went over the news dispatches of the day. They were abundant and conflicting. They came from headquarters at Taneytown, from Buford at Gettysburg, from scouts, from alarmed citizens, from all directions. They, however, forced the conclusion upon us, that Lee's infantry and artillery in great force were in our neighborhood."[1]

After some time, Howard returned to Emmitsburg where he issued orders for his corps to be prepared to march as soon as ordered. He then tried to catch some rest while the necessary preparations were made, but once more found his attempt

1 Howard report on Gettysburg, Aug. 31, 1863, Clements Library; Howard, "Gen'l O. O. Howard's Reminiscences," 241; Howard, *Autobiography*, I, 402-04.

thwarted by the evening's rapidly developing events. "It could not have been an hour before a loud knocking at the door aroused me" around 3:30 am. It was a new messenger, Lt. William Riddle, bringing orders from Gen. Meade. "I took the bundle of papers in my hand. The address was to Reynolds as the wing commander. To forestall the possibility of their loss between Emmitsburg and Marsh Run, I opened the dispatches, as was customary, read them, and sent them forward with a note." The papers instructed Howard to move the XI Corps to within supporting distance of the I Corps. Howard immediately dispatched an aide to Reynolds with the papers seeking further instructions.[2] In the meantime, the camps began to stir as orders filtered down to brigades, regiments, batteries, and supply trains. By sunrise the drowsy campsite had become a hub of activity.

In the 17th Connecticut, William Warren arose early to cook breakfast before the regiment fell in for roll call. Rowland Howard heard the bands playing "lively airs" and the drummer boys beating their instruments "merrily" while men packed their belongings before falling into ranks. Adj. Theodore Dodge wrote in his diary that morning the notation that a circular arrived from General Meade "calling upon every man and Officer to do his duty in the approaching Battle." Also making the rounds through the camps that morning was General Orders No. 17, issued by Howard to bolster the troops' morale: "During the late long and fatiguing marches I have noticed great diligence and cheerfulness in the performance of duty. Whatever march has been ordered, this Corps has accomplished. I cannot give too high commendation for the work performed and the spirit exhibited since we left Brooke's Station. Our Commanding General believes we shall soon meet the enemy. I need not refer to the issues involved in this struggle. Every friend of the country is looking to this Army with intense anxiety. If you are blessed with complete success, the war is over and the Country is saved. But if we fail the war is indefinitely prolonged. I feel that this Corps has special reasons for doing well and I doubt not that the next engagement will silence for ever every aspersion that has been carelessly or maliciously heaped upon us. I confidently expect a hearty co-operation from the officers and men of this Command."[3]

2 Howard, *Autobiography*, 402, 404; Howard report on Gettysburg, Aug. 31, 1863, Clements Library; Howard manuscript report on Gettysburg, Vertical File 5, GNMP; Howard, "Howard's Reminiscences," *National Tribune*, November 20, 1884; Bachelder, *History*, 241; William Riddle to Lt. Bouvier, Aug. 4, 1863, John Reynolds Folder, GNMP.

3 Warren diary, July 1, 1863; Rowland Howard, "The Story of Gettysburg," Bowdoin College; Dodge diary, July 1, 1863; General Orders No. 17, RG 393, Pt. 2, 5348, NARA.

While the troops prepared for the move, Howard communicated the line of march to the various commands. Schurz's Third Division would lead the column accompanied by Dilger's battery, to be prepared to move by 7:00 am. Von Steinwehr's Second Division, along with Wheeler's battery, to be ready by 7:30 am. The remaining three batteries would march between the Second Division and Barlow's First Division, the latter to be prepared to move by 8:15 am. At the end would be the baggage train followed by a regiment of the First Division acting as rear guard. With expectations high that there would be a confrontation, Howard was careful to divest his column of unnecessary encumbrances, specifying that "All empty wagons, surplus baggage, useless animals and impedimenta of every sort [is] to be sent to Union Bridge." He was also careful to impress upon the officers and men the need for speed: "The troops must be as light as possible so as to be able to move as rapidly as possible when and wherever ordered. On the march the troops must march in close Order, shortening the column as much as possible. Straggling must be prevented entirely. Whenever practicable the column must be shortened by forming column of platoons or companies."[4]

Howard's aide returned with orders from Reynolds directing the XI Corps to march to Gettysburg some eleven miles distant. The troops took to the road beneath a cloudy sky with the temperature already reaching 72° by 7:00 am. Lt. Col. Meysenburg found the road to Marsh Creek "passable" but suffering serious damage "from frequent use" so that in places it was "almost impassable." Soon the head of the column came upon the rear of the I Corps, its sluggish wagon trains clogging the road and slowing the march. To save time, Howard ordered Schurz, von Steinwehr and four of the artillery batteries to leave the direct route into Gettysburg along the Emmitsburg Road by turning right near the Moritz tavern onto a road through Horner's Mill to the Taneytown Road. Although two miles longer than the original route, it was clear of the detritus of the I Corps so the march would be unimpeded. Barlow was to continue along the main road in rear of the I Corps. His troops now in motion, and with specific marching orders, Howard turned temporary command of the corps over to Schurz and rode ahead with his staff through the fields adjoining the road to find out what was happening and where Reynolds wished his men placed when they arrived.[5]

4 Howard, Circular, July 1, 1863, RG 393, Pt. 2, 5321, NARA; *OR* 27, pt. 1, 747.

5 Meysenburg journal, July 1, 1863; Nofi, *Gettysburg Campaign*, 168; Michael Jacobs' observations, July 1, GNMP; Howard report on Gettysburg, Vertical File 5, GNMP; Chapman Biddle, *The First Day at Gettysburg*, Box B-32-1, GNMP, 24; Howard report on Gettysburg, Aug. 31, 1863, Clements Library; Howard, "Howard's Reminiscences," *National Tribune*, November 20, 1884.

Behind the general, his men labored over the rutted roads through a slowly warming morning. The column marched at common time of ninety steps per minute, covering about seventy yards in that time, but without the normal ten minute rest each hour. William Warren recalled that "Many of the boys fell out" after covering five or six miles without a break, while Adj. Dodge recorded in his diary around 10:00 am that "We have now crossed the Border and are in Pennsylvania. The marching is wretched and the atmosphere is so oppressively close that the men scarcely make any way at all, if we march ten miles to-day we shall do well." When a brief halt was finally ordered, William Southerton remembered that "The boys dropped to the ground almost like dead men, so terrific was the heat and humidity, and our woolen uniforms so unbearable."[6]

Stuck behind the slow-moving wagons of the I Corps, Barlow was determined not to lose any more time than absolutely necessary because of the obstructions before him. William Paynton in the 17th Connecticut recalled that the general issued stern orders that "straggling was strictly forbidden–that the ranks must be kept closed up, and regimental and company commanders would be held accountable for the violation of said order." Barlow's aides rode up and down the marching column to enforce the edict. "The day was very hot and the men became thirsty; the water in their canteens was consumed quickly," explained Paynton. "A soldier belonging to the 17th Regiment, while crossing a brook that ran by the roadside, stepped out of the ranks to dip a cup of water to quench his thirst." One of the general's passing aides observed the transgression and reported it to his commander. Barlow reacted in his usual fashion by immediately ordering Lt. Col. Douglas Fowler placed under arrest for failure to maintain discipline. Upon receiving the news, Fowler turned his sword over to Chaplain William Hall and rode to the rear of his regiment, the traditional place for an officer under arrest. When the column finally halted for a brief rest, men gathered around him vowing not to go into action unless he led them. Warning against anything rash, Fowler cautioned them to obey orders and soon the march resumed.[7]

☽ ☽ ☽

General Howard, with his staff and a small escort, trotted toward Gettysburg as quickly as the broken ground would allow. At some point near Marsh Creek the sound of artillery fire reached the group. Major William Riddle, one of General Reynolds'

6 Warren, diary, July 1, 1863; Dodge diary, July 1, 1863; Southerton, "What We Did There," 4.

7 Paynton, "From Virginia to Gettysburg and Back," manuscript, GNMP.

Lt. Col. Douglas Fowler, 17th Connecticut
U.S. Army Heritage and Education Center

staff, trotted up with orders for Howard to "Come quite up to Gettysburg." As the group continued forward nearing the vicinity of the Sherfy peach orchard, Howard asked the aide where Reynolds wished him to place his corps. "Stop anywhere about here," came the reply, "according to your judgment at present." From the rising ground around the orchard Howard could see, ahead and to his left, smoke rising about a mile and a half away. The sounds of both artillery and musketry were clearly audible as he watched men from the I Corps moving across the open fields into position along a slight ridge to the west of town. Turning to Captain Daniel Hall of his staff, Howard ordered the aide to locate Reynolds, report on the progress of the corps, and ask for specific orders on where the general wanted him to place it.[8]

Captain Hall spurred his horse north along the Emmitsburg Road. To the northwest he could see smoke rising from the fighting erupting beyond a seminary. In the distance he believed he could make out Reynolds from his corps headquarters flag, so he abandoned the roadway and spurred his mount across the open fields. He caught up with Reynolds near the front lines, presented Howard's compliments, and delivered the message entrusted to him. Reynolds responded that he had "encountered the enemy apparently in force" and to tell Howard to bring the XI Corps forward "as rapidly as possible." He did not specify an exact location for its deployment. Hall turned his horse back toward where he expected to find Howard, but went only a short

8 Howard, *Autobiography*, 409, 411; C. H. Howard manuscript on first day at Gettysburg, Box 3, C. H. Howard Papers, Maine; Hall to Howard, May 20, 1882, Howard Papers, VFM 917, OHS; Howard report on Gettysburg, Vertical File 5, GNMP; Howard report on Gettysburg, August 31, 1863, Clements Library; Howard speech on Gettysburg, Box 154, Folder 11 1/2, May 30, 1894, Bowdoin College; Riddle to Howard, April 3, 1864, Howard Papers; Hall to Howard, May 20, 1882, Howard Papers, VFM 917, OHS.

distance before Reynolds' orderly raced up to inform him that the general had been wounded.[9]

After dispatching Hall, Howard decided to familiarize himself with the area as quickly as possible. Seeking a better viewpoint than the Sherfy orchard he moved off to the right of the Emmitsburg Road onto Cemetery Ridge, moving north up the gradually rising ground to Cemetery Hill which provided him with a much better location for observation. Accompanied by Meysenburg, his assistant adjutant general, Howard swiftly moved his field glasses from left to right and back, taking in the general topography, the town, and the scene of fighting along a ridge to the west. Then, removing the glasses from his eyes, he turned to Meysenburg: "This seems to be a good position, Colonel." "It is the only position, General," the colonel replied.[10]

Realizing he would no doubt have to deploy Schurz's division as soon as it arrived, Howard sent an aide to carry a message to von Steinwehr to take possession of the hill as soon as he arrived. These were the first troops ordered to what would become the lynchpin of the defenses at Gettysburg. This done, the small group began to move once again toward town as Howard dispatched his brother Charles to find Reynolds to obtain information on the situation and any new orders. The general then entered town, his eyes fixed on the belfry of the court house where he hoped to gain a closer look at the battle lines to the west and the progress of the XI Corps to the south. Although Howard was unable to find any stairway leading to the desired surveillance position, Daniel A. Skelly, a local youth, approached with the suggestion that he try the Fahnestock Observatory on the roof of the building across the street. Ascending to the location, Howard was "delighted with the open view." Turning to the west, he could clearly see fighting around the railroad cut with a long line of Confederate prisoners being led to the rear.

In the street below, a cavalryman, Sergt. George Guinn, reined in his sweating horse. Looking up, he shouted "General Reynolds is wounded, sir." "I am very sorry," the general replied, "I hope he will be able to keep the field." Only a few moments later Major William Riddle arrived with the news that the general was dead. Almost immediately Captain Hall rode up: "General Howard, General Reynolds is dead and you are the senior officer on the field." "God helping us," Howard replied, "we will

9 Hall to Howard, May 20, 1882, Howard Papers, VFM 917, OHS.

10 Howard, *Autobiography*, 409-10; C. H. Howard manuscript on first day at Gettysburg, Box 3, Bowdoin College; Howard, "Howard's Reminiscences," *National Tribune*, November 20, 1884; Howard report on Gettysburg, Vertical File 5, GNMP; Howard speech on Gettysburg, Box 154, Folder 11 1/2, May 30, 1894, Bowdoin College; C. H. Howard, "First Day," 242.

stay here till the army comes." To Skelly, Howard appeared "perfectly calm and self possessed."[11]

Soon, Major Howard returned to confirm Reynolds' death. The general reacted quickly to the weight of the new responsibilities thrust upon him. He ordered Hall to ride as fast as he could to and XI Corps artillery chief, Major Thomas Osborn, to hurry the guns forward as quickly as possible and then to inform Schurz to assume command of the XI Corps. Next, he dispatched Captain Edward P. Pearson with instructions for Barlow and then to continue on south to find Gen. Daniel Sickles to ask that he move his III Corps forward "as quickly as possible." Another messenger, Capt. Abram Sharra of the 1st Indiana Cavalry, Howard's headquarters guard, raced toward Littlestown to locate Gen. Henry Slocum with a request "to hasten to Gettysburg with his corps." Finally, he sent instructions to Gen. Abner Doubleday, now commanding the I Corps, and Gen. John Buford, commanding the cavalry units, to report their situations. Having sent communications to all of the commanders in the area, Howard moved to Cemetery Hill where he established his headquarters in anticipation of holding the heights as a rallying point should the army be driven back from its forward position.[12]

☽ ☽ ☽

There were five regiments from Pennsylvania in the XI Corps. As each approached its home state colors were uncased and musicians prepared for the occasion. The regiments crossed the border "ruffling their drums, dipping their colors, and cheering as they stepped upon her soil." Shortly after Krzyzanowski's brigade crossed the Mason-Dixon Line into the Keystone State the muffled thud of artillery fire could be heard in the distance. An orderly soon arrived, bringing news of skirmishing. Gen. Reynolds was about to go into action, he said, and the XI Corps should move forward to support the I Corps as quickly as possible. The "march was

11 Howard, *Autobiography*, 411-12; Pfanz, *The First Day*, 138; C. H. Howard manuscript on first day at Gettysburg, Box 3, Bowdoin College; Hall to Howard, May 20, 1882, Howard Papers, VFM 917, OHS; Howard report on Gettysburg, Vertical File 5, GNMP; Howard speech on Gettysburg, Box 154, Folder 11 1/2, May 30, 1894, Bowdoin College; C. H. Howard, "First Day," 242; Howard, "Address at Syracuse University," 75. The soldier's name is often spelled Gwinn, but Daniel Skelly, who knew him, spelled it Guinn. Apparently Guinn lived only a few miles south of Gettysburg before the war.

12 Howard, *Autobiography*, 412; C. H. Howard manuscript on first day at Gettysburg, Box 3, Bowdoin College; Howard report on Gettysburg, Vertical File 5, GNMP; C. H. Howard, "First Day," 242; Howard report on Gettysburg, Aug. 31, 1863, Clements Library.

Col. James S. Robinson, 82nd Ohio
National Archives

hastened with all possible speed." A driving rainstorm began turning the earthen roads into a slippery goo, drenching the struggling troops. "Now commenced a most toilsome and fatiguing march," Adj. Albert Wallber recalled. "We reached the hilly country and, running, climbed rocky hills. The rain fell in torrents; the atmosphere was extremely sultry, so that the soldiers, burdened with their accoutrements, heavily-packed knapsacks, blankets, haversacks and arms could proceed onward only with the greatest exertion. But Orderlies, one after another, came galloping up, spurring us on in haste. We heard the roaring of cannon at a distance."[13]

Capt. Bernhard Domschcke rode his horse "Up and down miles of improved and unimproved roads, over fields and fences, across creeks and swamps filled by long rains the day before—then the command from Gettysburg: Come here as fast as you can! One of our hardest and most tiring treks began at once. Soon we reached the hilly region and scaled rocky heights on the run. Rain cascaded on soldiers scarcely able to proceed. Yet new orders demanded all possible speed." Those with footwear slogged along, water soaking their shoes while the mud sucked at their feet in an effort to tear the coverings from them. Col. James S. Robinson of the 82nd Ohio remembered how the column eventually halted a few moments to give the troops a brief rest. "The rain came down in torrents. The soldiers prepared to make their accustomed tin cup of coffee, when through the heavy mists we were startled by the dull, thudding sound, which only issues from the mouths of cannon, but when first heard leaves us in doubt whether it may not be thunder. We listen. In a few seconds all doubts are put to rest. . . . Aids came dashing along the line before we had time to fall in, with peremptory orders to *double-quick* our commands on that hot July day. How little men on horseback reflect

13 Lee, "Reminiscences of the Gettysburg Battle," 54-55; *OR* 27, pt. 1, 739-40; Howard, *Autobiography*, 408; Love, *Wisconsin*, 417; Wallber, "From Gettysburg to Libby Prison," 191-92.

on such an occasion. If they had once marched in the ranks they would never have issued such a ridiculous order."[14]

Adj. Dodge, one of those on horseback, thought the marching "leisurely enough" until Lt. Edward Brueninghausen, the assistant adjutant general for Krzyzanowski's brigade, "rode down the column," calling to Col. John T. Lockman to "Keep your men well in hand, Colonel, and close them up—there's fighting to do ahead!" Brueninghausen continued on down the line, delivering the same message to each regiment. "Now is the time to watch the countenances of the men," Dodge observed. "Here one whose face may be a shade paler, but his eye is none the less lustrous, nor his lips less firmly knit, as he weighs his inclination with his duty. Beside him lags a dead-beat, who five minutes hence will complain of sore feet, and make every excuse, and look for every chance to drop out and straggle; not far off, the bragging fellow, whom you would dub a lion from his words and a hare from his deeds; who will talk loud, and vent his gasconade on every side, but who will be as far to the rear in the coming broil as he can get, by skulking or deliberately running away. The boy, fair-faced and small, scarce eighteen years old, that trudges behind him, whistling to keep his courage up and drown the remembrance of mother's kiss and sister's smile left far behind at home, a pigmy compared with his file leader, and probably often a sufferer from the bully's coarseness and ill-nature, is yet an unconscious hero. *He* will be in line when the braggart is skulking in the rear; he will do the work which the dead-beat avoids; he will march on with sore and blistered feet; he will stick to the ranks till he is shot down and crippled. At such a time it is easy to tell who is to be relied upon, and who to be spotted as a shirk or a coward."[15]

About 10:30 am Schurz's division was passing Horner's Mill. There the rain ceased, revealing a bright, humid July day. Capt. Winkler, acting as an aide to Schurz, was riding at the head of the divisional column along with Capt. Hubert Dilger. From some distance in front of them, and off to the left, the sound of firing reached them, but Winkler thought little of it. "[I]t was the same kind of firing that we have heard very often on our marches of late," he explained, "and we attributed it to a cavalry fight." An aide to Gen. Howard approached with the intelligence that he had just passed "a high point about a mile to the left of the road where the firing could be seen plainly." Winkler and Dilger decided to have a look for themselves. They turned their horses to the left toward the hillock, but covered only a short distance when the firing stopped,

14 Domschcke, *Twenty Months*, 27; James S. Robinson, address at the dedication of the 82nd Ohio's Gettysburg monument. GNMP.

15 Dodge, "Left Wounded on the Field," 317-18.

so they turned back toward the laboring column. Along the way they "found several splendid cherry trees laden with ripe cherries and stopped to eat." When they finally rejoined the troops they found Schurz listening to firing ahead that had "re-opened and became quite fierce." Somewhere along the road they met Major Osborn who, after receiving Howard's order to hurry the batteries forward, "rode back to the several batteries and gave them orders to proceed to the front as rapidly as possible. Two of them I passed up to the head of the column, or near it, and then joined Howard at the front."[16]

Schurz sent an aide to Brig. Gen. Alexander Schimmelfennig, the next ranking officer, to place him in charge of the division with orders to move it along with all speed. Then, accompanied by the remainder of his staff, he rushed ahead to find out what was happening and where the division should be placed when it arrived. Within a few minutes "I met on the road fugitives from Gettysburg, men, women and children, who seemed to be in great terror. I remember especially a middle-aged woman, who tugged a small child by the hand and carried a large bundle on her back. She tried to stop me, crying out at the top of her voice: 'Hard times at Gettysburg! They are shooting and killing! What will become of us!'"[17]

Lt. Louis Fischer of the 74th Pennsylvania was marching with the division's pioneer company near the head of the column directly behind Schurz and his staff. About 10:00 am, by his reckoning, "the distant boom of cannon informed us of an engagement going on." Schurz immediately ordered the regiments forward at the double-quick, "this gait being kept up to the battlefield, with only short breathing intermissions." Off they went at 110 steps per minute that moved the column forward 86 yards every sixty seconds. Struggling forward, the troops fought to maintain their footing in the slippery mud. From above, a now unshielded sun beat down upon them without mercy. "Oh, that double-quick!" recalled William Southerton of the 75th Ohio. "Like a dog trot. Exhausting in the heat of mid-day. . . . Some dropped with sun-stroke and exhaustion. An ambulance drove along with the column and picked up all it could. The ambulance was only a jolty wagon, but little better than nothing. At times we checked for a little rest. Then hurried on at the double-quick. Blanket, blouse,

16 Winkler, *Letters*, June 26 to July 8, 1863; Crumb, *Eleventh*, 9, 59; Osborn, "Annals of the War," *Weekly Times*, May 31, 1879.

17 Schurz, *Reminiscences*, III, 4-5; *OR* 27, pt. 1, 727.

Col. George von Amsberg, 45th New York
National Archives

any article that could be disposed of was thrown away. Fields were dotted with the discard."[18]

Col. George von Amsberg, a native of Hildesheim who had commanded a Hungarian hussar regiment in the Austrian army before joining the Hungarian Revolution along with his troops, led the 45th New York. He had been on the road since 6:30 am marching alternately through a downpour that soaked uniforms, equipment and men, turning roads quickly into a slimy, slippery mud, and a sunny humidity that only magnified the sweat pouring from the men's bodies under their heavy woolen uniforms. Their hearts pounding from exertion mixed with the dread of approaching battle, the men were greeted near Marsh Run by another courier with orders to hurry. Col. von Amsberg ordered the double-quick for the final miles into town. The sweating column began to struggle. Men dropped out, recovered, strained to catch up, often only to fall out again from the exertion.[19]

18 Fischer, "At Gettysburg," manuscript version of an article submitted to the *National Tribune*, Dec. 12, 1869, 74th Pennsylvania File, GNMP; Southerton, "What We Did There," 5.

19 Zucker, *Forty-Eighters*, 272; Kaufmann, *Die Deutschen*, 478; *New York Monuments Commission Report*, I, 378; Ley to the New York Monuments Commission, Sept. 8, 1896, Grand Army of the Republic File, Department of New York Records, Box 25, Folder 19, 45th New York, New York State Archives (hereafter Ley letter); Christian Böhm, Address at the dedication of the monument of the 45th New York at Gettysburg, printed in German in Fox, *New York at Gettysburg*, I, 375-77 (hereafter Böhm address); Böhm address; Ley letter; Biddle, *The First Day*, 117; Louis Lindemeyer pension papers, *National Archives*; Francis Irsch pension papers, National Archives; *New York Monuments Commission Report*, I, 378. Various authors have suggested that there was an interval of time between the arrival of the last units of the I Corps and the first units of the XI Corps. Statements by veterans of the 45th New York and other regiments in first XI Corps brigade to arrive on the scene note that as they approached units of the I Corps were only then crossing fields toward Seminary Ridge preparing to reinforce units already engaged. This is further substantiated by Gen. Doubleday, commanding the I Corps, who asserted that "Howard's corps was already passing through the streets of the town, and the

Sweating, gasping for air, their legs tired with the weight of the miles, the men arrived at the outskirts of town. The I Corps was in trouble and needed support to prevent its right flank from being turned. The men of the XI Corps were about to be plunged once again into the vortex of mortal combat.

☽ ☽ ☽

Sometime around 11:00 am Schurz approached Gettysburg along the Taneytown Road. Spotting Howard's headquarters flag atop Cemetery Hill he spurred his horse up the slope. There he learned that Reynolds had been killed, Howard had command of the field, and he was now commanding the XI Corps. From his viewpoint he quickly drew a mental picture of the area, noting the I Corps engaged on the ridge to the west of town. As he and Howard surveyed the situation, messengers arrived from Doubleday and Gen. James S. Wadsworth, both indicating that Confederate reinforcements seemed to be arriving. Doubleday assured Howard that his left was secure, but his right was "hard pressed" by Rebels threatening to outflank the Union position.[20]

Confronted with an increasingly difficult situation Howard also lacked definite information on what was before him. As Schurz explained, "It was at the time difficult to see how far the ground was in our possession. Of the enemy we saw but little, and had no means of forming a just estimate of his strength. Either the enemy was before us in small force, and then we had to push him with all possible vigor, or he had the principal part of his army there, and then we had to establish ourselves in a position which would enable us to maintain ourselves until the arrival of re-enforcements." Briefly, Schurz surveyed the scene unfolding on the opposite side of town. "From where we stood we observed the thin lines of troops, and here and there puffy clouds of white smoke on and around Seminary Ridge, and heard the crackle of the musketry and the booming of the cannon. . . . Of the troops themselves we could see little."[21]

Howard saw the remaining I Corps troops filing across the open fields to the west of the Emmitsburg Road heading for the sounds of battle. Hopefully these reinforcements would stabilize the situation on Doubleday's front. Still smarting from

---

remaining divisions of the First Corps were almost up." For information on this statement, and general time estimates, see Beale, *Statements of Time*, 45.

20 Schurz, *Reminiscences*, III, 5; Howard, manuscript report on Gettysburg, Verticle File 5, GNMP (hereafter Howard ms report).

21 *OR* 27, pt. 1, 727; Schurz, *Reminiscences*, III, 6.

the criticism of him and his corps after Chancellorsville, he was ill-disposed toward risking additional censure by ordering a retreat. Schurz had informed Howard that two divisions of the corps would no doubt be arriving in a few minutes along the Taneytown Road and that the remaining division should be arriving on the heels of the I Corps along the Emmitsburg Road. Help was on the way. Howard made up his mind quickly: They would hold the advanced positions west of town. Turning to Schurz, he ordered him to take his First and Third Divisions quickly northwest to counter Confederate attempts to turn the Union position. Unlike Chancellorsville where he had paid a costly price for failing to establish an adequate reserve force, Howard further ordered Schurz to place his remaining division on Cemetery Hill as a rallying point in case a retreat became necessary. One battery was to accompany each division, with the remainder "to be put in position near me on Cemetery Hill." Thus, Howard made provisions for both of the two alternatives Schurz identified: Sending two divisions to bolster the I Corps but holding back one division and three batteries of artillery as a reserve and to protect a potential fall-back position.[22]

As the two generals conversed, the head of the XI Corps appeared in the distance along the Taneytown Road. Meysenburg timed its arrival at 11:00 am, although it may have been closer to 11:15. Schurz immediately rode in that direction. Meeting Schimmelfenning riding in advance of the troops, Schurz "turned over the command of the Third Division" with orders "to advance briskly through the town, and to deploy on the right of the I Corps in two lines." He sent an aide back along the road with orders for von Steinwehr to occupy Cemetery Hill with his division and for Major Osborn to place his reserve artillery on the hill. Another aide rushed off to find Barlow with orders to lead his division north through town in support of the Third Division. As he finished issuing orders, the leading regiment arrived at the double-quick. "The weather being sultry," Schurz noted, "the men, who had marched several miles at a rapid pace, were streaming with perspiration and panting for breath."[23]

The men were indeed fatigued. Some units made only two brief stops along the entire route of march; some none at all. Maj. Samuel Hurst in the 73rd Ohio recalled "The men suffered terribly from thirst and heat; but still we were urged forward." In the 33rd Massachusetts John Ryder described the experience of marching at the double

22 Howard report on Gettysburg, Aug. 31, 1863, GNMP; Schurz, *Reminiscences*, III, 7; Howard speech on Gettysburg, Box 154, Folder 11 1/2, May 30, 1894, Howard Papers Bowdoin; C. H. Howard manuscript on first day at Gettysburg, Box 3, Bowdoin College.

23 *OR* 27, pt. 1, 727. The Daily Log of the XI Corps notes at 11:00 am: "Head of column arrives at Gettysburg." This is the same time indicated in Meysenburg journal, July 1, 1863; Schurz, *Reminiscences*, III, 7-8; *OR* 27, pt. 1, 727; Schurz, "The Battle of Gettysburg," 275.

quick: "Imagine if you can what that meant to us, loaded with all our usual burdens, with a burning July sun and dust ankle deep, running for all we were worth! Before we had gone two miles half of the regiment lined the roadside. We were then permitted to rest ten minutes for the men to catch up. Then we continued until we reached the cemetery overlooking town. The sight that met our eyes beyond the village was enough to stir one's blood to fever heat."[24]

About five miles from Gettysburg one of Howard's aides delivered the order to Major Osborn to rush the artillery forward "as rapidly as possible." Osborn conveyed the order to Lt. William Wheeler, an attorney in civilian life, to push the 13th New York Independent Battery forward at a trot. "The roads were very stony, and my wheels were in very bad condition, but ahead I went; the gun-carriages rattling and bouncing in the air; feed, rations, kettles and everything else breaking loose from the caissons, the cannoneers running with all their might to keep up, for the road was so very rough, that I was afraid to have them mount, for fear of the repetition of the accident which befell us while trotting to Chancellorsville." On that occasion several men were thrown from the limbers and caissons and gravely injured. "For at least four miles the race continued, and I brought my whole Battery safely into position on the right of Gettysburg, but luckily did not have to fire immediately; my breathless cannoneers made their appearance one by one, and soon each detachment was full."[25]

For Capt. Michael Wiedrich's men, the "morning was beautiful and warm; cherries were ripe, and the men picked them as they went along. At about noon the bugle sounded, 'Cannoneers mount!' This had been expected for some time, and created no surprise, for shell had been seen exploding in the distance for some time; but not a sound could be heard, either of artillery or bursting shell. 'Trot' and 'Gallop' was sounded, and off they went towards the smoke and exploding shell, which seemed to be three or four miles distant."[26] The infantry, forced off the road into the adjoining fields by the passage of the artillery, found their hasty march all the more difficult.

Having ordered Schimmelfennig and Barlow to proceed through town, Schurz rode ahead to survey the situation. Capt. Winkler found him just north of town his eyes examining the right flank of the I Corps where Confederates were threatening to outflank Doubleday's position. At the head of the entire corps were the Third Division's pioneers. Hurrying past the Pennsylvania College, Lt. Louis Fischer quickly

24 Hurst, *Journal-History*, 65; Ryder, *Reminiscences*, 31.

25 *OR*, 27, pt. 1, 747, 752; Wheeler to grandfather and aunt, July 26, 1863, in Bershears, *Loyal Till Death*, 184.

26 *New York Monuments Commission, Final Report*, III, 1246.

Col. Stephen J. McGroarty, 61st Ohio
Library of Congress

went to work taking down "the post fences between the college and Hagy's house to let the infantry and artillery into the fields north of the road." The lieutenant "naturally turned my attention to the terrible but indescribably fascinating scene on the east slope of Seminary Ridge. The rebel infantry was coming down the Mummasburg road at a run, about 600 yards from me, and taking shelter on the southwest side of the road in the ditch behind the fence, fired into the exposed ranks of the 13th Mass. and 104th N.Y., who stood in an open meadow. I could see every man fall as he was hit by the enemy (who lost hardly any in this unequal contest), until of the original line of blue was left only a thin line, with great gaps at that."[27]

Immediately behind the pioneers came Dilger's battery. Clattering through town "on a swift gallop, its cannoniers bouncing high in their seats as the wheels revolve rapidly over obstructions in the roadway," the battery rushed out the north side of town where Schimmelfennig directed it into position in the open fields. Dilger quickly deployed a section on the highest rise between the Mummasburg and Carlisle roads, but Confederate Capt. Richard C. M. Page's four Napoleons of the Morris Artillery opened a hot fire on him that forced him to bring his remaining pieces into line to reply.[28] Dilger's guns were on their own when they arrived. Devoid of any infantry support, they made a tempting target for Rebel sharpshooters from Col. Edward A. O'Neal's Alabama brigade and Brig. Gen. George Doles's Georgia brigade which were moving south to threaten the Union flank.

Leading the infantry onto the field was the 61st Ohio, Col. Stephen J. McGroarty commanding, which emerged from town on the double quick moments after the

27 Winkler, *Letters*, June 26 to July 8, 1863; Fischer, "At Gettysburg," *National Tribune*, December 12, 1869.

28 Fischer, "At Gettysburg"; Barnett, "If Ever Men Stayed By Their Guns," 88-89.

Lt. Col. Adolph von Hartung, 74th Pennsylvania
U.S. Army Heritage and Education Center

artillery. There were only 143 men in the regiment's ranks that day because Lt. Col. William Brown had been detached with 103 officers and men on a reconnaissance to Mechanicstown (modern Thurmont) where they spent most of the afternoon. There may even have been fewer once deductions were made for stragglers and those on detached service. The regiment rushed north through the streets of town, passing the corner of Washington and Middle Streets where Michael Jacobs watched as the troops "flowed through and out into the battlefield beyond, a human tide, at millrace speed." McGroarty emerged to find Schimmelfennig who directed him to deploy into skirmish order in front of Dilger's battery to shield it from enemy sharpshooters. McGroarty's men immediately came under fire which they returned with vigor, pushing the Rebels back and protecting Dilger's men from immediate musket fire.[29]

Following the Ohioans in line came Lt. Col. Adolph von Hartung's 74th Pennsylvania which was even weaker, fielding no more than a mere 135 in its ranks. Schimmelfennig deployed them in skirmish order to the right of the 61st Ohio along a narrow lane running from the Carlisle Road toward Wilbur McLean's farm. All the while Rebel artillery played on the deploying Federals while skirmishers sent greetings in the form of deadly lead. One of those who went forward with the 74th was Lt. Emil Knoebel who recalled they deployed "as skirmishers and met with artillery fire with bombs and cannonballs. One cannonball went by so close to my head that the pressure almost knocked me down to the ground and did knock my cap off my head. For about an hour we were under heavy artillery fire." Lt. John F. Mader found himself "under a

29 Ley letter; Böhm address; *OR* 27, pt. 1, 734, 738; Thaddeus K. Miller Papers, VFM 2657, OHS; Stahl, "Pvt. John Wright," 56; Pfanz, *First Day*, 141.

Lt. Col. Adolphus Dobke, 45th New York
U.S. Army Heritage and Education Center

cross fire of the rebels shott & shell which made the air hideous with the whizzing. I am thankfull to the almighty God that I have escaped the iron hail."[30] The blue line was very thin with only 278 men covering a distance of about a half mile from the Mummasburg Road to the Carlisle Road, but it held, even pushing Rebel skirmishers back away from Dilger's gunners feverishly working their pieces.

The 45th New York emerged from Washington Street near the junction of the Mummasburg Road on the heels of the Pennsylvanians. With orders to support the right flank of the I Corps, Capt. Friedrich Irsch led Companies A, B, D and E out the Mummasburg Road to close with Doubleday's right flank. The regiment, Lt. Col. Adolphus Dobke promised, would move to support him as soon as it "had gained breath." Only 23 years of age, the German-born captain, had been a merchant in civilian life. Now he led his panting men out beyond the college toward the right flank of the I Corps, but Confederate infantry was already occupying the ridge and adjoining slopes leading up to Oak Hill. As Irsch advanced, his blue eyes detected Page's Morris Artillery firing from Rebel positions about midway up the hill on the extension of Seminary Ridge. Shells began to fall close by at the same time Major Eugene Blackford's Alabama sharpshooters appeared in the lane at the bottom of the slope to contest the Union advance. Spread out in the rye and wheat fields as far right as the Hagy apple orchard, Blackford's men opened an effective fire. Irsch deployed his men in skirmish order as directed, then pushed forward, driving the Rebels back despite growing artillery and musket fire. Finally, reaching a fence on the Hagy farm, with losses mounting, Irsch ordered his men to take cover behind the wooden fence rails, lying down but keeping up their fire. Despite growing opposition, Irsch succeeded in gaining a defensible position and providing

30 Emil Knoebel to C. Knoebel, Jan. 22, 1864, quoted in Kamphoefer and Helbich, *Germans in the Civil War*, 149; Baumgartner, *Buckeye Blood*, 90-91.

time for reinforcements to arrive. Blackford later reported his losses as "considerable."[31]

As Irsch fought against increasing Confederate resistance, help began to arrive. With the balance of the regiment formed, Lt. Col. Dobke ordered the remaining companies forward under the command of Major Charles Koch to support the embattled skirmishers. But Confederate reinforcements were also arriving. Gen. Robert E. Rodes' division completed its deployment on Oak Hill at the northern end of Seminary Ridge and Capt. W. P. Carter's King William Artillery joined Page's Virginia battery. The two Confederate batteries were a serious threat since they were well positioned to enfilade the entire I Corps line. To meet the danger, Dilger placed Lt. Clark Scripture's two-gun section somewhat forward on a rise. Page's battery, half way up the slope, opened fire on Scripture at a range of about 1,400 yards. When Carter arrived, Page moved a section forward to within about 800 to 1,000 yards of Scripture forcing the Federals to change position to throw off the accuracy of Southern gunners. Dilger, quickly sizing up the situation, moved his remaining four guns forward reducing the Federal disadvantage to 8-6. Yet, with six 12-pounder smoothbores, Dilger remained at a decided disadvantage because the Rebel batteries, emplaced at a higher elevation, could outrange his pieces.[32]

While Dilger re-deployed, the 157th New York arrived under Col. Philip P. Brown, Jr. Rushing out of town, it formed behind the right of the 45th New York as a support for the forward skirmish line, followed by the 82nd Illinois under Lt. Col. Edward S. Salomon which was directed into place behind the right of the 61st Ohio and in support of Dilger's battery. Salomon ordered Capt. Joseph Greenhut, his brother-in-law, to lead two companies of the 82nd to directly support Dilger's embattled artillerymen. Greenhut reported being "exposed to the fearful cannonade fire which the enemy opened in our front, and by which we had several of our men wounded." Capt. Matthew Marx "heard a horrible scream." Raising his head, since the men had been ordered to lie down to present a smaller target, he "saw Ernst Fuhrmeister, my sergeant, without any legs. A ball had torn one completely off and

31 Blackford quoted in Trudeau, "Taking Aim at Cemetery Hill," 48; Francis (originally Friedrich) Irsch pension papers, National Archives; Böhm address; Ley letter; *New York Monuments Commission Report*, I, 378; *Military Order of the Loyal Legion of the United States*, Circular #41, Series of 1906, #895, New York, October 1, 1906. The line where Irsch formed was about 100 yards behind the current location of the 45th New York monument. His men reached a point about 540 yards in advance of where a marker is located.

32 Schurz, *Reminiscences*, III, 8; *OR* 27, pt. 1, 754.

Col. Philip P. Brown, Jr., 157th New York
Karl E. Sundstrom

smashed the other one to pieces at the knee. The blood ran in streams." Near him lay Emil Giese and Friedrich Calmback [Kallenbach], their legs likewise shattered.[33]

The exploding shells disturbed Col. Brown's horse, so he dismounted and walked over to Dilger just as a gun fired, the shot flying over the Rebel battery, missing its mark by a considerable distance. According to Jonathan Boynton, the Rebels "yelled in derision" at the poor gunnery. Their derisive calls were short-lived. Dilger personally sighted the next piece then stood back as it fired. The shot hit the carriage of one of the Rebel guns dismounting the piece it carried. Moving to the next gun, Dilger again sighted it, stepped back, and the gunner fired the piece. The usual flame and smoke shot from the barrel, but nothing else happened. No strike was observed. "What effect, Captain Dilger?" asked Brown. Placing his binoculars to his eyes, Dilger looked for a few moments, then responded "I have spiked a gun for them, plugging it at the muzzle."[34]

33 Greenhut, speech at unveiling of 82nd Illinois monument at Gettysburg, September 3, 1891; Marx to *Illinois Staats-Zeitung*, published July 20, 1863, in Reinhart, *Yankee Dutchmen*, 94.

34 Brown to newspaper editor, July 27, 1863; Fischer, "The Battle of Gettysburg"; *OR* 27, pt.1, 754. This incident is often disputed with the claim that no corroborating evidence exists. However, civilian Jacob Hoke, writing about a tour of the battlefield on July 7, commented: "Returning to town we saw at the depot three or four disabled cannon. They were broken in various ways. One had been struck squarely in the muzzle by a solid shot one size larger than its calibre. The ball stuck fast in the muzzle and broke a piece out of it." See Hoke, *The Great Invasion*. Since there is no indication what portion of the battlefield this piece came from, a more interesting observation came from Justus M. Silliman, a soldier in the 17th Connecticut who was wounded and captured on July 1. He was taken to a Confederate field hospital on Oak Hill in the area where the batteries opposing Dilger had been located. Silliman stated: "I saw a rebel cannon which had been struck in its mouth by one of our shots and flattened out." See *Letters of Justis M. Silliman*.

To silence the pesky Dilger the Confederates trained some rifled pieces on his position. Now under fire from longer ranged, more accurate guns, Dilger sent a messenger galloping to the rear to request reinforcement. Back on Cemetery Hill, Major Osborn ordered Lt. Wheeler to move his 13th New York Independent Battery with four three-inch rifled guns from the reserve to support Dilger and place himself under the captain's command. Rushing through town, two of Wheeler's caissons broke down along the now rutted streets. The lieutenant left them and pushed on. Reaching the field he had to wait briefly while the pioneers filled a wide irrigation ditch with fence rails. This accomplished under fire, within a few minutes he unlimbered to the right of Dilger's position. Although he had only four guns, Wheeler's pieces were rifled and their longer range gave Dilger much needed support. Under their covering fire, the captain "instantly advanced Lieutenant [Christian] Weidman's section about 600 yards on our right, on the Baltimore and Harrisburg road." Covered by Wheeler's battery, Dilger ordered his men to fill in a ditch to his front, then advanced the remaining four of his pieces, the sections under Lt. Clark Scripture and Lt. William Dämmert, into a large wheat field and commenced firing. Wheeler then moved his own pieces forward to a position some fifty yards to the right of Dilger, but not before they had to withstand several minutes of Rebel fire while Lt. Louis Fischer and his pioneers chopped down a particularly resilient wood fence that blocked their way.[35]

Dilger's guns pummeled Page's battery. Looking on, Lt. Fischer and his pioneers were mightily impressed. "Within eight or ten minutes from the time that Capt. Dilger's gunners got orders to demolish the rebel battery they blew up two or three caissons and entirely disabled one or two of the guns, without losing any of their own." Years later when Schurz penned his memoirs he recalled how Dilger "dismounted four of the enemy's guns, as we observed through our field-glasses, and drove away two Rebel regiments supporting them." Dilger skillfully moved his guns about to foil Rebel attempts to gauge the range for accurate counterbattery fire. Major Osborn, who accompanied his batteries, reported that the Confederates had five guns dismounted in exchange for only one of Wheeler's pieces dismounted. The observant Lt. Fischer witnessed the result of the one-sided duel when "the remainder of the [rebel] battery limbered up and disappeared behind the rounding of the ridge."[36]

35 *OR* 27, pt. 1, 734, 747, 752, 754; Barnett, "By Their Guns," 89; Wheeler to grandfather and aunt, July 26, 1863, in Bershears, *Loyal Till Death*, 185-86; Fischer, "Gettysburg"; Ley letter; Böhm address; Naisawald, *Grape and Canister*, 356.

36 Schurz, *Reminiscences*, III, 8; Fischer, "Gettysburg"; *OR* 27, pt. 1, 747. Dilger also reported dismounting five Rebel pieces (see *OR* 27, pt. 1, 754).

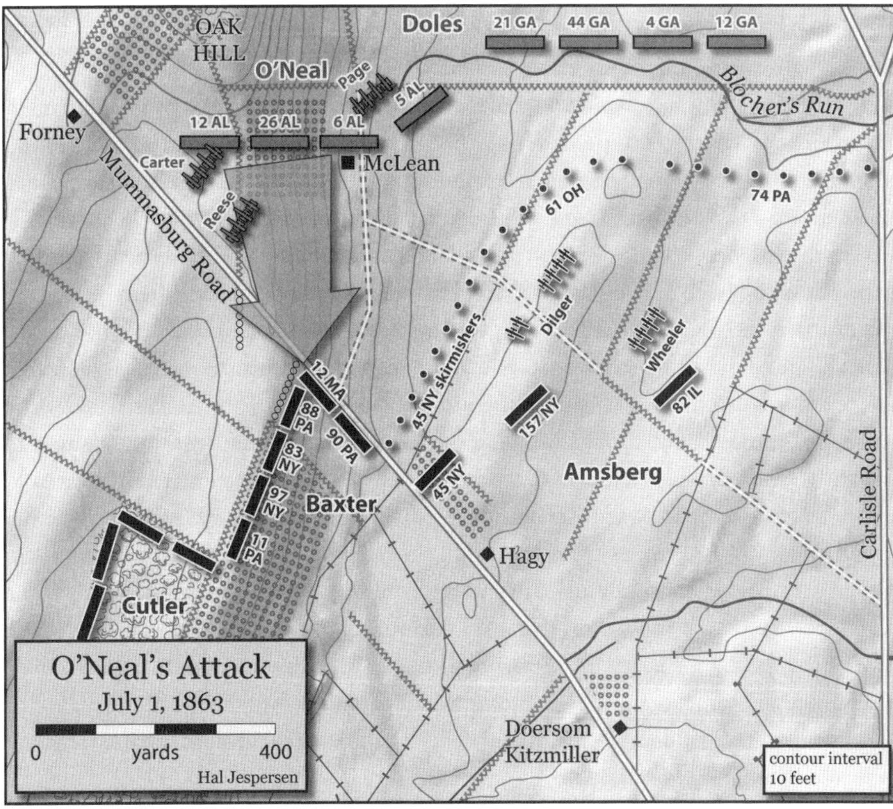

This map shows how the 45th New York and Dilger's guns were in an excellent position to pour enfilade fire into O'Neal's attack, as well as illustrating the perilously thin line that von Amsberg had to hold north of the Mummasburg Road.

The Federals' accurate fire decimated Page's battery which withdrew to escape the destructive shelling. Lt. Col. Thomas H. Carter, commanding the Rebel artillery battalion, confirmed in his report that Dilger "delivered a very destructive oblique fire on Page's battery. His loss here was heavy—2 men killed, 2 mortally wounded, 26 more or less badly wounded, and 17 horses killed and disabled." Among the wounded was Capt. Page of the Morris Artillery who was forced to relinquish command of his hard-pressed battery. It also forced Carter to shift the four rifled guns of Capt. William J. Reese's Jeff Davis Artillery left to support the two heavily engaged batteries.[37] Dilger's action forced the withdrawal of one battery and occupied the attention of Page

37 *OR* 27, pt. 1, 602; Macaluso, *Morris, Orange and King William Artillery*, 46-47; Barnett, "By Their Guns," 89.

and Carter so much that they were not able to deliver their potentially devastating discharges against the I Corps flank.

With support now at hand and Rebel artillerymen directing most of their attention to Dilger and Wheeler, Capt. Irsch led his command forward once again. Yet, no sooner had he begun to move than a strong column of Confederate infantry appeared. Col. Edward A. O'Neal's Alabama brigade rushed along the slope of Oak Hill, angling toward the gap between the 45th New York and the right flank of the I Corps. Sensing an opportunity, Irsch quickly ordered his men to change front, placing them directly on the exposed left flank of O'Neal's advance at a distance of only 50 to 100 yards. Opening fire, Irsch also sent runners to Dobke requesting support from the balance of the regiment and to Dilger asking the artillerist to fire into the Rebel flank. Both responded immediately, Dobke bringing the balance of the regiment into position to fire at the Confederates as they crossed his front, while Dilger redirected his pieces to fire canister into the exposed Rebel infantry. At the same time, the regiments on the extreme right of the I Corps opened fire into the front of O'Neal's men, catching them in a crossfire between their musketry and the flanking infantry and artillery fire of the XI Corps. "It was a terrible sight to see this splendid line annihilated in such incredible short time," Adj. Augustus Horstmann thought. "The effect of our rifles showed fearfully, while some, being hit, jumped several feet in the air falling either forward or backward to the ground, dead, others fell or sank to the ground without further movement, while the wounded tried to get shelter."[38]

Lt. Hubert Ley saw the "Confederate Brigade came charging down the hill near Mummasburg road driving in the right of the I Corps. Dilger's Battery and six companies of our regiment in their front, and the four companies on Oak Hill and at McLean's barn now in their flank and rear, as well as several regiments of the I Corps to the left of the Mummasburg Road gave them simultaneously fearful volleys, front, on both flanks, and rear." The Confederates "broke and ran for cover, and we all charged them from every quarter simultaneously and drove them upon the right of the I Corps and up to and across the Mummasburg Road where three entire regiments surrendered with their battle flags, but mostly to the I Corps, now in their front, and to the six companies of our Regiment." Colonel Hall of the 5th Alabama later wrote that "my command was under a front and enfilading fire, with no support, and suffering a very severe loss." Under this pressure, the Rebel advance ground to a halt. In his report on the campaign, Col. O'Neal explained that "We were compelled to fall back, as the regiment on the extreme left, being flanked by a superior force of the enemy, gave

38 Horstmann, account of the Battle of Gettysburg, GNMP.

way." The telling fire into the left flank of O'Neal's force came, of course, from the XI Corps.[39] That force was the 45th New York, backed by Dilger's artillery.

O'Neal's Confederates broke, some hugging the ground, some rushing back toward their line. A resounding "hurrah" rose from the Federals as Irsch ordered his men forward, rushing toward the McLean farm to press the Rebels before they could recover from their repulse. Companies A and B under Capt. Gustav Korn and Lt. Louis Lindemeyer pushed forward to the barn where Sergt. George Linder led a group that surrounded the structure, taking some 60 prisoners, and another dozen captives who had sought shelter in a nearby ditch. Others surrendered to Irsch or to the companies under Koch and Dobke, Lt. Ley estimating the total number at about 300. As the prisoners marched to the rear under guard, one of them asked whether Rudolph Schwarz might be among the Federals. As it happened, Corp. Schwarz, a tailor from Zwiebrucken, was a member of Company B, and had been among the men who captured the inquiring Confederate at the McLean barn. The corporal soon appeared, recognized the brother he had not seen since they both left Germany several years earlier, and the two exchanged a warm embrace. But duty called, cutting short the unlikely reunion. The Confederate marched to the rear under guard, while Corporal Schwarz rejoined Company B, only to be killed shortly after the touching reunion.[40]

☽ ☽ ☽

While Dilger and Wheeler exchanged fire with the Confederate batteries and Schimmelfennig pushed von Amsberg's brigade forward to protect the flank of the I Corps, the division's remaining brigade arrived under Colonel Wlodzimierz

39 Ley letter; Böhm address; *New York Monuments Commission Report*, I, 379; *OR* 27, pt. 1, 595, 734; *OR* 27, pt.2, 591; Horstmann, account of the Battle of Gettysburg, GNMP.

40 Ley letter; Böhm address; *New York Monuments Commission Report*, I, 379-81; Regimental Descriptive Book, 45th New York, NARA; *New York at Gettysburg*, I; *OR* 27, pt. 1, 734. A search of the available muster rolls and regimental papers for the units attached to O'Neal's brigade, available in the National Archives and the Department of Archives and History in Montgomery, Alabama, failed to locate any Confederate soldier by the name of Schwarz, or any reasonable variation, enrolled in any of the regiments of O'Neal's brigade. This is, however, not conclusive proof. Confederate records are incomplete, so Schwarz's enlistment may simply have been lost. Or, he may have enrolled under a different name, as some chose to do, or his name may have been different if he had been adopted or was a half-brother. Another possibility is that one of the six people listed in the Alabama archives with the surname of "Schwartz" or the one spelled "Swartz" may have served in more than one unit, being in O'Neal's brigade either before or after serving in the unit to which they are credited in the archives. Perhaps one day additional evidence will shed new light on this apparently touching reunion.

Krzyzanowski. As the troops marched Adj. Dodge found time to scribble an entry in his diary: "2 miles from Gettysburg. There is firing in the front. . . . It is not as yet very heavy." That would soon change. Adj. Alfred Lee in the 82nd Ohio recalled "hundreds of country-people, gathered by the roadside, dispensed food and drink and spoke words of encouragement to the hurrying soldiers. 'God bless you, boys!' exclaimed these rustic patriots, whose seriousness showed plainly enough that they realized, vaguely, perhaps, yet profoundly, that a tremendous crisis was at hand." When the column crested a small rise south of town, Lee's eyes observed "a wide scope of country, mostly open, and bounded by distant hills. Along the slopes of these hills, and issuing sometimes from clumps of timber, spasmodic puffs of powder-smoke betrayed the positions of the rebel batteries." Ahead of him, Lee saw the tail of the I Corps moving across the fields into position.[41]

The brigade had covered the distance from Emmitsburg, an average day's march in that era, in only four hours, the last ten miles with not a single rest stop. Sweating profusely, their ears picked up the rattle of musketry beyond and to the left of the village. Rushing toward the sound of the firing, Lt. Col. Hans Boebel raced his 26th Wisconsin the last mile into town at the double-quick, 140 steps per minute covering 109 yards each time the second hand completed a revolution. "Exerting what remained of our strength," Capt. Domschcke recalled, "we finally reached the town and hurried through its streets at double-quick." The sounds of battle brought to some a new surge of energy. "By this time every one has forgotten any symptoms of fatigue which may have been creeping over him, in the exciting anticipation of an approaching fray," explained Adj. Dodge. "Every one's blood flows quicker, every pulse beats louder, every nerve is more sensitive, and every one feels that he is living faster than he was half an hour since."[42]

As they trotted through the town citizens waved and cheered from their windows and porches. Some obliging Samaritans rushed forward offering buckets of water for the men to quench their thirsts. Here and there people held out loaves of bread or rolls to the soldiers. Two or three people offered warm greetings for Lt. Henry Hauschildt, a former resident of Gettysburg now serving with the 75th Pennsylvania. Exhausted, the men moved mostly by habit rather than through conscious effort. "We were wet as cats, hungry as wolves," commented Sergt. Karl Wickesberg in the 26th Wisconsin, "our thirst was satisfied by the good citizens when we ran in full gallop through their

41 Dodge diary, July 1, 1863; Lee, "Reminiscences of the Gettysburg Battle," 54-55.

42 Dodge, "Left Wounded on the Field," 318; Wickesberg to family, July 6, 1863; Domschcke, *Twenty Months*, 27; Karsten diary, July 1, 1863.

Adjutant Alfred Lee, 82nd Ohio
U.S. Army Heritage and Education Center

town." Lt. Lee sensed "the clanging of sabres, the clatter of horses' hoofs, the gleaming of arms, the sweaty, excited countenances of the troops, the shouts of command, and the booming of the deep-throated guns. Groups of men and women, terror stricken . . . stood showering upon us their benedictions. The prattling child joined the young maiden and the trembling matron in waving 'God bless you' to the soldiers."[43]

Moving rapidly through the streets, the brigade emerged from the north end of town. They were not novices to war. They knew what the firing meant, what horrors lay ahead of them, but they pushed on. Capt. Winkler, on Schurz's staff, sat astride his horse near an orchard as the troops emerged from town. To the left, the contest between Schimmelfennig and the Rebels still raged. Winkler directed the regiments into position to the west of the Carlisle Road as they arrived. Lt. Lee's 82nd Ohio emerged from town into the open field where it met a "lively" fire from Rebel guns whose "shot and shell" ricocheted "splendidly over the open fields." Col. James S. Robinson allowed the men to sit down and relax as best they could while sergeants called the roll. Lee was impressed that "the men quietly responded to their names amid the boom of cannon and the screech of exploding shells.[44]

Col. Franz Mahler let the 75th Pennsylvania relax to catch its collective breath, but there was little opportunity for rest as shells from Confederate rifled guns that overshot Dilger's position began landing uncomfortably close. One exploded directly in the

43 *Pennsylvania at Gettysburg Ceremonies*, I, 434, 438; Schurz, *Reminiscences*, III, 7; *OR* 27, pt. 1, 727; Wickesberg to parents, July 6, 1863; Baumgartner, *Buckeye Blood*, 41.

44 Lee, "Reminiscences of the Gettysburg Battle," 55.

Col. John T. Lockman, 119th New York
U.S. Army Heritage and Education Center

regiment killing one man and injuring two others. The dead man was the one-time resident of Gettysburg, Henry Hauschildt.[45]

The 119th New York halted in an orchard where the sergeants counted 16 officers and 284 men present for duty. Shells fell close by, some landing amid the troops. "We had a few minutes to ourselves," Dodge explained. "The men were allowed to rest in line, and each one sat or lay down in the most comfortable position just where he was, some reclining at full length and closing their eyes, some merely squatting down to discuss a hard tack and the situation." An aide from Krzyzanowski arrived with an order to occupy a nearby barn to prevent Rebel skirmishers from gaining the position, so Col. Lockman ordered Company H forward and they quickly obtained control of their objective. The position secured, Dodge sat with Col. Lockman under one of the apple trees discussing the state of affairs, speculating on what they would be called upon to do. Then they spoke briefly of those at home, passing between them messages for each other's family just in case the worst should befall either. After the two engaged in a brief prayer, Dodge took the opportunity to once again scrawl a note in his diary at 2:00 pm: "Beyond Gettysburg. We are engaged; we lie in column supporting a Battery with skirmishers in front. Shell are flying and bursting at a considerable rate. The Rebels are about half a mile off. The country is open and we can see everything. We see their Batteries are working hard. . . . Our Corps is to hold this position of Gettysburg. God grant we may have Victory!"[46]

In the 26th Wisconsin, located partially in the shade of an apple orchard and partially in a wheat field, Lt. Col. Hans Boebel rested his weary men. Despite the

45 *OR* 27, pt. 1, 745; *Pennsylvania at Gettysburg Ceremonies*, 434.

46 *Dedication of a Monument by the 119th Regiment*, 13; *OR* 27, pt. 1, 742; Pfanz, *First Day*, 220 (The barn may have been on the Crawford farm, or it could have referred to the buildings in the almshouse complex.); Dodge diary, July 1, 1863; Dodge, "Left Wounded on the Field," 319.

Lt. Col. Hans Boebel, 26th Wisconsin
Kenneth and Robert Medley

grueling pace of the march and the imminent threat of battle, there were remarkably few stragglers. Discounting a group of pickets under Lt. George Traeumer who had not yet caught up with the regiment and others on detached duty, the command counted only 16 officers and 293 men present for duty. With the sounds of battle all about them, the infantrymen knelt in silent prayer or meditation. They were an exhausted but resolute group of men. Only too well aware of the abuses heaped upon them after the Chancellorsville debâcle, and the crucial significance of this invasion of the North, they were determined to do their duty.[47]

☽ ☽ ☽

Barlow had been ordered to bring his division to a halt at a church about four miles south of Gettysburg, but by the time he reached that point heavy cannonading could be heard. Rather than stop, Barlow sent an aide, Capt. Edward C. Culp, forward to see what was happening and inform Howard that he was not going to stop at the church but continue on toward the engagement that was obviously in progress. Once in sight of Gettysburg Culp "struck across the fields, but before reaching the battlefield I met Capt. Pearson of Gen. Howard's staff, and repeated my order to him. Capt. Pearson replied: 'I was just on my way to Gen. Barlow. Ride back and tell the General, for God's sake, to push on with the utmost speed." The normally impatient Barlow did not wait for Culp's return, but dispatched a second aide, Capt. William Wickham, on the same mission. Culp met Wickham while returning with Pearson's message and the two returned to Barlow who already had his division "marching at almost a double-quick." On receipt of the information, Barlow, who was in advance of his men, ordered Capt.

47 *OR* 27, pt. 1, 742; Dodge, "Left Wounded," 317, 319; Fox, *New York at Gettysburg*, 15.

Capt. Edward C. Culp, 25th Ohio, an aide to General Barlow
U.S. Army Heritage and Education Center

Wickham "to return to the head of the column and urge the march as much as possible."[48]

Sometime between noon and 12:30 Barlow's division came into view. Leaving his chief of staff, Col. Charles Asmussen, at the headquarters on Cemetery Hill to make sure that his orders were carried out, Howard, accompanied by two or three staff officers, rode down to the junction of the Emmitsburg and Taneytown Roads where he met Barlow and rode with him through the town. Howard's intent was to visit the front lines in person to see for himself how things were going so he could judge what actions to take as the day unfolded. As they trotted through town, Howard noticed "a heroic young lady, regardless of her own safety and of the oncoming shells of the enemy, [who] bravely stood on the porch of her dwelling and silently waved her handkerchief while the divisions passed her. It was indeed a patriotic stimulus. How the men cheered her again and again as they marched by!"[49]

Reaching the north side of town, Howard conferred with Barlow while the latter's men emerged from town. Turning to Major Charles Howard, the general directed him to find General Buford and report on his situation on the far right east of Rock Creek. Then, turning his horse to the left, Howard rode behind Schurz's line but somehow managed to miss the general so the two did not confer. Instead, Howard continued on to Seminary Ridge where he passed behind the lines of Robinson and Wadsworth, stopping briefly to exchange information with the latter. Pushing on, he met

48 Culp, "Reminiscences of the Great Fight by a Participant," *National Tribune*, March 19, 1885.

49 Howard report on Gettysburg, Vertical File 5, GNMP (hereafter Howard ms report); Howard speech on Gettysburg, Box 154, Folder 11 1/2, May 30, 1894; Howard, *Autobiography*, 414.

Doubleday about a quarter mile "beyond the Seminary." The two discussed the situation after which Howard told Doubleday to hold on as long as possible then fall back to Cemetery Hill. His thirst for information satisfied, Howard rode back to Cemetery Hill, no doubt with a better picture of the actual ground and state of affairs.[50]

While Doubleday shifted troops to deal with an expanding Confederate front along Seminary Ridge and Schurz saw to the deployment of his troops north of Gettysburg, Howard received ominous news from Buford that a large force of Rebels was approaching Gettysburg from the north. They appeared to be in at least division strength with their leading elements only about four miles away. Meysenburg placed the arrival of this information at headquarters at 12:50. The advance of this Rebel force would place them directly on the open right flank of the Union position. Confirmation of the news came from Lt. Aaron B. Jerome of the Signal Corps: "Over a division of the Rebels are making a flank movement on our right. The line extends over a mile and are advancing skirmishing. There is nothing but Cavalry to oppose them." At nearly the same time, news arrived from Doubleday that Confederate prisoners identified the force he was facing as Hill's Corps and further reported that they expected the arrival of a division of Longstreet's Corps "in a short time." Howard sent his brother north on a reconnaissance to ascertain with certainty information about the Rebel force endangering his flank. He soon returned to confirm the threat, as did a message from Schurz who probably learned the information from Buford's cavalry.[51]

With the intelligence confirmed, Howard immediately sent an order to Schurz "to halt his command, to prevent his right flank being turned, but to push forward a thick line of skirmishers to seize the point first indicated, as a relief and support to the 1st Corps." He then dispatched an aide to Sickles near Emmitsburg again asking him to move to Gettysburg as rapidly as possible and to forward his message on to General Meade. Howard sent another communication to Slocum, some four or five miles away at Two Taverns, asking him to come up with "all possible speed." At about 2:00 pm he sent a brief report to Meade, but the communication did not arrive until at least 3:30 pm because the messenger had difficulty finding the commanding general's

50 Howard ms report; Howard speech on Gettysburg, Box 154, Folder 11 1/2, May 30, 1894; Howard, *Autobiography*, 414.

51 Howard ms report.; 1st Lt. Jerome, Signal Corps, note to Howard, no date, no time, RG 393, Pt. 2, Vol. 16, #5320, NARA; Howard report on Gettysburg, Aug. 31, 1863, Clements Library; *OR* 27, pt. 3, 488; Meysenburg journal, July 1, 1863; Bill Cameron, "The Signal Corps at Gettysburg," *The Gettysburg Magazine*, No. 3 (July 1990), 9.

headquarters. At 2:45 Howard sent another dispatch to Slocum asking "if he is moving to support. He is informed that our right is turned."[52]

Although the situation was serious Howard did not view it as critical. Doubleday was holding his own, Schurz had a stable position on the flank of the Rebels who were threatening the right of the I Corps, and von Steinwehr had come up, beginning to arrive about 1:00 pm. It had been a fatiguing march. For some, the sounds of imminent action stirred an adrenaline induced burst of energy. "Tired limbs, blistered feet and sore muscles no longer absorbed our thoughts or drew upon the will power," explained Lt. Lucian Smith of the 136th New York, "the whole man was charged as if by magic; quickened and apparently refreshed to a degree not explainable, and hardly to be appreciated by those who have never experienced the wondrous power of a battle already begun, and toward which one is rapidly marching. Nothing escapes observation: every fence and field, the whole topography of the country, the expression on comrades' faces, the tone of command, all are indelibly stamped on mind and memory to a degree that time itself does not efface."[53]

Von Steinwehr ordered Col. Orland Smith's brigade into position to support the artillery and placed Col. Charles Coster's brigade guarding the approaches from town. Coster moved the 73rd Pennsylvania into cornfields at the base of Cemetery Hill, deploying the men as skirmishers across the Emmitsburg Road and Baltimore Pike. He pushed the 27th Pennsylvania forward to High Street where it turned right to take possession of the German Reformed Church, Union School, Adams County Jail, and the surrounding houses on the outskirts of town to prevent Rebel sharpshooters from getting into them. He held his two largest regiments, the 134th and 154th New York, back on Cemetery Hill to support Wiedrich's battery. Orders arrived for the men to get a quick meal and clean their muskets for action, but apparently some of them did not heed the latter injunction. Corp. George Warner noticed that "Many of them failed to remove the moisture from the tubes of their guns, so that when they were finally

52 Howard, *Autobiography*, 416; Howard, "Commencement Address," 75; Howard speech on Gettysburg, Box 154, Folder 11 1/2, May 30, 1894; Howard ms report; Meysenburg journal, July 1, 1863. Meysenburg did not mean the right flank had been pushed back since that had not yet occurred; what he meant was that the advancing Confederates would arrive overlapping the right flank of the Union line.

53 "Report of Colonel A. B. Underwood," Dec. 9, 1881, Vertical File 4-10l , GNMP; Smith, "Recollections of Gettysburg," 298.

brought to close quarters with an overwhelming foe with empty guns, they had no time to remedy the fault."[54]

When the troops arrived, Elizabeth Thorn, the wife of the cemetery gatekeeper who was off serving in the army, and her daughter were busy baking bread. "As fast as I could cut the hot bread they took it out of my hands and eat [*sic*] it. Every vessel I had in the house, all the tin cups and tumblers were out along the old pump inside the gate and the vessels were kept filled with water for the thirsty soldiers and were quickly emptied. They would take a drink and hurry off and this lasted until the pump broke. . . . Shortly afterwards a big man with straps on the shoulders came along and asked me whether there was a man about who could point out the roads." Thorn volunteered to go herself. The unidentified officer objected that it was too dangerous, but the plucky woman replied that she "thought there was as much danger inside as outside the house" and the officer finally agreed. "He made me walk to the east or south-east of the horse to protect me from any bullets." As they moved north, they met soldiers who gave her "three cheers." After pointing out the location of the roads to York, Booneville, and Harrisburg the two returned to Cemetery Hill, the officer being careful all the way to keep the brave lady on the side of the horse away from the fire.[55]

"[W]hen we reached the cemetery," Henry Henny observed, "the artillery drove into the burial ground, crushing over tombstones and graves regardless of everything but the supreme necessity of getting their guns into position to open fire upon the Rebel renegades." Corp. Newell Burch and his friends in the 154th New York took advantage of the respite to catch their collective breaths, "fill canteens, clean & load guns [and] get a bite of tack & sow belly." Lt. Smith's "first thoughts were of the seeming desecration, as we trod beneath our feet the grass-grown mounds which marked the resting place of the dead, but other thoughts and scenes soon engrossed our attention." Capt. J. W. Hand in the 136th New York found himself "filing through the lines of marble slabs and over the low grassy mounds" in the Evergreen Cemetery, an experience in which he found "a grim suggestiveness." He wondered whether "the pious Howard [was] taking this method of impressing on our minds the old lesson of mortality, and giving us an opportunity to 'view the ground where we must shortly lie?'"[56]

54 *OR* 27, pt. 1, 720; Bates, *History of Pennsylvania Volunteers*, 390; Conklin, *Under the Crescent and Star*, 101-02.

55 Thorn, "Experience During Battle," 2.

56 Henny diary, evening July 1, 1863; Burch diary, July 1, 1863; Smith, "Gettysburg," 299; Hand, "A Graphic Account of the Battle by a Eleventh Corps Captain."

☽ ☽ ☽

Carl Schurz's original orders were to push two divisions through town, protect the right flank of the I Corps, and take up a position to extend the I Corps line north along Seminary Ridge, occupying Oak Hill in the process. To carry out these instructions he ordered Schimmelfenning to hurry directly north through town and form on the right of the I Corps in the vicinity of the Mummasburg Road. Then, riding to the head of Barlow's division which had just appeared, he ordered Barlow to keep to the main road through town, then go into position to extend the XI Corps line to the right of Schimmelfennig. Schurz then spurred his horse through town to see for himself what was happening. What he found was terrain ill-suited for an infantry fight. Although the I Corps held positions beyond the crest of Seminary Ridge, the ground the XI Corps emerged onto from the streets of Gettysburg was relatively flat with some low undulating mounds but no militarily significant features upon which to anchor a line of battle. Further, by the time the XI Corps began deploying, it was obvious that the northern end of Seminary Ridge and its extension onto Oak Hill were already occupied by Confederate infantry in significant number. Even when his entire two divisions were in place, to assume the offensive and seize the ridge he would have available less than 6,000 men who would have to cross an open plain and attack up a significant hill defended by superior numbers of Confederates supported by artillery. Schurz immediately recognized the difficulty, if not impossibility, inherent in this assignment.

Climbing to the roof of the Hagy home, the general did not have long to ponder what was to be done. Reports soon reached him that a large Confederate formation was moving from the northeast well-positioned to come in behind the flank and rear of any Union line established along Seminary Ridge and Oak Hill. Almost immediately an aide arrived from Howard confirming the report and passing along new orders. Schurz was to "halt his command" so as not to be outflanked, but to "push forward a thick line of skirmishers to seize the point first indicated."[57] Although clearly revoking the previous order, the new directive required him to simultaneously guard his flank and push forward skirmishers to take "the point first indicated," presumably the extension of the ridge upon which the I Corps was in action. By this time that position was occupied by Gen. Robert Rodes' division, his artillery already playing on Schimmelfennig's troops as they emerged from town onto the plain. Quite clearly, Howard did not appreciate at a distance the impossibility of the latter command. An assault that would have been most difficult for Schurz's entire force was impossible for a mere skirmish line. Schurz

57 Schurz, *Reminiscences*, III, 8; Schurz, "Gettysburg," 276; *New York at Gettysburg*, I, 378.

of course recognized that he would be unable to "seize" the ground in question, but he could push forward skirmishers and he could take action to protect his own flank from the approaching Rebel column to the northeast.

When finally established, this skirmish line stretched for about one-half mile with three regiments deployed as skirmishers and two held in reserve, one behind each flank. This deployment was in strict conformity with the accepted textbook regulations for establishing skirmish lines and their supports. Beyond this, Schurz faced another disadvantage aside from the flat terrain and the arrival of Rodes' division of Confederates—the impending arrival on the field of Gen. Jubal Early's Rebel division on his flank. Further, the extent of ground he was required to cover—initially nearly 1,300 yards from the end of the I Corps line northeast beyond the Hagy farm then northeast-by-east in an arching circle to the Carlisle Road—was impossible to cover adequately with the number of troops available. As a general rule, a brigade of about 1,500 men deployed in the standard double battle line with reserve would cover about 500 yards. Clearly, von Amsberg's brigade was woefully inadequate in numbers. Even deployed in skirmish order, with proper supports and the prudent precaution of holding back some reserve, Schurz could not possibly hope to occupy the front in question with anything more than a thin skirmish line with large gaps between its various segments.

Although many authors have criticized Schurz for not connecting physically with the I Corps, leaving a gap between the two, this was not necessarily a fatal weakness. Given the lack of troops on hand and the requirement that he both protect his right flank and support the I Corps to his left, Schurz deployed von Amsberg's brigade to perform the latter task as best he could. Col. Krzyzanowski, in reserve, massed in closed double column of companies in and around an orchard behind the right flank of von Amsberg's deployed brigade. The positioning of Krzyzanowski's brigade has often been misunderstood. Comments have varied from criticism of Schurz for not deploying the brigade earlier, to the silly comment by one author that the brigade had to be held in closed columns behind the line lest it run away. The placement of Krzyzanowski's brigade, and its formation, were calculated and perceptive decisions by Schurz designed to provide a reserve to counter a number of possible Confederate threats. Closed column was a formation designed to expedite movement. Troops in this formation could move quickly and transform into battle formation in a relatively short time through several methods of deployment. It was an ideal formation for a unit intended as a reserve to be deployed to the point of crisis as quickly as possible.

From his position to the right of and behind von Amsberg's brigade, Krzyzanowski would be available to either support von Amsberg if Rodes launched a serious assault, or move to the left to bring force upon the flank of any attempt by the

Rebels to attack the seemingly exposed flank of the I Corps. By adopting this deployment, Schurz was able to place some pressure on the Confederates as he believed Howard wished him to do, while at the same time maintaining a position and a mobile reserve sufficient to support the I Corps or his own skirmish line as needed. The positioning of Krzyzanowski was neither haphazard nor the result of circumstance; it was a conscious decision by Schurz that appears well conceived when taken in the context of his orders, the exigencies of the moment, and the extended ground he was trying to defend north of town. To deal with the second portion of Howard's order, Schurz instructed Barlow to deploy his division to the right of Schimmelfenning's division, with one brigade extending the XI Corps line and the other formed *en echelon* in a refused position to the right rear.[58] This would not only protect the right flank, but it would also place Krzyzanowski behind the approximate center of Schurz's line in position to come to the aid of Barlow's division should the Rebels threaten that flank. Given the scarcity of troops, Schurz clearly attempted to form as short a line as possible to cover the right flank of the I Corps and the roadways into town from the north, while keeping his regiments well in hand and in immediate supporting distance of one another.

Aside from the scarcity of troops, the other difficulty Schurz faced was terrain. The corps had been ordered to a relatively flat plain exposed to fire from Rebel guns along the slopes leading up to Oak Hill, while offering virtually no physical features upon which to establish a defensive line. Faced with this quandary, it appears that Schurz's intention was to form a line from the position occupied by von Amsberg east toward the county almshouse, making use of the latter's buildings and trees as the only defensible features on that portion of the field. Had he formed his line closer to town, Rebel sharpshooters could have occupied the almshouse grounds, using the cover there to fire at the Federals much as Confederates later used the buildings of the Bliss farm on July 2. If one draws a straight line from the Hagy farm near the flank of the I Corps through the almshouse property to Rock Creek, the defensive line Schurz intended to occupy is approximately 2,000 yards. If the brigades of von Amsberg, Ames and von Gilsa had been deployed along the line Schurz envisioned, leaving Krzyzanowski in reserve, they could have covered approximately 1,500 yards. Adding the batteries of Dilger and Wheeler, the straight-line distance of something like 2,000 yards could have been covered, albeit loosely, while still maintaining a brigade in reserve.

58 *OR* 27, pt. 1, 727; Schurz, *Reminiscences*, III, 8; Schurz, Carl. "The Battle of Gettysburg," 276.

With Barlow's second brigade *en echelon* behind his right, Schurz's right flank would be covered to Rock Creek, with the stream and a small stand of woods along its banks offering at least some modicum of protection. Further, the ground east of Rock Creek could be covered by Buford's cavalry, one brigade of which under Col. Thomas Devin was present when Schurz began his deployment. It was also within range of artillery support from the guns that Howard had placed atop Cemetery Hill. In fact, those guns were specifically sited to fire at a distance rather than to cover the immediate slopes up the hill. Further, we know that these guns were within range of the ground along Rock Creek because Devin later complained that shells from these Federal guns fell among his troopers. Thus, the line Schurz appears to have envisioned would gain some flank protection from Rock Creek and Devin's cavalrymen while using the almshouse site to defensive advantage along a portion of his front. Aside from placing his units in the buildings and streets of the town itself, this was the only logical defensive position that could be formed across the plain.

While it has been argued by some writers that the ground north of the almshouse sloped upward, thereby giving the Confederates a potential advantage for their artillery, this consideration, given the relative indefensibility of *any* position north of Gettysburg, would seem to be, on balance, not necessarily fatal, especially given the very gentle upslope. The Confederate guns on Oak Hill enjoyed much better positions already. Converging fire from Rodes's and Early's batteries would make the seeming "high ground" exceptionally difficult if not impossible for any Federal force to hold. While Barlow's division on the right of Schurz's line would have to face Early's guns in any event, by placing his troops along the almshouse line Schurz opened the distance to Oak Hill, thereby lessening the accuracy and effectiveness of the guns located there. Further, while the forward position on Blocher's Knoll faced wooded area to its front and on both flanks, seriously limiting the field of fire of any Federal infantry deployed there, the almshouse line provided an open field for defensive fire at least 500 yards deep. A Confederate force approaching the line Schurz envisioned would thus have had to cross considerable open space that could be raked by both infantry and artillery fire.

Having ordered his limited number of troops into positions he believed gave them the best opportunity to fulfill his orders, Schurz sent Capt. Winkler to Cemetery Hill to request that a reserve brigade be sent forward to reinforce Barlow's division on the right flank then turned his attention to the growing fight on von Amsberg's front. By this time Dilger was in action and Capt. Irsch's skirmishers from the 45th New York had pushed back Major Eugene Blackford's Alabama sharpshooters to the ridge where Rodes was deploying his division. But Schurz's attention was drawn to a rising crescendo of musketry from the far left in front of Brig. Gen. John C. Robinson's division of the I Corps where O'Neal's and Iverson's brigades were just launching their ill-fated assaults. Robinson's men, bolstered by the cover of a stone wall, unleashed killing volleys into O'Neal's attackers, while the 45th New York fired into the Rebel flank and Dilger's Battery poured shell and canister into the badly exposed Confederates. Both Union corps were holding their own.

☽ ☽ ☽

Francis Barlow was not a happy man as he led his division through Gettysburg. He did not like being in the XI Corps, he particularly did not like commanding German troops, and he was still angry that his orders limiting the number of men who could go for water were not always being obeyed—deliberately disobeyed he thought. His lead brigade that afternoon should have been led by Col. Leopold von Gilsa, but he was already under arrest for supposedly refusing Barlow's order at Middleton on June 28. To make matters worse, Barlow held little confidence in the diminutive German. Schurz felt otherwise. With combat already begun, he ordered von Gilsa's release. Reluctantly, with combat perhaps only minutes away, Barlow sent a message to von Gilsa suspending his arrest until after the battle was over. Receiving the message from one of Barlow's aides, von Gilsa made a production of spurring his horse through the streets to the head of his column shouting "By order of General Schurz I take command of my brigade." On seeing their leader the men "shouted lustily." "Far down the road," an onlooker observed, "behind the passing regiments, a roar of cheers began. It rolled forward, faster than the running of the men who made it—like some high surge sweeping across the surface of a flowing sea. Its roar of cheering neared and neared, until we saw a group of officers coming at a brisk trot, with the mighty cheer always at their horses' heels. Among them rode one man in colonel's uniform who held his head high and smiled. He was an officer, a favorite with the soldiers, who had been under arrest until the eve of the battle. Now, released he was on his way into action, and the whole brigade that knew him was greeting him with the chorus of the lungs."[59]

The band of the 153rd Pennsylvania struck up martial airs as townspeople continued to line the streets. A young girl wearing a white dress emblazoned with the stars and stripes "standing near the middle of the street" caught the attention of Levi Walters. "She was handing out water in a tin dipper, taking it from a tub which her father, a man of about fifty, kept filling with buckets carried from his house nearby." As he rushed along through the streets at the double-quick Reuben Ruch marveled how

59 Keifer, *153rd Pennsylvania*, 257; Pfanz, *Culp's Hill*, 29.

Reuben Ruch, 153rd Pennsylvania
Keifer, *History of the One Hundred Fifty Third Regiment Pennsylvania Volunteer Infantry*

the ladies of the town "stood along the sidewalks with buckets of water, and doing all they could for the men. God bless them. Cannon were booming, and musketry rattling, while wounded were being brought back through the town. By all appearances the ball was on." Ruch soon experienced another reception he found less inviting. "As soon as we got clear of the town we received another reception, but this one in the shape of solid shot, shells . . . and everything that could be shot out of a cannon. Here we got the same old command to forward double-quick, and away went for the big red barn at the Almshouse. The shells were coming pretty thick before we reached the barn. Some were going over us, and some did not quite reach us. A shell exploded right over the column, and every man dodged for the instant."[60]

Once the exhausted men reached the almshouse Barlow allowed them a few moments to remove their knapsacks and catch their breath while still formed in a battalion in mass. The men loaded their weapons. Major John Frueauff in the 153rd Pennsylvania made use of the time to call his men about him. As Ruch recalled it, the major told them that they were a nine-months' regiment and their term of service had expired on June 22. Their enlistment obligation had been fulfilled. None of them had to be there if they did not want to be. Frueauff explained the situation and the obvious danger they were marching toward. As Ruch recalled, the major said "If there was a man in ranks who did not wish to go into battle; he should step out, that it was no disgrace; but that the enemy was in our native state, and that the people of Pennsylvania looked to us for relief, and that it was our duty to protect our homes." When the brief

60 Kiefer, *153rd Pennsylvania*, 177, 209-10.

speech was over, Ruch recalled that "we gave three cheers and not a man stepped out of the ranks."[61]

The last brigade to arrive was commanded by Brig. Gen. Adelbert Ames following in the footsteps of von Gilsa's men. Ames had an estimated 1,269 men with him, less stragglers and those assigned to detached duty—probably no more than 1,150 actually present. The 75th Ohio approached at the double-quick but slowed somewhat upon entering the confines of town. William Southerton noticed the "Townspeople were excited and scared to death, hurrying and scurrying in every direction." Leading Company D, Capt. Mahlon B. Briggs found time for a brief stop by Miss Kate Wattles of West Middle Street, probably to quench his thirst with one of the cups of water being proffered. As he gulped the refreshing drink, the young girl wrote a message in his "Soldier's Textbook": "Capt. Briggs / Don't forget God's will be done / Go forward into the fight / Think of friends and home / God is with you /I pray God protects you / Sincerely Kate W Gettysburg." The booklet was later found on the field north of town. Inside someone had written "Gettysburg July 12, 1863 Pick up on battlefield." Wounded shortly after the chance meeting, Capt. Briggs died on July 3 at the age of 22.[62]

The order to hurry reached the 17th Connecticut about the time the men began to hear the booming of guns and see hazy clouds of smoke in the distance. W. W. Paynton recalled: "The next hour was a trying one to men of weak nerves, and many a poor soldier expressed in his blanched face a fear that he would blush to speak, for there are none so brave but at the approach of battle feel a vague sense of impending danger and perhaps death. The bravado and bluster of camp life is all gone in the face of the enemy, and it is a remarkably courageous man that can look into the mouth of a twelve pound Parrott gun, or the muzzles of a regiment of infantry, and not feel a quiver of fear. For my part I felt that sense of uneasiness that is born of uncertainty, and I wondered what would be my fate and how I should acquit myself in the struggle that was so near at hand."[63]

61 Biddle, *First Day*, 118; Kiefer, *153rd Pennsylvania*, 209-10. In reality, the term of the 153rd had not expired, but apparently the major and many, if not most, of the men believed that it had since there was a squabble following the battle when the men determined to head home only to be told they had a few additional days of service remaining. Nevertheless, at the time they believed they were free to decide whether to go into battle or not. It is to their credit that no one refused.

62 Baumgartner, *Buckeye Blood*, 45; Southerton, "What We Did There," 5; 75th Ohio File, GNMP.

63 Paynton, "From Virginia to Gettysburg and Back," manuscript, GNMP.

Rowland Howard was surprised by the civilians' behavior. "As we passed through the principal street, the inhabitants thronged us with refreshments. The sight was a novel one, coming so unexpected, created quite an impression. I expected to find the place deserted, knowing that spherical case and 'round solids' were not calculated to promote good fellowship, hence the surprise. One of the number, a young girl of no ordinary attraction, claimed my attention in particular. . . . She held a plate of cakes with one hand, the other being used in administering to the thirst of the wearied boys, from a pail that stood by her side. An Officer seeing her exposed condition, ordered her to retire. 'Why should I fear,' she proudly asked, 'They are fighting for me and I will not leave them!'" William Warren's company rushed through town "in such as hurry, we could hardly stop to get anything to eat, we were on business & we soon had all we wanted." Emerging from town "we halted in a meadow by the road, close column in mass, for a rest." Warren "dropped like a dead person, all exhausted & tired."[64]

Leading the Connecticut regiment was its lieutenant colonel, Douglas Fowler. He had been placed in arrest by Barlow for allowing too many men to go for water at a time. As the sounds of battle approached, Fowler wanted desperately to lead his men in the coming fight. No longer willing to play a passive part riding behind his regiment, he went over Barlow's head, appealing directly to the acting corps commander. In his reminiscences Schurz explained it this way: Barlow was "a strict disciplinarian, and one of the coolest and bravest in action. In both respects he was inclined to carry his virtues to excess. At the very time when he moved into the firing line at Gettysburg I had to interfere by positive order in favor of the commander of one of his regiments, whom he had suspended and sent to the rear for a mere unimportant peccadillo."[65] Fowler resumed command of his regiment at once. Barlow, already unhappy, had one more reason to be resentful.

☽ ☽ ☽

While the balance of the troops arrived, Schimmelfennig continued to be actively engaged. Under increasing fire from Oak Hill, Dilger expertly moved his pieces about to avoid giving the Rebel gunners a stationery target for too long. Although his maneuvers reduced casualties among the gunners, Rebel overshoots landed among the 157th New York "doing much injury." The artillerymen also took fire. One Rebel shell "struck a driver of a gun" in Wheeler's battery "and swept him and his two horses right

64 Warren diary, July 1, 1863; Rowland Howard, "The Story of Gettysburg," Bowdoin College.

65 Schurz, *Reminiscences*, III, 7-8.

away," while nearby an infantryman's leg was "taken off by a shot, and whirled like a stone through the air, until it came against a caisson with a loud whack." Back on Cemetery Hill Lt. Bayard Wilkeson's Battery G, 4th U. S. Artillery arrived, its laboring horses covering the last two miles at a trot. Meeting him as he appeared, Major Osborn ordered him to hurry his six 12-pounders ahead to report as quickly as possible to Barlow north of town.[66]

Several errant shells landed among the 82nd Ohio in support behind the Union batteries. Musician Joseph Gillis, a nineteen-year-old shoemaker from Delaware, Ohio, "had to march through an open field to a cluster of woods. We played the tune called 'The Yankees Are Coming.' It is a very quick piece and pretty. The rebs let go solid shot. The first went about three feet from the back drummer, and you ought to have seen him juke. Several came very close until we got to the woods." A fragment of shrapnel tore Maj. David Thomson's coat without injuring him, while a large piece of shell struck Sergt. Major Jasper Snow's "cheek just scratching it from the temple to chin, back, cutting his ear and the side of his neck. That side swelled up immediately as though he had mumps, yet he was not off duty. Several of our boys were torn to tatters, their blood and flesh scattered over their comrades. Yet those brave boys stood still and awaited for their turn patiently." It must have seemed like an eternity, but finally the order came to move forward. Gillis watched as "the Regt. was formed. The Col said, 'Musicians to the Hospital, March.' I bid goodbye to the boys and left, and we just got about five or six rods to the rear when the 82nd went in on their nerve."[67]

In Krzyzanowski's brigade the 26th Wisconsin made ready for battle. The musicians, who functioned as stretcher bearers during times of battle, were sent to the rear to await developments. While they awaited the call, Rebel artillery on Oak Hill found the range, sending shells arching through the humid summer sky toward their position in what Lt. Karl Karsten pronounced "a strong artillery fire." We "were assigned to a position in an open field to the north of the town," Adj. Wallber recalled, "with orders to lie down to escape the shot and shell which came flying over our heads."[68]

It was now mid-afternoon. Dobke's men, and indeed the entire brigade under von Amsberg, had fought well. Arriving on the battlefield exhausted from a demanding

66 Cook, *Letters of George Arrowsmith*; Wheeler to grandfather and aunt, July 26, 1863, in Bershears, *Loyal Till Death*, 186; *OR* 27, pt. 1, 747, 756.

67 Gillis to sister, July 22, 1863; Baumgartner, *Buckeye Blood*, 42; Thomson to family, Aug. 5, 1863.

68 Wallber, "From Gettysburg to Libby Prison."

Musician Joseph Gillis, 82nd Ohio
Joseph H. Gillis

forced march, they had gone directly into action, pushed back picked sharpshooters, captured the Hagy and McLean farms and aided in repulsing assaults on the I Corps. Dilger and Wheeler were giving the Rebel batteries on Seminary Ridge a drubbing. The 61st Ohio had pushed back Rebel sharpshooters, clearing the immediate field of that menace. Company H from the 119th New York in Krzyzanowski's brigade seized the Crawford barn to deny its protected position to Southern sharp- shooters and two companies from the 153rd Pennsylvania in von Gilsa's brigade had seized the almshouse buildings. With the arrival of Wilkeson, Schurz had three batteries, Dilger's and Wheeler's supporting the right of the I Corps and Wilkeson's in support of Barlow's division holding the right of the XI Corps line. Every attempt by the Rebels to turn the I Corps flank had been thrown back, Major Eugene Blackford's picked sharpshooters had been driven from their positions, and a large number of Confederate prisoners taken. Both of Schurz's divisions were now in place: Schimmelfennig had von Amsberg holding the left of his line linking with the I Corps while Barlow had his two brigades massed near the almshouse and in echelon with the right brigade refused to protect the flank. Krzyzanowski's brigade was drawn up in reserve in position to support any portion of Schurz's line that might be threatened. To the right, beyond Rock Creek, Buford's cavalry were in place to prevent any wide flanking move by whatever Confederates might be approaching down the Harrisburg Road. Climbing once more to the roof of the Hagy home, Schurz surveyed the situation. Everything appeared stable. Perhaps a brief sense of relief passed through his mind.

Chapter 11

"Keep Cool and Aim Well"

Afternoon, July 1, 1863

WHEN BARLOW'S DIVISION BEGAN ARRIVING he first directed it into position in accordance with Schruz's orders with Leopold von Gilsa's brigade, the first to arrive, in proximity to the almshouse and Adelbert Ames' brigade refused *en echelon* on von Gilsa's right.[1] While the troops caught their breath from their exhausting forced march, Barlow surveyed the field. Several hundred yards to his front he spied Blocher's Knoll, a small rise at the end of a gradually rising plain. Most likely thinking that the elevated ground would make a better defensive position for his division, he ordered his men forward without regard to Schurz's directive, the effect this might have on the rest of the Union position or, for that matter, with no thought to his own flanks.

Von Gilsa aligned his regiments with the 54th New York on the right, the 68th New York in the center and companies A and B of the 153rd Pennsylvania on the left, all deployed in skirmish order to cover the amount of ground and to better deal with Confederate skirmishers to their front and in the wheat fields to their left. The remaining eight companies of the Pennsylvania regiment, by far the largest in the brigade, formed behind the line in battle order as a reserve. Von Gilsa, still mounted, rode behind the skirmish line to provide encouragement and direction. Reuben Ruch, with the reserve, clearly heard the colonel shouting encouragement. "He told them not to shoot unless they saw something to shoot at, as ammunition was worth money, and they must not waste it. Just at this time the bullets commenced to whistle and some of

1 Kiefer, 153rd *Pennsylvania*, 28-29.

the boys on the skirmish line were trying to dodge them. The general told the boys to never mind those that whistled, as long as they whistled they were all right."[2] Miraculously, von Gilsa was not hit despite making quite an inviting target.

While they advanced, Confederate artillery took them under fire. Captain Friedrich Otto von Fritsch, a member of von Gilsa's staff, recalled advancing "over an open field, toward the Harrisburg road, where we were heavily bombarded. Large shells and six-pounders passed close over our heads, many officers dismounted or bent low whenever they felt the pressure of the air created by the shot." Despite the sharpshooters and the shelling, von Gilsa's skirmishers quickly drove back the Rebels until they reached and seized the knoll. With the objective in his possession, von Gilsa closed up his skirmishers into a thin line on the northern slope. Half of the 68th New York he placed in skirmish order to protect the exposed left flank where Rebel sharpshooters were still active. Though offering a small rise to protect the troops from direct musketry from the north and east if they lay down, and a wooded area with shade and some apparent protection, von Fritsch found Blocher's Knoll to be "a hot place for us. Trees were felled everywhere by the cannon balls, and one unfortunate soldier was nailed by a six-pounder against a big tree. I got hold of his bushy hair and pulled him down, as he presented a ghastly appearance." The men were ordered to sit down while the officers conferred with Barlow riding ahead of Ames' brigade which he was holding in reserve. Von Fritsch was leading the 68th New York's skirmish line. The captain "rode up and down, encouraging the men to keep cool and aim well, and soon we drove the Confederate skirmishers back" across a small brook just south of the Blocher homes. "But now I noticed heavy columns approaching in front, and from the right. We fired, and then I ordered the commanding officer of the skirmishers to fall slowly back into the woods and fire from tree to tree."[3] Von Fritsch reported a large Rebel column approaching.

☽ ☽ ☽

From his position along the Mummasburg Road Carl Schurz was busy monitoring the situation. Knowing that Confederate troops were reported approaching from the north, he felt "much anxiety about my right, which was liable to be turned if any of the enemy's forces were advancing by the Heidlersburg road." Turning to Capt. Frederick Winkler, he ordered the aide to ride quickly to Howard on Cemetery Hill to request a

2 Kiefer, *153rd Pennsylvania*, 210-11.

3 Kiefer, *153rd Pennsylvania*, 211; Butts, *Gallant Captain*, 75-76.

brigade be sent forward from the reserve to form *en echelon* on his right near the railroad depot. The general's intent was "to have that brigade in readiness to charge upon any force the enemy might move around my right." Winkler galloped through town, found von Steinwehr on Cemetery Hill, and delivered the request. It is not clear if Howard had returned from his visit with Doubleday by this time, but the commanding general later wrote that "I had then only two small brigades in reserve, and had already located three regiments from these in the edge of the town and to the north, and I felt sure that I must hold the point where I was as an ultimate resort. Therefore I at first replied that I could not spare any troops."[4] The captain turned his horse around and hurried back to deliver the disappointing response.

While Winkler completed his mission, the sound of firing increased off to the left where the I Corps was heavily engaged. Observing the action from the Hagy house, Schurz made sure that no crisis existed, then turned to his right to monitor progress on that front. He could not believe what he saw. Against his specific orders Barlow's entire division was in motion, moving north away from its assigned position. Rather than linking to Schimmelfennig's division as Schurz ordered, Barlow had already lost contact. "[A]t the same time," Schurz "saw the enemy emerging from the belt of woods on my right with one battery after another and one column of infantry after another, threatening to envelop my right flank and to cut me off from the town and the position on Cemetery Hill." The situation had suddenly become critical. "We could hardly hope to hold out long against such a superiority of numbers, and there was imminent danger that, if we held out too long, the enemy would succeed in turning our right flank and in getting possession of the town of Gettysburg, through which our retreat to the defensive position on Cemetery Hill would probably have to be effected. For this reason I was so anxious to have one of the reserve brigades posted at the entrance to the town to oppose the flanking movement of the enemy which I saw going on."[5]

Why Barlow disobeyed his orders has never been clearly established. Howard rode with him through town and accompanied him as he deployed. What Howard may or may not have said to Barlow has not, to date, come to light. Whether he altered Schurz's orders to Barlow without informing Schurz, or whether Barlow decided to act on his own initiative is uncertain, although it may be deduced from some of Barlow's post-war writings that he felt the position assigned to him a poor one and believed moving to higher ground would place his command in a better position, much the same rationale used by Gen. Daniel Sickles to move his entire III Corps out of position

4 *OR* 27, pt.1, 728; Howard ms report.

5 *OR* 27, pt. 1, 728; Schurz, *Reminiscences*, III, 9-10.

on the following day, and with much the same eventual result. Howard later wrote in the *National Tribune* that "Barlow made one strong effort to advance his lines, but as soon as I heard of the approach of Ewell and saw that nothing could prevent the turning of my right flank, the order of advance was countermanded, except to press out a skirmish line."[6] Although this statement clearly indicates Howard was aware of Barlow's advance, it does not prove that Howard was aware at the time that Barlow's move violated Schurz's orders.

What is certain from this is that regardless of the exact circumstances, Howard countermanded the earlier orders and replaced them with a directive to only advance skirmishers. So Barlow in effect disobeyed both the orders he received from Schurz and those from Howard. In his memoirs Schurz was generous, commenting only that Barlow must have either "misunderstood my order, or that he was carried away by the ardor of the conflict."[7] No doubt there was more to it than this. Could bias have been a contributing factor? Barlow did not like serving with or commanding "German" troops, so he no doubt disliked even more serving under the command of a German. Did this prejudice figure into his disobedience of Schurz's orders and his failure to even so much as communicate his intent to his immediate commanding officer? And this was only minutes after Schurz had overruled Barlow's orders placing Colonels von Gilsa and Fowler under arrest. Could Barlow's temper have gotten the best of him?

Regardless of Barlow's motivations, his disobedience of orders presented Schurz with a very serious problem. Rather than a continuous position running from the Hagy farm to Rock Creek, with a wide field of fire to its front, Barlow's unauthorized movement forward meant not only that his left flank broke contact with the right of Schimmelfennig's division, thereby creating a gap, but it also exposed the right of the XI Corps line to being taken in both its flanks and its rear. Instead of refusing his right as Schurz had ordered to protect the right flank of the entire I and XI Corps position, Barlow's new alignment left him in an exposed position where both of his flanks were "in the air" and Schurz's carefully prepared position in shambles. Capt. Winkler having returned from his unsuccessful attempt to get a reserve brigade sent forward from Cemetery Hill, Schurz dispatched him to Barlow at once, with words of caution and perhaps an order to cease his unauthorized move. The captain quickly found Barlow. Whatever message he brought back was apparently not recorded, but Schurz quickly dispatched Winkler back to Barlow a second time to advise the general that his flank was about to be turned.

6 *National Tribune*, November 20, 1884.

7 Schurz, *Reminiscences*, III, 9.

The term "almshouse" is deceptive. As seen in this photograph, it was a large complex of buildings that would have made an excellent anchor for the line Schurz was trying to construct across the plain north of town if it had not been for Barlow's unauthorized advance.

Gettysburg National Military Park

Schurz sent an order to Schimmelfennig to reestablish his connection with Barlow's division, a move forced upon him but which he recognized "made still thinner a line already too thin." He also "hurried one staff officer after another to General Howard with the urgent request for one of his two reserve brigades to protect my right against the impending flank attack by the enemy."[8] To carry out Schurz's order, Schimmelfenning could only push von Amsberg's slender line of skirmishers farther north to regain contact with Barlow, lengthening the line and further thinning it by stretching the distance between soldiers and units. In fact, this was a mere skirmish line with no force behind it at all. Only two regiments were available to form a normal line of battle, far too few to resist any serious assault. By this time Confederate artillery was already opening on Barlow's command and Gen. Jubal Early's division was formed, ready to strike. Time had run out.

☽ ☽ ☽

While von Gilsa's small force dueled with Confederate sharpshooters, nineteen-year-old Lt. Bayard Wilkeson arrived to reinforce Barlow with his Battery G, 4th U. S. Artillery. Wilkeson left one section under Lt. Christopher F. Merkle south of the York road near the almshouse where he immediately opened fire with solid shot against one of the Confederate batteries. The other two sections unlimbered east of the

8 Schurz, *Reminiscences*, III, 9-10; *OR* 27, pt. 1, 728.

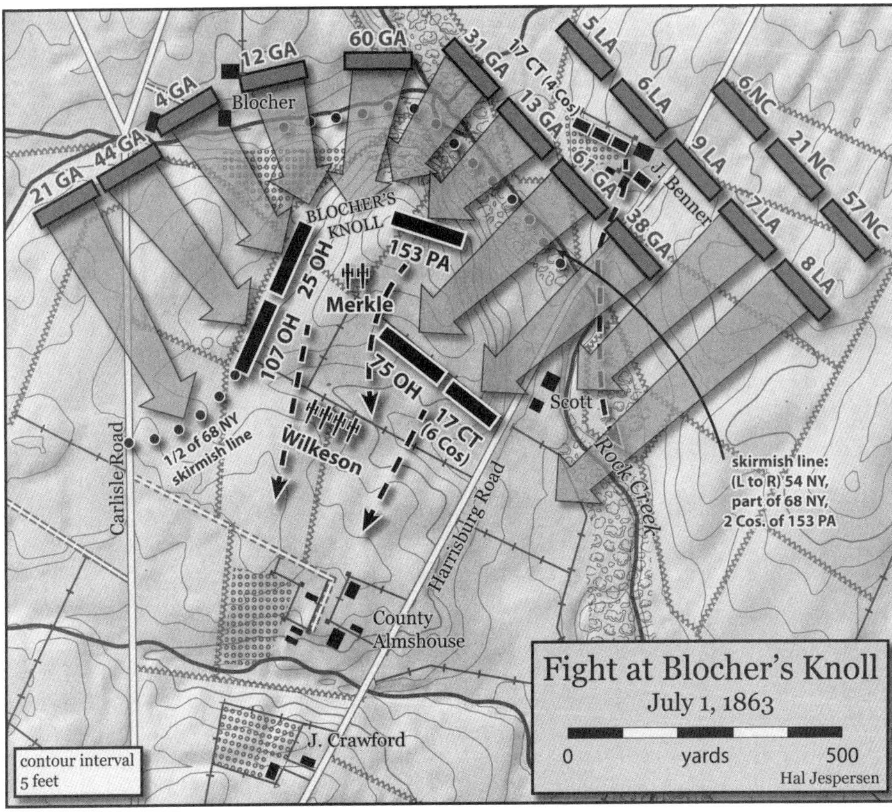

almshouse where they quickly opened fire. Within the Rebel lines, Gen. Early and his aide Major John Warwick Daniel sat astride their horses next to Captain A. W. Garber's battery watching the Federals deploy. From their vantage point they saw "A Federal Battery, plainly in sight, galloped to meet [Early's deployment]. . . . One of its earliest, if not its first shot, struck a brass Howitzer of Garber's company in the mouth, and that ended its military service." Yet, while Wilkeson's opening fire proved accurate, his guns immediately came under fire from Rebel infantry and two batteries which shifted their attention to him. Almost immediately a shell fragment tore into the lieutenant's right leg. Four of his men carried him from the field mortally wounded. Lt. Eugene A. Bancroft, a bookkeeper from Chicago, took command, wisely shifting the position of the pieces regularly to prevent the Confederates from blanketing his guns.[9]

9 *OR* 27, pt. 1, 756-57; Daniel account, Jubal Early Papers, Box B-41, GNMP; Barnett, "By Their Guns," 92.

Major Allen G. Brady, 17th Connecticut
U.S. Army Heritage and Education Center

Behind Wilkeson, Justus Silliman and his comrades in the 17th Connecticut "were obliged to pass through a raking crossfire from a Rebel battery on our right, but most of their shells passed over us." While they waited, many of the men fired off their muskets to make sure they worked after passing through the downpour along their march. Ames soon ordered part of the 25th Ohio forward to provide support for Wilkeson and sent an aide, Lt. Charles E. Doty, to Lt. Col. Fowler in the 17th Connecticut to sieze a small wooden bridge and occupy a brick house east of Rock Creek. Fowler asked for volunteers. Capt. Henry Allen offered his Company F, soon to be joined by companies A, B, and K. Major Allen G. Brady, who Fowler placed in charge of the mission, had already been passed over for promotion twice, the second time after Chancellorsville where he led the regiment after his colonel was seriously wounded and lieutenant colonel killed. Instead, Fowler had been promoted over his head. Apparently Governor William Buckingham had something against Brady, but the major appears not to have held it against Fowler. Brady dispatched two companies to occupy the bridge while the other two continued on to take possession of Josiah Benner's home. Once across the creek they immediately ran into skirmishers from Early's approaching division. A hot fire fight began with Brady's men pushing the Rebels back, one company proceeding around each side of the Benner home. Lt. Col. Hilary P. Jones' artillery opened with "shot, shell, grape, and canister" that stalled progress. Brady dismounted to continue the advance, but Jones' artillery soon set fire to the house. Unable to advance any farther, Brady spread his men out behind whatever cover they could find.[10]

10 Marcus, *New Canaan Private*, 41; Hamblen, *Connecticut Yankees*, 18, 20-21; Niven, *Connecticut for the Union*, 234; *17th Connecticut Volunteers at Gettysburg*, 10; OR 27, pt. 1, 717.

After withstanding concentrated artillery fire for about half an hour Bancroft withdrew the two advanced sections of Battery G somewhat to lengthen the range, and hopefully decrease the accuracy of the Rebel fire. While he did so, von Gilsa was becoming increasingly concerned as his skirmishers reported large numbers of Rebels massing to their front. Early's division was forming, connecting with Brig. Gen. George Doles' brigade from Rodes' division deployed in the lowlands east of Oak Hill. The vulnerability of the position Barlow chose quickly became evident. Doles brought to the field about 1,300 men, now aligned directly on the exposed left flank of von Gilsa's small force of less than 900 men. To the north of Blocher's Knoll, Early began deploying Brig. Gen. John B. Gordon's Georgians, 1,800 strong, in his first line, supported by Brig. Gen. Harry Hays' 1,200 Louisianians, and Col. Isaac Avery's 1,200 North Carolinians with Brig. Gen. William "Extra Billy" Smith's 800 Virginians in reserve. Doles and Gordon alone outnumbered von Gilsa by about three and one-half to one; if one counts Hays, Avery and Smith then the Confederate advantage rises to six to one. And this does not count Jones' artillery battalion of sixteen guns. With these pieces moving into battery, Early outnumbered Bancroft's guns by more than two and one-half to one and could also count on the guns from Oak Hill that were within range of Barlow's positions.[11] Nor was von Gilsa's position easily defensible. Both of his flanks were completely in the air while the woods covering his front dramatically reduced his effective field of fire. The colonel quickly sent a messenger to Barlow requesting immediate support.

Whether he realized it by now or not, Barlow had placed his entire division in a completely untenable position. With Ames' brigade aligned behind von Gilsa, and no significant force of any size to guard its flanks, the division was positioned in a very vulnerable salient approachable by Confederates on three sides and also from the rear by any of Early's troops who bypassed Barlow's right flank east of Rock Creek. Further, the separation caused by Barlow's precipitate move exposed Schurz's entire force to possible defeat in detail. Barlow's division stood no chance against the approaching Confederate tide that outnumbered him in total by about three to one. Whatever modest advantage he may have felt he was gaining from the small rise of Blocker's Knoll was more than offset by the completely exposed position in which he left his own division, and by extension Schurz's entire force.

Receiving von Gilsa's request for reinforcement, Barlow ordered Ames to send his 107th Ohio forward. When the regiment was momentarily held up until a rail fence could be removed, Ames became impatient with the seeming failure to execute his

11 *OR* 27, pt. 1, 756; Gottfried, *Maps*, 298, 492, 496, 501, 507, 523.

Col. Seraphim Meyer, 107th Ohio, in a postwar photograph. *Ohio History Connection*

orders and also with the conduct of the regiment's commander, Col. Seraphim Meyer, who appeared to "crouch down upon his horse" amid the bursting shells. Irate that Meyer was not projecting the correct image before his troops, Ames approached and "reproved him . . . for his apparently cowardly conduct and unnecessary dodging."[12]

Once the fence had been removed and its commanding officer "reproved," the 107th Ohio moved forward, deploying into refused formation on von Gilsa's left to protect his flank. As they advanced, Frederick Nussbaum was horrified to see a shell take off the arm of Maj. Augustus Vignos then bounce up and kill the horse of another officer. Another almost completely severed the leg of Lt. William Fisher. Barlow then sent the 25th Ohio to strengthen von Gilsa's inadequate second line and support Wilkeson's section positioned on the left. This raised von Gilsa's strength to about 1,500 muskets, slightly less than half of what Doles and Gordon could bring to bear on his position. Barlow also ordered the remainder of Ames' division, the 75th Ohio and six companies of the 17th Connecticut, forward to form a reserve immediately behind von Gilsa on Blocher's Knoll.[13] About this time the very active Capt. Winkler came thundering up with the second message from Schurz warning Barlow that his flank was about to be turned. But by this time it was too late, Early's artillery was already in action and his division was formed, ready to strike.

☽ ☽ ☽

12 Baumgartner, *Buckeye Blood*, 47.

13 Smith, *107th Regiment Ohio*, 225; Browne letter to John Bachelder, Apr. 8, 1864, in Ladd, *Bachelder Papers*, I, 148; Gottfried, *Brigades*, 311.

Jubal Early's Confederate division could not have arrived on the field in a better position if it were planned in advance. George Doles' brigade of Rodes' division holding the Confederate left had been deployed in the plain below Oak Hill to outflank the Federal I Corps position. The arrival of the XI Corps turned the tables. Both Doles's and Major Eugene Blackford's sharpshooters were pushed back until Rodes became concerned for the safety of his own flank. But then, from out beyond the Union right, Rodes spied the head of Early's column, 5,158 men coming right down on the exposed flank of the Federal position. Early deployed his division with Gordon's Georgia brigade on the right, Hays' Louisianians in the center straddling the Harrisburg Road, Avery's North Carolinians on the left and Smith's Virginians in reserve supporting Jones' artillery battalion. To Gordon's right stood Doles' brigade, the two in perfect position to turn Barlow's flanks and strike his center at the same time.[14]

Col. von Gilsa had deployed the 54th New York in skirmish order below Blocher's Knoll stretching left from Rock Creek where its right ended along the banks of the stream. To its left lay a portion of the 68th New York and two companies of the 153rd Pennsylania extended the skirmish line. Covering almost 750 yards through heavy underbrush, this advanced line was thinly held with an average of one man every two yards and with its field of fire seriously restricted by woods that provided cover to an approaching Rebel force until it was within almost a hundred yards of the Federal position. His main line, located toward the crest of the knoll some 100 to 130 yards behind the skirmish line, was drawn up in a conventional battle array with the 153rd Pennsylvania on the right and the 25th Ohio in the center, a total of about 620 men deployed in two lines covering a little over 150 yards.[15]

On the left of von Gilsa's battle line lay the 107th Ohio in a refused position to protect the left flank with the balance of the 68th New York stretched out in skirmish order southwestward to the Carlisle Road, the total flank position covering some 550 yards with an average of only one man per yard (or one every two yards if in a standard double line). While the New York skirmishers were located in a relatively open grain field, a gap existed between their right and the left of the 107th Ohio. To make matters worse, the Buckeyes found most of their front obstructed by an orchard. Two sections of artillery under Lt. Bancroft lay behind them while within supporting distance Ames held the 75th Ohio and six companies of the 17th Connecticut, a total of some 650 men. Thinly held, the position's flanks were completely in the air and its nearest

14 *OR* 27, pt. 2, 479, 468.

15 Kiefer, *153rd Pennsylvania*, 140.

support, Krzyzanowski's brigade, lay over 800 yards away. It was no wonder that von Gilsa excitedly rushed another aide back to Barlow asking to further reinforcement.[16]

On the 153rd Pennsylvania's skirmish line, Sergt. William R. Kiefer could see movement among the woods and underbrush to the front of his position. Turning to Lt. J. Clyde Millar, Kiefer pointed across the opening to the woods, telling the officer that "by crouching down, I could see their legs up to their knees. I did so, and saw the force was a large one." Alarmed, Millar "ran back up the slope to report the fact, when I met Adj. [Howard J.] Reeder with drawn sword, who said, 'Go back and hold your line at all hazards.'" While Millar and Reeder spoke, skirmishers from the 31st Georgia pushed forward against the advanced position of the 68th New York twice, only to be driven back both times by accurate Federal fire. But all was not well. When Millar returned to his company he was surprised to see some of his men wounded by musket balls coming from behind. Angrily, he ordered a corporal to rush back to the main line to stop the friendly fire. But when the soldier returned he brought even more disturbing news. The seemingly errant fire was not coming from friendly forces, but from Confederates who had worked their way around the flank and rear of Barlow's position.[17]

☽ ☽ ☽

"Forward, Georgians!" Early's staff officer John Daniel heard Gordon yell the order that put his brigade in motion. Looking from near the Benner home his eye caught a scene he would never forget: "And steadily forward across the yellow wheat fields we saw the line of Georgians, Louisianians, and Carolinians roll, their burnished bayonets making a silver wave across a cloth of gold. Now they disappeared in the copse of woods along the stream; then comes the wild cheer, and the crashing volley, and a cloud of smoke wraps the combatants." On the receiving end of the assault Capt. von Fritsch peered north from Blocher's Knoll to see a sight he would also never forget. "The Confederates approached slowly and in magnificent order, and after the first volley of our men they sent a strong volley in return. Our men, now standing, fired twice more, then the Confederates charged through the creek, screaming savagely."[18]

16 Ibid.

17 Kiefer, *153rd Pennsylvania*, 140-41, 211; Millar to Bachelor, Mar. 2, 1886; *OR* 27, pt. 2, 492; Nichols, *A Soldier's Story*, 116.

18 Daniel, *Speeches and Orations*, 81, Jubal Early Papers, Box B-41, GNMP; Butts, *Gallant Captain*, 75.

As Gordon's men burst upon von Gilsa's skirmish line, Doles' Georgians rushed across the fields and orchards east of John Blocher's home to throw their weight against the flank held by the 107th Ohio and a portion of the 68th New York, the defenders outnumbered by about two and one-half to one. Von Gilsa's skirmish line fell back up the slope where it rallied behind the battle line. Gordon's Confederates followed closely behind, while Doles pressed his attack against the left flank and Hays' brigade began fording Rock Creek behind von Gilsa's right threatening him with encirclement. Despite the shock of the assault and the impossible position von Gilsa's men found themselves in, they fought back desperately. In the forefront of Doles' assault, the 21st Georgia was subjected to what one veteran described as "a galling fire" that Henry W. Thomas of the 4th Georgia recalled "doing considerable execution." Advancing against what Major W. H. Willis of the 4th Georgia called "stubborn" resistence, Col. D. R. E. Winn fell mortally wounded as did Col. Samuel P. Lumpkin at the head of the 44th Georgia.[19]

In Gordon's brigade, Captain W. L. McLeod leading the 38th Georgia was killed crossing Rock Creek as the Rebels charged into what George W. O'Neal in the 31st Georgia described as "stubborn resistance." G. W. Nichols, fighting in the same regiment, was surprised by the determined Federal opposition: "We met the enemy at Rock Creek. We attacked them immediately, but we had a hard time in moving them. We advanced with our accustomed yell, but they stood firm until we got near them. They then began to retire in fine order, shooting at us as they retreated. They were harder to drive than we had ever known them before. Men were being mown down in great numbers on both sides." "As my command charged across the ravine and up its steep declivity," Gordon later reported, "the fight became on portions of the line a hand-to-hand struggle." The conflict was so fierce that Capt. William J. Seymour, viewing the assault from his position with Hays' brigade, described von Gilsa's resistence as "a heavy fire. The musketry was very severe and we feared that Gordon would be borne back." Gordon called the Federal stand "a most obstinate resistance."[20]

19 Thomas, *Doles-Cook*, 7-8; 4th Georgia File, GNMP; *OR* 27, pt. 2, 584.

20 Hudgins manuscript, 38th Georgia File, GNMP; O'Neal manuscript, Co. G, 31st Georgia File, GNMP; Nichols, *A Soldier's Story*, 116; Gordon, *Reminiscences*, 114; Jones, "A Louisiana Tiger," manuscript, Hays Brigade File, GNMP; White, *History of the 31st Georgia*, 92. It is difficult to ascertain Confederate losses since sources are contradictory and the same author sometimes cites different figures. Further, some units either did not submit casualty reports or they were lost. Then too, the Confederates tended to count "wounded" differently than the Union forces, thus reducing the number of actual Rebel casualties.

Col. Andrew Harris, 75th Ohio
U.S. Army Heritage and Education Center

With the situation deteriorating by the minute, Barlow ordered up his reserve in a desperate attempt to stabilize his position. Receiving the order, Adelbert Ames turned to Col. Andrew Harris of the Ohio regiment and ordered him to "fix bayonets, pass to the front between the 107th and 25th Ohio, and if possible check the advance of the enemy." A graduate of Miami University in Ohio, Harris would one day become governor of the state. "We passed to the front as ordered," Harris explained. It was a fearful advance and made at a dreadful cost of life. We could go no further, halted and opened fire. The enemy was close and still advancing. We checked them in our immediate front, but they continued to press on around both flanks. Our situation was perilous in the extreme." Thick, swirling musket smoke covered the battle line, artillery roared along both flanks, the din of battle magnified by the screams of the wounded and the constant discharge of Bancroft's supporting guns to the rear. William Southerton recalled "How frantically we gnawed paper from cartridges! Loaded rifles! Oh, golly! The Johnnies were coming! And coming fast! A large force of infantry was coming right at us. . . . What a horrible roar of battle! Smoke and fumes thick and acrid. One could scarcely see the comrade beside him. Casualties were terrible. Oh, so many were killed or wounded there."[21]

At one point Lt. Col. Jeremiah Williams of the 25th Ohio saw his color bearer and his Rebel counterpart striking out at "each other with their flag-staffs!" Confederate Gen. Gordon never forgot the incident, writing in his memoirs more than forty years later about "This lion-hearted color bearer" who "stood firmly in his place, refusing to fly, to yield his ground, or to surrender his flag. As the Confederates crowded around him and around the stalwart men who still stood firmly by him, he became engaged in personal combat with the color-bearer of one of my Georgia regiments. What his fate

21 Harris to Bachelder, Mar. 14, 1881, and Sept. 18, 1882; Bachelder Papers, GNMP; Southerton, "What We Did There," 5-6; Baumgartner, *Buckeye Blood*, 49.

was I do not now recall, but I trust and believe that his life was spared." Caught in a deadly crossfire between Doles's and Gordon's brigades, the Ohioans suffered heavily from the effects of the enfilading fire. Shot down, Lt. Col. Williams was unable to escape and fell into the hands of the Confederates, destined to spend eight months in Libby Prison.[22]

In the 17th Connecticut, as shells shrieked overhead, occasionally bursting to spray the waiting men with hot shrapnel, Lt. Col. Douglas Fowler sat atop his white horse joking with his men to keep up their spirits, calling on them to only "Dodge the big ones boys." When Ames' order arrived, the colonel directed his men forward. Lt. C. E. Doty watched as "Colonel Fowler at once rode to the front and gave the command to deploy columns, and swinging his sword, said: 'Now, Seventeenth, do your duty! Forward, double quick! Charge bayonets!' And with a yell, which our boys know how to give, they charged."[23]

As it approached Blocher's Knoll, the regiment ran headlong into the Confederates. Fowler's officers called to their commander "to persuade him to dismount during the battle, but he refused, fearing he might be deemed cowardly." In a few minutes, a whizzing shell fragment nearly decapitated the colonel, splattering his blood and brains onto Adj. H. Whitney Chatfield. Horrified by the sight, Fowler's men hesitated before slowly turning to move ahead. As they reached the slope leading up to Blocher's Knoll, two color bearers were shot and killed in quick succession carrying the state flag, as was Color Sergt. Edwin D. Pickett when he grasped the fallen standard and Corp. Henry Burns after him. Lt. James Mayne bent down, rolled Burns's body off the fallen colors, gathered them up, and carried them away to safety. Similarly, when Sergt. Cyrus T. Batchelder dropped the national colors, John Hayes retrieved the silk banner, only to be quickly wounded. Daniel S. Garritt picked up the flag, soon dropped it, and the ensign was transferred into the hands of Jimmy Hayes. In minutes 33 men fell. One was Justus Silliman, knocked unconscious by a minié ball that "glanced across the top of my head."[24] Seeing the command caught in a crossfire, Ames sent Lt. Doty through the maelstrom with an order for the regiment to retire. We were "cut to

22 Williams to Bachelder, June 18, 1880, in Ladd, *Bachelder Papers*, I, 668; Dreese, *Never Desert the Old Flag!*; Bishop, *Union Regimental Commanders*, 49.

23 17th Connecticut web site, http://members.aol.com/clonch/the17th2.htm; Hamblen, *Connecticut Yankees*, 23-24.

24 *Seventeenth Annual Reunion of the 17th Regiment Connecticut*, 23; Peck, "First Day at Gettysburg"; Paynton, "From Virginia to Gettysburg," manuscript, GNMP; Warren diary; Hamblen, *Connecticut Yankees*, 23-24; Dreese, *Never Desert the Old Flag!*, 43-44.

pieces" recalled Lt. Albert W. Peck, "and having no troops in our rear to support us, we fell back."[25]

Adj. Chatfield and Sergt. Major Fred Betts tried to drag Fowler's body to the rear, but had to abandon it or be surrounded themselves. Just as they gave up, Jimmy Hayes came by carrying the regiment's national colors, only to be shot through the leg. Betts scooped up the colors, as he had at Chancellorsville two months before, and carried them from the field. Somehow in the chaos someone remembered to send an order to Major Brady east of Rock Creek to retire back through town to the rallying point on Cemetery Hill.[26]

Amid the chaos, Barlow sat atop his horse directing his men, shouting words of encouragement. Capt. Edward Culp was just returning to him when the general shouted "What is that skirmish line stopping for?" and spurred his horse toward the front line. Culp rode alongside him, noting the large mass of Confederates whose numbers appeared to increase every moment. Barlow turned to Culp, ordering him to rush to Howard to request more artillery support. Culp had not yet covered twenty rods when "Gen. Barlow was severely wounded, and all but one of his staff officers and orderlies killed or wounded."[27] Ames assumed command, but the situation was hopeless. Walking wounded were drifting to the rear, Rebels were encircling what was left of the position on the exposed knoll, Barlow and several other key offices had been killed or wounded. Some units still held out but how much longer they could stand without being completely encircled could be measured in minutes.

With the situation deteriorating, Lt. Bancroft's guns switched from spherical case to canister. Merkle's section had been "engaged [with] one battery of the enemy for a few moments with solid shot, and then directed my attention to the Rebel infantry as they were advancing in mass upon us. I used shell and spherical case shot at first, and, as the line of the enemy came closer, and I ran out of shot, shell, and case shot, I used canister." When his supports retired, Bancroft limbered his two sections and headed toward town, picking up Lt. Merkle's section along the way. Bancroft halted briefly to replenish the ammunition chests of his limbers, but the Rebels continued to adance. Merkle, with the Confederates approaching uncomfortably close, "fired two double rounds of canister . . . then limbered up." When orders arrived to retire to Cemetery

25 Peck, "First Day at Gettysburg"; Peck, "Second Day at Gettysburg," manuscript, 1887, GNMP.

26 Paynton, "From Virginia to Gettysburg"; Peck, "Second Day at Gettysburg"; Warren journal.

27 Culp, "Reminiscences of the Great Fight by a Participant."

Hill, Bancroft proceeded in good order back through town. In addition to Wilkeson, the battery lost one man killed, five severely wounded, and four missing, along with 17 horses killed, but successfully brought off all of its guns.[28]

With Ames busy trying to rally his wavering line and no further reserves at hand, Col. Harris found his position untenable. "Four of the twelve officers who made the advance with us were dead or dying. Half the residue were dangerously wounded and lay bleeding on the ground. One fourth of the men were dead or dying, and at least half of the residue were wounded and unable to stand in rank. Without orders I began to fall back," covering the retreat with his regiment as best he could. "The whole division was now retiring. . . . My regiment being in the rear drew most of the enemy's fire, but as we retired in the skirmish line, our loss on the retreat was slight. It was while we were thus retiring, and while I was walking along side of my color bearer that Gen. Ames notified me that I must turn over the command of my regiment and take command of the 2d brigade, which I did at once."[29]

In the wake of the Federal retreat, C. D. Grace, advancing with Doles' brigade, marveled at the "fearful slaughter, the golden wheat-fields, a few minutes before in beauty, now gone, and the ground covered with the dead and wounded in blue." Major Andrew Pitzer of Early's staff noticed an officer lying on the field. Dismounting, he found the man to be Barlow with what appeared to be a mortal wound. Pitzer ordered some men to carry the general to the shade of the nearby woods, gave him a canteen of water, and went on his way to do his duty with Early's division. Later, some of Barlow's men who had been captured placed him on a blanket and carried him to the home of Joseph Benner where he was placed in a bed and attended by two Confederate surgeons, both of whom, along with a captured Federal surgeon, believed the wound to be mortal.[30]

28 *OR* 27, pt. 1, 756-57.

29 Harris to Bachelder, Mar. 14, 1881, Bachelder Papers, GNMP.

30 Grace, "Rodes's Division at Gettysburg," *Confederate Veteran*," n.d., Vertical File 49-e, GNMP; Welch, *Boy General*, 86; Barlow account, Vertical File 5, GNMP; Keene, "History Restored." In Gordon's memoirs he describes himself as finding and aiding Barlow without any mention of Pitzer (Gordon, *Reminiscences*, 151), but Barlow does not mention Gordon in any of his contemporaneous writings and does mention Pitzer. Although it is possible both Gordon and Pitzer came across Barlow, given the lack of any mention of Gordon by Barlow at the time it may well be that it was Pitzer who rendered the aid. Perhaps Gordon came along as this was in progress and either ordered the general attended to or simply became aware of it as he passed along in the process of directing his brigade. Capt. James A. Scrymser seems to confirm Gordon's story in his *Extracts from Personal Reminiscences of James A. Scrymser in Times of Peace and War* (1915, 5-6), but this appeared well after the fact and after the publicity surrounding Gordon's claims.

☽ ☽ ☽

Shocked to see Barlow's Division in its advanced position, Schurz realized that his command was in serious trouble. Rebels were already threatening to cut Barlow's division off from town. Immediate action was essential. After Capt. Winkler returned from delivering the warning to Barlow, Schurz dispatched the captain once again to Howard to request reinforcements. Schurz next rode over to Col. Krzyzanowski commanding his reserve brigade in hopes of providing immediate support to his imperiled flank. Looking out over the field, Major Benjamin Willis of the 119th New York could see that Barlow's division was already wavering as Schurz approached. Between his position and Barlow's lay close to 800 yards of mostly flat, wide open fields broken only by an occasional wooden fence. Commanded by Confederate batteries, there were no natural obstacles to provide even partial cover or upon which to anchor a battle line. Adj. Alfred Lee could clearly see that "their shot and shell ricocheted splendidly over the open fields."[31]

Edwin Southard found the "thunder of the cannon was terrific now, for our own artillery were firing over our heads as we of the infantry lay flat on the ground. So the horrible, screaming, hurtling messengers of death flew over us from both sides. Solid shot, fragments of shells dropped among and around us. Sometimes a shell buried itself in the ground, and exploding hurled a cloud of earth and dust high into the air; the heavier portions rained down upon us, while the lighter floated away, and joining with the smoke of the heavy guns and the volleys of musketry, made still more dense the heavy atmosphere. In such a storm it seemed a miracle that any were left alive."[32]

Adj. Lee, who was nearby when Krzyzanowski received the order to advance into the bedlam, noticed how the brigade commander's "face grew pale and distressed." The order to fall in passed quickly among the regiments. In moments they were off across the fields, moving in double column of divisions to hasten their arrival where needed. A few precious moments were lost as they encountered several fences "which had to be taken down under a heavy fire of musketry from the enemy." Lee observed that "The enemy's batteries completely swept the plain from two or three directions. The shells and shot howled, shrieked and plunged through the air like infuriated demons. There was no shelter, not even a stump or tree. Now a huge iron nugget plowed its way through the living mass, leaving in its track eight poor fellows torn and

31 *OR* 27, pt. 1, 742; Lee, "Reminiscences of the Gettysburg Battle," 55.

32 *OR* 27, pt. 1, 742; Edwin Southard, "Graphic Description," *National Tribune*, August 19, 1897.

Col. Franz Mahler, 75th Pennsylvania
U.S. Army Heritage and Education Center

bleeding. The deadly 'thug,' and a submissive groan or two is all that is heard. Again and again the jagged fragments of iron sweep destructively through the ranks, but there is no wavering." The 82nd Ohio advanced into the deadly barrage, but "before the regiment fired a shot it lost twenty men killed and wounded."[33]

Krzyzanowski's brigade had just torn down a fence east of the Carlisle Road when Barlow's division began retiring. Slightly in advance of the other units, the 184 men of Col. Franz Mahler's 75th Pennsylvania made contact first when they ran into the advanced position of Col. John T. Mercer's 21st Georgia. Major August Ledig could clearly see the Rebels some 100 yards away in a wheat field. "[W]e charged upon them and drove them back. We halted, and opened fire on the enemy." Col. Mercer recalled that his Georgians "Having attracted their fire, and finding their force too strong for the exposed position we then occupied, we fell back some 40 yards to a lane, where we awaited their approach. By lying down, we hid ourselves from them till they had approached within a few yards, when we commenced firing, and advanced." By now Barlow was in full retreat, leaving Doles and Gordon to focus their efforts on Krzyzanowski who was forced to deploy his brigade under fire from both converging artillery and increasing musketry. The gentle rolls in the terrain at first hid the Rebel battle lines from view, but soon Adj. Lee spotted them "As they came up out of the willows their serried muskets dazzled . . . and their banners seemed to flaunt an audacious challenge. On they came, one line after another in beautiful array, while our own line with equal steadiness advanced from the opposite direction. Soon the combatants were close enough almost to read the names on each other's battle-flags."[34]

33 Lee, "Reminiscences of the Gettysburg Battle," 56; *OR* 27, pt. 1, 745; Baumgartner, *Buckeye Blood*, 41; Reid, *Ohio in the War*, 474.

34 *OR* 27, pt. 1, 745, and pt. 2, 584; Baumgartner, *Buckeye Blood*, 54.

With his brigade caught in a crossfire of 48 guns positioned to sweep the plain, Krzyzanowski deployed the 26th Wisconsin on his right, with the 119th New York to its left followed by the 75th Pennsylvania and 82nd Ohio. As at Chancellorsville, the brigade's right flank was unprotected save by the scattered fugitives from Barlow's division. Lt. Col. Hans Boebel hastened the 26th Wisconsin into line only some "one hundred yards from the rapidly advancing enemy."[35]

The men formed amid the nightmare of whistling minie balls punctuated by exploding shells. "Fire!" A volley burst forth from the Badgers. In their exposed position, Rebel fire cut through their lines. A ball caught the colonel in the right leg. He gallantly refused to leave the field, but then a shell fragment caught Boebel in the same leg, slashing the flesh and crushing the bone. Major Heinrich Baetz [Bätz], a native of the Duchy of Hesse and a merchant and Register of Deeds in Milwaukee when the war broke out, fell painfully wounded. Command of the regiment devolved on the senior captain, John Fuchs. Sergt. Karl Wickesberg thought the "bullets came as thick as hail." Within minutes Confederate fire killed or wounded every member of the color guard. Men fell by the scores. Of the 32 men present on the field with Company G, only seven survived unhurt. Riddled by enemy fire in their exposed position, the men fired at will as fast as they could reload. In the chaos, their faces streaked with sweat mixed with the gunpowder from their cartridges, the thick smoke covering the line, the screams, the bloodshot eyes contorted with tension and fear, Krzyzanowski pronounced it "a portrait of hell."[36]

Yet the hell was not one-sided. Facing Krzyzanowski's brigade was Captain William Evans in the 4th Georgia who found the "Yankees were in large numbers, and fought more stubbornly than I ever saw them, or ever want to see them again. Several times we were not fifty yards apart. Twice the Yankees fixed bayonets and thought they were going to meet us hand to hand, but our boys raised a shout and rushing forward, pushed them back, fighting us all the time." N. E. Scott in the 12th Georgia explained that "The yankees would walk back about ten steps and load and fire at us. We got in about fifty yards of the yanks. Several times."[37]

35 *Annual Report of the Adjutant General of the State of Wisconsin*, 403.

36 Flower, *History of Milwaukee*, 997; Quiner, *Military History of Wisconsin*, 280; Krzyzanowski, *Wspomnienia*, 79.

37 Evans to sister, October 9, 1863, United Daughters of the Confederacy, Bound Typescripts, Vol. 10; Scott to father, July 16, 1863, Rare Book, Manuscript, and Special Collections Library, Duke University.

Spurring his horse along the lines, Krzyzanowski yelled encouragement. As the animal jumped to clear an intervening fence a lead ball tore into it. The stricken animal plunged to earth hurling its rider through the air. The colonel came down hard upon his chest, the animal landing on the left side of his body. Pain shot through him as he fought for breath, each convulsion of his chest bringing a torment of agony, then he passed out. Assistant Surgeon Charles Stein of the 58th New York rushed to his colonel's aid. He found Krzyzanowski unconscious, his breathing greatly impaired. Exactly what happened next is unclear, and in the tumult of the frenzied combat it is uncertain whether there was a rapid transition in command or whether the regiments simply continued to resist as best they could. The next ranking officer was Col. Franz Mahler in the 75th Pennsylvania, but he was hardly in a position to leave his regiment. Fighting on their home soil, the Pennsylvanians displayed an obstinate determination as their ranks were torn to pieces. Mahler and his horse were both hit almost simultaneously, with the stricken animal falling atop the officer pinning him underneath. Though in pain, he managed to free himself with the help of some nearby soldiers. Sergt. Hermann Nachtigall saw his colonel rush "to the left flank of the regiment which was under heavy fire. While he roused the men to bravery with his speech, he was cut down by another bullet, falling not far from the lifeless body of his brother, Lt. Louis Mahler. Carl Schurz, directing his troops from near the front, saw the colonel fall. The two were longtime friends having served together at Festung Rastatt in 1849 during the "Springtime of Nations." Schurz spurred his horse over, dismounted, and conversed briefly with his stricken friend: "Now with death on his face he reached out his hand to me on the bloody field of Gettysburg to bid me a last farewell." Lt. T. Albert Steiger carried Mahler to a field hospital where he would die from his injuries on July 5. Major August Ledig took command of the Pennsylvanians with the Rebels rapidly closing in only some forty yards away and pouring lead into his left and rear. Surrounded by death and destruction, Schurz was struck by the scene. "Regiment stood against regiment in the open fields, near enough almost to see the whites in one another's eyes, firing literally in one another's faces."[38]

With Krzyzanowski and Mahler both down, command of the brigade devolved on Col. James S. Robinson of the 82nd Ohio. As the regiment deployed, Adj. Lee saw the Rebels sweeping across the fields. "Their movements were firm and steady, as usual, and their banners, bearing the blue Southern cross, flaunted impudently and seemed to challenge combat. On they came, one line after the other, in splendid array." They were

38 Krzyzanowski pension application, NARA; Nachtigall, *Geschichte des 75sten Regiments*, 5-6, 8, 21-22; *OR* 27, pt. 1, 745; Schurz, *Reminiscences*, Vol. III, 10, 12.

within only 75 yards, he estimated, so that "the names of battles printed on the Confederate flags might have been read, had there been time to read them." As he took in the scene, "By common impulse the whole line immediately delivered its fire, and the reverberations of the cannon were drowned by the volleys of musketry, which roared across the meadow. The enemy's musketry responded instantly to our own, and the combatants, standing like duelists, scarcely more than seventy-five yards apart, blazed away into each other's faces. Not many minutes elapsed before the ground was strewn with arms and accoutrements, with the bodies of the wounded and the dead." Lee experienced distinct uneasiness as "bullets hummed about our ears like infuriated bees."[39]

Lt. Col. David Thomson's horse was shot three times and he was hit twice by spent balls that left only painful black and blue patches on his skin. Every field officer in the regiment had his horse shot from under him. "From this point we were gradually being pressed back by the power of overwhelming numbers," Col. Robinson observed. "The men stubbornly contested every inch of ground. Our position was in every respect untenable." Outflanked, with enfilade fire ripping through the ranks, the colonel ordered the brigade to retreat toward town firing at will. Before it was over, seventy percent of the Ohioans would be casualties, including 19 of their 22 officers.[40]

The 119th New York was in similar distress. The order given, the regiment pushed forward "in line of double columns at deploying distance, forward through the fields, tearing down the fences in our way, or climbing them in confused ranks, and re-forming on the other side."[41]

Dodge was atop a new mount that was not entirely at ease with the bursting shells. Each time one exploded the horse threatened to bolt, forcing Dodge to exert every effort to hold her in place. As they began the advance, the horse was "scared by an explosion altogether too near for her sensitive nerves." The horse bolted forward, carrying Dodge "far beyond our line, and in disagreeable proximity to where I knew the enemy to be, creating a peal of laughter, at my expense, through the whole brigade . . . and completely shocking my sense or propriety and military punctilio. But worse was to come." Dodge no sooner regained control of his mount and returned to his correct position in the regiment than another shell burst sent the skittish horse off "in a

39 Lee, "Gettysburg Battle," 56; Lee, "Disadvantages Under Which it Fought," *Weekly Press* (Philadelphia), XXIX, January 26, 1887, 1; Baumgartner, *Buckeye Blood*, 55.

40 Robinson, dedication of the 82nd Ohio monument, GNMP; Baumgartner, *Buckeye Blood*, 57.

41 Dodge, "Left Wounded," 319.

Maj. David Thomson, 82nd Ohio
U.S. Army Heritage and Education Center

diametrically opposite direction. This was insufferable, it looked so very like running away, which, in a physical point of view, it in truth was. This 'bolt' occasioned another laugh, at which I began to get nettled." Regaining control once again, Dodge returned to the regiment to find most of the officers dismounting as they drew near to the enemy. Dodge followed suit, handing the reins of his horse to "a stray drummer."[42]

Col. John Lockman managed to get his men into line just before the appearance of Rebel infantry and in the few moments that followed some of his men, perhaps motivated by the high anxiety or the wish to strike back in some way as shells raked their lines, fired off their muskets without orders. Adj. Dodge heard a "volley of oaths from the delinquents' supervisors" and witnessed several receive "a sound rap over the head . . . by a testy file closer." The adjutant felt another "moment or two of breathless anxiety and impatience, and the irregular line of butternut and gray hove gradually in sight—their officers all mounted, waving their swords and cheering on their men." With the enemy now in sight, Lockman gave the order to "Fire!" A flash, a loud explosion, a cloud of smoke and the lines were fully engaged. Dodge was surprised that the volley "in no way checked the enemy's advance, but it drew their fire; and they continued slowly to push on, keeping it up in a desultory manner as they drew near."[43] The Rebels drew to within a hundred yards as the two lines continued to rake each other with angry volleys.

Dodge estimated that "every five or six seconds some poor fellow would throw up his arms with an 'ugh!' and drop; then pick himself up, perhaps, and start for the rear. Another would drop flat on his face, or his back, without a sound; another break down, and fall together in a heap. Still another would let drop his gun, and holding his

42 Dodge, "Left Wounded," 320.

43 Dodge, "Left Wounded," 320-21.

shattered arm, would leave the ranks; or, perhaps, stay by to encourage his comrades. One brave boy near me, I remember, shot in the leg, sat there loading and firing with as much regularity and coolness as if untouched, now and then shouting to some comrade in front of him to make room for his shot." Five minutes, ten minutes, the deadly contest continued with neither side "showing symptoms of wavering." The ground became increasingly covered with the dead and wounded, while a steady stream of walking wounded wound to the rear. "Under the never-ceasing encouragements of the officers, generally taking the form of 'Give 'em—, boys!' or, 'Knock spots out of them, boys!' or, 'Rake—out of 'em, boys!' this familiar synonym for heat creeping into almost every admonition, our men, though with thinned ranks and ghastly wounds staring them in the face on every side, kept unflinchingly up to the mark."[44]

After twenty minutes or so the Rebels resumed their advance, the lines of the 119th being taken at the same time under canister fire enfilading them from the right. The line fell back some twelve to fifteen yards, then steadied as the remaining officers rushed about shouting orders and encouragement to their men. Dodge was with them, "rushing about, ordering and entreating, gesticulating and threatening" when suddenly "I was knocked clean off my feet by an excruciating blow (so it felt) on my right foot; our line passed over me in retreat, and I found myself in the disagreeable position of being between two fires (neither side having ceased their fusillade), and with redoubled prospects of being taken prisoner. . . . It was not a pleasant position. After their line had passed me, and I was a prisoner, my sword and belt was taken away. I then cut off my boot and bound up my ankle with my pocket handkerchief. After a while an Orderly Sergeant of the 119th [New York], who was also taken prisoner, came up to me, and with the help of a Confederate soldier, got me to a grove in the rear. Here he helped me bind up my wound afresh, and then I waited till after dark, when they came and carried me on a stretcher to Mr. Benner's."[45] Confederate fire also found Col. Lockman, inflicting a painful wound.

Looking to his right, Alexander Schimmelfennig could clearly see Confederate troops moving into the gap between von Amsberg and Krzyzanowski's brigade, threatening the flanks of both. Turning to Colonel Philip Brown of the 157th New York, he ordered him to move quickly to support the endangered position. Brown, who had ordered his men to lie prone to lessen the target while in support of Dilger's battery, ordered them to their feet, then to "change front forward on the first

44 Dodge, "Left Wounded," 321.

45 Dodge, "Left Wounded," 321-22; Dodge diary, July and July 3, 1863; Brewster to Dodge diary, July 28, 1863.

company," all the while under fire. Brown stationed himself on the left of his regiment with Lt. Col. George Arrowsmith, who, though ill, disobeyed his physician's advice to enter the battle with his regiment, on the right. Moving obliquely to the right, crossing a fence, and pushing through a large wheat field Brown directed his men onto the exposed flank of the 44th Georgia which, its attention fixed on its fight with Krzyzanowski's brigade, did not notice the Yankees' approach until a volley ripped through their ranks from a distance of only 30 to 40 yards. Major W. H. Peebles of the Georgia regiment, "made a wheel to the right, faced the new foe, and began to fire upon him. Thus checked in his movement, he faced us, and opened a severe fire upon us." The 4th Georgia also wheeled into position to support the 44th and the two opened fire on the 157th New York which continued to return fire at will.[46]

With his attention firmly on the two regiments to his front, Brown did not notice the 21st Georgia approaching his exposed left flank along a sunken farm lane near the John Blocher home. Suddenly, without warning, the Rebels poured in a devastating volley that quickly changed the balance of the firefight. Taking brutal fire from front and flank, Brown saw his men "falling rapidly" with the Rebel position "taking the form of a giant semi-circle" that was rapidly encircling him. Schimmelfenning saw Brown's predicament as well. Quickly he sent an aide with an order for Brown to withdraw at once, but the aide had his horse shot from under him and the order was not delivered. Brown heard someone at a distance who "hallooed to me to retreat," but without a direct order he attempted to hold his increasingly untenable position with his "rapidly diminishing numbers." A bullet smashed through Lt. Col. Arrowsmith's forehead, killing him instantly.[47]

Jonathan Boynton found the "noise of shells and bullets hurtling through the air was terrible." When the Rebels charged "I found myself near a fence over which rushed the Confederates and ordered me to surrender. I dropped my gun, and stood facing the grey boys at attention. . . . In a moment they were interviewing me. 'What regiment? Who commands the army?' I answered the best I could. One said, 'Yank, don't be skeered. We won't hurt you all'." With no support at hand, his regiment in the process of being overrun, Brown finally ordered a retreat on his own responsibility, but the regiment was wrecked. Brown's horse was killed beneath him, but he miraculously escaped the encirclement on foot, only to be wounded as he made his way toward

46 Brown to newspaper, July 27, 1863, GNMP; "Battle of Gettysburg," manuscript, GNMP; Place to Brown, GNMP; Boynton, "Reminiscence"; *OR* 27, pt. 2, 58, 586; Boynton memoir.

47 Applegate, *Arrowsmith*, 217; "Battle of Gettysburg"; Place to Brown, GNMP.

Lt. Col. George Arrowsmith, 157th New York, killed at Gettysburg
Karl E. Sundstrom

town. Despite the handicap, he managed to remain with the remnant of his regiment until it reached Cemetery Hill.[48]

During the hand-to-hand mêlée, Capt. J. H. Connolly commanded Company E, 44th Georgia. As he urged his men forward he came upon Lt. Frank Gates "who was badly wounded and was suffering for water, as he lay in the wheatfield; and as I passed him I gave him my own canteen of water." Twenty-three years later Connolly noticed a letter in the *Atlanta Constitution* in which Charles O. Newton, corresponding secretary of the One Hundred and Fifty-Seventh Regimental Association, sought to make contact with Georgia veterans in anticipation of the commemoration planned in Gettysburg on the twenty-fifth anniversary of the battle. Out of curiosity, Connolly wrote to Newton in Homer, New York, to inquire whether the wounded officer had survived. He went on to say that he had "a strong desire to visit this historic battlefield, and now since I have the opportunity of meeting with the men who faced us so bravely on that day of strife, my desires are doubly strong, and if circumstances will allow, I will be there, and perhaps many others." Gates, it turned out, had survived and "distinctly" remembered the Confederate's act of kindness.[49]

The 157th New York brought 350 men into the action and lost 307, an 87.7 percent loss. By the time this deadly encounter had run its course. Col. Robinson ordered Krzyzanowski's brigade, with regiments from Early's division moving around its right flank threatening to cut it off from town, to retire. In the thick of the fight, Schurz sent orders to the survivors from Barlow's division and Krzyzanowski's brigade to retire to the almshouse to avoid the encirclement, but once the retreat began it was difficult to stop. Nevertheless, several units, along with individuals and small groups,

48 Boynton, "Reminiscence"; Bishop, *Gettysburg Battlefield*, 51.

49 New York Monuments Commission, *Final Report on the Battlefield at Gettysburg*, III, 1060-61.

did rally to a line being formed at the almshouse. Among them was Capt. John Fuchs, now the senior officer of the 26th Wisconsin, who fell rallying his men. Nearby were Cols. Seraphim Meyer and von Gilsa directing men into this new improvised defense line. Off to the right, between the almshouse and Rock Creek, Ames, now commanding Barlow's division, also worked to form an effective defense. Spotting Col. Harris, he ordered him to assume command of his former brigade, bypassing Meyer who was next in line by virtue of seniority. Despite the somewhat haphazard nature of the new formation, it still managed to acquit itself well for some minutes. Among the attackers was G. W. Nichols of the 61st Georgia. He was impressed as the Federals clung to the almshouse position where "the Yankees stopped and made a desperate stand. Their officers were cheering their men and behaving like heroes and commanders of the 'first water'."[50] But resistance was by now useless.

Amid the chaos, Carl Schurz saw the situation was hopeless. Barlow's position had been untenable. Now most of his division was in precipitate retreat as the enemy threatened to cut it off from the village. He had done all that he could by throwing in his only reserve to try to stabilize the situation, but it was too far gone. Krzyzanowski's brigade had been caught in the open and overwhelmed by Doles and Gordon attacking its completely vulnerable position. Schimmelfennig had endeavored to help, but the 157th New York was all but destroyed in the attempt. To make matters worse, "At that moment it was reported that the right wing of the First Corps, which had fought heroically all day, had been pressed back, and one of General Doubleday's aides-de-camp [Lt. David Slagle] brought me a request for a few regiments to be sent to his assistance. Alas, I had not a man to spare, but was longing for reinforcements myself." Schurz had no other reserve, not even a single regiment, every unit he had was already engaged. Helpless to assist, he sent the messenger back with word that he had no one to send.[51]

From prisoners, Schurz knew he faced at least two Confederate corps. If all of those troops were up they would easily outnumber the entire I and XI Corps, perhaps by two-to-one or more. "We could hardly hope to hold out long against such a

50 Place to Brown; Brown to newspaper, July 27, 1863; Nichols, *Soldier's Story*, 116; Baumgartner, *Buckeye Blood*, 54.

51 *OR* 27, pt. 1, 727-28; Schurz, *Reminiscences*, III, 11; Doubleday, *Chancellorsville and Gettysburg*, 146.

superiority of numbers, and there was imminent danger that, if we held out too long, the enemy would succeed in turning our right flank and in getting possession of the town of Gettysburg, through which our retreat to the defensive position on Cemetery Hill would probably have to be effected."[52]

Turning to Capt. Winkler, Schurz ordered his aide to ride as quickly as possible to Howard's headquarters to once again request immediate reinforcement. It was much too late to save his right flank, but Schurz at least hoped that a fresh brigade would allow him to stabilize his situation long enough to withdraw to a more defensible position where his men could rally and continue the fight. Yanking his horse's bridle in the direction of town and digging his spurs into the animal's flanks Winkler "dashed through the town to the other side, where the reserves were stationed, as fast as my horse could carry me." As he approached Cemetery Hill he could see the reserve was still in place, no one had been sent forward after he delivered Schurz's earlier request. Winkler delivered his message, and, no doubt animated by the urgency of the situation, he "urged haste impetuously." Whether by previous order, or in response to the new request and Winkler's animated appeal, Col. Charles Coster's brigade quickly fell into marching order and was "set in motion at once."[53]

While Winkler rode for help, Schurz again turned his attention to the crisis at hand. Confederates were "pressing on with great vigor" against the impromptu almshouse line. Others, on the opposite side of Rock Creek, were rushing past its open right flank with some already behind the imperiled position. They need only cross the small creek to cut his entire command off from any retreat through town to their rallying point on Cemetery Hill. From Schimmelfennig came a report that his position was being threatened on its left,[54] no doubt the result of the difficulty that prompted Doubleday to seek help but a few minutes earlier. Schurz did the only thing he could. He sent an order to Ames, desperately trying to contest the Rebel advance, to fall back to the outskirts of town. He sent another order to Schimmelfennig to withdraw his troops immediately back toward town so as not to be cut off. Schurz planned to form another line on the outskirts of town.

☽ ☽ ☽

52 Schurz, *Reminiscences*, III, 9-10.

53 Winkler letter home, July 6, 1863; *OR* 27, pt. 1, 720, 728.

54 *OR* 27, pt. 1, 728.

Ames' position at the almshouse would have been untenable even for a well-manned, stable line since both its flanks were completely in the air. As it was, he was trying to cobble together a defense from the remnants of several regiments from different commands. Watching Ames struggle to form an organized defense, Adj. Peter Young of the 107th Ohio was mightily impressed with the general's demeanor. "Allow me here to state that such imperturbable coolness as Gen. Ames displayed in the trying hours of the first day under the most galling fire, I but seldom saw in my army experience; he has the highest admiration and regard of all under his command who ever fought under his guidance."[55]

Amid the bedlam von Gilsa called for some men near him to catch his runaway horse, mounted the skittish animal, then rode about trying to encourage the men to hold out. Reuben Ruch was struck by how the colonel "rode up and down that line through a regular storm of lead, meantime using the German epithets so common to him. I could hear the words 'rally boys.'" The order to retire must have come as a relief to both officers, but it did not mean the killing and maiming would stop. As Schurz explained, "the task . . . of breaking off an engagement . . . becomes very difficult in a fight at very close quarters. Still, the [men], when ordered to do so, fell back in good form, executing its retreat and fighting, step by step, with great firmness."[56]

Much of Ames' line consisted of survivors of Krzyzanowski's brigade who rallied in the orchard to the left of the almshouse. When the order to retreat finally arrived, Confederates were in some places within twenty yards of the 26th Wisconsin's position. All of its field officers were already casualties and the firing line was becoming "confused" as both of its flanks came under severe pressure. The men had to retreat across an open field raked by deadly fire that added greatly to the casualty list. Retiring toward Gettysburg, bullets slashed through Sergt. Karl Wickesberg's right arm and wrist. Another shot Capt. Franz Lackner through the right calf. He continued on, limping to a field hospital that had been set up in a village church.[57]

As Adj. Albert Wallber headed for town "a fragment of a shell threw me down. I was stunned, but not hurt. In coming to, I found myself inside the Rebel lines. A soldier shouted several times, 'where is an officer?' Upon seeing me lying on the ground, he

55 Young to Bachelder, Apr. 12, 1867, in Ladd, *Bachelder Papers*, I, 311-12.

56 Keifer, *153rd Pennsylvania*, 215; Schurz, *Reminiscences*, III, 11.

57 *OR* 27, pt. 1, 745; Arnold to mother, Oshkosh Public Museum, Oshkosh, Wisconsin; Wickesberg to parents, July 6, 1863; Lackner diary, Dec. 22, 1863; Wallber, "From Gettysburg to Libby Prison," 192; Winkler to Gaylord, Aug. 25, 1864; *Annual Report of the Adjutant General of the State of Wisconsin*, 403.

leveled his gun and was about to pull the trigger, when an officer of his company stepped in front of me and beckoning to his men said: 'Come on, my brave boys, come on.' It was a sorrowful sight passing over the battle field. Many a friend lay there lifeless; others, more or less seriously wounded, begged for water, but my captors refused to allow me to render assistance and after relieving me of my sword and revolver, told me to walk back. In doing so, I went across the battle field of the Rebels, where the dead outnumbered the wounded, mostly shot in the head or through the breast, which proved that the aim of our soldiers was good."[58] When the remnants formed on the outskirts of town, only four officers in the entire regiment remained uninjured.

By the time the order to retire reached the 75th Pennsylvania, Maj. August Ledig saw the Rebels pressing in, threatening to cut off his line of retreat. Sergt. Hermann Nachtigall followed the major's directions to retire back across the wide fields, well aware that "in order to obtain a piece of safety, garden fences had to be torn down, since all the roads and avenues were already in the possession of the enemy." Col. Robinson, commanding the brigade, realized that, by the time his retreating troops reached the outskirts of town, "The enemy was on our right front, right flank and in our rear." Coming upon Heckman's battery unlimbering near the northeast edge of the village he stopped to help direct its fire but a "ball entered through the shoulder and passed forward through, coming out below the neck to the left." Robinson was the third leader the brigade lost that day. He survived the very serious wound, and the war, but when he died in 1892 the cause of death was listed as "Results of Army Wound." Lt. Col. David Thomson took command of the survivors to rally them at the town limits.[59]

☽ ☽ ☽

On Cemetery Hill, Oliver Otis Howard was becoming increasingly concerned with the progress of the battle. Lt. David Slagle arrived at his headquarters from Doubleday and Capt. Winkler reappeared from Schurz, both bringing news of intensifying Rebel pressure along with requests for reinforcements. News arrived that Barlow had been

58 Wallber, "From Gettysburg to Libby Prison," 192.

59 Robinson, address at 82nd Ohio monument, GNMP; Thomson letter to "My dear boy," July 5, 1863, Thomson Papers, in possession of Ms. Mary Geiger; Lee to Bachelder, Feb. 16, 1888, Ladd, *Bachelder Papers*, III, 1527; Robinson Pension Files, RG 94, Records of the Adjutant General's Office, Book Records of Volunteer Union Organizations, NARA; *Pennsylvania at Gettysburg Ceremonies*, 434. In the 75th Pennsylvania, 55 percent of those who fought north of town became casualties; *OR* 27, pt. 1, 744.

seriously wounded.[60] Using his field glasses Howard tried to keep himself informed of the progress of the battle, but the distance made it difficult. He had only two small brigades of Adolph von Steinwehr's division as a reserve, along with two reserve batteries. No doubt he was greatly conflicted. All of the evidence suggested it was becoming much more difficult for Doubleday and Schurz to hold out, yet the specter of Chancellorsville, only two months before, still hung over his head. In the wake of that disaster criticism fell upon him from the press, detractors within the army, and his own officers and men. Supporters urged him to request a transfer and, if not granted, to resign outright. Now he found himself in the middle of another battlefield crisis, this time with the entire responsibility for whatever decisions were made. His command was clearly outnumbered and in danger of being driven from the field. But, if he ordered a retreat would he be criticized anew? If he did not and his command was forced from the field, would he still be criticized as at Chancellorsville? What should be done?

Unwilling to risk censure by ordering a retreat before it was absolutely necessary, Howard resisted committing any of this small reserve force as long as he could, but once Winkler arrived with news of the critical situation facing Schurz he finally relented and agreed to let von Steinwehr send a brigade to help out. Through his glasses he could see Rebels flanking the almshouse position even as the reinforcements were moving out. Turning to Capt. Wiedrich, Howard ordered him to fire on the Confederates with his 3-inch rifled guns. The battery immediately opened fire, but its shells fell short causing great consternation among the 17th Pennsylvania Cavalry on Buford's skirmish line among whom they fell. Buford quickly dispatched an aide to Howard to stop the firing. Howard explained that "The reason of this irregularity [the shells falling short] was the poor quality of the ammunition there used."[61]

With his right clearly being turned and hard-pressed to hold against superior numbers, Howard "now sent again to General Slocum, stating that my right flank was attacked, and asking him if he was moving up, and stating that I was in danger of being turned and driven back." Earlier he had sent an aide, Captain Edward P. Pearson, "to General Sickles, requesting him to move up to Gettysburg as rapidly as possible. Owing to difficulty in finding Sickles' headquarters, this message was not delivered until 3:30 p.m." Howard dispatched another message to Doubleday and Schurz: "Hold

60 C. Howard manuscript on first day at Gettysburg, Box 3, Bowdoin College, Brunswick, Maine; Barthel, *Abner Doubleday*, 150.

61 *OR* 27, pt. 1, 751; Biddle, *The First Day*, 119; Wiedrich to Steinwehr, July 10, 1863, Civil War Collection Folder, 1st Regiment Light Artillery, Battery I, Box 3, Folder 14, Buffalo and Erie County Historical Society; *OR* 27, pt. 1, 703; *New York at Gettysburg*, III, 1247.

out, if possible, awhile longer, for I am expecting General Slocum every moment." If he was to hold out much longer Howard needed help, and he needed it now. He dispatched yet another messenger, Capt. Daniel Hall, to find Slocum asking him to "move up as rapidly as possible." When Hall found the general he was struck by his seeming reluctance to move. Hall later called Slocum's "conduct on that occasion anything but honorable, soldierly or patriotic."[62]

Turning to examine the field from the heights Howard saw that "the enemy renewed his attack on the First Corps." Messengers continued to arrive from both fronts. "Earnest requests were made upon me for re-enforcements, and General Schurz . . . asked for a brigade to be placed *en echelon* on his right. I had then only two small brigades in reserve, and had already located three regiments from these in the edge of the town and to the north, and I felt sure that I must hold the point where I was as an ultimate resort. Therefore I at first replied that I could not spare any troops, but did afterward permit General Steinwehr to push out Colonel Coster's brigade beyond the town, to cover the retreat." But the calls for help kept coming. Those "from Doubleday and Wadsworth were stronger than ever."[63]

When Capt. Edward P. Halstead, Doubleday's assistant adjutant general, arrived with yet another urgent request, Howard still held out hope that the lines to the west and north of Gettysburg could be held. According to Halstead he "looked the picture of despair." Halstead relayed the message to which Howard replied: "Tell General Doubleday that I have no reinforcements to send him." But then, a moment later, the general told Halstead to "Go to General Buford, give him my compliments, and tell him to go to General Doubleday's support." Next, Howard ordered Capt. Lewis Heckman's Battery K, 1st Ohio Light Artillery, to report to Schurz. He also sent an order to Schurz to "send one regiment to Wadsworth, as his front was the place at that moment of the hardest pressure,"[64] but Schurz was in no position to help anyone; all of his men were engaged and he needed reinforcement himself.

No sooner had Howard dispatched his order to Schurz than "the firing, growing worse and worse, showed me that the front lines could not hold out much longer." Summoning another aide, he dispatched the rider to Doubleday to let him know that

62 *OR* 27, pt. 1, 703-04; C. Howard, "First Day at Gettysburg," 254; Meysenburg journal, July 1, 1863; Pfanz, *Culp's Hill & Cemetery Hill*, 94; Meysenburg journal, July 1, 1863; Howard speech on Gettysburg, May 30, 1894, Box 154, Folder 11½, Bowdoin College.

63 *OR* 27, pt. 1, 704; Howard speech on Gettysburg, May 30, 1894, Box 154, Folder 11½, Bowdoin College; Howard, *Autobiography*, I, 417.

64 Halstead, *First Day*, 5; Halstead, "Incidents of the First Day," 285; Howard, *Autobiography*, I, 417; Barthel, *Abner Doubleday*, 151.

Major Charles Howard, an aide to his brother General Howard
Karl E. Sundstrom

"if he could not hold out longer, he must fall back, fighting, to Cemetery Hill and on the left of the Baltimore pike." At the same time he sent another order to Buford "to make a show of force opposite the enemy's right, which he immediately did." But even as the rider sped away, the situation was changing by the second. Howard could see both the flanks in danger of being turned—the I Corps left and the XI Corps right—while Rebel infantry was pushing steadily against Wadsworth's I Corps position. Recalled Howard: "[I]t was not long before I was satisfied that the men were giving way at different points on the line, and that the enemy, who overreached both flanks, were steadily and slowly advancing."[65]

Now desperate for help, Howard sent his brother off to find Slocum "to inform him of the state of affairs, requesting him to send one of his divisions to the left, the other to the right, of Gettysburg, and that he would come in person to Cemetery Hill." The major found Slocum who told him that the XII Corps was already in motion "but that he did not wish to come up in person to the front and take the responsibility of that fight." Apparently Slocum, recalling Meade's caution not to bring on a general engagement until the army was reunited, feared censure if he took command of an action of which he thought the commanding general might disapprove. After delivering the message, the major spurred his horse back toward Gettysburg as quickly as possible, arriving just about the time that the first retreating troops were beginning to emerge from the town.[66]

Finally, Howard could wait no more. "[F]inding that I could hold out no longer, and that the troops were already giving way, I sent a positive order to the commanders

65 *OR* 27, pt. 1, 704; Howard, *Autobiography*, I, 417; Howard speech on Gettysburg, May 30, 1894, Box 154, Folder 11½, Bowdoin College.

66 *OR* 27, pt. 1, 704; C. Howard, "First Day at Gettysburg," 258.

of the First and Eleventh Corps to fall back gradually, disputing every inch of ground, and to form near my position, the Eleventh Corps on the right and the First Corps on the left of the Baltimore pike." Meysenburg pegs this at 4:10 pm. Howard also "instructed Buford to pass to the extreme left and extend the new line, making with his cavalry all the show possible." As soon as he received the order, Schurz sent aides rushing to Ames and Schimmelfennig ordering them to retire to the edge of town, then to continue through to Cemetery Hill as best they could.[67]

67 *OR* 27, pt. 1, 704; Howard, *Autobiography*, I, 417; Meysenburg journal, July 1, 1863; Ames, *Adelbert Ames*, 131.

Chapter 12

"The Situation Calls for Stubborn Fight"

Late Afternoon, July 1, 1863

BY THE TIME ALEXANDER SCHIMMELFENNIG received Schurz's order to retire his position was little more than a salient vulnerable to Rebel assault on three sides. He immediately ordered von Amsberg to retire toward town. The 82nd Illinois, in support of Dilger's and Wheeler's guns, was the only regiment that was not mostly strung out on the skirmish line, or shattered as was the 157th New York, so von Amsberg assigned it, supported by the 61st Ohio, to cover the retreat as he attempted to disengage. At the same time, Dilger and Wheeler, who had by this time changed from counter battery fire to canister so they could rake the Rebel infantry flanking them on the right, began to withdraw. Dilger ordered "all the pieces back excepting one section of each battery, commanding with them the entrance of the town as long as possible. The two rifled guns had to retire first." Lt. William Wheeler "did not leave this position until the enemy was almost in rear of my battery. I then moved back to a point on the road near the town, and held this until the enemy were again nearly behind me, and the infantry supports had withdrawn. While moving across the field to this point, a shot struck the axle of one of my pieces and broke it, dismounting the piece. I slung the piece under the limber with the prolonge, and carried it for some distance until the prolonge broke, when I was obliged to abandon the gun." Dilger and Wheeler used the same "leap-frog" tactic to retire that they used to advance, with one gun retiring while the other fired alternately until they reached the outskirts of town. Looking on, Captain Leonidas Jewett of the 61st Ohio, supporting the batteries, thought that he "never saw a more orderly retreat."[1]

1 *OR* 27, pt. 1, 753-54; Naisawald, *Grape and Canister*, 359. Wheeler recovered the lost gun on July 5 and found it still in operable condition. He also took possession of an abandoned piece

Col. Adolph von Hartung was wounded just as the retreat began, a musket ball shattering his left leg, but his 74th Pennsylvania fell back through the fields west of the Carlisle Road under the command of Lt. Col. Alexander von Mitzel accompanied by the few survivors of the 157th New York, while the 45th New York retired along the Mummasburg Road back toward the seminary where it had its field hospital. Lt. Hubert Ley recalled the regiment retiring "leisurely" while "on our left we could see the broken lines of our First Corps left being turned and pressed towards the western outskirts of the town." Adj. Augustus Horstmann noticed that "the 1st Corps on our left gave way & exposed our left flank at the same time heavy columns were moving on us in front & on the right in overwhelming forces."[2]

Lt. Col. Adolphus Dobke relayed the order to retreat to the regiment which "rallied in line, and in splendid style retreated to the seminary, where it was ordered to halt and cover the retreat of the First and Eleventh Corps through Gettysburg" with its left anchored on the seminary buildings and the regiment stretching right across the road. "We made preparations to defend the College," Ley wrote, "and as the enemy in our front pressed very feebly forward, expected to make a stubborn stand there; although we saw the left of the First Corps, broken to pieces, and pursued by the overwhelming numbers of the enemy, making for the left of the town." Although the Rebels kept a respectful distance behind, the entire defensive position was rapidly collapsing with the 45th New York still in a precariously exposed location. Dobke watched with increasing anxiety as "all sorts of missiles found their way through houses, fences, and gardens, and it was evident that to stay much longer would be certain destruction."[3]

After fifteen to twenty minutes that seemed an eternity, the division bugler sounded "Retreat," followed by the "Double-Quick," but Dobke ordered his men to ignore the double-quick so they would not lose cohesion while they retired. When his men reached the outskirts of town "suddenly a few regiments of the First Corps were thrown in the way." Rather than push into the crowd in front of him and risk his men becoming entangled in the disorder, Dobke moved two streets to the east before again turning south. By now Rebel skirmishers were pushing in close behind the retiring

---

from another corps, thus leaving the Gettysburg battlefield with one more gun than when he arrived. See letter of William Wheeler to grandfather and aunt, July 26, 1863, in Bershears, *Loyal Till Death*, 184.

2 Ley letter; Bishop, *Gettysburg Battlefield*, 52; Horstmann, Battle of Gettysburg, GNMP.

3 Ley letter; *OR* 27, pt. 1, 734; New York Monuments Commission Report, I, 379; Böhm address.

Capt. Friedrich "Francis" Irsch, 45th New York, was recognized for his valor and professional conduct on July 1 with the Medal of Honor.
New York State Military Museum

column, while musket balls swept in from the west along the cross streets making it equally dangerous to remain or push on. Reaching a corner, balls began to enfilade the column severely wounding Major Charles Koch. Recognizing the imminent danger, Dobke hurried his men into the protected alleys to either side of Christ Lutheran Church. The quick decision provided protection from Confederate fire, but safety was merely temporary. Only upon entry did Dobke realize the alley was a cul-de-sac. They were trapped.[4]

Christian Böhm, a member of Captain Irsch's command, now acting as rear guard, recalled the terrible scene. "At every western street corner enemy bullets pierced our ranks; so we turned against the enemy enabling our brothers to retreat under cover; and so the bloody street battle continued. When bullets began raining from the east as well, it meant saving the regimental colors. So Colonel Dobke and the brave Captain Korn led the head of the column into a protected alley by the church . . . and the rear guard reached the alley under heavy attack from east and west alike. Then the bad news from the head of the column: We are in a blind alley—men and colors must escape over fences to the nearby cemetery."[5]

Hastily, men at the front of the column scrambled over the confining fences, making way for the color guard so the banners consigned to their care would not fall into the hands of the enemy. They moved as fast as they could, but by the time Irsch's rear guard arrived the street was under a deadly Confederate crossfire. Dobke reported

4 New York Monuments Commission Report, I, 380; *OR* 27, pt. 1, 734; Böhm address.

5 Böhm address.

that "about 100 men . . . extricated themselves from this trap, ran the gauntlet, and arrived safely at [Cemetery Hill]." Behind them they left four companies cut off from escape by the Confederate crossfire. "Comrades," Irsch yelled above the musket fire and whizzing minié balls, "it is too late for quick retreat; the situation calls for stubborn fight, imprisonment or death!" The captain ordered his men to use anything they could to blockade the alleyway and street. Stray refugees from other regiments arrived to bolster the force under Irsch's command to somewhere between 200 and 600 men—there would never be anything approaching an accurate count. According to Ley, "Lieutenant [John] H[enry] Ahlert had taken possession of some houses near the Eagle Hotel into which we all retreated, covering the Lutheran church opposite, being assisted by many soldiers of other regiments of the First and Eleventh Corps, we broke down the fences in the yards, and Captain [Henry] Dietz gained more houses up to an alley near Market Place, occupying windows, barns and alley-ways, from which the enemy was continually harassed and several attempts of the enemy to dislodge us were refused."[6]

A similar fate befell the 74th Pennsylvania, among the last to enter the town. Lt. Louis Fischer with the pioneers stood on a box at the "corner of the college" and "as far as my eye could reach I saw thousands of Ewell's men come toward the rear and right flank of my corps, completely enveloping it." As he watched, artillery pummeled the retreating troops, Rebel infantry caught them in a crossfire. "The wounded are coming in constant streams across the fields toward me, until every room in the large college is filled to overflowing. . . . South of the college grounds a stone bridge spans a brook. The arch is considerably elevated above the surrounding level. Word is passed from man to man to not go over the bridge but walk through the deep mire. Rebel infantry in the houses east of it are raking it with their fire. Lieut. [Wilhelm] Roth, of my company scorns the idea of any Rebel hitting him, and marches over the bridge. A dull thud, and his reeling body sinks to the earth before me; but I take [the route] through the mire."[7]

6 New York Monuments Commission Report; *OR* 27, pt. 1, 734; Böhm address; Ley, letter; Schurz, *Reminiscences*, Vol. 3, 18-19.

7 Fischer, "At Gettysburg"; a letter from one of Roth's comrades placed his death in a more heroic light for his brother. He says that Wilhelm was "Struck by two Balls one through the Breast and one through the head he died the Death of a Hero, in him we have lost a patriotic and Daring Soldier as well as a much beloved comrade." See Letter from John Zela, Captain, Company K, to Charles Roth, near Warrenton, August 5, 1863, Civil War Miscellaneous Collection, USMHI.

"Things were getting hot," Lt. Col. von Mitzel understated, "I had two horses shot under me." The dwindling group made it to town only to find it "already in the enemy's hands." Trying to find a way through the labyrinthian back alleys, Maj. Gustav Schleiter with about 21 men found an escape route back toward Cemetery Hill, but von Mitzel and the balance of the rear guard were cut off, surrounded, and eventually forced to surrender.[8]

☽ ☽ ☽

Capt. Frederick Winkler rode north through town past groups of refugees from Barlow's division who were "crowding the sidewalk on both sides." Emerging from town he spotted Schurz and spurred over to report that help was on the way. All about him were troops in a retreat that appeared "less orderly than it should have been." Gaining Schurz's attention, Winkler pointed to the head of Coster's brigade just then beginning to emerge from the village. About this time a message arrived from Schimmelfennig advising that he was being flanked on his left as the I Corps fell back and the order arrived from Howard to retire through town to Cemetery Hill. Schurz could only hope to use Coster to "check the enemy long enough to permit Barlow's Division to enter the town without being seriously molested on its retreat."[9]

In the 154th New York Charles McKay was appalled by the scene that met his regiment as it rushed through town. "All around was confusion and disaster." The brigade double-quicked along Baltimore Street, turned right on High Street, then left onto Stratton Street. As it passed the German Reformed Church at Stratton and High Streets the regiment began to come under artillery fire. Sergt. John F. Wellman saw shells "shrieking closer to their heads, and every shot a little closer. . . . I looked for some disorder, but I swear to you today, not one man broke step from the head of the column to the rear."[10]

When Coster reached a position opposite the railroad depot on the north side of town he detached the 73rd Pennsylvania to form there as a brigade reserve. This left him with only 936 officers and men. Schurz joined him near the German Reformed Church about the same time the column came under artillery fire. Fragments from one of the first shells tore into Jerome Myers' knapsack. Henry Teller heard the German

8 Valuska, and Keller, *Damn Dutch*, 142.

9 Winkler letter home, July 6, 1863; Hitz, *Letters of Frederick C. Winkler*, 70; *OR* 27, pt. 1, 729.

10 McKay, "Three years or During the War With the Crescent and Star," 131; Conklin, "Long March," 51.

Lt. Col. Daniel B. Allen, 154th New York
U.S. Army Heritage and Education Center

exclaim "Dey will haf to schoot petter as dat if dey want to kill me."[11] A hesitant chuckle briefly relieved the tension of those who heard.

Placing himself at the head of the column, Schurz "led it out of the town, and ordered it to deploy on the right of the junction of the roads east of the railroad depot, which the enemy was fast approaching." The general's intent was to protect his open flank while the survivors of Barlow's and Schimmelfennnig's divisions retired. At Schurz's direction, Coster turned the column east toward John Kuhn's brickyard where he ordered "Halt, front, right dress." In the lead, the 134th New York entered the brickyard property through a carriage gate. It formed behind a wooden post and rail fence, the regiment straddling Stevens Run with its right flank ending in a wheat field. The 154th New York formed to its left "in front of the kilns."[12]

Charles McKay noticed that the "ground in our front was higher than at our position, gently rising until, 40 rods away, it was perhaps 20 feet above us and covered with wheat just ready for the sickle." The rise obstructed his view so that he could not see the approaching enemy. Lt. Col. Daniel B. Allen was concerned that while the higher ground to his left front "protected the left of our line" it "also prevented its firing, except obliquely to the right. Our left ought to have been advanced upon this higher ground where we could observe the whole movement of the enemy, and doubtless would have been, except for a strong post and rail fence which occupied the

11 Dunkelman, "Coster Avenue Mural," 5, Verticle file 4-9g, GNMP; Conklin, "History of the 134th N.Y." Coster had 438 men in the 134th New York, 224 in the 154th New York, and 274 in the 27th Pennsylvania. For this, see Dunkelman and Winey, "Brickyard Fight," 20; Cosgrove, *History of the 134th New York*, 80.

12 *OR*, 27, pt. 1, 729; Dunkleman, *Hardtack Regiment*, 19; McKay, "Crescent and Star," 131; Dunkelman, "Coster Avenue Mural," 5; Dunkelman and Winey, "Brickyard Fight," 20.

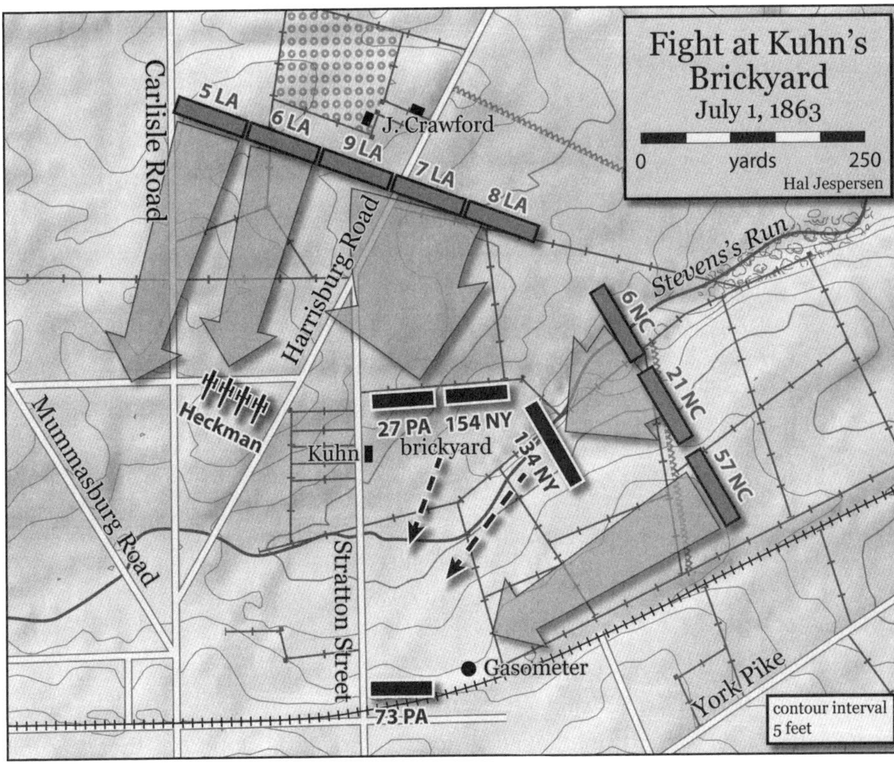

same position. . . . The enemy consisting of Early's whole division came down upon us almost before we had got in line."[13]

The 27th Pennsylvania completed Coster's line with its left end resting on the intersection with Stratton Street. Two sections of Heckman's battery unlimbered in an open field to the west of the intersection. Lt. Charles M. Schiely's section of two guns went into battery on the right, with Lt. Columbus Rodamour's section to the left and slightly behind him. Both sections opened fire as soon as they unlimbered. "We commenced giving them our best wishes in the shape of shell and canister," explained Quartermaster Sergt. Cecil C. Reed, a twenty-year-old native of Cleveland, Ohio, "which mowed them down like wheat. But on they came, closing up their ranks whenever they were torn asunder by our shots, and they were not idle all the time either; they were pouring in their volleys with telling effect. Our men were falling fast

13 McKay, "Crescent and Star," 131; Dunkelman and Winey, "Brickyard Fight," 20; *Final Report on the Battlefield at Gettysburg*, III, 1051.

Lt. Col. Lorenz Cantador, 27th Pennsylvania
Library of Congress

and they were coming so close that some of their skirmishers were literally blown to pieces from the muzzles of our guns."[14]

The hasty deployment left a gap between the 134th and 154th New York. Lt. Col. Lorenz Cantador of the 27th Pennsylvania spotted the opening and ordered one battalion of his regiment to move into the gap, but "owing to the din and confusion of the battle, the order was only partially executed" with about fifty men under Lt. Adolphus Vogelbach moving to close the opening.[15] Despite Cantador's quick action, the position was not ideal since the ground rose in front of much of it restricting the field of fire forward while a small depression where the Pennsylvanians formed also made it impossible for them to offer effective support to those on the right. But time had run out, there could be no further advance. As it was, the rapid approach of the enemy gave them precious little time to deploy into line of battle before the storm struck.

Apparently there was just enough time for Corp. Emil Preiser to pen a brief entry onto a page of his New Testament. "On our left Artillerymen ready their lanyard. I am praying and hoping that the attack of the Rebels of missing us. Gettysburg July first. God help us." Wounded during the ensuing combat, Preiser made it to the XI Corps hospital on the Spangler Farm where his testament was found by Peter D. Swisher after the owner's death on July 7.[16]

Coster's three regiments numbered only slightly more than 900 officers and men. Bearing down on them were Hays' and Avery's brigades of Early's division, a force of about 2,500 fresh troops that had thus far been only marginally engaged. The two brigades advanced in concert with Hays deploying his five Louisiana regiments to each

14 Dunkelman, "Coster Avenue Mural, Gettysburg," 5; Baumgartner, *Buckeye Blood*, 61.

15 Conklin, "History of the 134th N.Y."; Bates, *History of Pennsylvania Volunteers*, 390-91.

16 Preiser prayerbook.

Lt. Col. Alan H. Jackson, 134th New York
U.S. Army Heritage and Education Center

side of the Harrisburg Road. Avery's three North Carolina regiments moved forward through the fields on either side of Stevens Run.[17] The Rebels overlapped Coster's line on each flank in a repeat of the same problem that earlier plagued Barlow and Krzyzanowski.

The 134th New York barely finished deploying when Avery's Confederate brigade burst upon it only some 60 yards away. "Evidently," concluded Lt. Benjamin F. Sheldon, "they deemed themselves sufficiently strong for us as they advanced upon us in splendid style; but if this was the idea they embraced, they were a little mistaken in their notion, as our boys certainly gave them to understand that free soil was no place for traitors to the time honored flag of our fathers."[18]

Lt. Col. Alan Jackson immediately gave the order to fire and the first volley the regiment ever fired in combat swept across the field. On the receiving end of the volley, Capt. Neill W. Ray in the 6th North Carolina observed that "the enemy seemed to fight with more desperation and gallantry than we had been accustomed to in our engagements with him in Virginia." Col. Archibald C. Godwin of the 57th North Carolina on Avery's left flank found the fire "very destructive," but it could have been more so. Corp. George Warner found that "many" of the men who had "failed to remove the moisture from the tubes of their guns" while on Cemetery Hill found that in this crisis they would not fire. It was a rookie mistake that would cost the regiment dearly. While the 6th and 21st North Carolina assaulted from the front, Godwin led his regiment around the exposed right flank of the New Yorkers catching them in a destructive enfilade fire. Capt. James Dart said the "contest was severe, and the struggle

17 Dunkelman, "Coster Avenue Mural," 5; Conklin, "History of the 134th N.Y."

18 Cosgrove, *History of the 134th New York*, 80.

great. We fought an overwhelming force, yet not a man flinched from the stern duty before him, but fought nobly until compelled to retire."[19]

"My poor regiment was horribly cut to pieces," Lt. Col. Jackson lamented, "I never imagined such a rain of bullets." Despite the destruction, his regiment held out some 20 minutes against the onslaught as Godwin's men moved from flank to rear, catching them in a deadly salient. Godwin believed the Federals were "stubbornly holding their position until we had climbed over [a fence] into their midst." Briefly a hand-to-hand struggle raged until Jackson, now nearly surrounded, finally acknowledged the hopelessness of the situation and ordered a withdrawal. Those who could escape fled across the open fields, crossed the railroad tracks, heading for York Street in the hope of reaching Cemetery Hill. Sergts. Robert O. Seaman and John J. Carroll raced as fast as their legs would carry them in an attempt to save the regiment's colors. A minié ball hit Seaman severely wounding his right arm. When he fell, Carroll picked up the fallen banner and attempted to escape with both, but he soon went down, shot three times with wounds in both legs. Hastily, Carroll tore the state colors from their staff and wrapped them around his body, hiding the banner beneath his clothing. Carroll would be a prisoner until July 4 without the Rebels ever discovering that he had secreted the regimental colors beneath his sack coat. As he struggled, an officer he did not know scooped up the national colors as he ran for the rear. Jackson stayed until it appeared all the men who were going to get away were hastening to the rear, then attempted to make his own escape. By then, Godwin's troops had cut his escape route. Unwilling to surrender, he managed to enter the Henry Meals home unseen in the confusion. There Mrs. Meals hid him, along with Levi Moore from his regiment, in a loft over her kitchen for the next two days until the two finally donned disguises and "braving the fire of their own pickets, they made it back to Cemetery Hill."[20]

William Warner took "refuge under a barrel in another citizen's cellar" and also managed to escape detection. The 134th carried about 400 officers and men into action that day. Later that evening only five officers and 27 men answered the roll call. By the following morning when those on detached service and the walking wounded returned, its numbers increased to only about 100.[21]

19 Cosgrove, *History of the 134th New York*, 80; *OR* 27, pt. 2, 484; Conklin, "History of the 134th N.Y."; Conklin, "Long March to Stevens Run," 50.

20 *OR* 27, pt. 2, 484; Cosgrove, *History of the 134th New York*, 81-82; Conklin, *Crescent and Star*, 110-11; Conklin, "History of the 134th N.Y."

21 Conklin, "History of the 134th N.Y."; Cosgrove, *History of the 134th New York*, 76, 84, 255, 375; Conklin, *Crescent and Star*, 112, 114. London-born Carroll was shot in the right knee requiring the surgeons to remove 77 bone fragments.

In the 154th New York Lt. Col. Allen was not happy with the location of his 265 men. "Our regiment was unfortunate in the position assigned it, or rather where it happened to fall, here on this low ground, where nothing could be seen of our immediate left. . . . Even from the right of my regiment, where I immediately went as soon as we came to a front and the firing commenced, I could see nothing of how far the enemy's right extended to our left." Even before it completed its deployment bullets began to zip overhead or through the ranks. Allen reported the enemy "came down upon us almost before we had got in line."[22]

Charles McKay was fascinated with "how the Confederate line of battle looked as it came into full view and started down toward us. It seemed as though they had a battle flag every few rods, which would indicate that their formation was in solid column." Allen ordered the men to "reserve our fire until the enemy were close enough to make our volley effective." Once the Rebels crested the rise to begin their descent the distance quickly diminished. "Fire!" The order brought forth "a blaze of fire" as a volley leapt forth. According to McKay, "our fire did good execution when we opened, and their line was stopped in our front." Lt. Alanson Crosby was even more enthusiastic: "Not a man flinched or gave an inch to the overwhelming force opposed to them. There they stood, firm as the Pyramids, fighting with the desperation of a forlorn hope, a murderous fire all the time raking them in front and flank."[23]

Allen was holding his own for the moment, but the crisis on the right of the 134th New York soon uncovered his flank making his position untenable as Confederates began to move in behind his regiment. "I relied upon orders for withdrawing the regiment in case we were in danger of being flanked in that direction," he recalled. "We stopped the enemy and were holding them in our front, but their line so far overlapped the One hundred and thirty fourth on our right that they swung around almost in their rear, and had such an enfilading fire upon them and our whole line, that that regiment was compelled to give way, and I immediately gave orders for my regiment to fall back."[24] Allen did not know it, nor did Jackson, but seeing the crisis developing on his right, and being able to see the rest of Hays' brigade approaching along the Harrisburg Road, Coster ordered a retreat. For some reason, the order never reached the two New

22 Fanton, "Battle on the Brickyard Wall," 35-36; Alanson Crosby to friend, Feb. 28, 1864, 154th New York File, GNMP; *New York at Gettysburg*, Vol. III, 1051. For the number present and other data see Dunkelman, "'We Were Compelled," 34-56.

23 McKay, "Crescent and Star"; Dunkelman, "We Were Compelled"; Letter, Lt. Alanson Crosby to friend, February 28, 1864. For the number of men it carried into action see Dunkelman and Winey, "Brickyard Fight," 19.

24 Fanton, "Battle on the Brickyard Wall," 35.

York regiments. By the time their colonels decided, on their own responsibility, to retire, it was too late to carry out a well-organized withdrawal.

Allen retreated toward Stratton Street thinking to fall back on the 27th Pennsylvania and, if necessary, continue the retreat along the road into town. Cresting the rise, he was astonished to find the Pennsylvanians "had been withdrawn without my knowledge, and that the enemy had outflanked us to a much greater extent upon our left than on the right; that their line had advanced unopposed down the road and across the open field beyond. The ground directly in rear of the position which we had occupied was cut up into village lots surrounded by board fences, so that retreat was greatly impeded in that direction." In an instant, Hays' and Avery's men were in among the Federals prompting another short but violent hand-to-hand confrontation. Lt. Vogelbach's small contingent of Pennsylvanians attempted to cut their way to safety, but the lieutenant was seriously wounded and the command surrounded. Allen found his regiment "compelled to cut our way through them and in doing so our losses were heavy." In the brickyard, James Quilliam was not fast enough. "The regiment started back double quick i got up and went as fast as any of them but when we got to the road it was full of rebbels and they were comeing up behind us so there we had to stay and but few got away they made us lay down our guns and marched us of."[25]

In the 154th New York, Lewis Bishop stood erect among the chaos waving the national colors, with Corp. Albert Mericle nearby holding aloft the state banner. When the retreat began it quickly degenerated into a race for the village for those who managed to escape the encirclement. A bullet hit the flag staff between Bishop's hands, then another sliced through his leg, but Bishop refused to yield his flag until a second ball shattered his other leg. Unable to continue, he surrendered the colors to Gilbert M. Rykert but he took only a few steps before falling wounded. John A. Bush picked up the fallen banner only to be wounded. Mericle also attempted to save the colors in his care but he was shot down near Stevens Run. First Sergt. James W. Bird picked up the state colors and brought them to safety. Heading to the rear, Capt. Matthew B. Cheney saw a flag lying on the ground. Thinking it belonged to his regiment he grabbed it as he rushed along. Although seriously wounded, he managed to carry it to Cemetery Hill only to find that it belonged to the 134th New York.[26]

25 New York Monuments Commission, Final Report, III, 1051; Fanton, "Battle on the Brickyard Wall," 35; Dunkelman, *Brothers One and All*, 132-33.

26 John F. Wellman to Ellicottville Post, Sept. 5, 1888, 154th New York File, GNMP; Conklin, "History of the 134th N.Y."; Bates, *History of Pennsylvania Volunteers*, 391. The fate of the colors of the 134th and 154th New York is extremely confusing. See Dunkelman, "Additional Notes," 79-85.

While the chaos of the brickyard fight unfolded, Capt. Lewis Heckman's Battery K, 1st Ohio Light Artillery fired into the Confederate advance. Heckman, a German-born baker in civilian life, found the "enemy was already in range when my battery went into position. I unlimbered, and commenced firing as soon as possible, as the enemy were close to me and advancing." During the thirty minutes his men worked the guns out in the open field the four pieces poured 113 rounds of canister into Hays' brigade which the Confederate general described as "unusually galling," so much so that it held up Hays causing his men to lag somewhat behind Avery's. Capt. Michael O'Connor of the 6th Louisiana expressed surprise at the "stubborn resistance" his men met. Yet the encounter was not one-sided. Although supported by the 27th Pennsylvania until Coster ordered its withdrawal, Heckman came under counter battery and musket fire, costing him one officer seriously wounded along with two men killed, ten wounded, and nine horses according to Major Thomas Osborn, who was on the scene.[27]

"We found it would not be very healthy for us to remain," Sergt. Cecil Reed understated, "and we commenced making preparations for a retrograde movement; but when we came to move off the battery we found that [Schiely's] section had lost nearly all their horses, so we had to abandon it, not however until the guns were well spiked and rendered unserviceable to the enemy. We finally came off with two guns." Disengaging was not easy. As the sergeant described, "The boys used their revolvers with telling effect on the Rebels. All of our officers' horses were shot from under them. Captain Heckman ran a very narrow escape; he had just dismounted when his favorite horse fell, pierced by two balls, but it was not long until he had the saddle off and was again mounted on a fresh horse. After he had got the battery off he rode back through the fire of the enemy to see if any of the boys were left on the field. We cannot compliment our Captain too highly for the interest he took in our welfare, and the daring deeds he performed that day will be long remembered by us."[28]

Confederate shells dropped among the streets and the troops retreating through the northern edges of town. Minié balls sliced through the air, eventually enfilading the Federals as they tried to find a safe route through the town. In the 154th New York one of the lead missiles went through Lt. Salmon Beardsley's canteen, bruising his hip. Feeling the warm liquid flowing down his leg, he feared the worse, but "soon found that I was only scared by the watter running down from my *wounded* canteen instead of

27 *OR* 27, pt. 1, 747, 755; *OR* 27, pt. 2, 479; Gannon, *Irish Rebels*, 187; Cosgrove, *History of the 134th New York*, 82; Naisawald, *Grape and Canister*, 360; Dunkelman, "Coster Avenue Mural," 5.

28 Baumgartner, *Buckeye Blood*, 62.

blood from my body." Another ball sliced into Sergt. Amos Humiston of the 154th New York as he attempted to escape. Desperately wounded and unable to continue, he sat down, took out of his pocket an ambrotype portrait of his three young children, his eyes exploring their features one more time as he bled to death. Following the battle a burial detail would be touched by the scene. The photo of the unknown children would be circulated throughout the North until at last someone recognized them and the last thoughts of Sergt. Humiston became a *cause célèbre* throughout the North. With the assistance of northern Sunday schools, Dr. John F. Bournes led a fund-raising drive that collected enough money to open the Soldiers' Orphans Home in the same Baltimore Street house that served as Howard's headquarters during the battle. It opened in 1866 with Phylinda Humiston as the wardrobe mistress and her three children as residents.[29]

☽ ☽ ☽

29 Dunkelman, "Additional Notes," 74; Dunkelman and Winey, "Hunt for Sergeant Humiston," 29-31; Dunkelman, *Gettysburg's Unknown Soldier*, 181-82.

Opposite page:
The photo that stirred a nation. From left, Frank, Frederick and Alice Humiston
Library of Congress

Right:
Sergeant Amos Humiston, 154th New York
Dunkelman and Winey Collection, St. Bonaventure University

After reporting to Schurz and directing him to Coster's approaching column, Capt. Winkler spied a portion of the survivors of Krzyzanowski's brigade formed into ranks near the Carlisle Road "among them thirty-two men with the colors of the 26th Wisconsin, but without any officer; we rode by them and they called out to me and, with the General's permission, I sent my horse away and took command of this gallant squad." Winkler "formed my little band in two ranks and had them sit down in the road. It was useless, of course, to try to resist the long Rebel forces that were then approaching, but we could delay them and thus ensure a safe retreat to the rest of our troops." To his right, the violent contest in the brickyard raged until Coster was driven from the field. With no further orders, Winkler was reluctant to withdraw even though it was obvious nothing more could be done. "We were not fired upon and I had an excellent opportunity to look on. There was a long line of battle approaching on each side of the road." As he contemplated the situation, Capt. Alexander Maluski, Krzyzanowski's aide, rode by with orders to "fall back." Winker retired to "a little white cottage where the little remnant of our brigade went into the yard and from there fired another volley at the advancing line on the right flank. My men went in, fired, and then followed the rest, running into the city."[30]

After delivering the order to Winkler, Maluski also fell back to the "little white cottage" where "I was riding my horse in front of the infantry so that this retreat would be an orderly one. The enemy saw this and, having a long-range rifle, aimed at me. The bullet hit my *portmanteau*, breaking its contents of personal items, flattening a watch and lodging in it. Another four inches higher and it would have pierced my body." Busy

30 Winkler letter home, July 6, 1863; Maluski reminiscences.

Capt. Alexander Maluski, 58th New York, an aide to Col. Krzyzanowski
U.S. Army Heritage and Education Center

directing his men, Schurz never noticed until later that his "horse had a bullet hole clean through the fatty ridge of the neck just under the mane."[31] Others had similar narrow escapes.

Several regiments claimed to have been the last to exit the field into town. Of course, since the brigades retreated along different routes, within the limited scope of individuals the claims were probably each correct for their immediate surroundings. "I believe," wrote Major Benjamin Willis of the 119th New York, "we were the last regiment to reach the foot of Washington street, where we again took a position to cover the town, and held the enemy in check until our trains of baggage-wagons and ambulances had withdrawn to the rear. This movement was a success, in part due to a section of Captain Dilger's renowned battery, planted upon an eminence near the square in the town of Gettysburg."[32]

Still hoping that a stand could be made in the outskirts of the village despite the order to retire, Capt. Winkler was mortified to see the remaining units in full retreat. "I felt furious when I saw the 1st Division all crowding the sidewalks; think of it, it was a northern village. I had ridden up and down its streets from one end to the other three times that day and everywhere there were manifestations of joy; handkerchiefs were waving everywhere, and ladies stood in the streets offering refreshments to the soldiers as they passed. It seemed so awful to march back through those same streets whipped and beaten. It was the most humiliating step I ever took."[33]

☽ ☽ ☽

31 Maluski reminiscences; Schurz, *Reminiscences*, III, 12.

32 *OR* 27, pt. 1, 742.

33 Winkler, *Letters*, 71.

Taken from the top of Cemetery Hill looking toward town along the Baltimore Pike, this photograph clearly shows the rough stone fences constructed by farmers to mark their fields. In the bottom right and center left can be seen gaps in the wall where the stones were cast aside, mostly likely for the movement of Wiedrich's battery into position to the right. Notice also how rough the "walls" are and how low in comparison with the people and the wagon.

Library of Congress

As Schurz's order to withdraw circulated, the units that continued to resist along the outskirts of town began attempting to disengage and withdraw. Looking out over the scene from his position on Cemetery Hill, Col. Adin Underwood in the 33rd Massachusetts "watched them as they stubbornly retreated, turning every few rods to fire a volley, facing in every direction. Batteries limbered up, galloped back, and then halted and fired grape and canister."[34] It was clearly a fighting retreat.

Major David Thomson assumed command of the 82nd Ohio, and briefly Krzyzanowski's brigade. He was the fourth brigade commander in an hour. With the adjutant wounded, Thomson quickly deputized another, but while seated atop his horse giving the man instructions a 12-pound shot struck the new adjutant killing him instantly and splattering remains for yards around. Thomson was struck twice by spent balls, "yet not hurt beyond a bruise." Two balls cut holes in his boots, shell fragments tore his coat, and later that evening he counted more than twenty bullet holes in the regiment's colors. William Paynton saw what he thought was an abandoned gun just

34 Underwood, *Three Years' Service*, 118.

outside town, no doubt one of Heckman's. As he rushed to escape, "the rebels were crowding, yelling and making for that gun. Just as I came opposite to where the gun was, some 'Yankee' boys ran out to the gun and finding it loaded they fired into that crowd of yelling rebels, and reloaded and fired it several times, until I turned off into another street and lost sight of them."[35]

The remnant remaining of the 26th Wisconsin fell back along Carlisle Street to the town square. A woman there noticed Sergt. Karl Wickesberg, his wrist bleeding from a gunshot wound suffered as the regiment withdrew toward town. "[S]he called me into the house, washed my wound and bandaged it," he later recalled with thanks. "Men horses, teams and artillery poured in by cross roads from the west together with those coming from our direction crowded the square." Winkler passed directly through the town square and headed south. "We took things leisurely," he recalled, adding, "There was no close pursuit, no firing into the city of any moment." Reaching Cemetery Hill, Winkler and his small command went into position where directed behind some stone walls.[36]

Capt. Hubert Dilger unlimbered a section of guns in Gettysburg's main square, from which he could sweep the approaches along York, Chambersburg, and Baltimore streets. By the time he attempted to withdraw his pieces, he later explained, "The main road was completely blockaded by artillery, infantry, and ambulances, and I took the first road to the left, marched around the town, and rejoined my command on Cemetery Hill."[37]

Col. Seraphim Meyer was also in the town square rallying some of his 107th Ohio when Adj. H. Whitney Chatfield of the 17th Connecticut, apparently unaware that Ames had ordered Harris to command the brigade, approached with the news that Meyer was now the senior officer in the brigade. Before he could act, another aide rode up with an order to turn his regiment over to the senior captain, but *not* to assume command of the brigade. Mystified by the sudden order, he had no time to react before yet another aide arrived with an order for him to lead his regiment toward the southern end of town. Now completely confused by the contradictory orders, Meyer turned command of the 107th Ohio over to Capt. Otto Weber and, with bugler Conrad

35 Thomson to Mary, July 16 and Aug. 5 1863, Thomson Papers in possession of Ms. Mary Geiger; Paynton, "From Virginia to Gettysburg."

36 Wickesberg, *Letters of Sergeant Charles Wickesberg*, letter of July 6, 1863; Winkler, "Reminiscence," Milwaukee County Historical Society.

37 *OR* 27, pt. 1, 754.

Hornung in tow, headed south. The two of them made it. Weber did not. Lingering too long, he was captured by advancing Rebels.[38]

Here and there other units continued to resist as they moved through town. Capt. Jacob Gross of the 82nd Illinois found that "all proceeded in good order until we were attacked by the enemy in the streets of Gettysburg, where we became engaged in a bloody hand-to-hand fight, losing many in killed, wounded and prisoners." Captain Joseph Greenhut of the same regiment recalled that "It was in this retreat through the town that our regiment suffered most severely, the Rebels coming in through the side streets, which compelled us to fight our way through the entire town. Besides the killed and wounded we suffered in this street conflict, a number of our officers and men were cut off and captured by the enemy. It was a fearful struggle against great odds, and as our regiment covered the rear of our brigade in that retreat, it has been a surprise to me that we were not entirely annihilated or captured in our endeavor to force our way through the town up to Cemetery Hill. Each of us can, however, vividly recollect the hairbreadth escapes experienced on that occasion without any allusions on my part . . . down through the entire rank of offices and men, none will ever forget that terrible day." Lt. Col. Salomon, already twice wounded, found himself in "a cul-de-sac, where I was compelled to have a heavy, tight board fence knocked down to make it possible to proceed. That accomplished, we had to pass through an enfilading fire of musketry."[39]

Major Allen Brady, whose four companies of the 17th Connecticut were still skirmishing with Confederates east of Rock Creek, received an order from Gen. Ames to withdraw into town and take command of the regiment since he was now the senior surviving officer. Brady had some difficulty disengaging Company K, which was in very close contact with the enemy, but successfully "fell back in good order, skirmishing with the enemy, who advanced as we retreated, and tried to cut us off and capture us before we got to the town, but we foiled them in this attempt by making a circuit and entering the town near the upper end, and soon joined the remainder of the regiment." By the time Brady arrived in the village, he found the Rebels already penetrating its streets. Ordering his men into line, he "fired several volleys into the ranks of the enemy, which thinned their ranks and retarded their advance."[40]

38 Meyer to Meysenburg, July 5, 1863; testimony at the court martial of Col. Meyer, File #nn163, RG153, Records of the Office of the Judge Advocate General (Army), Court-Martial Case Files 1809-1894, National Archives; Baumgartner, Buckeye Blood, 64-65.

39 Gross, *82nd Illinois*, 34, 36; Jacob Gross, *82nd Illinois*, 36.

40 *OR* 27, pt. 1, 717-18. Brady's four companies resisted Early's advance all afternoon, losing two officers wounded, three men killed, and four men captured.

Once in town the troops arriving along several routes from the north and west converged to create some confusion in the village streets. The most serious problem occurred west of the town square where units of von Amsberg's brigade encountered retreating troops from Robinson's division of the I Corps, becoming entangled as the former entered from the north and the latter from the west. Although men from both corps acted as rear guards, once the streets became congested traffic slowed considerably which allowed some of the Rebels to move around the west side of the town far enough south to enfilade some of the streets that Federals would have to cross to reach Cemetery Hill. This set up several intersections swept by deadly cross fires that either prevented some Federals from escaping or made the attempt very costly if they did so. Dead-end streets heightened the confusion. Few Union officers knew which streets led where, causing several groups to go astray while trying to find a way through the crowded roads or while looking for a passage free from Confederate fire.

Capt. Edward Culp, an aide on Barlow's staff, walked his horse calmly back through the streets until he spotted a wounded captain from his regiment, the 25th Ohio, holding onto a lamppost for support. Culp stopped to offer assistance, but soon "discovered that I was liable to become a prisoner. I dashed up a street to find it absolutely blocked with ambulances and abandoned wagons and caissons. I was still riding my horse, and too valuable a one to lose; besides, he had stood my friend in several hot places, and was reliable as steel. As a last resort, I rode up the steps of a veranda, opened the hall door and rode through the hall into a large sitting room in which the frightened family were gathered. I asked if there was a lane back of the lot I could get out through, and a young lady of perhaps 16 quickly opened the door, and requesting me to follow her tripped lightly through the house and to the back of the lot, where she commenced to let down some bars. Telling her not to mind, but get back and to the cellar as quickly as possible, I jumped my horse over the bars and just saved myself from a trip to Libby prison."[41]

Sergt. Arthur W. De Goyler of the 134th New York made it to "the foot of Main Street, where there is a large square. Here the bullets were flying like hail and the street was blocked up with men, artillery, ambulances and horses, so I ran into a yard and went into the house and sat down, as I was very tired and overheated. In the house were a good many of our wounded boys of the 134th. In a few minutes the Rebels came into town and a Rebel cavalryman came to the door and ordered all who were not wounded to come out. Just then the lady who lived in the house came into the room. Well, she told me to come with her, and with three others she took us upstairs and hid us away."

41 Baumgartner, *Buckeye Blood*, 64.

The sergeant remained in hiding until July 3 when he noticed that Union soldiers who were identified as aides in the hospitals were allowed to walk about town. Fastening a white string around his arm, as the hospital attendants were identified, he ventured outside where he found the Rebels "friendly, giving me drink, and food, which I stood much in need of." He remained in town until it was re-occupied by Federal troops, then rejoined his regiment.[42]

Capt. Friedrich Otto von Fritsch "rode behind our men into the town and saw many captured by Grey-coats everywhere." Passing a building that had been commandeered as a field hospital he stopped briefly to speak with a surgeon he recognized, but "Some twenty Confederates came rushing on, hollaring at me to surrender. One excited fellow got hold of Caesar's bridle with his left hand and was ready to plunge his bayonet into me with his right, screaming: 'Surrender! Get down, you damned Yank!' 'You be damned,' I answered, and cut off his hand with my Saxon sword. Then I started off, gave spurs to my horse, but to my horror found myself in a yard surrounded by high fence rails. They shot at me from behind and demanded surrender. Caesar, with an enormous effort, jumped the fence and made off towards Cemetery Hill. Reaching the arch, I dismounted and examined my horse; the poor fellow had been shot twice. My left leg was wounded, my left shoulder strap had been shot away and the shoulder was badly scratched; one bullet had damaged my saddle, and when I tried to replace my sabre, I found the scabbard bent. I had hurt my right knee badly on the fence, and torn off one of my stirrups." He bound a handkerchief around a "slight but painful flesh wound above the ankle" and proceeded to rally the troops as they emerged from the southern edge of town.[43]

Another of those caught in a similar situation was Schimmelfennig. Among the last to leave the field, he continued attempting to organize an effective rear guard action as the troops struggled to find their way through town. Turning into an alleyway off Baltimore Street to escape musketry, he suddenly found himself confronted by a high fence with no way out. Enemy soldiers barred any thought of retracing his steps. When they began shouting for him to surrender, the general quickly dismounted and attempted to climb over the fence. One of the Rebels got close enough to strike Schimmelfennig with the butt of his rifle. Falling over the fence, the general played dead hoping his pursuers would continue on their way. Perhaps because he had on an ordinary cavalryman's overcoat over his general's uniform the Rebels did not recognize the prize in their grasp. When they had left the area, Schimmelfenning crawled slowly

42 Conklin, "Long March," 53.

43 Butts, *Gallant Captain*, 77.

Dr. Franz Hübschmann, 26th Wisconsin
Milwaukee County Historical Society

over to a small wooden structure with straw and the remnants of food on the floor apparently meant to feed hogs. Later that evening Catharine Garlach came out back to feed her livestock, only to be surprised by the general motioning to her with his finger to his lips for her to be quiet.[44]

Catherine's daughter Anna thought "It was remarkable that he was not captured. The Rebels had torn down fences from Breckinridge Street southward through the yards, and there were Rebels on all sides of us, and any movement of his in daytime might have been seen from a number of points. On the second day, Mother made a pretense of going to the swill barrel to empty a bucket. In the bucket, however, was water and a piece of bread, and instead of these going into the barrel they went to the general in hiding. Mother was so afraid that she had been seen and the general would be found that she did not repeat this."[45]

In the field hospital Dr. Franz Hübschmann of the 26th Wisconsin received an order to evacuate, the Federals were retreating with the Rebels close behind. A native of the Duchy of Weimar, the doctor had been a member of the convention that drafted Wisconsin's constitution when it applied for statehood, served as a presidential elector and state senator, and was one of the founders of the Milwaukee *Banner and Volksfreund.* He elected to remain behind to treat the wounded. Nine men from his regiment volunteered to remain with him as hospital stewards, hoping the humanitarian nature of their work would spare them from imprisonment.[46]

44 Schurz, "Battle of Gettysburg," 284; Wheeler, *Witness to Gettysburg*, 174; Gettysburg Profiles: A La Cartes De Visite, http://stevehblogdotcom.wordpress.com/2013/01/30/catharine-garlach/.

45 Wheeler, Witness to Gettysburg, 174.

46 Osten, "Huebschmann," 1; Flower, *History of Milwaukee*, 1011-12.

Emil Frey, 82nd Illinois
Emil Spiess, *Illustrierte Geschichte der Schweiz*

Amid the fury that reigned outside, Hübschmann and his volunteers worked feverishly to tend the ever-lengthening line of wounded awaiting their care. Eventually, some 500 patients crowded the hospital and its environs. While they worked, shells fell in the fields nearby and Southern skirmishers sent their deadly missiles whining through the streets outside the hospital's windows. Annoyed by the dangerous conditions, the doctor's concern grew until he could restrain himself no longer. Setting aside his instruments, he walked out the door into the nearby field where his large frame, conspicuously clad in a blood-spattered white coat, made an excellent target. Ignoring the danger, he lifted his arms above his head as if to signal a halt, and in a "booming voice" he "implored the troops to stop firing on the wounded and pick on healthy soldiers who could defend themselves." The firing ceased. "Few could forget the courageous 'Dutch' doctor," a witness recalled, "who, with his energetic interference, saved many lives."[47]

In town, regiments, small groups, and individuals tried to find their way through crowded streets and a labyrinth of alleyways to the perceived safety of Cemetery Hill. Caught in a cul-de-sac with members of the 82nd Illinois, Adj. Emil Frey's horse was wounded but he believed it his duty to remain mounted to cheer the troops. Along with 76 men of his regiment he found himself surrounded, probably near the group that formed in the buildings near the Eagle Hotel. "I am still sure I could have escaped had I not thought it my duty and a point of honor to remain on horseback to the last moment." Captured with his men, Frey was sent to Libby Prison. For a long time he was one of three officers threatened with execution in retaliation for the planned

47 Milwaukee Features File, Microfilm #450, Milwaukee County Historical Society; Osten, "Huebschmann," 1.

Col. Charles R. Coster, 134th New York, commanded a brigade at Gettysburg.
U.S. Army Heritage and Education Center

execution of a captured Confederate office. Surviving the ordeal, he went home to Europe after the war where, following a distinguished political career, he was elected president of the Swiss Federation.[48]

The rest of the regiment, which turned down a different alleyway, escaped. When they at last made it to Cemetery Hill and Lt. Col. Salomon "congratulated myself that I had extricated my command from the most perilous position it ever occupied, and when I saw my men safely placed behind a stone fence in Cemetery Hill, a platoon of Confederates crossed the road right behind me, shouting to me to surrender. I did not surrender, but put the spurs to my horse to follow my command, when the whole platoon fired, and my horse, pierced by a number of bullets, fell dead, burying me under him. At that time the soldiers of my regiment saw my predicament, they opened fire on the enemy and under the protection of this fire a great number rushed forward, rescued me and carried me across the wall to a place of safety. While I was severely hurt by the fall, I found myself able to continue on duty." Capt. George Heinzmann later recalled that Salomon spit up blood during the rest of the engagement.[49]

The survivors began arriving at the rallying point, yet the peril, the maiming and dying was not over.

48 Meier, *Swiss Officer*, 10-11; Gerling, *Swiss Community*, 14; Rappolt, *Letters of Emil Frey*, 155, 162, 193-94; Frey, "My American Experiences," 136.

49 Salomon, "Gettysburg," 6; Eric Benjaminson, "A Regiment of Immigrants: The 82nd Illinois Volunteer Infantry and the Letters of Captain Rudolph Mueller," *Journal of the Illinois State Historical Society*, Vol. 94, No. 2 (Summer 2001), 158.

Chapter 13

"We Need Help Now"

Evening, July 1, 1863

WHILE THE XI CORPS STRUGGLED to extricate itself from the streets of Gettysburg, Howard continued to hope for the early appearance of reinforcements. In Emmitsburg Maj. Gen. Daniel Sickles, commanding the III Corps, faced a quandary. On the march north, only a day after Meade had assumed command of the army, the new leader rebuked Sickles for allowing his wagon train to obstruct the road, thereby delaying the progress of other units. This was followed a day later by another reproach about the slow progress of his marching column. Clearly, Sickles was already in Meade's dog house when, on the morning of July 1, his predicament became even more problematic. That morning Sickles dispatched Major Henry Tremain to find Reynolds to obtain an update on the situation and any orders he might have for the III Corps. Tremain found Reynolds already engaged at Gettysburg and returned with instructions for Sickles' command to "come up." In the meantime, however, Sickles received an order directly from Meade to hold his corps at Emmitsburg to protect the army's trains and flank. But then an aide from Howard arrived breathlessly explaining that the I and XI Corps were in action a few miles away and in desperate need of help. A troubled look coursed his face as he read the message. "General Reynolds is killed. For God's sake, come up.—Howard."[1]

If Sickles complied, he risked the censure of the commanding general for ignoring his orders. If he did not comply, he might be accused of failing to respond to the pleas

1 Swanberg, *Sickles the Incredible*, 202; Keneally, *American Scoundrel*, 275.

of a general whose troops were already engaged and in real need of assistance. Sickles thought for only a moment before ordering Maj. Gen. David Birney to march his division to Gettysburg immediately, followed by Brig. Gen. Andrew Humphreys' division. Sickles reasoned that he could comply with Meade's orders by holding men under Brig. Gen. Charles Graham at Emmitsburg while still "marching to the guns" with the rest of his III Corps. Turning to the aide, Sickles hastily penned a message for him to carry back to General Howard: "I have at this moment received a communication from an officer of the staff and also two written communications dated at one and half past one p.m. I shall move to Gettysburg immediately."[2] Sickles, however, was still some eleven miles distant. His troops could not be of immediate help, but at least Howard could be assured that if he and his XI Corps could hold out a while longer, help was on the way.

Closer at hand was the XII Corps under Maj. Gen. Henry W. Slocum. The orders for the day issued by Meade called for Slocum to march to Two Taverns and halt there to await further directives. This location placed him in position to support Reynolds or fall back to the defensive line tentatively sketched by Meade along Pipe Creek. Slocum later claimed that he "received no word from General Howard, but started as soon as we heard of the battle, and marched at once to the field of Gettysburg, arriving there about 5 p.m. on the first day."[3] A wealth of evidence suggests otherwise.

By 11:00 am the XII Corps had arrived at Two Taverns, a relatively easy march of some five miles from Gettysburg along the Baltimore Pike. Later testimony by several men in the corps including the official reports of Lt. Col. Charles Morse of the 2nd Massachusetts and Col. William Packer of the 5th Connecticut asserted that from Two Taverns they could hear the sounds of a fight in progress in the direction of Gettysburg, yet no orders were forthcoming to move in that direction or, as far as they knew, to investigate. The papers of Gen. Howard and his aide Major Charles Howard, as well as the XI Corps daily log and Lt. Col. Meysenburg's diary, provide ample evidence that multiple messages were sent to Slocum apprising him of the situation and asking for help. Aside from the earlier messages, these missives included one sent as Early's division was going into position prior to its attack on Barlow which the corps'

2 Meade, *With Meade at Gettysburg*, 88; Sickles, Newton and Butterfield, "Further Recollections of Gettysburg," in Cozzens, *Battles and Leaders*, Vol. 6, 278; Sickles, Gregg, Newton, and Butterfield, "Further Recollections of Gettysburg," 262; Sickles to Howard, 3:15 pm, July 1, 1862, RG 393, Pt. 2, 11th Army Corps, Letters Received, 1863-1864, BOX 1, NARA.

3 Slocum to Sidney G. Cooke, May 16, 1866, in Cooke's "The First Day at Gettysburg."

daily log recorded as: "Gen Slocum asked if he is moving to support. He is informed that our right is turned."[4]

This last reference was apparently the message delivered by Major Howard: "I was sent back to Slocum on the Baltimore Pike as all the other Staff Officers were otherwise occupied and was directed to request him to bring up his Corps as soon as possible and take position on the right, filing in to the right of Culps Hill, and to come up in person, even in advance of his troops, in order to survey the situation from the commanding eminence of Cemetery Hill." The major reported that he delivered the message to Slocum in person but the general was not inclined to move to Gettysburg. "His exact words in reply I remember but will not now put them on record." Major Howard galloped back to Gettysburg "as quickly as possible." Returning, the major found Howard at his headquarters on Cemetery Hill along the Baltimore Pike where he reported that he had met with Slocum who was reluctant to move to Gettysburg. In a letter dated only six days after the battle, Major Howard commented that Gen. Howard "had hoped that Slocum would come up to assist in the retreat as he was but two miles away but he was too willing to demonstrate the fitness of his name 'Slow come' in saying he would not assume the responsibility of that day's fighting & of those two corps."[5]

It appears that Slocum did not get his corps in motion to Gettysburg until late that afternoon. Only when Capt. A. G. Mason from Meade's staff arrived, probably somewhat after 3:00 pm, with written orders for Slocum to "push forward with all possible dispatch," did he finally move.[6]

☽ ☽ ☽

On Cemetery Hill the initial appearance of occasional walking wounded turned into a steady stream followed by the first groups of retreating troops. Looking to the northeast, Howard spied a line of battle approaching the town. When he did not

4 Meade, *With Meade at Gettysburg*, 88; Allers, *Fog of Gettysburg*, 78; Daily Log of 11th Corps, July 1, 2:45 pm.

5 C. Howard manuscript on the first day, Bowdoin College; C. Howard to Whittlesey, July 9, 1863, Bowdoin College. Pfanz states that Capt. Addison G. Mason of Meade's staff later arrived at Slocum's headquarters with a message urging that "corps commanders push forward with all possible haste." Mason met Lt. Col. Hiram C. Rogers, Slocum's adjutant general, who directed him to Slocum who had by then set the XII Corps in motion but still refused to come forward himself to take command. See Pfanz, *Culp's Hill & Cemetery Hill*, 94, 97.

6 *OR* 27, pt. 3, 465; Himmer, "Meade's Lost Afternoon."

quickly order fire placed on them, Capt. Stephen M. Weld, a former aide to Reynolds who offered his services to Howard, blurted out "General, those are the rebs, why don't you fire at them!" Unconvinced even when another line came into sight behind the first, Howard sent Weld into town to find "general Schurz, to see how he was getting on. Just before I got to him the Rebels got into the town and began firing. As I passed by a board fence along the road, I could hear the bullets come crashing through, making an unpleasant noise about one's ears. I found our men running back, the enemy having flanked us, and General Schurz was riding up the street, when I saw him." Weld briefly spoke to Schurz, then spurred his horse back toward Cemetery Hill amid the zipping and clattering of minié balls to report that the troops they had seen approaching were indeed Rebels and the corps was in retreat having both of its flanks turned.[7]

While several of the XI Corps units fought rear guard actions in the streets of Gettysburg, Schurz moved through town to Cemetery Hill where he began to rally the retreating units. For a while he contemplated organizing an offensive to re-take the town and link up with some several hundred men under Capt. Friedrich Irsch of the 45th New York who were surrounded in positions around the Eagle Hotel, but Howard had only a single fresh brigade and Wiedrich's battery with which to hold the heights against the advancing Rebels. He had nothing left with which to launch even a limited offensive. His priority was to rally the retreating troops as quickly as possible and get them into a manageable defensive position. Sitting on his horse near the general, Major Charles Howard noticed "Some sharpshooters had got possession of some of the houses and the bullets began to strike about us on the west side of Cemetery Hill. The troops were not in compact order as they came from the town and there seemed a little hesitation at first to face about and file off into the fields."[8] With bullets beginning to sing around the rallying point, Gen. Howard had to act fast to protect the position or risk his chance to hold Cemetery Hill.

Though shaken from their prolonged ordeal, Maj. Brady's 17th Connecticut fell in with little difficulty but were reluctant to advance when ordered to move forward to duel with the Rebel sharpshooters. "I can tell you," Lt. Albert Peck admitted, "the loss of the brave Colonel Fowler and Captain Moore took some of the zeal out of our boys for a while, and when we were ordered forward, after reforming on the hill, there was a little hesitation." When Howard approached the regiment Major Brady heard him ask "if he had troops brave enough to advance to a stone wall across a lot toward the town,

7 Weld, *War Diary and Letters*, 233 and letter to father, July 3, 1863, 236.

8 C. Howard manuscript on the first day, Bowdoin College.

and said he would lead them. We replied, 'Yes, the Seventeenth Connecticut will,' and advanced at once to the place indicated, remained a few moments, and again advanced across another lot still nearer the town and behind a rail fence at the upper end of the town, which position we held until late in the evening, exposed to a galling fire from the enemy's sharpshooters."[9]

Lt. Peck recalled that "General Howard took our colors and moved forward, and our boys followed with a cheer." Major Howard confirmed that "At this point Gen. Howard galloped up to one regiment of the Eleventh Corps and taking a flag in his one hand placed it upon the stone fence. The troops raised a cheer and followed him and it was not long before we had a continuous line of rifles behind the stone fence." Major Brady was impressed that the general "was in the thickest of the battle, regardless of danger." Von Gilsa was there too, doing a kind of triage as the men arrived, sending the wounded on to the hospital and rallying the others to their colors.[10]

Thankful to have reached Cemetery Hill, Corp. Frederick Nussbaum of the 107th Ohio stopped to retrieve something from his knapsack when Gen. Howard approached. "General Howard did all he could to get the boys to rally again. . . . sabre in his only hand, he entreated the boys by yelling at the top of his voice, 'Rally Boys! Rally Boys! Let us regain the name we lost at Chancellorsville.'" As he watched, Schurz and Doubleday joined Howard in rallying the men and determining where they would be placed. When the roll was called, the 107th counted only eight officers and 171 men out of the 458 it took into action but a few hours earlier—a loss of 60.9 percent.[11]

Col. Seraphim Meyer, still baffled by the seemingly contradictory orders he received in the town square, exited the southern end of the village to find a large group of men milling about in the fields on the eastern side of Cemetery Hill. Turning his horse, he rode over to get them organized and into position when Lt. Col. Meysenburg and Major Howard joined him in the effort. Once the men were in order and in position, Meyer spotted Ames and rode over to report. According to Lt. Edward Culp who was nearby, Ames replied pointedly "Mr. Meyer, so long as I have a Sergeant left to command the Second Brigade your services will not be required. Your place is in the rear." Stunned and at a loss for words, Meyer retired, but remained around Cemetery Hill for the next three days to offer what assistance he could. On July 5 he was further

9 Peck, "First Day at Gettysburg"; *OR* 27, pt. 1, 718.

10 Peck, "First Day at Gettysburg"; C. Howard manuscript on the first day, Bowdoin College; Howard, *Autobiography*, I, 419; *OR* 27, pt. 1, 718; Kiefer, *153rd Pennsylvania*, 216.

11 Baumgartner, *Buckeye Blood*, 66, 68.

shocked when Ames had him arrested and charged with "misbehaving in the presence of the enemy and cowardice."[12]

On the crest of the hill, Wiedrich's battery joined in the effort to halt the Confederate advance. The captain "opened with shells on their columns with good effect." In the advancing Confederate lines, Col. Archibald Godwin in the 57th North Carolina of Avery's brigade attempted to press on through the outskirts of town toward Cemetery Hill. "The shells from the enemy proving very effective, we were soon after halted in a depression on the hillside, and the men ordered to lie down." Major Campbell Brown, one of Ewell's staff officers, also noted the continued Federal resistance during the retreat. "There were some sharpshooters in the upper end of the place, firing on us apparently from the houses & now & then hitting somebody. By the time we got into the town, the enemy had crowned the top of Cemetery hill with a battery supported by quite a long line of infantry & opened on us in the hollow."[13] Clearly, Brown found continued Union fire, perhaps from Capt. Irsch's surrounded command, annoying and the developing defensive line about Cemetery Hill formidable.

With the Federals in full retreat, Col. Charles Wainwright, commanding the I Corps artillery, arrived on the scene. "I reached the top of the hill almost as soon as my first battery. Here I found General Howard, who expressed pleasure at seeing me, and desired me to take charge of all the artillery, and make the best disposition I could of it: saying that he would instruct Major Osborn to take his orders from me. The General pointed out to me how he should form the two corps; stating that this spot must be held until the rest of the army came up. I have since heard it said that General Hancock claims to have been in command at this time. I neither saw nor heard anything of him, and the troops certainly were posted as General Howard told me he meant to put them."[14]

Wainwright placed most of the I Corps batteries to the left behind where that corps was to form, directing the XI Corps batteries to the vicinity of the cemetery where they could sweep the space between the ridges in the event of any Confederate assault. Seeing four of Capt. Michael Wiedrich's guns already in place in front of the cemetery gatehouse, he rode quickly over to confer with the battery commander. "In

12 Culp, "From the 25th Ohio," *National Tribune*, June 4, 1885; Meyer to Meysenburg, July 14, 1863; testimony of Meyer court martial; Baumgartner, *Buckeye Blood*, 65.

13 *OR* 27, pt. 1, 751 and pt. 2, 484; Brown manuscript, Richard S. Ewell Papers, Box B-41, GNMP.

14 Nevins, *Diary of Battle*, 237.

case you are charged, you will not limber up under any circumstances, but fight your battery to the last!" Gen. Howard also approached the German battery from Buffalo calling out "Boys I want you to hold this position at all hazards. Can you do it?" Shouts of "Yes Sir!" filled the air. Howard later confirmed that once the Federals had been "driven out of the town, and the enemy made his appearance in our front, [Wiedrich] received him with canister, which checked his progress, and gave our troops time to rally in rear of the battery, to advance on the enemy again, and to drive him back into town."[15]

Under the cover of Wiedrich's guns and the skirmishers forming along the stone walls, other units were rallied into a defensive line. Von Steinwehr stretched the 55th Ohio, which had not as yet been engaged, along the Emmitsburg Road north to where the town's houses began. Then he placed part of the 73rd Pennsylvania, which had suffered few casualties as Coster's reserve regiment, into the buildings and yards along both sides of Baltimore Street to deny them to the approaching Rebels. Capt. Daniel F. Kelley took three companies along the east side of Baltimore Street while three others moved up through a wheat field on the west side and two proceeded directly up Baltimore Street. They made it as far as the Winebrunner home and tannery where they came under Confederate fire and retired to defensive positions in and around the Welty house. The Rebels occupied the McCreary house, a nearby brickyard, and the Winebrunner's house and tannery.[16]

Von Steinwehr placed the balance of the Pennsylvania regiment, comprised of Companies G and I, inside Snider's Wagon Hotel at the junction of the Emmitsburg Road and Baltimore Pike. There, the Keystone men "punched holes in the roof, and through those holes and the windows and other openings in the building, acted as sharpshooters against the enemy in the tan-yard and other buildings. The rifle shots from the hotel can be seen upon the buildings on the street to the left and front, in the window of one of which buildings eleven of the enemy were killed as they attempted to fire."[17]

The hotel was an exceptionally important position, resting as it did as a veritable fortress astride the approach from the village. In Confederate hands it would have

15 Nevins, *Diary of Battle*, 238; Schaefer, "Wiedrich's Battery"; Fuerschbach, *Wiedrich's Battery*, 22; *OR* 27, pt. 1, 751.

16 Pfanz, *Culp's Hill & Cemetery Hill*, 133-34, 138.

17 Quote from Ker to Nicholson, May 1, 1894, 73rd Pennsylvania Infantry File, GNMP; see also Conklin, "History of the 134th N.Y."; Pfanz, *Culp's Hill & Cemetery Hill*, 54, 133-34, 138. Later that night Company B was also moved into the hotel.

made Cemetery Hill untenable. In Union hands it proved a key obstacle to any further Rebel pursuit. Confederate Major Campbell Brown clearly noted that "While Genl. Ewell & the rest were reconnoitering the Cemetery Hill, a sharp skirmish fire was kept up on both sides, or rather a fire of sharpshooters. Some of these (Federals) had got into secure cover in some detached buildings on the edge of the town & behind stone walls, barns, &c, & were firing down the main street, at every one who showed himself." The 6th Louisiana reported facing "very severe" fire in town from both muskets and artillery.[18]

Most of the regiments belonging to the I Corps skirted the southern end of the town where they were able to march through the open fields in good order. Those units with Brig. Gen. John C. Robinson's division at the northern end of the Union line on Seminary Ridge faced the same conditions trying to find their way through Gettysburg that faced the XI Corps. One of these was Lt. Col. Rufus Dawes leading the survivors of the 6th Wisconsin south along Washington Street. "We hurried along, not knowing certainly that we might not be marching into the clutches of enemy." Nearing the southern edge of town, the colonel was greatly relieved when "the colors of the Union, floating over a well ordered line of men in blue, who were arrayed along the slope of Cemetery Hill, became visible. This was the seventy-third Ohio, of Steinwehr's division of the eleventh army corps."[19]

Schurz noted that "in whatever shape the troops issued from the town, they were promptly reorganized, each was under the colors of his regiment, and in as good a fighting trim as before, save that their ranks were fearfully thinned by the enormous losses suffered during the day." The remnants of Krzyzanowski's battered brigade began arriving at Cemetery Hill as the sun began to sink toward the horizon. By this time their colonel, now conscious though in great pain with his breathing labored, had recovered sufficiently to direct them into position, which he did despite Schurz's suggestion that he seek medical attention. Survivors of the 26th Wisconsin under Capt. Winkler formed behind a low stone wall near the base of the hill with their flank resting on the Baltimore Pike. As they awaited further developments, Sergt. Karl Karsten counted six separate bullet holes through the rubber blanket he carried slung over his shoulder, a miraculous escape for one who emerged unscathed from the maelstrom north of Gettysburg. His wound having been dressed at the hospital, Capt. John Fuchs

18 Brown manuscript, Ewell Papers, Box B-41, GNMP; Gannon, *Irish Rebels*, 187.

19 Quoted in Stuart Dempsey, "'The Heaviest Skirmishing,'" 44.

The Wagon Hotel was located at the junction of the Baltimore Pike (left) and the Emmitsburg Road (right). The hotel and the buildings to its right were securely held by the XI Corps throughout the battle preventing the Rebels from advancing directly from town toward Cemetery Hill. *Library of Congress*

soon returned to resume command of the regiment while it worked to fortify its new position.[20]

The 119th New York, Lt. Col. Edward F. Lloyd now commanding, emerged from town, according to Major Benjamin Willis, "in most excellent order, taking a position along a stone wall by an orchard, on the edge of the town. In this position we remained until near nightfall, when we moved in a corn-field on the west side of the road from Emmitsburg to Gettysburg, between the cemetery and the town." Lt. Col. David Thomson led the survivors of the 82nd Ohio as it came into view of those waiting on Cemetery Hill. He recalled that Krzyzanowski had approached him north of town and "ordered us to march to the opposite side of the town, which we accordingly did in most excellent order, taking a position along a stone wall by an orchard, on the edge of the town."[21]

Major Thomas Osborn met Lt. Christopher F. Merkle arriving with a section of artillery, ordering him, in Merkle's words, to "take up a position with my section on the right of Captain Wiedrich, and about 100 yards north of the graveyard, on a small range of hills. At the same time he ordered me to get another gun from Lieutenant Bancroft and place it in the road or pike."[22]

20 Schurz, *Reminiscences*, III, 12, 20; *Annual Report of the Adjutant General of the State of Wisconsin*, 403; *Milwaukee Sentinel*, January 11, 1875, 8; *OR* 27, pt. 1, 740; Winkler to Gaylord, Aug. 25, 1864; Karsten diary, July 1, 1863.

21 *OR* 27, pt. 1, 742, 744; Reid, *Ohio in the War*, 474.

22 *OR* 27, pt. 1, 757-58.

With surprising quickness, Howard, energetically assisted by the other surviving officers of both the I and XI Corps, was able to stop the general retreat, direct fire from Wiedrich's battery against Rebels attempting to skirt the eastern side of the town, place men in strategic buildings on the southern edge of town where they could command the approaches to the hill from that direction, and establish a solid line of troops behind the stone walls and rail fences stretching from Ziegler's Grove on the left to Culp's Hill on the right. It was a strong position, but open to being turned on each flank if reinforcements did not appear soon. To keep the Rebels at bay, Howard and Schurz ordered sharpshooters into the town's outlying buildings to arrest the enemy's advance. In the 8th Louisiana, J. Warren Jackson and his fellow Tigers "formed line of battle in town & Co. I had to go out as skirmishers—the enemy were posted on Cemetery Hill about 600 yds from town & had command of every place near town or around it—our position was a poor one and as we deployed we were subjected to a galling fire from their sharpshooters. Nobody hurt and we soon laid low in the grass but their position was such a good one that they could see us and they kept up their firing and I spent about 2 hours as miserably as I ever did in my life." Schurz was surprised that "All this was accomplished in a very short time."[23]

☽ ☽ ☽

Back in Taneytown, Gen. George Gordon Meade tried to figure out what was happening. Since he received an initial report of the opening combat from Capt. Stephen M. Weld who Reynolds sent for that purpose, no further information arrived except for a chilling note from Gen. John Buford reporting that it appeared an entire Confederate corps was approaching Gettysburg. The worst place for a commanding general to be was in the dark, but that is exactly where Meade found himself. No further information reached him from the front until Major William Riddle, Reynolds' aide-de-camp, brought the sad news of the general's death. Whatever the exact circumstances at the front, Meade knew it was time for him to act. Riding the short distance to the headquarters of the II Corps with his chief of staff, Gen. Daniel Butterfield, he found Gen. Winfield Scott Hancock to whom he had only that morning been explaining his plans for meeting the Rebel invasion. For this reason, Hancock believed, Meade ordered him to immediately turn his corps over to Gen. John Gibbon,

23 Jones, "Going Back," 12, 55-60; Fuerschbach, *Wiedrich's Battery*, 23; O.O. Howard to O'Donnell, March 9, 1891, Northwest Corner CW Roundtable, USMHI; Schurz, *Reminiscences*, III, 15.

then proceed to Gettysburg to take command of the forces and determine whether the army ought to consolidate there or retire behind Pipe Creek in keeping with Meade's earlier thinking.[24]

While Gibbon prepared the II Corps to move toward Gettysburg, Hancock headed for the embattled crossroads. Buford, unaware of his approach and deeply concerned over the increasing Confederate forces pressing toward town, sent a hasty note off to Gen. Alfred Pleasonton: "At the present moment the battle is raging on the road to Cashtown. . . . General Reynolds was killed early this morning. In my opinion there seems to be no directing person." To this he added a postscript: "We need help now."[25]

Hancock arrived near Cemetery Hill as Howard was busy rallying his troops. Directing his horse toward the hill, Hancock passed along the line of von Steinwehr's reserve brigade under Col. Orland Smith hunkered down behind the stone fences along the rising slopes. Encountering Capt. John D. Madeira, Smith's acting assistant inspector general, Hancock inquired whose brigade it was. Madeira responded, then directed him to Col. Smith where the introductions were necessarily hasty. "My corps is on the way," Hancock told the colonel, "but will not be here in time. This position should be held at all hazards. Now, Colonel, can you hold it?"

"I think I can," Smith responded.

"Will you hold it?" Hancock pointedly asked.

"I will."[26]

Some twenty feet away, Andrew Sweetland in the 55th Ohio watched the scene as "Hancock turned to the regiment, threw up one arm full length, and said in a strong, firm voice: 'Gentlemen, I want you to hold this line if all hell comes,' We threw up our caps and shouted: 'We will, General.'"[27]

Satisfied, the general continued on up the hill. Hancock approached Howard and the two engaged in a very brief conversation. Howard described it thusly: "He said that he had been sent up from Taneytown by General Meade to represent him on the field. After he had said this to me and knowing he was junior to me in rank I never thought otherwise than that he was in the nature of a staff officer of Meade's and pleasantly replied, 'There is no time to talk, Hancock, you take the left side of this road and I will

24 Gambone, *Hancock at Gettysburg*, 22-24; Meade to Hancock at 1:10 p.m. on July 1, 11th Army Corps, Letters Received, 1863-1864. RG 393, BOX 1, Pt. 2.

25 Gambone, *Hancock at Gettysburg*, 27.

26 Osborn, *Trials and Triumphs*, 97.

27 Baumgartner, *Buckeye Blood*, 66.

take the right and put in these troops.' Without a further word he, like the gallant soldier he was, rallied the troops to the left of the pike and led them into place. Soon I saw him take Wadsworth's division behind me over to Culp's Hill to my right; I thought nothing amiss, for it was the right thing to do and such as an aide-de-camp to the commanding general with authority might do."[28]

Other versions, including Hancock's, painted a scenario where Hancock announced that he had been sent by Meade *to take command* of the field. In some renditions Howard demurred, noting that he was senior in rank. In other versions, he outright refused to take orders from Hancock. Quite possibly, Howard actually did believe at the time that Hancock was sent as Meade's representative and nothing more. The battle had been raging since early morning, Howard had hurried forward and been engaged ever since arriving in riding along the lines, sending messages to various commands and to Sickles, Slocum, and Meade, and attempting to manage a battle over which he could exert little or no real influence. He had been under great mental and physical strain for hours. Retreating troops were streaming in; the sharp sounds of battle surrounded the scene. Is it so improbable to believe that Howard did not fully understand Hancock's brief explanation of his mission? Years later when he penned his memoirs Schurz may well have unintentionally identified exactly this when he wrote: "And in this preparation Howard, in spite of his heart-sore, cooperated so loyally with Hancock that it would have been hard to tell which of the two was the commander, and which the subordinate."[29] Perhaps this impression was fueled because Howard really did not see Hancock as commanding the field.

And there is more. Howard later claimed that Meade's order placing Hancock in command "was not received by me until evening." A communication he sent to Meade dated 5:00 pm noted Hancock's arrival and said "I am still holding on at this time. Slocum is near, but will not come up to assume command." This clearly gives the impression he considers himself still in command. Both the daily log of the XI Corps and the journal of its assistant adjutant general, Lt. Col. Theodore Meysenburg, recorded that Howard turned command over later that evening to Gen. Henry Slocum. And when Gen. Sickles arrived, clearly much after Hancock's arrival, he sent the following message to Chief of Staff Daniel Butterfield, obviously still concerned whether the commanding general would approve his decision to move to Gettysburg: "General Howard commands. My impression is, if I may be allowed to make a

28 Howard manuscript report on Gettysburg, Vertical File 5. GNMP ; C. Howard manuscript on the first day, Bowdoin College.

29 Schurz, *Reminiscences*, III, 14-15.

suggestion, that our left and rear is not sufficiently guarded, nothing less than the earnest and frequent appeals of General Howard and his supposed danger could have induced me to move from the position assigned to me on General Orders, but I believed the emergency justified my movement. Shall I return to my position at Emmetsburg, or shall I remain and report to Howard?"[30] Clearly, Sickles believed that Howard was in command.

Regardless of what transpired between Howard and Hancock, immediately after the conversation Major Howard watched Hancock as he "passed over to the South of the Pike" where he "was occupied with the 1st Corps the rest of the afternoon."[31] In the coming years this brief encounter would take on unwarranted major proportions as partisans of Howard and Hancock jockeyed to portray their favorite general as the person in charge, the hero of the day. Whatever transpired, Hancock quickly crossed the Baltimore Pike, spoke to Doubleday, and made dispositions for the remnants of the I Corps. The only major change attributed to him was sending Gen. James S. Wadsworth's division over to occupy Culp's Hill on the Union right,[32] an astute move—one that Howard recognized as prudent and fully approved—since those heights were critical to the defense of Cemetery Hill. What is important is not who was technically in command, because in reality in this time of crisis the two generals quickly agreed to split responsibility for establishing the defenses. Both went about their tasks with energy and professional judgment that reflected well on each.

Aside from any command decisions he may or may not have made, Hancock's arrival proved an elixir to many of the disheartened soldiers, which members of the XI Corps were only too willing to admit. "Under the circumstances," Schurz observed, "the appearance of General Hancock at the front was a most fortunate event. It gave the troops a new inspiration. They all knew him by fame, and his stalwart figure, his proud mien, and his superb soldierly bearing seemed to verify all the things that fame had told about him. His mere presence was a reinforcement, and everybody on the field

30 Howard account of Gettysburg, Verticle File 5, GNMP; Meade, *With Meade at Gettysburg*, 86; Daily log, XI Corps, July 1, 1863; Meysenburg journal, July 1, 1863. In his *Autobiography*, page 422, Howard says he was not aware of Hancock's real status until around 7:00 pm. Both the corps Daily Log and Meysenburg record the arrival of the XII Corps at 7:00 pm with the notation that Howard turned command over to Slocum. Meysenburg also adds the information that the III Corps was "near." Sickles to Butterfield dated 9:30 p.m., July 1, 1863, Henry Hunt Papers Box B-11, GNMP.

31 C. Howard manuscript on the first day, Bowdoin College.

32 Howard to O'Donnell, Mar. 9, 1891, Northwest Corner Civil War Roundtable, USMHI.

felt stronger for his being there."[33] While many writers agreed with Schurz that Hancock's presence was an energizing factor, no doubt much of the renewed enthusiasm was from the troops' recognition that if Hancock was there his II Corps was probably not far behind. Reinforcements were on the way, perhaps almost at hand.

Howard, apparently anxious to send Meade his version of events as soon as possible, sent the following message to the commanding general at 5:00 pm. "General Reynolds attacked the enemy as soon as he arrived, with one division, about 10:45 a.m. . . . I pushed on as fast as I could by a parallel road; place my corps in position on his right. General Reynolds was killed at 11:15 a.m. . . . I assumed command of the two corps (First and Eleventh), and sent word to Slocum and Sickles (Twelfth and Third Corps) to move up. I have fought the enemy from that time to this. . . . The First Corps fell back when flanked on its left, to a stronger position, when the Eleventh Corps was also ordered back to a stronger position. General Hancock arrived at 4:00 p.m., and communicated his instructions. I am still holding on at this time. Slocum is near, but will not come up to assume command."[34] At least in Howard's mind, he was still in command of the field.

☽ ☽ ☽

In town, Confederate troops searched the buildings, basements, and alleyways looking for Union soldiers who had been cut off during the retreat. Well into the night they rounded up strays to be sent off to prison camps. Yet, along Chambersburg Street, west of the main square, resistance continued. Under Capt. Friedrich Irsch, several hundred men, cut off from any escape, isolated by a ring of encircling Rebels, fought on despite dwindling ammunition. Lt. Hubert Ley described how they broke down fences to build barricades across alleys and placed men in the upper windows of the hotel and nearby houses and barns "from which the enemy was continually harassed and several attempts of the enemy to dislodge us were refused."[35]

On they fought, their ammunition rapidly being depleted, until around sundown an officer appeared in the street with a flag of truce demanding their surrender. Irsch refused, "saying that he expected every moment to be relieved." The Confederate informed Irsch that he was surrounded. The whole town was in Confederate hands and

33 Schurz, *Reminiscences*, III, 14.

34 *OR* 27, pt.1, 696. The times, of course, are debatable as it seems no one's watch was set to the same time as anyone else's on that day.

35 Ley letter.

XI Corps troops under Capt. Friedrich Irsch held out stubbornly in and around the Eagle Hotel until their ammunition was exhausted and all hope of relief gone.
Gettysburg National Military Park

the Federals had retreated to a position south of town. No rescue would be forthcoming. He then invited Irsch "to come out under a safe conduct, and see the hopelessness of further defense." Irsch accepted and "was taken to the Market Place where a Brigade of infantry and a battery were drawn up." In the market place Irsch observed Gen. Ewell engaged in conversation with another officer about an order from Gen. Lee to assault Cemetery Hill. Continuing on, he found "Baltimore Street up to the base of Cemetery Hill was filled with Confederate troops; the eastern and western outskirts were full of the enemy, and the fields in front of the town were massed with infantry and artillery, and no Federals in sight, excepting such as had taken refuge in cellars and houses brought out as prisoners."[36]

The situation was indeed disheartening. There appeared to be no hope of rescue. Irsch returned to his disparate command, called the officers together, explained what he had seen, and asked their opinions. Ammunition was nearly exhausted, darkness was falling, they were surrounded, and there did not appear that any attempt was going

36 Schurz *Reminiscences*, III, 18-19; Ley letter.

to be made to break through to them that night. They had already held out several hours. Irsch, along with the other officers, "ordered their men to destroy their arms and ammunition and throw them into the wells, and then all formally surrendered." The defiant Federals were marched off to various Rebel prisons, many to die in captivity. Capt. Irsch was taken to Richmond's Libby Prison. He escaped once, only to be recaptured. On May 27, 1892, he was awarded the Medal of Honor for "Gallantry in flanking the enemy and capturing a number of prisoners and in holding a part of the town against heavy odds while the Army was rallying on Cemetery Hill."[37]

☽ ☽ ☽

Out on the field north of town, some of Barlow's men who were Confederate prisoners constructed a makeshift stretcher from a blanket and carried him to the home of Joseph Benner where he was fortunate to be given a bed. Three Confederate surgeons examined him, all concluding that his wound was mortal. A Federal physician who examined him the following morning reached the same conclusion, but offered some glimmer of hope. Once the intestines were cut there was no hope, but were they cut? Barlow was taken to the home of Miss Jane Smith where the women bathed his wounds regularly with cold water and surprisingly he not only continued to live, but over time would recover to fight again during Grant's Overland Campaign and the Siege of Petersburg. Yet, he would never again fight with the XI Corps, and that suited his men just fine. William Simmers in the 153rd Pennsylvania quipped that "Billy Barlow continued the scourge of the division, until a chance bullet at Gettysburg lowered the petty tyrant from his exalted position and freed the division of his presence. The short reign of this individual forms an epoch in our history, which will never be forgotten by those who had the misfortune to serve under him."[38]

Adj. Theodore Dodge of the 119th New York lay in agony from his shattered leg and ankle, but once the Rebel battle lines passed over him he was greatly relieved and thankful that "The Confederates treated me kindly." A captain demanded his sword and belt, which he turned over without protest, but when he was quizzed about the Union troops involved and their commanders he refused to reply and the captain did not press the issue. Sergt. Joseph Waechter from his regiment had also been captured and, with the help of a Rebel soldier, assisted Dodge from the field. Another passing Confederate officer offered Dodge his canteen to wash his wound. The group stopped

37 Ley letter; Arrington, *Medal of Honor at Gettysburg*, 6.

38 Welch, *Boy General*, 86-87; Simmers and Bachschmid, *Volunteer's Manual*, 26.

to rest in the shade of woods along a small stream. A Rebel surgeon stopped, and had four men place Dodge on a stretcher. Carried from the field, he was taken to the Benner home where he had the further good fortune to be placed in a real bed. A Southern commissary officer from Gordon's brigade brought him some food, while a Louisiana slave kept Dodge's mind off his predicament as much as possible by conversing with him in French.[39]

Once the Rebel battle lines passed over him, Alfred Lee felt reasonably certain he would not be hit again since the fighting had moved on toward town. His only concern would be how the enemy would treat a wounded Union officer. When a Rebel approached with a captured officer's sword on a belt "thrown over his neck," Lee hesitantly asked how the wounded were to be treated. He received the reassuring reply "you need not be afraid. Ten minutes ago I would have shot you in a minute; but now that you are a prisoner you shall not be disturbed." When a battery unlimbered nearby, two of the artillerymen "very gently removed me to a place of greater safety" so he would not be trampled by the horses. They brought him water, along with another wounded lieutenant who they spoke to "sympathizingly" and attempted to make as comfortable as possible despite his great distress. Soon a cavalryman appeared "clad in the usual gray homespun." He promised to "get you a surgeon or an ambulance if I can." Lee was thankful, and impressed: "Our own comrades-in-arms could not have given us more faithful attention." Eventually the cavalryman left and darkness descended over the field. "All was silent, except for the occasional lamentations of some severely wounded soldier." Just as he began feeling really alone, the cavalryman returned with a Union surgeon and a wagon to transport Lee and a nearby wounded German soldier to "a large brick mansion near the railway station," the home of a "Mrs. S." Lee offered his thanks and inquired as to his benefactor's rank. He was a private from Lynchburg, Virginia, named James Marks, an orderly assigned to Gen. Early's headquarters.[40]

The year after the war ended, on February 2, 1866, Lee experienced "one of the most singular surprises of all my life." While sitting in his office, who should appear at the door but Marks who decided to look him up while passing through on his way to Cincinnati "where he expects to go into business."[41]

39 Dodge diary, July 2 and 28, 1863.

40 Lee, "Reminiscences of the Gettysburg Battle," 54, 57-59.

41 Alfred Lee to Robinson, Feb. 2, 1866, Robinson Papers, Ohio Historical Society, MSS 29, Box 1.

☽ ☽ ☽

Losses among the regiments clinging to Cemetery Hill were severe. Only Wiedrich's battery and Col. Orland Smith's brigade, barely 1,600 men, had been held in reserve under the immediate command of von Steinwehr and had not yet been engaged. The remaining defenses were held by regiments that were often no larger than companies, by men who were already exhausted from marching what would normally be a good day's distance through a rain storm and under the hot July sun only to be traumatized by the violence and death they witnessed all about them.

Maj. James C. Carmichael took out a pencil on the evening of July 1 to tabulate the results of a roll call in the 157th New York on the outside of an envelope. Aside from the major, a total of 51 men remained—four sergeants, eight corporals, and 39 men. The next morning, 56 answered the roll call. A few stragglers and lightly wounded appeared during the day, along with a portion of Company K that had been detached as provost guard on July 1, yet the entire regiment still numbered somewhat under 100. Coster's brigade had been nearly destroyed. Of the three regiments directly engaged on July 1, the 134th New York recorded losses of 63 percent, the 27th Pennsylvania 39 percent, and the the 154th New York a staggering 78.1 percent. Philo Markham reported that only 18 men from the Hardtack Regiment answered the roll call atop Cemetery Hill that night. Over the next two days a few would wander in, but the regiment still numbered less than a standard company.[42]

The 74th Pennsylvania carried 15 officers and 120 men with it into the fields north of town. It arrived back on Cemetery Hill with only four officers and eighteen men capable of bearing arms. With Barlow seriously wounded, Ames now commanded his division and Col. Andrew Harris the brigade. With Lt. Col. Fowler killed, command of the 17th Connecticut devolved on Major Allen G. Brady. Of the 369 who answered to their names at the roll call that morning, 207 became casualties, a loss of 56.1 percent. The 75th Ohio reported bringing 292 men onto the field, losing 63 killed, 106 wounded, and 34 captured and missing—a total loss of 203 or 69.5 percent. In the 25th Ohio, which suffered a loss of 188 men, all of the field officers and every captain were among the casualties. The senior surviving officer was 1st Lt. John H. Milliman. In the 107th Ohio the adjutant, Lt. Peter F. Young, found himself in command. Young's regiment took 434 men into the fight on July 1. A roll call that night showed only 171 capable of bearing arms. The other regiments in the brigade each numbered less than

42 Bracy, *157th New York Volunteer*, 35; Dunkelman, *Brothers One and All*, 94, 131.

Capt. Emil Koenig, 58th New York
U.S. Army Heritage and Education Center

100. The 153rd Pennsylvania had taken about 550 men into the fight north of town. It lost 267, or 47 percent.[43]

In Krzyzanowski's brigade, every one of the regimental commanders were killed or wounded. More than half of the men who fought in its ranks that afternoon did not answer when the roll was called on Cemetery Hill. The 75th Pennsylvania brought 184 officers and men onto the field, suffered 28 killed in action, 100 wounded, and 6 captured. Col. Mahler was mortally wounded. Less than fifty remained unscathed. Counting the lightly wounded who remained in the field, only some 70 were able to rally around Major August Ledig that night. The 82nd Ohio took 19 officers and 236 men into action; only two officers and 89 men remained unscathed. The 26th Wisconsin brought about 350 into action and lost over 200. The 119th New York had some 260 men in its ranks, but lost half. Only 130 were left to answer the roll that evening.[44] The brigade lost more than half of those actually engaged that day.

☽ ☽ ☽

Even as the shattered, traumatized regiments went into position, the first trickles of reinforcements began to arrive. These were largely XI Corps units that had missed the day's fighting. Captain Emil Koenig had been ordered to take some 100 men of the

43 *Pennsylvania at Gettysburg Ceremonies*, I, 430; Harris to Bachelder, Mar. 14, 1881; Browne to John Bachelder, Apr. 8, 1864, in Ladd, *Bachelder Papers*, I, 148; "Seventeenth Regiment," 34; Young to John Bachelder, Apr. 12, 1867, in Ladd, *Bachelder Papers*, I, 310; Keifer, *One Hundred Fifty Third Regiment*, xxv.

44 Nachtigall, *75th Regiment, Pa. Vols.*; Valuska and Keller, *Damn Dutch*, 144; Taylor, *Philadelphia in the Civil War*, 101; *Pennsylvania at Gettysburg*, Vol. 1, 434; *OR* 27, pt. 1, 744; Thomson to Mary, Aug. 5, 1863 and to Mary, July 16, 1863; Reid, *Ohio in the War*, 474-75; Fox, *New York at Gettysburg*, Vol. 2, 808, 810.

58th New York on a scouting expedition off toward Creagerstown on the night of June 30. Returning to Emmitsburg early the next morning he found another group from the regiment that had been on picket duty the night before, but the rest of the brigade had departed. Koenig pushed the men forward arriving around 3:30 pm. As they approached an unknown officer asked them to halt and provide support for a battery, which the captain did since he did not know the location of his own corps. Later, Schurz arrived to approve his location. After dark, Koenig's men were withdrawn to a reserve position in a second line established behind the stone fences at the base of Cemetery Hill.[45]

Lt. Col. William Brown arrived with a detachment of 104 men from the 61st Ohio that had been on a reconnaissance to Mechanicstown when their regiment left Emmitsburg. Trying to catch up, Lt. Anthony Grodzicki found the hurried pace "very hard" on the men which was compounded by the difficulty they had finding their regiment once they arrived. Nevertheless, the newcomers more than doubled the number of the regiment's survivors. Another 100 men from the 82nd Illinois arrived who had missed the first day's fight while on a reconnaissance to Fairfield, Pennsylvania. Lt. George Traeumer arrived from Emmitsburg with a detail of the 26th Wisconsin that had been assigned to picket duty south of that town the night before. Capt. Fuchs ordered Traeumer's group over the stone wall at the base of Cemetery Hill to take possession of the nearest buildings in Gettysburg for use as picket posts and sharpshooter positions. Pressed spiritedly by Rebel skirmishers, they lost two killed and two wounded but carried out their assignment, holding the buildings for the rest of the battle.[46]

Major George Benson Fox had been sent with 100 men of the 75th Ohio on reconnaissance toward Greencastle. Although recalled after covering only six miles, the rutted roads from the traffic that had preceded them and the clutter of ponderous wagons crowding the roadways in the wake of the corps prevented them from arriving until after the fighting north of town was over. "Some of the men with me could not keep up as twas so hot and Rainy," Fox recorded. He arrived at the head of his detachment somewhere between 5:00 and 6:00 pm. "Genl Ames ordered us to hold the position at all hazards. Our boys said they would."[47]

45 *OR* 27, pt. 1, 739-40.

46 Baumgartner, *Buckeye Blood*, 88-89; *OR* 27, pt. 1, 733, 740; *Annual Report of the Adjutant General of the State of Wisconsin*, 403; *Milwaukee Sentinel*, January 11, 1875, 8; Schurz, *Reminiscences*, III, 20; Winkler to Gaylord, Aug. 25, 1864; Karsten diary, July 1, 1863.

47 Fox to father, July 4, 1863; Baumgartner, *Buckeye Blood*, 68-69.

Around 10:00 pm Lt. Col. Detleo von Einsiedel arrived from Emmitsburg at the head of the 41st New York which had been left behind to guard the ammunition train. He brought with him 14 officers, 187 enlisted men, and 17 musicians who he placed in position behind a stone fence along the Baltimore Pike.[48] Yet important as these additions were in that time of crisis, more troops would be needed, *many* more troops, and they were required immediately. Would they arrive in time?

☽ ☽ ☽

Despite the success in rallying the troops, and the trickle of reinforcements beginning to arrive, a great deal of apprehension gripped those on Cemetery Hill. Were the Confederates being reinforced? Were they reforming? Would they continue their attack? Gen. Hancock "sat down on a stone fence on the brow of the hill from which he could overlook the field." Schurz approached him, taking a seat alongside. "Through our field glasses we eagerly watched the movements of the enemy. We saw their batteries and a large proportion of their infantry columns distinctly. Some of those columns moved to and fro in a way the purpose of which we did not clearly understand. I was not ashamed to own that I felt nervous, for while our position was a strong one, the infantry line in it appeared, after the losses of the day, woefully thin. It was soothing to my pride, but by no means reassuring as to our situation, when General Hancock admitted that he felt nervous, too." They believed they held a strong position with artillery well-posted, but still the number of available troops was small. As they sat watching, attempting to divine the Rebels' intent, endeavoring to determine if their deployments around the hill could in any way be strengthened, they frequently looked behind them in the hope of sighting the advance of approaching support. Gradually, Schurz noted, they "observed to our great relief that the movements of the Rebel troops looked less and less like a formation for an immediate attack. Our nerves grew more and more tranquil as minute after minute lapsed, for each brought night and reinforcements nearer."[49]

Sunset on July 1 occurred at 7:33 pm. In the waning minutes of daylight help began to arrive. Advance units of the XII Corps finally made an appearance on the right flank while messages from the III Corps reported it was not far off. Sickles arrived in advance of his laboring columns soon after. He quickly found Howard to report that Birney's leading division should be in sight in but a few minutes. Slocum arrived in the

48 *OR* 27, pt. 1, 713; Martin, *Bornemann's Regiment*, 149.

49 Schurz, *Reminiscences*, III, 14-15; Schurz, "The Battle of Gettysburg," 277-78.

Elizabeth Thorn provided valuable intelligence about the local geography to Gen. Howard, gave water and food to the officers and men of the XI Corps, and served dinner to Howard, Slocum, Sickles and other officers.
Gettysburg National Military Park

wake of his leading regiments, still apparently reluctant to take command. Nevertheless, as soon as he appeared Howard formally turned over to him command of field.[50] The sun was setting. The lingering twilight was fast giving way reassuring all of the diminishing likelihood of a renewed Rebel assault that night.

Horrified to receive Meade's order for Hancock to replace him, Howard now had a few spare moments to pen a hurried note to the commanding general, clearly concerned about how his conduct of the day's engagement was being viewed. "General Hancock's order, in writing, to assume command reached here at 7. At that time, General Slocum being present, having just arrived at this point, I turned over the command to him." He went on to explain that he believed he handled the two corps well after Reynolds death. If reinforcements had arrived earlier the initial position might have been held, but it not possible when outflanked. With no other option, he retired to what he judged was a good position, yet judged his relief by Hancock indicated Meade's displeasure. It "has mortified me and will disgrace me. Please inform me frankly if you disapprove of my conduct to-day, that I may know what to do."[51]

50 Daily Log of XI Corps, July 1; Schurz, *Reminiscences*, III, 16; C. Howard manuscript on the first day, Bowdoin College.

51 Howard manuscript report on Gettysburg, Vertical File 5, GNMP. The Daily Log of the XI Corps, listed under 7:00 pm, notes: "Gen Hancock arrives on the field bringing with him the

With the arrival of Slocum, Hancock left to find Meade while Howard, Sickles, and Slocum adjourned to the cemetery gatehouse where they enjoyed the hospitality of Elizabeth Thorn who served them "two good sized dough cakes I had made, pan cakes, three pieces of meat I had, apple butter and coffee." Howard, who had eaten nothing since early morning, "was nearly famished." Over four decades later he gratefully recalled in his autobiography "Those refreshments have never been forgotten." Nor was he the only Howard who was thankful. After the generals had finished, Major Charles Howard knocked on the door looking for something to eat. Mrs. Thorn gave him a piece of pie. He thanked her, turned, and walked away eating it as he went. More than a year later when several officers visited the battlefield Major Howard again knocked on the gatehouse door. When Mrs. Thorn appeared he handed her a silver dollar in payment for the pie.[52]

It was a warm evening, recorded as 74° as late as 9:00 pm. The warmth, combined with the lengthy tensions and exertions of the day, caused many of the men to quickly fall into a deep sleep once night fell and the immediate dangers appeared to pass. Looking about him in the growing darkness, Schurz could just make out men lying among the gravestones in the cemetery, some wrapped in cloaks, others with nothing to cover them but the open sky. "There was profound stillness in the graveyard, broken by no sound except the breathing of men and here and there the tramp of a horse's foot; and sullen rumblings mysteriously floating on the air from a distance all around."[53]

"What will the morrow bring forth is now the question being asked," thought Jacob Smith in the 107th Ohio, "and weighing heavily upon the hearts of our troops tonight as they lay upon their arms." In the 73rd Ohio Maj. Samuel Hurst "lay down and slept heavily after the fatigue of the day. We lay on the grass, among the neatly-trimmed graves; and some, with no irreverence, rested their heads on the green hillocks for pillows, and slept without a superstitious dream, but with the assurance that to-morrow's sun would bring earnest and bloody work."[54]

order directing him to assume command of the left wing. Gen Howard turns the command over to Gen Slocum & resumes command of his corps."

52 Howard Speech on Gettysburg, May 30, 1894, Box 154, Folder 11 1/2 Howard Papers Bowdoin; Thorn, "Experience During Battle," 2; Howard, *Autobiography*, I, 419; "Mrs. Thorn's War Story," *Gettysburg Times*, July 2, 1938; "Mrs. Thorn's Story," *Grand Army Scout and Soldiers' Mail*, Vol. 5, No. 36, 6.

53 Nofi, *Gettysburg Campaign*, 168; Schurz, *Reminiscences*, III, 20.

54 Smith, *107th Regiment Ohio*, 90; Hurst, *Journal-History*, 68.

Chapter 14

"A Place to try a Man's Courage"

July 2, 1863

CLOAKED IN DARKNESS DURING THE first hours of July 2, apprehension played on the minds of those awake on Cemetery Hill. While some of the exhausted troops fell asleep, others remained awake or found only fitful repose. Henry Henny described the experience: "We slept in the cemetery last night. The moon shone most of the night. . . . All night could be heard the rumble of cannons and artillery, moving into position along Cemetery Ridge. We could hear the shouting of the men as they rode their horses over the soft ground. Fences were being leveled and everything was gotten into shape for the struggle which seemed imminent on the following day."[1]

Darkness had long before descended when Gen. George Gordon Meade, arrived on the field with his staff making an impression on Schurz still vivid in his mind when he penned his memoirs: "His long-bearded, haggard face, shaded by a black military felt hat the rim of which was turned down, looked careworn and tired, as if he had not slept that night. The spectacles on his nose gave him a somewhat magisterial look. There was nothing is his appearance or his bearing—not a smile nor a sympathetic word addressed to those around him—that might have made the hearts of the soldiers warm up to him; or that called forth a cheer. There was nothing of pose, nothing stagey, about him. His mind was evidently absorbed by a hard problem. But this simple, cold, serious soldier with his business-like air did inspire confidence. The officers and men,

1 Henny diary, July 2, 1863.

as much as were permitted, crowded around and looked up to him with curious eyes, and then turned away, not enthusiastic, but clearly satisfied."[2]

Given the traumatic events of the previous day, and Howard's genuine fear that Meade disapproved of his conduct, Howard was both anxious and apprehensive. Nervously, he approached his commander. No doubt greatly relieved, he heard Meade congratulate him on his handling of the troops. Though possibly with some understandable exaggeration, he later recalled Meade "virtually apologizing for the previous seeming discourtesy." Meade next asked for Howard's opinion of the position the army held. Howard replied that it was "a strong position," an assessment Sickles quickly seconded. "I am glad to hear you say so, gentlemen, for it is too late to leave it."[3] Meade then announced that he had ordered the entire army to concentrate on Gettysburg.

Already the badly needed reinforcements were beginning to arrive. Geary's and Williams's divisions of the XII Corps and Birney's division of the III Corps arrived before nightfall on July 1. Humphrey's division of the III Corps began arriving shortly after midnight, and the rest of the army was moving to Gettysburg as fast as possible.[4] The battle to save the Union would be waged on these hills and fields.

☽ ☽ ☽

Union officers, those who slept at all, were up and about well before dawn on July 2. Roll calls that morning revealed how weak the XI Corps was after its July 1 ordeal. Schurz, back in command of his division, reported only about 1,500 effectives available, while Ames, now in command of Barlow's division, reported about 1,150 men ready for duty. Von Steinwehr fared somewhat better with an estimated 2,850 available on the morning of July 2. Exclusive of those on detached service in the hospitals, with the trains, and elsewhere, this left the XI Corps with only 5,500 effectives or possibly less.[5] During the morning and afternoon a few men continued to filter in from detached duty, the lightly wounded returned from the hospital, and some

2 Schurz, *Reminiscences*, Vol. 3, 20-21; Meysenburg journal, July 2, 1863, notes Meade's arrival at 3:30 am.

3 Howard account of Gettysburg, Vertical File 5, GNMP; C. Howard ms on first day, Bowdoin College; Howard speech on Gettysburg, May 30, 1894, Box 154, Folder 11 1/2, Bowdoin College.

4 Stackpole, *They Met at Gettysburg*, 117.

5 Schurz to Meysenurg and Ames to Meysenburg, July 2, 1863, RG 393, Pt. 2, 11th Army Corps, Letters Received, 1863-1864, Box 1, NARA.

others arrived to raise the total slightly, but the corps had been hurt badly during the first day's fighting.

Gen. Adelbert Ames moved along the line held by the remnant of his division, a mere shadow of what it had been the previous morning. He chatted briefly with the men, telling them they must hold their position "at all hazards." They replied that they would. Maj. Thomas Osborn spent most of the night checking on the position of his guns. He found the space atop Cemetery Hill so limited that they had to be placed at half their normal 14-foot interval. Continuing his inspection, one of the sights that came to view gave him pause. Behind Cemetery Hill, across the open fields, Rock Creek flowed through a low break in the hills. To Osborn's eye, this looked like an excellent gap for the Confederates to exploit, especially since there was only "a thin picket line" guarding the approach. Osborn quickly reported the weak point to Howard, then "withdrew two batteries from Cemetery Hill, separated them into sections of two guns each and put them into position. These ten guns, spreading over a front of more than a half mile, could bring a converging fire upon the head of a column coming through the narrow pass along the bank of Rock Creek."[6]

Gen. Henry Hunt, the army's chief of artillery, spent the morning inspecting the positioning of guns on Culp's and Cemetery Hills. Hunt at first questioned Osborn's deployment of artillery without infantry support, but when he understood the situation he ordered additional guns from the Artillery Reserve to bolster Osborn's line. Continuing his inspection, Hunt found "The men of both Corps, 11th & 12th, there were hard at work on their entrenchments of earth, stones & logs and were in capital spirit, as merry as crickets, and I felt that in such a state of affairs Lee might attack and be hanged, that we would hold every thing until all our army was up that evening."[7]

☽ ☽ ☽

The first grey rays of impending daylight streaked the eastern sky before the 4:36 am sunrise. Witnesses agreed that when the sun finally emerged it appeared especially bright. Jacob Smith in the 107th Ohio was struck by the "fresh, balmy and pleasant" dawn. "The sun shone mildly through an atmosphere still smoky from yesterday's

6 George Benson Fox, Papers, MS755, Cincinnati Historical Society; Cole, *Civil War Artillery*, 209; Crumb, *Eleventh*, 21-22.

7 Hunt to Col. Gantt, Aug. 19, 1886, Box B-11, GNMP; Hunt to Gantt, Sept. 4, 1886, Box B-11, GNMP.

conflict giving it the appearance of a huge ball of fire."[8] By daybreak, the position of the XI Corps stretched north along the Taneytown Road from a point just north of Ziegler's Grove to the junction of the Emmitsburg Road, turned right to Baltimore Street, then angled back to the northern base of Cemetery Hill before breaking right to cover the base of the hill to the rising ground where Culp's Hill began. Von Steinwehr's division held the Taneytown and Emmitsburg Road portions of the line with Coster's brigade along the former and Smith's the latter. The 55th Ohio was in position along the Emmitsburg Road between the intersections of the Taneytown Road and the Baltimore Pike. When the line bent east, Ames's division took over with Harris's brigade formed at a ninety degree angle around the base of Cemetery Hill, the right being extended by von Gilsa. Lacking enough troops to fill the space, the 33rd Massachusetts was detached to anchor the right flank between von Gilsa and the slope of Culp's Hill. Schurz's division was largely in reserve, though several regiments furnished skirmishers. Von Amsberg's troops were mostly backing Smith's brigade in a second line of defense while Krzyzanowski was in reserve in and around the Evergreen Cemetery.

Dawn found the men on Cemetery Hill kneeling uncomfortably behind stone walls, lying next to whatever cover they could find, peering out of the few buildings they occupied, or huddling behind the grave stones of the cemetery for protection. The position held vital importance because artillery posted on the hill could command the Federal line which spread out to the left along Cemetery Ridge. To the right, the Union lines stretched across wooded Culp's Hill where Slocum's XII Corps held that flank, hooking to the right at its end near Spangler's Spring. To the left the position wound south along Cemetery Ridge with the I Corps linked to the left of the XI and Daniel Sickles's III Corps extending the line to the low-lying area abutting Little Round Top. Buford's ever-present cavalry covered both flanks.

The darkness had barely begun to retreat when the crack of rifle fire announced that sharpshooters were opening the day's action. William Paynton in the 17th Connecticut observed that "the public buildings and churches that were used as hospitals were filled with Rebel sharpshooters—those demons of modern warfare, who would send their death dealing messengers into the ranks of our artillery and infantry." The men on both sides hated sharpshooters. It was one thing to lose one's life in a battle, quite another to fall victim to what many termed "assassins" or

8 Quoted in Archer, "The Hour Was," 15.

"murderers," men who singled out targets solely for the purposes of spreading fear and adding to the casualty list.[9]

One of the hottest skirmishes to develop that morning took place along the Emmitsburg Road. About 350 yards in front of Col. Orland Smith's position the gently rising land formed a crest before it sloped in a somewhat steeper grade another 900 yards to Seminary Ridge. Just to the western side of the crest lay a wooden fence. Once daylight came, Southern sharpshooters positioned behind this fence began to fire at Federals on Cemetery Hill. Because of their close proximity and slightly elevated position, their fire was noticeably accurate. To eliminate the problem Smith ordered two companies from the 73rd Ohio and two from the 136th New York to clear the menace. Lt. Samuel Fellers from the Ohio regiment led a portion of the attack. "The boys (who were deployed five paces apart) all sprung to their feet, and advanced as steadily as Iron, and picked every Rebel as fast as one showed his head above the wheat." Fellers' company and the others "drove them [the rebels] out of reach of our gunners," but it was not quite as easy as the lieutenant made it sound. Fellers' company began the attack with 36 men. When it was over 23 had been killed or wounded.[10]

George Metcalf described how "We ran about sixty rods forward, but before we had gone half that distance, the first line of Rebel skirmishers broke and ran before us. I saw about ten rods ahead of me, a rail pile made into a sort of breastwork. I made up my mind to reach this pile and stop whether the rest of the company did or not, for the bullets came too thick to expect to escape for much longer. I ran or tried to run as I never ran before. It seemed I would never reach the place, and in my anxiety to get there, my head wanted to go faster than my feet could carry it. As a result, I fell forward when within ten feet of the rail-pile. . . . I counted out fifty-four [percussion] caps and laid them on a rail, so as to be handy when loading, for I did not dare rise over the top of the rail-breastwork to load, so loaded my gun lying on my back. . . . I began to load and shoot, and the two comrades with me did the same. I took deliberate aim and discharged my gun 53 times—at a Rebel every time. We three would shoot together, often by calling "One, Two—fire," and watch for the result. Whether we actually hit anyone or not, we could not tell."[11]

But this was hardly the end of the fighting and dying on this part of the field. The 1st South Carolina sent in reinforcements to force the Federals back, Smith responded

9 Paynton, "From Virginia to Gettysburg and Back," manuscript, GNMP; Mesnard, "Reminiscence," manuscript, Civil War Miscellaneous Collection, USMHI.

10 Dempsey, "Heaviest Skirmishing," 49-50.

11 Metcalf, "Reminiscence," Gregory Coco Collection, USMHI.

with more troops to retake the position, and as the day progressed Smith found himself facing a steady influx of new Confederates from Col. Abner Perrin's South Carolina brigade and Brig. Gen. James Lane's North Carolina brigade. Smith countered by sending in his own reinforcements from the 55th Ohio as the two sides alternately claimed and gave up the important position along the fence. About 6:00 pm the Rebels made a determined effort to take the position once and for all. They were able to gain a small foothold, but as the sun set most of the disputed territory was still a no-man's-land between the contending lines.[12]

For the 55th Ohio the day was especially fraught with danger since portions of the regiment not only engaged in Smith's duel with the Carolinians, but was also subject to fire from the buildings on the outskirts of town off to their right. Henry Henny noticed that Rebel sharpshooters occupied a brick building and punched holes in the wall from which they were able to shoot in relative safety. Located in some barns nearby, another group of Rebels opened fire on anyone exposed on Cemetery Hill. Howard asked for volunteers to eliminate the threat and Benjamin Pease from the 55th Ohio responded. Pease jumped from behind his cover "charged up to a brick barn, from which the fire had been especially annoying, and pounding on the closed doors with the butt of his musket, called loudly on the inmates to surrender. One by one the Rebel soldiers on the inside dropped their guns and crept forth, till five had given themselves up. They were chagrined to find their captor had no support; but it was too late, and they sullenly preceded him to the Union lines, which cheered the valiant soldier again and again."[13]

In another incident, skirmishers from the 55th Ohio took possession of a barn in which they found a dozen refugees from the 143rd Pennsylvania of the I Corps who had not been able to reach the new lines on Cemetery Hill during the retreat the previous day. Aside from rescuing the men, the Ohioans, according to Corp. Simon Hubler of the 143rd, opened fire through openings along the barn's heavy beams, keeping up their fire for an hour or more despite the constant rattle of Confederate minié balls on the structure's outside walls.[14]

The shelling and continuing skirmish fire sent a steady stream of wounded climbing back over the stone wall the regiment was holding. Col. Gambee ordered others to take their place, but a wounded sergeant protested that "No one can stay out there under that cross fire." As Hartwell Osborn observed, "a rush over mostly open

12 Dempsey, "Heaviest Skirmishing," 50-51.

13 Henny diary, July 2, 1863; Osborne, *Trials and Triumphs*, 258.

14 Baumgartner, *Buckeye Blood*, 78, 80.

Col. Charles B. Gambee, 55th Ohio
Trials and Triumphs

space, and rushing against trained and barricaded sharpshooters is not conducive to long life."[15] But it had to be done.

Gambee turned to Lt. Frederick H. Boalt: "Take your company out there." Luther B. Mesnard was ill. Unable to march, he had ridden in an ambulance to Gettysburg the day before. Although under orders from his regimental surgeon to avoid any work, he could not stand the thought of his comrades being subjected to deadly sharpshooter fire while he remained in safety behind the lines. Ignoring the doctor's directive, he joined Lt. Boalt's company in the front lines just in time to advance over the stone wall into the open fields in an attempt to drive back Rebels who had worked their way into excellent positions to take Cemetery Hill under rifle fire. "Boalt drew his sword and we were out there in a jiffy, but how the lead did fly. A half dozen men were sent to a small brick barn to the right. As I was kneeling in the grass capping my gun a ball from the right struck my gun-stock, stinging my little finger, and bruising my knee severely, and spoiling my gun. I picked up another gun, and suggested to Boalt that we charge on the post and rail fence behind which the rebs were, as I thought they were *too close.* The word was given and we got there. There was wheat standing on the other side of the fence. I raised up behind a post to look over as a bullet struck the edge of the post and glanced past my ear sending splinters into my forehead."[16]

"Boy it was a bad place," William Southerton remarked. One ball struck him in the right arm, but to get back to the field hospital he had to brave the open space between the advanced position and the main line. Taking a deep breath, he bolted for the rear. "The bullets seemed to come criss cross from every way, but I was just ahead of them."[17] To the amazement of all, he made it.

15 Mesnard, "Reminiscence," 36; Osborn, *Trials and Triumphs*, 97.

16 Mesnard, "Reminiscence," 36.

17 Ibid.

Lt. Frederick H. Boalt, 55th Ohio
Firelands Historical Society

From the outlying buildings of Gettysburg, including a church steeple, sharpshooters trained their weapons on Federal officers moving about Cemetery Hill. George Roth in the 153rd Pennsylvania marveled as Col. von Gilsa strode about, walking back and forth in plain sight of the enemy to encourage the troops. Isaac Smith called to him that he had better get down out of the fire, to which the colonel replied "Perhaps I had better; for they may keep on shooting at me all day." Twelve volunteers, their rifles fitted with Swiss-made telescopic scopes, silenced one group of the troublesome Rebels, although firing continued sporadically all day. Deployed in the Wagon Hotel between the southern end of town and at the base of Cemetery Hill, men of the 73rd Pennsylvania held a critically important position. Having "punched holes in the roof, and through those holes and the windows and other openings in the building, acted as sharpshooters against the enemy in the tan-yard and other buildings" the regiment kept up a hot fire all day. In 1894 Capt. William Kerr wrote that "The rifle shots from the hotel can be seen upon the buildings on the street to the left and front, in the window of one of which buildings eleven of the enemy were killed as they attempted to fire."[18]

Lt. Albert Peck was in the front lines with the 17th Connecticut. "There was a well near the brick house where we supposed the Officers commanding the pickets line had their headquarters, and there seemed to be an old fashioned windlass to draw the water. We saw the Johnnies try to draw water a number of times during the day, but I do not think they got much, as our boys would let them get the bucket part way up, when they would send some minnies after them, and they would let the bucket drop and seek

18 Kiefer, *History*, 161, 163; Simonhoff, *Jewish Participants*, 77-78; Ker to John P. Nicholson, May 1, 1894, 73rd PA File, GNMP.

shelter behind the house. Of course this seemed like fun to our boys, but probably it was not much fun for the thirsty Johnnies."[19]

Under the continuing hot fire, nineteen-year-old Charles Stacey, a native of England serving in the 55th Ohio, volunteered to go forward to an exposed position behind a tree stump to try and locate the Rebel sniper positions. There, between the lines, he was able to spot two Rebels "across a narrow wheat field who were doing the most damage. They saw me at the same time but I was quicker then they were, and I guess I disabled one of them [with] the first shot as only one shot came from there and then I disabled the other as no more shots came from that point after I had fired four shots." When the Rebels located his position they brought an entire line of fire against him. "[T]his whole line would fire on me but I would drop down" and the "splinters from the top of the fence would fly all over me." Stacey held his exposed position for some four hours, firing at Rebels attempting to move to positions where they could fire on the Union line. He believed that "my company did not have a man touched during the time I was out and I destroyed the Sharpshooters. I don't believe any man ever had a line of battle fire at him as many times as I was fired at and live to tell of it."[20] The company remained in its advanced position until eventually relieved when its ammunition was depleted. Stacey's bravery was later recognized with the Medal of Honor.

Although Federals found the Confederate fire accurate and unrelenting, the Rebels were no less impressed. John A. McPherson in Col. Isaac Avery's brigade was "uneasy all the time balls hissing all round us. . . . [T]he Sharp-shooters kept up a brisk fire all day, so that a man could not show himself along the line without being shot at." Similar feelings gripped Lt. J. Warren Jackson in the 8th Louisiana whose regiment "posted some advance skirmishers and reserves behind a plank fence at the edge of town. If any one showed themselves a volley was poured into us. We had to crawl to get to regimental headquarters and run like '240' the last 30 yards."[21]

Capt. William J. Seymour, an aide on the staff of Gen. Harry Hays, found himself hugging the ground behind "a very low ridge which only partially covered us from the enemy's fire. It was almost certain death for a man to stand upright, and we lost during the day, forty-five men in killed and wounded from the fire of the enemy's

19 Peck, "Second Day at Gettysburg."

20 Stacey to Ford L. Stacey, Norwalk, Ohio, Apr. 13, 1918, in the possession of John L. Harris.

21 John A. McPherson to Col. I. T. Avery, Aug. 3, 1863, GNMP; Jones, "Going Back," 55-60; Fuerschbach, *Wiedrich's Battery*, 23.

This postwar photograph of Charles Stacey, 55th Ohio, shows him wearing the Medal of Honor he was awarded. *Libbie Romigh*

sharpshooters, who were armed with long ranged Whitworth rifles that could kill at a distance of twelve hundred yards."[22]

As the morning wore on and the temperature climbed, the intensity of the skirmish fire likewise rose. In the 17th Connecticut, William Paynton and four comrades were ordered into a field in an advanced position where they sought cover behind a low stone wall "near the brow of the hill" in the shade of an apple tree. "We were annoyed very much by frequent shots striking the ground around us, and also the tree under which we were. No one was hit as yet, but we did not like to be shot at in that way and not know where it came from." To determine the origin of the shots, "Our boys would hold a cap on the end of a ramrod just above the level of the fence to see them send a bullet through it." After several shots, "Finally we discovered that the shots came from what appeared to be a hog-pen situated at the rear of a house about two or three hundred yards distant. We proposed to drive those chaps out. So it was decided that four of our party should load and fire a volley into that hog-pen, and one of us reserve his fire to see the effect of the volley. As I was on the outpost, it was left to me to hold the reserve fire. As the smoke of the volley cleared away, three or four rebs were seen to clamber out of that hog-pen. Just as the last one was throwing his leg over the top board, I sent a 'minnie' after him, and he went over sooner than he intended. The others turned to assist in carrying him off, but that little party under the apple tree made it too hot for them and they left him to his fate."[23]

Nearby, Lt. Col. Edward Salomon in the 82nd Illinois realized something had to be done about a particularly nasty nest of enemy sharpshooters in and around the

22 Jones, *Memoirs of Captain William J. Seymour*, 73.

23 Paynton, "From Virginia to Gettysburg and Back."

Capt. Joseph B. Greenhut, 82nd Illinois, in a postwar photograph
Chicago History Museum

McCreary and Welty houses. Turning to Capt. Joseph B. Greenhut, he ordered the officer to take a group of skirmishers forward to dislodge the Rebels. Born in Austria, Greenhut was one of the regiment's Jewish officers—he was also married to Salomon's sister. If anyone realized the danger of what he was about to enter it should have been him since he had previously been wounded serving with the 12th Illinois earlier in the war. No doubt he instantly knew that his forty men were to embark on what seemed "a forlorn hope" against the houses about one hundred yards away. But Greenhut knew what he was doing. Salomon looked on in amazement as the captain "directed his men to avail themselves of every chance and opportunity of protection in the advance upon these houses from which a continuous, deadly fire was pouring forth, he was constantly and conspicuously exposed, challenging the admiration of thousands who looked on."[24]

In an expertly led attack, Greenhut's men cleared the buildings, receiving "the cheers of his comrades and the congratulations of his fellow officers for this brilliant and heroic action." Salomon was so impressed with Greenhut's courage that he later nominated him for the Medal of Honor. It was refused on the grounds that if he were awarded then everyone who took part in the action would have to be similarly awarded—a patently absurd argument that clearly was not applied in other cases. Instead, the captain received a letter of thanks from the War Department for his actions.[25]

In another act of heroism, when Schurz called for volunteers to run across an open space to take possession of some "barns and houses at the edge of the Southern portion of the town" from which Rebel sharpshooters were proving particularly

24 Dluger, "Fighting for the Cause," 20, 41-42.

25 Salomon, "Gettysburg," 11; Dluger, "Fighting for the Cause," 42.

annoying, Sergt. Charles Link and nine men from the 45th New York stepped forward. Over the next two days every one of the ten was either killed or wounded, but "they did such effective work that our artillery was unmolested from this source" for the rest of the engagement.[26]

Despite the successes, by late afternoon there remained some Confederate marksmen whose whereabouts eluded the men in blue. These continued to pick off officers and artillerymen atop the hill whenever they exposed themselves. A prime target was Wiedrich's battery that spent the morning exchanging occasional shots with two Southern batteries placed directly north of it. The men serving the pieces could clearly hear the zip of balls as they whistled past the makeshift emplacements, or the occasional dull thwak as lead found flesh and bone. One particularly annoying sharpshooter ensconced in the steeple of the St. James Lutheran Church wounded Lt. Christian Stock, Lt. Nicholas Sahm, and several enlisted men in the area. Try as they might, nearby Federals could not get a clean shot at the well-protected Confederate. Though the artillerists were tempted to reply, they had orders not to discharge their pieces into the town. The Rev. T. P. Bucher recalled that after the firing had gone on for some time the artillerists began to run around, jump up and down, and otherwise draw attention to themselves. When the Rebel marksman leaned out of the steeple window to observe the strange behavior the gunner on one of the pieces, disregarding orders, pulled the lanyard sending a round shot screaming out from amid the fire and smoke. The minister recorded that the missile struck only a foot or so above the astonished Rebel who quickly abandoned his post, rushing down the stairs, through the door and into the street "swearing he could not stand such shooting as that."[27]

Clearing the church steeple relieved those on the hill from one particularly effective marksman, but did not eliminate further threats from behind fences, the upper floors of buildings, and other hiding places. Col. Salomon asked for volunteers to drive a group of annoying sharpshooters out of a peach orchard. Several men quickly assented, but John Ackerman of Company K, who Salomon knew to be "a dare-devil fellow, who was ever ready to volunteer when danger was greatest," remained silent. Turning to him, Salomon asked why he did not speak up. Gravely, the private explained that he had a premonition that he would be killed that day. He would not volunteer, he answered, but would go forward if ordered. Salomon ordered him forward, but only a few moments after he set out Ackermann was back "looking pale and disturbed." No one, he declared, could possibly survive the fire sweeping the field

26 Ley letter; Böhm address; *OR* 27, pt. 1, 736; Fox, *Final Report*, I, 381.

27 *OR* 27, pt. 1, 751; John B. Linn diary, GNMP; Fuerschbach, *Wiedrich's Battery*, 26.

and orchard. The colonel relented, relieving him from the attack and ordering him back to his company. Ackermann moved to where his unit was and stretched out behind the safety of a stone wall, a look of great relief on his now relaxed face. A few minutes later a shell exploded above the line sending a jagged piece of shrapnel through Ackermann's head, killing him instantly.[28]

☽ ☽ ☽

Throughout the morning and early afternoon of July 2 men simultaneously dueled with Rebel marksmen and listened to the sounds of battle echoing down the line from the Round Tops, the Peach Orchard, the Wheatfield, and Cemetery Ridge where Confederate infantry launched a series of determined assaults on the left of the Union position. As the turmoil increased, Meade began to shift reinforcements into the area, eventually removing all but one brigade of the XII Corps from Culps Hill to stop the Rebel assaults. In the XI Corps some of the artillery was realigned to bear on the threatened portion of the line and two guns from Wiedrich's battery under Lt. Christopher Schmitt were moved to the Evergreen Cemetery where they unlimbered to fire in support of Union troops near Little Round Top. In Wheeler's battery "our boys all stood on tiptoe to watch the contest. Just then General Howard rode along and said, 'Never mind the left, boys; look out for your own front'; and sure enough, a few minutes afterward, we saw puffs of smoke . . . then the boom of the guns and the bursting of the shells among us."[29]

Shortly after 3:30 pm, fifty-five guns from A. P. Hill's and Richard S. Ewell's corps opened fire on Cemetery Hill. Their most advantageous position was atop Benner Hill overlooking and only some 1,000 yards from their target. Major Joseph W. Latimer placed four batteries totaling fourteen guns in position. Col. Adin Underwood in the 33rd Massachusetts was inspecting his regiment's position along the base of Cemetery Hill when "Whizz came a round shot over the heads" of his men "and plunged into the earth with a dull sound. A shell came shrieking and hissing in its track and exploded itself into destructive atoms; in almost a moment of time a hundred shot and shell were tearing about, bursting into fragments that hurried away many a brave life. Splinters of gun carriages, pieces of tombstones, even human legs and arms and palpitating flesh were flying about in every direction." Shells came from so many angles that

28 Salomon, "Gettysburg," 11.

29 Remington, *Battery I, First N.Y.*, 21; *Buffalo Evening News Magazine*, July 2, 1955; Wheeler to grandfather and aunt, July 26, 1863, in Bershears, *Loyal Till Death*, 187.

Underwood twice moved his men from one side of a stone wall to another, eventually leaving them on the side nearest the Confederate lines as the safest place during the bombardment. Adj. Augustus Horstmann in the 45th New York believed shot and shell descended on the Federal position "in such terrible profusion that the whole air appeared to be charged with whistling, sizzling & and humming fragments of iron, tearing to pieces everything in their path, the shells exploding, by whole battery charges, incessantly for 3 hours over us in front, to the right & left & behind us, with terrific report, furrowing deeply through the ground, breaking cannon & caisons, exploding ammunition wagons, knocking over the monuments and gravestones in the cemetery, killing our Artillerists & infantry alike on every step. . . . It is a wonder that our whole corps did not become deaf from the noise, which inspired terrible awe into our very souls. Men, who never prayed before, did so now fervently, to be delivered from such a hell & even the stoutest men trembled in their boots, some so violently that it was fortunate they were lying on the ground."[30]

Col. Charles S. Wainwright was sitting on a stone fence conversing with Gen. Ames when the Confederate guns opened. He did not like the odds. "The rebel guns had the advantage of us. They were on higher ground, and having plenty of room were able to place their guns some thirty yards apart, while ours were not over twelve; and the two faces of our line meeting here, the limbers stood absolutely crowded together."[31]

Capt. James H. Cooper's Battery B, 1st Pennsylvania, immediately opened counter battery fire, hitting a Confederate caisson that exploded sending debris in every direction. Capt. James Stewart's gunners in Battery B, 4th U.S. Light Artillery, gave three cheers for the Pennsylvanians, but almost immediately one of their own caissons blew up with similar pyrotechnics and destruction. "Then the hurrah was on the side of the Johnnies," Stewart observed. "It was the cleanest job I ever saw. The three chests were sent skyward and the horses started off on a run toward the town, but one of the swing team got over the traces, throwing him down and causing the rest of the team to halt."[32]

In the 82nd Illinois, Lt. Col. Edward Salomon was riding about checking on his troops when the bombardment began. Capt. Matthew Marx was struck by how Salomon "stood in front of the regiment so calmly, like we were having a dress parade, laughing and joking with the officers and soldiers, and how our boys laughed and joked

30 Underwood, *Three Years' Service*, 123; Horstmann, Battle of Gettysburg manuscript, GNMP.

31 Nevins, *Diary of Battle*, 243; Cox, *Culp's Hill*, 89, 91.

32 Cox, *Culp's Hill*, 92.

among one another that the Rebels aimed so poorly that most of the balls went over us; however, one hit in our regiment and smashed into the head of a soldier in Company K, who was killed immediately." Salomon narrowly avoided a similar fate. A "solid shot ricocheted, knocked off the right foreleg of my horse, and passed right through the body of my Adjutant's horse, throwing us both to the ground without any serious injury."[33]

Adj. Eugene Weigel had a somewhat different recollection of his experience. "There was crashing and howling and hissing as if all the devils in hell had been let loose." When it began his horse "went crazy so that I had to dismount and hold him by the reins. As I stood there a 6-lb. shell came flying, went through my horse's chest and hit me in the stomach so hard that I was hurled 3-4 feet. Thereupon I was carried to the rear, half unconscious." In addition to the dead horse, a canteen Weigel had slung around his shoulder hanging over his abdomen also cushioned the blow. "It had been flattened like a pancake but had repelled the shell." Stunned, Weigel survived. He was able to return to his regiment the following morning but his abdomen remained blue and sore for some time.[34]

Frank Smrcek in the 26th Wisconsin confided to his diary that "we had to endure a violent shell fire. It began at 2:30 and lasted far into the night. The shells fell like peas on our heads." William Southerton found it much more dramatic than falling peas. "What a furious bombardment. It swelled to a roar! A horrible roar! Artillery on the crest above us turned and opened up on the Rebel line there, then swept all along Seminary Ridge, north of the college. Oh, my! How terrific the roar! On and on, incessantly, for three hours! During all those horrible hours our regiment never fired a shot. There was no Rebel infantry in front of us, that we could see."[35]

On the left of the XI Corps line along the Emmitsburg Road, James S. Jones in the 136th New York believed he was on the receiving end of "the very worst of the cannonading, which was terrific." He was "exposed to a cross fire from 3 ways" while "the shell rained in on Cemetery hill tairing up graves, knocking monuments & iron fences killing horses & men & knocking guns endways there was some noise when

33 Marz letter to *Illinois Staats-Zeitung* published July 20, 1863, in Reinhart, *Yankee Dutchmen*, 95; Dluger, "Fighting for the Cause," 39.

34 Weigel to family, July 9, 1863, in the possession of Eric Benjaminson; Benjaminson, "A Regiment of Immigrants," 47, 158.

35 Southerton, "What We Did There."

those cannons all got to playing." Despite the terror, the only immediate casualty was the top of one of the regiment's flagstaffs that was sliced neatly off by a Rebel shot.[36]

Maj. George Benson Fox, commanding the 75th Ohio, found the bombardment worse than anything they faced at Chancellorsville. "[W]e were in a very hot place, but hugged the Stone wall" for protection. With a temperature over eighty degrees, the sun beating down relentlessly and constantly under the strain of sharpshooters and exploding shells, by mid-afternoon those on the firing lines were in some cases short of ammunition, and in nearly all cases hungry, their mouths parched with thirst. "Of all the places in battle excuse me from supporting a battery where one has nothing to take up his mind but to lie waiting to be killed or wounded and no chance to fire at the enemy unless he should advance to capture the battery," confessed John Ryder. "That was the hottest place I was ever in. The air was literally filled with exploding shells and I expected every moment would be my last. Finally our gunners got the range and soon dismounted their cannon and blew up their caissons, so they were glad to withdraw from our view and cease firing."[37]

The rain of shrapnel was particularly heavy in the Evergreen Cemetery as Rebel guns trained on the batteries atop Cemetery Hill overshot their mark to rain death and destruction among the supporting troops to the rear. Exploding shells cracked the headstones in the cemetery where the men crouched nervously behind the stone walls and grave markers, seeking what little protection they offered. The 58th New York found itself on the receiving end of much of the Rebel barrage. Flying pieces of jagged metal killed Adj. Louis Dietrich and Louis Krause, while others mortally wounded Capts. Edward Antoniewski and Gustav Stoldt. Fragments sliced into several others. A shell fragment found Capt. Frederick Stowe, the son of noted abolitionist Harriet Beecher Stowe, the author of the influential *Uncle Tom's Cabin*, who was serving on von Steinwehr's staff. Carried to the division field hospital, the captain was attended by Surgeon Robert Hubbard. Nor was the corps hospital on the Baltimore Pike behind the hill spared. Surgeon Henry Van Aernam told his wife that "The situation of our hospital was such that the shells that passed over our line of battle, either in front or right or left, would fall [near the hospital] . . . the shells were frequent, and familiar

36 Jones letter, Sept. 15, 1863, 136th New York File, Box B-16, GNMP; Smith, "Recollections of Gettysburg," 136th NY File, GNMP.

37 Fox to father, July 4, 1863; Ryder, *Reminiscences*, 34.

visitors. There were five horses killed by shells right about the hospital—two men wounded—and several horses wounded."[38]

On the crest of the hill where much of the Rebel barrage was aimed, Wiedrich's gunners worked their pieces to keep up their counter battery fire. To the captain, it appeared that at least three separate enemy batteries were aiming their fire directly at him, yet the damage remained surprisingly slight. In Dilger's battery a shell struck and dismounted one piece, while a 20-pounder parrot shot tore away the pistol hanging from Lt. Z. Clark Scripture's left hip without so much as touching him, sliced off Alonzo Slisby's left hand above the wrist, then buried itself into the ground. Slisby died three weeks later. Also mortally wounded was Green Brockway. Darwin Cody "stood within ten feet of [both] when they were shot. There was a place to try a man's courage. I hope I never shall be in quite as close quarters again. I was hit once but soon got over it." Earle Rich in the 33rd Massachusetts witnessed "a cannonball hit the man standing along side of me squarely in the chest. I'll never forget the sound of that hollow thump when it hit him; the impact knocked him back at least ten feet. My God, what a horrible sight."[39]

While the shells scattered their deadly shrapnel, Capt. von Fritsch watched as "cartridges were distributed, and, now and then, a box of crackers was carried to a starved regiment." In the 136th New York, a call was raised for a volunteer to run the gauntlet back to a nearby spring for water. "No one at first spoke," recalled Lt. Lucian Smith. "Then tall Tom Nelson said 'I'll go.' 'Take my canteen too, Tom. Take mine and mine came from a dozen half famished soldiers. And Tom did take them until strapped and hanging to him were twelve canteens. He climbed over the fence. No one tho't he would return. We watched him thro' the crevices in the wall. He kept straight on to the spring, and filled every canteen with a cup, and came back unhurt, cheered and welcomed by us all. Tom Nelson was a hero. His name is unknown to fame. He belongs to that countless number of brave men, who when duty pointed the way followed in it."[40]

Another intrepid soul was a cook in the 82nd Illinois, who manhandled a large kettle up to the front line during the height of the bombardment. "Coffee for Company D," he exclaimed. But the words no sooner left his lips than a shell burst close by,

38 *Final Report on the Battlefield at Gettysburg*, I, 431; Hubbard to wife, July 14, 1863; Van Aernam to Lis, July 30, 1863. He was Chief Surgeon of the 1st Brigade, 2nd Division, XI Corps.

39 *OR* 27, pt. 1, 751-52; Dilger's Battery Papers, GNMP; Baumgartner, *Buckeye Blood*, 90-91; Rich, *Cape Cod Echoes*, 44.

40 Butts, *Gallant Captain*, 83; Smith, "Recollections of Gettysburg."

Capt. Frederick Stowe, the son of noted abolitionist Harriet Beecher Stowe, served on Gen. von Steinwehr's staff.
U.S. Army Heritage and Education Center

knocking the kettle and its precious liquid from his hands. "You scoundrels!" the infuriated cook yelled, shaking his fist at the Rebel lines. "Wait till I get you; I'll fix you for that!" Although deprived of their coffee, the men at least enjoyed a hearty laugh as the cook retired to brew another batch of the stimulating elixir. Then, as shells continued to burst with regularity, incongruously out of place amid the cacophony of exploding ordnance and ricocheting fragments, some of the men detected the unmistakable sounds of familiar waltzes and polkas drifting their way across the plain from some unseen Confederate band. Intended, no doubt, to relieve the tension of the sweating Rebel artillerymen, the ironically appropriate European tunes helped calm the frayed nerves of those holding Cemetery Hill.[41]

Also within the Rebel lines was Francis C. Lawley, a correspondent from the *London Times*, who searched the full extent of his vocabulary to explain what he witnessed. "Vain indeed would be the attempt to portray the scene which the Cemetery hill . . . presented to the spectator. If it had not been reserved for me to listen next day to a still more awful din, I should have fancied that no such scene had ever before saluted mortal eye or ear. A thick canopy of smoke, constantly rent by bright darting flashes of flame, cast its dense pall over the struggling, bleeding thousands who toiled and died in its centre, while out of the opaque gloom, as though from the bowels of the earth, one deep prolonged bellowing roar never ceased to issue. Through the deepening twilight and on far into the night the fierce struggle continued, until, in the gloom, the dazzling parabolas of flame, bursting into sparkling jets and coruscations as the shells cracked and exploded, made a ghastly pyrotechnic display."[42]

41 Salomon, "Gettysburg," 14; Pula, *For Liberty and Justice*, 136-37.

42 Lawley, "The Battles of Gettysburg," *London Times*, August 18, 1863, in GNMP Folder B57-22/246010.

While the Federals suffered under the Rebel bombardment, counter battery fire dealt death and destruction among the Southern gunners. The Chesapeake Artillery was particularly decimated, losing three of its guns. Adj. Robert Stiles was appalled at the destruction. "Never, before or after, did I see fifteen or twenty guns in such a condition of wreck and destruction as this battalion was. It had been hurled backward, as it were, by the very weight and impact of metal from the position it had occupied on the crest of the little ridge, into a saucer-shaped depression behind it; and such a scene it presented—guns dismounted and disabled, carriages splintered and crushed, ammunition chests exploded, limbers upset, wounded horses plunging and kicking, dashing out the brains of men tangled in the harness; while cannoneers with pistols were crawling around through the wreck shooting the struggling horses to save the lives of wounded men." When it was all over, Latimer's batteries had been badly mauled, suffering a crippling 22 killed and 29 wounded. Thirty horses were killed. So was Major Latimer.[43]

☽ ☽ ☽

Dusk was rapidly settling over the battlefield by 7:00 pm, little more than half an hour before the official sunset at 7:33 pm, but the temperature still hovered just under eighty degrees with heavy humidity. By now most of the troops were hopeful that the day's travails would soon be at an end. They were wrong.

On the far Confederate left Maj. Gen. Edward Johnson had just completed preparations for sending three brigades—sixteen regiments and one battalion containing about 4,700 men—slamming into the XII Corps lines holding Culp's Hill. Though a strong defensive position, the prescient precautions of Brig. Gen. George S. Greene who ordered his men to dig elaborate entrenchments further enhanced the position's natural strength. By late night the site was indeed formidable, but the weakness was manpower. One by one during the day units had been hastily withdrawn to reinforce the threatened Union left where Gen. James Longstreet's assault had broken through the III Corps, threatened the fragile Northern grasp on Little Round Top, and driven to the very slopes of Cemetery Ridge itself before finally being hurled back. By the time Johnson launched his attack, only Greene's brigade—five New York

43 Cox, *Culp's Hill*, 91, 99; Jorgensen, "Joseph W. Latimer," 34. Pfanz, *Culp's Hill & Cemetery Hill*, 187-88, lists Latimer's losses as 10 men killed and 40 wounded, as well as two caissons blown up, a limber chest hit with a solid shot, 27 horses killed and many others wounded. Latimer had fired 1,147 rounds.

regiments numbering only some 1,400 men—was left to oppose the Confederate onslaught.[44]

The Rebels made little headway against Greene's well-prepared defenses, but gradually, pushing farther to their left, they were able to locate and flank the Union position. Some of Greene's men were already running low on ammunition, his right threatened with imminent collapse for lack of manpower to oppose the Rebel flanking movement. Greene sent a desperate plea to Gen. James Wadsworth, whose division of the I Corps lay next in line, and to Howard. Both responded with Howard dispatching four regiments from von Amsberg's brigade. These included the 82nd Illinois, 45th New York, 61st Ohio, and 157th New York. All of the regiments were engaged heavily the previous day and could muster, in total, not more than 475 men. Lt. Col. August Otto of the 58th New York, serving on Schurz's staff, stepped forward as a volunteer to lead the force. "Somehow," Howard later wrote, "it always affected me strongly to behold a hearty and fearless young man, after receiving an order, set forth without reluctance to execute it under such circumstances that there were few chances of ever seeing him again. So I felt as Otto went forth that night into the gathering gloom."[45]

According to the Daily Log of the XI Corps, firing broke out on Culp's Hill about 8:00 pm. Though trying to reconcile times at Gettysburg is a near impossibility, this does generally coincide with the sunset time reported by other sources. Lt. Col. Dobke of the 45th New York groped his way forward for "a mile through the complete darkness in the woods" all the while becoming more frustrated because "while the regiment marched in the darkness through the woods, under guide of a staff officer, the march was considerably delayed by a number of general staff officers, each exerting himself to give his orders, and so, by movements, counter-movements, halts, &c., some time elapsed before the regiment found itself in the right place." The two regiments fell in on the very left flank of Greene's line next to the 102nd New York which was running low on ammunition, taking the place of the 60th and 139th New York which retired to replenish their ammunition. Dobke's regiment "pushed up to the stone fence through an incessant shower of bullets, and shared well in the defense of this position."[46]

44 Meade, *With Meade at Gettysburg*, 130-31.

45 Meade, *With Meade at Gettysburg*, 131; Schurz, *Reminiscences*, III, 24; Howard, *Autobiography*, I, 428; Report of 3rd Brigade, 2nd Division, XII Corps, July 12, 1863, RG 393, NARA.

46 *OR* 27, pt. 1, 735; Horstmann, Battle of Gettysburg, GNMP; Daily Log of 11th Corps, July 2, 7:45 pm. One brigade of Schurz's division was ordered to support of Gen. Ames. At 8:00 pm firing broke out on the right and Slocum was engaged.

Lt. Col. Salomon's experience was similar. "I entered the woods, it being very dark, so that the position of the enemy could only be distinguished by the flashing of the guns, and before we were aware of it, were close up to their lines, and for ten minutes engaged in a hand-to-hand fight." Capt. Jacob Gross was a little more graphic, recalling that "we charged bayonets and drove the enemy from the field with wild hurrahs."[47]

The 82nd Illinois engaged with the Louisiana regiments of Nicholls's brigade under the command of Col. Jesse Williams, helping to drive them from "the line of rifle pits they had captured an hour before." For the next few hours the two XI Corps regiments shared in the defense of Greene's position until about 2:30 am when they were finally recalled to Cemetery Hill. Later Salomon proudly wrote that "My command was praised for the part it took in this action by Generals Schurz, Howard and Slocum."[48]

The 61st Ohio and 157th New York, only slightly over 100 men in total, moved off to the right in the darkness, falling in with the 137th New York on the extreme right flank of Greene's line at exactly the time that the Federals were flanked and in danger of having their whole line rolled up by Brig. Gen. George Steuart's Virginia brigade that had worked its way around the right flank of the 137th New York, and thus of Greene's position. In the process, a staff officer directed the 157th New York into woods so dark the men could barely see, assuring them there were no Rebels ahead. Without warning they came upon Steuart's brigade which fired a searing volley toward the New Yorkers, most of it fortunately high, causing few casualties. One of those shot was George H. Davis the color-bearer. In the darkness no one noticed that the colors had fallen to the ground, so when the regiment withdrew to the edge of the woods they were inadvertently left there to be retrieved later by a member of the 37th Virginia. When clear of the woods and again at least able to distinguish some shapes in the darkness, Capt. Frank Place, along with Marcus Livingston and Francis Gault, went back in an attempt to locate the missing colors in the dark, but with visibility very limited they lost their way. Approaching what he thought was a group of Union pickets behind a stone wall, Capt. Place found out too late that they were Confederates and all three were taken prisoner. In a letter to his father, Marlow D. Wells claimed that at the end of the fight on Culp's Hill only sixteen men were left present for duty in the 157th, which might be an exaggeration—but only slightly—and clearly shows the reduced state of its

47 Salomon, "Gettysburg," 9-10; Gross, 82nd Illinois, 36.

48 Salomon, "Gettysburg," 9-10; *OR* 27, pt. 1, 735; Ley letter.

Lt. Col. Edward S. Salomon, 82nd Illinois
U.S. Army Heritage and Education Center

fighting capabilities. By the next day, when pickets, the slightly wounded, and those detailed to other duties returned, the regiment still fielded only 86 muskets.[49]

When the action on the southern end of the Union line ended in the growing twilight, Meade was able to readjust his lines so that most of the troops borrowed earlier from the XII Corps were gradually relieved. When the 82nd Illinois began to withdraw an officer approached Salomon offering what he thought would be thanks for the services Salomon's regiment had rendered. "If you had been here yesterday instead of that damned XI Corps, we would have not been driven back." Greatly offended, Salomon shot back "You are a miserable hound sir, I and my regiment belong to the same XI Corps you are speaking of and we did no worse fighting yesterday."[50]

With the position secure, Slocum and Greene rode over to Howard's headquarters to thank him and his men for their support, particularly singling out Lt. Col. Otto for praise. Greene's report of the action noted that "These regiments rendered good service being sent into the trenches to relieve our Regts as their ammunition was exhausted and their muskets required cleaning." They stayed until relieved by the brigades of Brig. Gen. Henry Lockwood and Col. Charles Candy, "having rendered good service and efficient aid." Later Wadsworth also appeared to thank Howard and Schurz for the support rendered by the XI Corps.[51]

☽ ☽ ☽

49 Cox, *Culp's Hill*, 145; Bracy, *157th New York*, 37; Wells to father, July 9, 1863, New York State Division of Military and Naval Affairs; Murray, "The 157th New York," 40-41.

50 Schurz, *Reminiscences*, III, 352; Pfanz, *Culp's Hill & Cemetery Hill*, 214.

51 Report of 3rd Brigade, 2nd Division, XII Corps, July 12, 1863, RG 393, NARA; Howard, "Gen'l O. O. Howard's Reminiscences of the War of the Rebellion," *National Tribune*, January 1, 1885; Schurz, *Reminiscences*, III, 24.

On a flat paper map the Cemetery Hill position looks impressive. Its height portrayed with bold hash marks, artillery positions noted by the images of small guns, and its base and left flank covered by stone walls behind which thick solid lines indicate the entrenched positions of infantry, at first glance one wonders how any attacking force could succeed. No doubt it appeared that way to the Confederates as well. From their vantage points in the attics, lofts, and church belfries of town they could easily see the concentration of Federal artillery crowning the heights, as well as the sturdy-looking stone walls that sheltered infantry waiting in seeming security to deal sweeping volleys of death upon anyone foolish enough to attack. Yet the apparent strength of the position belied some serious weaknesses.

Though it was the prominent rallying point for retreating Federals on July 1, and served as the lynchpin of the Union defense throughout the next two days, East Cemetery Hill formed a salient protruding out at the apex connecting the Federal line running south along Cemetery Ridge with the positions around Culps Hill that stretched eastward. Aside from the notorious defensive weakness of a salient, the Rebels surrounded it with artillery so that if one drew a complete circle with Cemetery Hill as its center, Southern batteries could place converging fire on the hill from positions along three-quarters of that circle. Similarly, Rebel sharpshooters in the town were in range of gunners working the Federal pieces, officers attempting to direct their men, or any careless person who showed himself for more than a few brief seconds.

To make matters worse, the Union batteries atop Cemetery Hill had not been placed there with the immediate defense of the position in mind. Wiedrich's battery of 3" ordnance rifles were placed there specifically because the range of their guns would allow them to support, at least to some extent, the Federal position north of town and rain shells on any Confederates moving south. Next to Wiedrich lay Capt. R. Bruce Ricketts' combined Batteries F and G, 1st Pennsylvania Light Artillery, from the artillery reserve. Ricketts brought with him six guns, but they were also 3" rifles. The Union command was obviously thinking of long-range dueling with Rebel artillery, for which the rifled guns were excellent choices. But they were not good for close-in defense since they normally were not suited for firing canister. They could do so in an emergency, but a few discharges of the tightly packed round balls would destroy the rifling, rendering the pieces useless for their primary purpose.

Not only were the guns ill-suited to close defense, but their position atop a steep slope, recessed back from the crest, created an effective blind spot that prevented the guns from being used effectively in their own defense. They could hit targets at a distance, but once attackers closed on the hill they could not even be seen until they rushed over the crest of the hill, mere feet away from the gun emplacements. At best, alert gunners might get off one shot if their pieces were loaded, primed, and at the proper elevation. Artillerist Edward Whittier explained: "These batteries had absolutely no point blank, and were prevented by the sharp descent of the eastern face of the hill, from exerting any control over that portion of his front which an artillerist holds as his dearest possession, leaving in its place a 'dead angle,' large and of terrible significance, in the place of ground where guns can vex and tear assaulting columns with canister."[52] Though ten pieces of artillery gave the appearance of strength, they were nearly useless for close in defense against infantry.

Yet another disadvantage of the position was the topography approaching it from the north and northeast. Running east from the town were a series of fairly sharp ridges intersected by two small streams. The ridges were ideal for hiding a gathering or approaching assault. Above Winebrenner's Run rose a "ridge with an elevation of 424 feet" which "covers this stream from view of the crest of East Cemetery hill its line affording admirable cover for an attack."[53] It was in this exact "dead spot," secure from the eyes of curious Federals, where the Confederates assembled for their assault. As one approached the Federal position, ridges hid much of an attacking force until close to the infantry defenses, while a ridge running northeast to southwest guarded the Rebel left flank from artillery fire from Culp's Hill.

The troops chosen to make the charge were two veteran brigades, Hoke's North Carolinians under the command of Col. Isaac Avery and the brigade of Louisiana "Tigers" under Brig. Gen. Harry Hays. Both had spent an uncomfortable day dodging Federal sharpshooters, the lucky ones being able to enjoy the shade inside some building while the unlucky ones had to sweat it out under the hot sun in the July humidity. Around dusk, when most of the troops—officers and men alike—believed the day's bloodletting near an end, Capt. William Seymour, Hays' aide, noticed their division commander making his way toward them. "Presently the old General [Early] reaches us, and after inquiring whether we are ready, gives the order to charge." Capt. R. J. Hancock observed "Hays, who was no man to deceive his men nor anyone, rode along the line about dusk and told his men that Gen'l Early had said we must go [to] Cemetery Hill and silence those guns." "I felt as if my doom were sealed," thought Lt. R. Stark Jackson in the 8th Louisiana, "and it was with great reluctance that I started my skirmishers forward." Capt. Seymour noted the lack of enthusiasm also, but interpreted it differently. "The quiet solimn [*sic*] mien of our men showed plainly that

52 Whittier, "The Left Attack," 85.

53 Scott, "The Cemetery Hills," manuscript, Verticle File 4-10q, GNMP.

This photograph of the northern base of Cemetery Hill clearly shows the ridge fronting the Union position that shielded Confederate attackers until very close to the defense line.
Library of Congress

they fully appreciated the desperate character of the undertaking: but on every face was most legibly written the firm determination to do or die."[54]

The Rebels formed near the home of William Culp about 1,000 yards from the farthest part of the federal line. In Avery's command, Major James Beall of the 21st North Carolina "hailed with delight the order to again meet the veteran foe, regardless of his advantage in numbers and position." One wonders how many of his men, looking across at the steep slopes, the artillery emplacements, and the stone walls felt the same enthusiasm. Col. Hamilton Jones, leading the 57th North Carolina, believed "the line advanced in beautiful order, and as it pointed to the south-west there was a glint all along the line of bayonets that was very striking and marked how beautifully they were aligned."[55]

In a nearby church being used as a hospital for the wounded, Reuben Ruch of the 153rd Pennsylvania looked out the window mesmerized by the scene unfolding before his eyes. He watched intently as the Rebels formed lines, then moved out. "[B]etween the Rebel and Union positions was a ridge about six or eight feet high. The Johnnies started stooped over, scattered like a drove of sheep, till they got to this ridge. Then

54 Seymour journal, July 2, 1863, GNMP; Hancock and Jackson quotes from Gottfried, *Brigades*, 504.

55 Whittier, "The Left Attack," 85; Clark, *North Carolina Regiments*, Vol. II, 136, and Vol. III, 415.

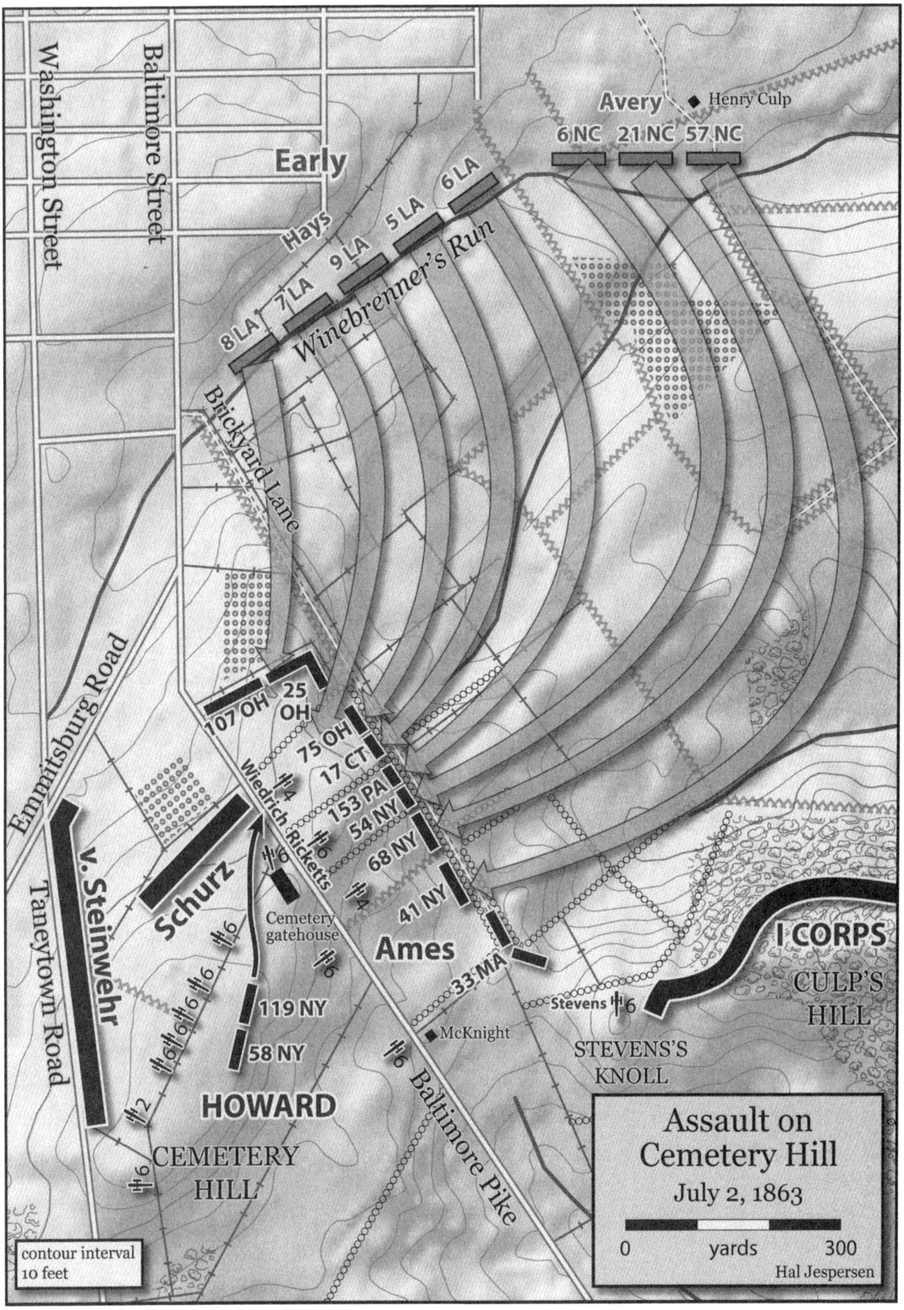
Washington Street
Baltimore Street
Early
Hays
8 LA
7 LA
9 LA
5 LA
6 LA
Avery
Henry Culp
6 NC
21 NC
57 NC
Winebrenner's Run
Brickyard Lane
Emmitsburg Road
Taneytown Road
v. Steinwehr
Schurz
107 OH
25 OH
75 OH
17 CT
153 PA
54 NY
68 NY
41 NY
33 MA
Wiedrich
Ricketts
Cemetery gatehouse
Ames
119 NY
58 NY
McKnight
HOWARD
CEMETERY HILL
Baltimore Pike
Stevens
STEVENS'S KNOLL
I CORPS
CULP'S HILL
contour interval 10 feet
Assault on Cemetery Hill
July 2, 1863
0 yards 300
Hal Jespersen

every man took his place, and giving the Rebel yell . . . they closed up like water, and advanced on a double-quick."[56]

☽ ☽ ☽

Across the sharply undulating fields from where the assault began, the Federals also believed the day's fighting had finally come to an end. Atop Cemetery Hill the gunners were at their pieces, but no one expected any major action in the dwindling twilight after sunset. Below them, at the northern base of the steep hill, infantry used a small stone fence as an impromptu breastwork. Ames's brigade held the left with the 107th Ohio facing generally north toward town in a refused flank position. Next to the right was the 25th Ohio at the point where the line turned southeast along the Brickyard Lane, then the 17th Connecticut and 75th Ohio. Von Gilsa's brigade prolonged the line along the base of Cemetery Hill with the 153rd Pennsylvania, 54th New York, 68th New York, and 41st New York. The 33rd Massachusetts from Col. Orland Smith's brigade held the far right, beyond which Battery E of the 5th Maine Light Artillery from the I Corps, Lt. Edward N. Whittier commanding, lay on the western slope of Culp's Hill.

Although the position may have looked strong from across the open fields, the stones averaged only about two to three feet in height and there were few troops to man the line. After the crippling losses of July 1 the manpower allotted to the defense of this critical sector of the Union line was not nearly as strong as it should have been. Ames's division (formerly Barlow's) numbered barely as many men as a normal brigade did in mid-1863. The most carefully reconstructed estimates for the evening of July 2 are those of researcher John M. Archer. According to his calculations, on the morning of July 2 the regiments in Harris's brigade (formerly Ames) numbered no more than 688. Von Gilsa's brigade counted only some 708. Thus the entire division numbered only 1,396, with fewer than that in line when deductions are made for those on detached duty. Probably no more than 1,200, at most, were available to occupy the position. Added to this should be the 461 members of the 33rd Massachusetts filling the gap between the Eleventh Corps and the Maine battery on the slope of Culp's Hill.[57]

56 Keifer, *History*, 219-20.

57 Archer, "*The Hour Was One of Horror*," 82-87; Martin, *Bornemann's Regiment*, 149. See also Ames to Meysenburg, July 2, 1863, RG 393, Pt. 2, 11th Army Corps, Letters Received, 1863-1864, Box 1, NARA.

Given the alignment, the right flank was clearly the strongest with the only two unscathed regiments assigned to that position: the 41st New York which had been on detached service on July 1 and the 33rd Massachusetts which had been held in reserve that day. Deducting the approximate footage held by the Massachusetts regiment on the right, Ames's division was expected to cover some 600 yards of front. With the available men he could form only a thin line with no provision for a reserve to handle any crisis that might develop. There was also no ready reserve since von Amsberg had been dispatched to aid Greene's defense of Culp's Hill and had not yet returned.

As evening descended the sudden crashing rattle of musketry from Culp's Hill announced the beginning of the Rebel assault on Greene's position. Over time, the noise receded, and with it much of the anxiety the men felt about their advanced position. Ames did not share their relief. He worried about a soft spot along the Birckyard Lane where the defenders appeared quite thin in the area where the two brigades joined. To strengthen the position, he ordered the 17th Connecticut to move men into the thin gap. Somehow, the orders were either incorrectly given or went terribly awry. In the 17th Connecticut Major Allen Brady received the order to fill the gap and quickly moved his entire regiment into the position indicated, almost directly below Wiedrich's Battery. No one arrived to take their place. Col. Harris was horrified to observe that "In moving the 17th C. V. . . . their place at the wall was left vacant, thus endangering the left flank of the 75th O. V. I. and the right flank of the 25th O. V. I. Before I could make any arrangements to remedy this breach in the line the attack of the enemy on Cemetery Hill was made."[58] The timing could not have been worse. The Confederate assault had begun.

☽ ☽ ☽

Sometime around 4:00 pm Companies B and I of the 33rd Massachusetts, along with two companies each from the 17th Connecticut and 41st New York, were sent out through the fields north of Cemetery Hill to form an advanced skirmish line between the Rebels occupying the town and the Union positions. One of them was John Ryder. "We went out a little over half a mile where we could see the Rebel infantry across a little valley within easy gunshot. We exchanged a few shots with their skirmishers but for some reason they were unusually quiet, the cause of which we soon discovered. . . . Just as it was getting a little after sunset four lines of battle suddenly appeared in front rapidly advancing towards East Cemetery Hill and our infantry lines at its base." The

58 *OR* 27, pt.1, 716, 718; Harris to Bachelder, Apr. 7, 1864, in Ladd, *Bachelder Papers*, I, 138.

John Ryder, 33rd Massachusetts. The image on the left was taken in 1864 and that on the right in 1916.
Providence Public Library

skirmishers quickly retired toward their own lines. "How we are going to get into our lines without being shot by our own men was a cause of great anxiety, but we saw a little space in the line where the fire was held up, and our colonel was standing on the wall saying, 'These are our skirmishers, don't fire on them.' We jumped the wall and lay down quickly back of it. The next man on my right was our color bearer, Sergeant Edgar Bumpus." Not everyone made it. In the 17th Connecticut Lt. Milton Daniels reported that one of his men was killed by "lead wadding" from a Federal artillery discharge.[59]

On the Confederate right, opposite Col. Harris's command, the Louisiana Tigers burst from their cover near Winebrenner's Run, rushing at the double-quick across an open space and a corn field toward the northwest base of Cemetery Hill. Within seconds the alert Federals loosed a volley, but most of the fire went high because of the undulating ground. In the Rebel ranks Capt. William Seymour noticed the Federal line explode in fire and smoke, "But we are too quick for them, and are down in the valley in a thrice, while the Yankee missiles are hissing, screaming & hurtling over our heads, doing but little damage."[60]

Wiedrich's battery opened fire, but since its guns were unable to depress sufficiently its charges also went high. R. J. Hancock of the 9th Louisiana noted that "the enemy's cannon lighted up the heavens but most of the charges they shot over us." Gen. Hays noticed the same tendency of the Federal artillery to fire too high, which he attributed to the dwindling light. "Owing to the darkness of the evening, now verging into night, and the deep obscurity afforded by the smoke of the firing our exact

59 Ryder, *Reminiscences*, 34-35; Hamblen, *Connecticut Yankees at Gettysburg*, 58.

60 Jones, "A Louisiana Tiger," Hays Brigade File, GNMP.

locality could not be discovered by the enemy's gunners, and we thus escaped what in the full light of day could have been nothing else than horrible slaughter."[61]

In the 17th Connecticut Major Brady recalled that "the enemy were discovered advancing rapidly upon us on our right and a full brigade obliquely toward our left. When within 150 paces of us, we poured a destructive fire upon them, which thinned their ranks and checked their advance. We fired several volleys by battalion, after which they charged upon us. We had a hand-to-hand conflict with them, firmly held our ground, and drove them back." There was much more to the story. Perhaps confused by his regiment's move to the right, when the firing began the major suddenly feared that his men were shooting into their own skirmishers. "Our boys commenced firing, when Major Brady ordered them to cease firing as we were firing on our own men; the firing ceased for a moment, when the boys saw the Rebel line approaching and commenced firing again."[62]

Brady's gaffe does not seem to have been fatal. Capt. Seymour encountered "a heavy line of Yankee infantry greet[ing] us with a destructive volley, and many of our noble fellows go down before it killed and wounded." J. Warren Jackson in the 8th Louisiana rushed forward "over fences, ditches, thro marshy fields and we 'botch up' at a stone fence behind which Mr. Yank had posted himself and he did not want to leave."[63]

The Tigers recoiled before the steady fire, rallied, then came on again. Some reached the wall where the fighting became hand-to-hand. Capt. Henry P. Burr "grabbed a 'Johnnie' by the collar of his coat during the fight, and drew him over the wall and made him a prisoner." Burr's haul was the color bearer of an unrecorded Rebel regiment. Amid the turmoil Lt. Milton Daniels noticed George Woods and William Curtis sitting down, firing and reloading so calmly "you would have supposed they were shooting at a target." Woods shot: "He won't come any further, will he, Bill?" Curtis fired: "I got that fellow, George." And so on. "[T]hey kept it up that way, perfectly oblivious to danger themselves." All around them chaos reigned. Corp. George Scott shot one Rebel as he tried to pass over the wall, then took a captain prisoner. The fighting was intense, personal, brutal. "[W]ith bayonets & clubbed guns we drove them back," explained J. Warren Jackson in the 8th Louisiana, while Major Brady found that "the rebels succeeded in getting in our rear." Fighting front and rear,

61 Sauers and Tomasak, *Ricketts' Battery*, 93; Jones, "Twice Lost," 91; *OR* 27, pt. 2, 480.

62 *OR* 27, pt. 1, 718; Peck, "Second Day at Gettysburg."

63 Jones, "Louisiana Tiger," GNMP; Jones, "Going Back," 55-60; J. Warren to brother, July 20, 1863, 8th LA File, GNMP.

his regiment again "drove them back and held our position," but a shell fragment slashed into the major's shoulder leaving a painful wound.[64] With Rebels all around them, fighting as a pocket surrounded by the enemy, Brady and his embattled Nutmegers held their position throughout the confusing fight despite the fact that some of the enemy passed to their rear.

Lt. Oscar Ladley in the 75th Ohio "lay behind a stone wall" looking out over the field at the Rebel advance. "They came on us about dark yelling like demons with fixed bayonets. We opened on them when they were about 500 yards off but still they came their officers & colors in advance. . . . I was standing behind the wall when they came over. A Rebel officer made at me with a revolver with his colors by his side. I had no pistol nothing but my sword. Just as I was getting ready to strike him one of our boys run him through the body so saved me. . . . I never saw such fighting in my life. It was a regular hand to hand fight."[65]

Nearby, William Southerton and his comrades heard the "cursing screaming hordes" as they "came rushing at us. Louisiana Tigers!" The "crackle" of the Ohioans' "rifle fire was incessant," but in a flash figures in grey and butternut appeared across the fence from Southerton. "John North, standing beside me was pulled over the wall and taken. George Humphrey was shot and captured. The Tigers had gained the wall! . . . There stood the major of the Tigers! Right on top of the wall! He carried their flag! A flash of steel! Lorenzo Dowler stabbed the major through with his bayonet. The Rebel fell headlong over the rocks as a force of his men sprang to the top of the wall. Oh, the burst of fire! Screaming of dying men! We ran our bayonets right through [them]! Catching those Tigers as they leaped down among us. What horrible slaughter! A lull for a minute or two. The Tigers' flag! What a scramble as the flag was torn into pieces! Our boys pounced upon the rag as if a piece of it would be the greatest badge of bravery they would ever get their hands on. Andrew Jackson got the biggest piece. He shoved it down into his pocket. He kept it as long as he lived, and gave it to one of his sons."[66] The Rebel banner that was captured was never identified since it had been torn to pieces as souvenirs.

Next to the 75th, the wide gap created by the movement of the Connecticut regiment was covered by only a handful men of the 25th Ohio quickly moved into the space by an alert company officer who found his flank suddenly unprotected. In fact, following its losses on July 1 the entire 25th Ohio mustered less than a regulation

64 *17th Connecticut Volunteers at Gettysburg*, 25; Warren journal; OR 27, pt.1, 718.

65 Becker and Thomas, *Ladley Letters*, 142-43.

66 Southerton, "What We Did There," 10.

Lt. Oscar Ladley, 75th Ohio
Wright State University

company under the command of Lt. William Maloney. On the far end of the line, the 107th Ohio found itself overlapped on the left while Rebels moved through the lightly held gap on its right. Capt. John M. Lutz ordered a quick withdrawal to prevent the 107th from being taken in the rear. His regiment rallied behind a stone wall near the top of the hill.[67]

While Hays's brigade struggled to break through the Federal defense, to his left Col. Isaac Avery led his North Carolinians across open fields toward the position held by von Gilsa's brigade. Avery's men had a greater distance to move to the attack, but they also had the benefit of some sharp ridges which afforded at least some protection part of the way. Looking out over the darkening field, Lt. Edward Whittier could not believe what he was seeing. Up from the plain arose rank after rank of Rebel soldiers aiming for a point to the left of his 5th Maine Battery on the western slope of Culp's Hill. Whittier immediately opened fire with spherical case shot. As he watched in amazement, the Rebel assault "swept past the left flank of my guns within short canister range; shutting out the right half battery so that these guns could not be brought to bear on those troops which were hastening to gain a new position and re-form on ground from which they could, with better hope, charge the crest of East Cemetery Hill. The trails of the left half battery were swung sharp and hard to the right, the right half battery was hastily 'limbered to the rear,' and in the darkness, hurried to a new position on the left of the guns remaining in the works, so that the whole battery was once more effective, and this time, with double canister, pouring a most destructive, enfilading, demoralizing, fire into a confused mass of the enemy, struggling in the uncertain shadows at the base of the hill."[68]

67 *OR* 27, pt. 1, 719-20; Young to Bachelder, Apr. 12, 1867, Ladd, *Bachelder Papers*, I, 310.

68 Whittier, "The Left Attack," 88-89.

The sudden explosion of Whittier's guns into the darkness jolted Col. Underwood in the 33rd Massachusetts. He "had no knowledge that the enemy was advancing, when suddenly, right over my head, it seemed, there was a blaze, a crash, and a roar, as if a volcano had been let loose." Col. Archibald C. Godwin saw the 57th North Carolina, closest to Whittier's guns, come "under a terrific fire." To escape the deadly artillery, and realign his brigade toward the objective of East Cemetery Hill, "Colonel Avery now ordered a change of front, and succeeded in wheeling the brigade to the right, a movement which none but the steadiest veterans could have executed under such circumstances." His men sprinted forward, but "The enemy's batteries now enfiladed us, and a destructive fire was poured into our ranks from a line of infantry formed in rear of a stone wall running at a right angle with our line of battle and immediately below the batteries." When it was over, Whittier reported that his guns expended "the entire contents of the limber chests."[69]

When the Rebels came within range, John Ryder heard Col. Underwood shout "Fix bayonets and remember Massachusetts!" Then came the command to fire! The 33rd fired volley after volley while the butternuts continued to be raked by Whittier's guns. Underwood heard "the roar of guns, and down drop the colors and color bearer, and heaps of those brave traitors. Groans and shrieks fill the air. A fearful destruction of life!" As canister shredded the onrushing lines, shouts of "Good for Maine!" rose from the Massachusetts defenders. "My regiment opened a severe musketry fire on them," Col. Underwood reported, "which caused gaps in their line and made it stagger back a little. It soon rallied and bravely came within a few feet of our wall, though my men clung unflinchingly to it and steadily poured in their fire. I ordered them to fix bayonets to be ready for the enemy."[70] On the North Carolinians rushed, but the 33rd held steady, its left flank guarded by the 41st New York.

In the 41st, Sergt. Carl Bornemann found himself caught in "a hand to hand conflict, carried on with the valor and vindictiveness of desperation. The arms of ordinary warfare were no longer exclusively used. Clubs, knives, stones, fists—anything calculated to inflict pain or death was now resorted to. Now advancing, then retreating, this sort of conflict continued for fully three-quarters of an hour. At one time defeat seemed inevitable. Closely pressed by the enemy, we were compelled

69 Whittier, "The Left Attack," 87; *OR* 27, pt. 2, 484; Whittier to XI Corps Adjutant, July 16, 1863, Bachelder 5th Maine File, GNMP.

70 Ryder, *Reminiscences*, 35; Underwood, *Three Years' Service*, 130; "Report of Colonel A. B. Underwood, Thirty-third Massachusetts Regiment, U.S. Volunteers," Dec. 9, 1881, Vertical File 4-10l, GNMP.

Sergt. Carl Bornemann, 41st New York
David Martin, *Carl Bornemann's Regiment*

to retake our first line of defense, but even here the enemy followed us, while the more daring were resolutely advancing towards our lines." A bullet glanced off a stone catching Bornemann in the face near his eye. Stunned, the sergeant reeled and fell to the ground beneath a tree, his face bleeding profusely. Regaining his senses, he wiped the blood from his face, struggled to his feet and continued rallying his men to resist the onslaught. For his bravery he was later promoted to lieutenant. The regiment would lose fully thirty percent of its men defending East Cemetery Hill that night.[71]

Because of the galling fire directed into the left of Avery's attacking columns from Whittier's guns and the muskets of the 41st New York and 33rd Massachusetts, the Confederates quite naturally drifted to their right away from the greatest danger. As a result, the weight of their attack fell on the Union line held by the 54th and 68th New York and a portion of the 153rd Pennsylvania. The defenders fired volley after volley into the Rebels, but the howling wave kept coming until the foremost attackers were vaulting the low stone wall. Sergt. Henry Michel, color bearer of the 54th New York, was among the first to be killed. A soldier nearby picked up the fallen banner, but was promptly wounded, as was a third man who came forward to rescue the colors.[72] Greatly reduced in number, the two New York regiments began to fall back up the hill opening a gap in the line through which more Rebels rushed.

71 Simmers and Bachschmid, *Volunteer's Manual*, 28; Martin, *Bornemann's Regiment*, 157-58.

72 Fox, *New York at Gettysburg*, I, 404; *A Brief History of the 54th Regiment N. Y. Vet. Vol. Infantry (Hiram Barney Rifles)* (New York: A. H. Kellogg, 1888), n.p.

With the Pennsylvania regiment, von Gilsa ordered the men to hold fire thinking the approaching troops were his own skirmishers. When Lt. Clyde Millar approached to ask for permission to fire, von Gilsa still refused until Lt. William Beidelman ignored his brigade commander by ordering Company F to open fire. The rest of the regiment quickly followed, but by then it was too late. Lt. Millar watched horrorstricken as the "first rebel line passed over and up towards the batterys [*sic*] the second line and our line met" in "a promiscuous fight" with "muskets being handled as clubs; rocks torn from the wall in front and thrown, fists and bayonets used."[73] Some of the men stood and fought it out with the Rebels along the stone wall while the others joined the New Yorkers in a retreat up the hill.

The retreat uncovered the left flank of the 41st New York which suddenly found itself taking fire from flank and rear. The four companies on the left bent back, some eventually retiring while the rest doubled back to form a near right angle still firmly holding position on the flank of the 33rd Massachusetts which also found itself fired into from the rear.[74]

While the fierce fight still raged along the base of Cemetery Hill, the few Confederates from the two brigades who made it through the gaps in the Union line or vaulted over the wall and continued up the hill found that once they were free of the Federal infantry at the wall they were in a blind spot below the summit where the artillery could not be depressed far enough to fire on them. Likewise, infantry atop the hill could not fire until the attackers appeared over the crest. This effectively limited fire on the assailants to a single volley of musketry or one pull of the lanyard on an artillery piece once they appeared. Before either could reload the Rebels were among two sections of Capt. Michael Wiedrich's battery. An Alsatian by birth, the captain had been a shipping clerk in civilian life and was the commander of the "Light Artillery Company," a solidly German unit attached to the 65th Regiment, New York State Militia. On January 18, 1861, long before the firing on Fort Sumter, the unit offered its services to Governor Edwin D. Morgan "for the defense of the Union." Now, two and a half years later the battery's surviving veterans found themselves engulfed in the turmoil of a murderous hand-to-hand confrontation. They had been ordered several times during the past two days not to retreat, they must hold their position at all costs—for these gunners the moment of truth had arrived.[75]

73 Millar to Bachelder, Mar. 2, 1886, GNMP; Keifer, *History*, 141-42.

74 Martin, *Bornemann's Regiment*, 158; Underwood, *Three Years' Service*, 130.

75 Capt. Michael Wiedrich File, Buffalo and Erie County Historical Society; Schaefer, "Wiedrich's Battery," in the Michael Wiedrich Papers; *Buffalo Courier*, April 16, 1899.

Capt. Michael Wiedrich, Battery I, 1st New York Light Artillery
National Archives

"[U]p the Hill we go," wrote Gen. Hays' aide, Capt. William Seymour, "and, after a short struggle, the much coveted crest and its now silent batteries are ours." But it was not that easy. At the gun emplacements, Rebels appeared on the embrasures. Nearby, Lt. Paul Bachschmid of the 153rd Pennsylvania watched as "One of the first Rebels to reach the guns threw himself over the muzzle and called out to the gunners 'I take command of this gun.' The German gunner replied 'Du sollst sie haben!' [You shall have it]. He pulled the lanyard and blew the Rebel to kingdom come." Nothing remained but a spray of blood and small bits of human flesh spattered here and there. Another witness to the event was less gruesome in his description. William Simmers commented simply that "the soul of the departing Rebel had taken its flight to the realms of everlasting peace."[76]

Adj. Peter Young rallied with the 107th Ohio at the batteries. Young saw his color bearer, Sergt. Christian Taifel, "flaunting them in the faces of the Rebels," fall wounded. Young reached out and grabbed the colors, handed them off to someone else, then fired his pistol at Arthur Duchamp who was advancing with the colors of the 8th Louisiana. Duchamp fell. Young sprang forward, but another Rebel, Corp. Leon Gusman scooped up the fallen banner. In an instant, he fell wounded, whether by Young or someone else was impossible to tell. Young wrestled the flag from Guzman

76 Jones, "Going Back," 12, 55-60; Rollins, *Damned Red Flags*, 133; Fuerschbach, *Wiedrich's Battery*, 23; Simmers and Bachschmid, *Volunteer's Manual*, 30.

but was immediately shot in the left lung and arm. Sergt. Major Henry Brinker caught the adjutant as he fell. A grayclad lieutenant followed Young, but Lt. Fernando C. Suhrer slashed his shoulder with a saber. The Ohioans came away with the colors of the 8th Louisiana. Soldiers "conveyed [Young] to the Cemetery Gate pump where refreshing water somewhat allayed the burning fever and saved my life."[77]

The fight was short, but sharp. In the confusion one Confederate grabbed onto already-wounded Lt. Nicholas Sahm from Wiedrich's battery and manhandled him over the revetment where he disarmed the officer and headed off down the hill with his captive. Somewhere along the way Sahm managed to escape minus his sword. Fortunately for him, his name was engraved on the blade. The following winter a Rebel officer was taken captive with the sword that, thanks to its identifying marks, eventually made it back to its original owner who was then serving in Bridgeport, Alabama.[78]

While the mêlée took place in Wiedrich's battery, Avery's men struggled to push through the gap created in von Gilsa's line. Federals shot Avery down, his wound proving mortal. Major Samuel McD. Tate led the 6th North Carolina in a last desperate charge of about 75 Tarheels over the crest of the hill and into Ricketts's battery while von Gilsa's rallied men fired into their flank as they approached the gun embrasures. Hand-to-hand fighting engulfed the battery in what Lt. Charles Brockway described as "the wildest confusion. Friends and foes were indiscriminately Mixed, and our brave men, though outnumbered and without arms, by means of handspikes, rammers and stones . . . made a sturdy resistance."[79]

One of the attackers attempted to capture the battery guidon but its bearer, James H. Riggin, used his revolver to shoot the intruder. Riggin was quickly shot down by another Confederate who attempted to make off with the banner and a horse, but Lt. Brockway saw what was happening. Amid the confusion he "picked up a stone, and in a most unmilitary manner, broke the fellow's head." Leading the assault, Major Tate noted the ferocity of the opposition, commenting that "The enemy stood with a tenacity never before displayed by them." Samuel W. Eaton of the 57th North Carolina recorded in his diary later that night that "We were under a desperate fire, only a few

77 Young to Bachelder, April 12, 1867, in Ladd, *Bachelder Papers*, I, 311-12; Rollins, *Damned Red Flags*, 133; Nussbaum, "Louisiana Tigers and the 107th Ohio," *National Tribune*, July 15, 1909.

78 Fuerschbach, *Wiedrich's Battery*, 23; Crumb, *Eleventh*, 27.

79 *OR* 27, pt. 2, 485; Archer, "The Hour Was," 66; Dreese, *Old Flag*, 67.

Drawing of the July 2 attack on Cemetery Hill by Alfred R. Waud. *Library of Congress*

got to the batteries and could not hold them. . . . There was harder fighting today than ever I knew of before."[80]

☽ ☽ ☽

As darkness fell, Howard and Schurz stood near the cemetery gatehouse discussing the days' events. The deadly afternoon artillery barrage had long since diminished to an occasional shell or two. Reinforcements had been hurried to Greene on Culp's Hill where the decrease in firing seemed to indicate that the Federal position was holding firm. It looked to the two as if the army had withstood the Confederates' best efforts to dislodge them; now it was time to think about any necessary readjustments in their dispositions before the next appearance of the sun brought any new attacks. Behind the two generals, in the cemetery itself, Col. Krzyzanowski sat with the remaining XI Corps reserve, the 58th and 119th New York regiments. With portions of each regiment on picket and among the sharpshooters manning the corps's

80 Dreese, *Old Flag*, 67; *OR* 27, pt. 2, 485; Tate to governor of North Carolina, July 8, 1863, 6th North Carolina file, GNMP; Samuel W. Eaton diary, in 57th North Carolina File, GNMP.

advanced positions, there were less than 400 men available when suddenly the unmistakable sounds of furious combat reached them. Instantly, the colonel knew this was no simple skirmishing. Shouting to be heard above the crash of battle, he ordered the two regiments to fix bayonets and form as quickly as possible.[81]

Howard and Schurz "were suddenly startled by a tremendous turmoil at Wiedrich's and Rickett's batteries." Schurz quickly asked permission to order up the reserve, to which Howard instantly agreed. Accompanied by an aide, Captain Julius Schenowsky, Schurz sprinted over to where Krzyzanowski's command lay, but found it already forming with the 119th New York getting underway as the 58th New York fell into line. Schurz joined Krzyzanowski at the head of the troops, turned, and led them off toward the endangered batteries at the double-quick. When Schurz arrived at the batteries, he "found an indescribable scene of melee. Some Rebel infantry had scaled the breastworks and were taking possession of the guns. But the cannoneers defended themselves desperately. With rammers and fence rails, hand spikes and stones, they knocked down the intruders. Our infantry made a vigorous rush upon the invaders, and after a short but very spirited hand-to-hand scuffle tumbled them down the embankment."[82]

Outside the embrasures, Capt. Alfred Theinhardt of the 41st New York rallied a large number of von Gilsa's retreating men behind a stone wall where they continued to resist. Sergt. Bornemann, bloodied from the wound in his face, was among those pushed up the hill who rallied at the guns. So were men from the 153rd Pennsylvania. "Here our reverses ended," William Simmers proudly asserted. "Determined to conquer or die in the attempt, our men now threw themselves up on the enemy with a resolution and a fury that soon compelled him to retire. The batteries were saved, the day ours, Chancellorsville redeemed!"[83]

Lt. Lucian Smith in the 136th New York, looking across the slope of Cemetery Hill from his position to the left of where the Confederate attack hit, could see "the flashing in the dark like the red tongues of serpents of each piece as it was discharged, the cheering of men as they came on or went back, the shrieking of the wounded." The same sights and sounds reached von Steinwehr who also responded quickly to the crisis, dispatching portions of the 27th and 73rd Pennsylvania. Advancing rapidly across the slope, William Levey found "A fierce hand to hand conflict ensued in which

81 Schurz, *Reminiscences*, III, 25.

82 Schurz, *Reminiscences*, III, 25; Howard, *Autobiography*, I, 429. Howard claims he ordered Schurz to send reinforcements.

83 Simmers and Bachschmid, *Volunteer's Manual*, 30.

gunstocks, revolvers, swords, bayonets and even stones were used." Seeing the relief forces approach, Capt. Friedrich von Fritsch "joined and charged with them down the hill. They drove the Confederates back over the wall and then we lay down as our cannons were firing very close over our heads."[84]

With the Confederates already driven from Wiedrich's battery by the counterattack, and a small number of North Carolinians hanging on in Ricketts's emplacements, Colonel Samuel S. Carroll's brigade of the II Corps appeared on the scene. Having been sent by Gen. Hancock when the sounds of battle reached his headquarters, the brigade approached from behind the cemetery, which brought it in on the right flank of Ricketts' battery. In the full darkness of the nighttime struggle, Major Tate of the 6th North Carolina saw that all around him his men were dying. Looking to his rear he could see nothing but darkness, no hint of any supports rushing to join them. With only a handful of men left, he issued the order to withdraw.

In the dark it was nearly impossible to tell friend from foe. While the last of the North Carolinians were rounded up amid Ricketts' guns or retired down the hill into the darkness, Carroll's 14th Indiana arrived, charged into Ricketts's battery, and cleared it of the few remaining Tarheels. During the assault the color bearers of the 21st North Carolina suffered repeated losses. Four men in succession were shot down carrying the banner. During the retreat Corp. Eli Wiley brought the flag successfully off the hill but was shot down after crossing back across the stone wall at the base of the slope. In the darkness and confusion no one noticed the banner lying on the ground next to its dead bearer. When daylight finally arrived the next morning Oliver Root, a soldier in the 14th Indiana of Carroll's brigade spotted the fallen color, retrieved it and was later awarded the Medal of Honor despite the fact that all he did was retrieve a trophy that should rightly have been the prize of the soldier or regiment that had killed its original custodian[85]

☽ ☽ ☽

When night and the mutual exhaustion of both armies finally brought a merciful end to the day's fighting Maj. Samuel Hurst became aware of "the most distressful wail we ever listened to. Thousands of sufferers upon the field, and hundreds lying between

84 Smith, "Recollections of Gettysburg"; Conklin, "History of the 134th N.Y."; Butts, *Gallant Captain*, 85.

85 Sauers and Tomasak, *Ricketts' Battery*, 99, 110; Dreese, *Old Flag*, 80. Most likely the troops responsible for shooting the Rebel color bearer were members of the 17th Connecticut.

Musician Richard Enderlin in the 73rd Ohio crawled out beyond Union lines to save the life of a fallen comrade. He was awarded the Medal of Honor for his courageous act.
Gettysburg National Military Park

the two skirmish lines, who could not be cared for, through the night were groaning . . . they were the mingled cries of friend and foe, borne to us on the night-breeze, as a sad, wailing, painful cry for help."[86]

German-born Richard Enderlin migrated from his native Baden to Chillicothe in 1854. He enlisted in Cincinnati as a musician in Hurst's regiment, the 73rd Ohio. Although musicians were detailed as stretcher bearers and not expected to fight in the ranks, Enderlin voluntarily took a musket that dreadful day. In the fields before his position lay hundreds of wounded men caught between the fire of the contending sides. Gradually, they crawled to safety, were taken prisoner, or expired. That night the suffering moans of one of the wounded that remained alive between the warring sides became too much for Enderlin to endure. The repeated plaintiff cries for water particularly stirred him. Slipping over the protective wall, the musician crawled out into the field using the growing darkness to cover his moves, gradually wiggling forward until he was within the enemy picket lines. Reaching the wounded soldier, "under a sharp fire," he dragged the helpless form back through the field to the safety of the Union lines. For his bravery he received the Medal of Honor. The man he rescued was George Nixon, whose great-grandson Richard would one day become president of the United States.[87]

In the wake of the fighting on Cemetery Hill someone called William Southerton's name. It was his close friend Norman Brooks who had been shot through the face. Southerton was horrified by the sight. Brooks had torn a piece of cloth from his pants leg to press against the gaping wound, but Southerton could easily see that "part of his

86 Quoted in Dempsey, "Heaviest Skirmishing," 51-52.

87 Arrington, *Medal of Honor*, 4; Baumgartner, *Buckeye Blood*, 85; Pfanz, *Culp's Hill & Cemetery Hill*, 150.

jaw was shot away, many of his front teeth were gone." Southerton helped his friend to the rear. "The farther I went the more terrible. Dead horses strewn about in every shape. Some had been blown to bits. Bodies of our men had been gathered up and removed. Seemingly no end to the battlefield! And, oh! What destruction of our battery on the crest! Horses and pieces of horses lying all about." The hospital lay along the Baltimore Pike a few hundred yards east of the hill's crest. "There was no mistaking the way to the hospital. Such a line of wounded men! Many on stretchers, many hobbling trying to make it under their own power. . . . Dr. [Charles L.] Wilson was working frantically near a wide open doorway. He recognized us as I led Norman to him. If any one could help us, Dr. Wilson could. Other surgeons were working just as frantically. All by the light of a few lanterns hung on the walls. Hay was strewn about on the floor for beds for the wounded. At the doorway I saw a huge stack of amputated arms and legs, a stack as high as my head! The most horrible thing I ever saw in my life! I wish I had never seen it! I sickened."[88]

The frightening scenes about the field hospitals were for many too gruesome to behold. Everyone knew the standard treatment for a leg or arm wound where the bone was broken was amputation, so some of the ambulatory wounded simply refused to go to the hospital, preferring instead to rely on their friends or their own ingenuity to save their extremities from the surgeon's knife. "Hospital!" an alarmed Earle Rich of the 33rd Massachusetts responded. "Hell, if I had turned myself into one of those places I would not have had my leg today. It did not bleed to amount to anything; the only time it hurt was when I put a cud of tobacco in the hole to keep the flies out and kill the germs."[89]

In the 73rd Pennsylvania Andrew Diembach and several comrades tried to assist a badly wounded Confederate. "We carried him to the pump back of the cemetery gate. He was moaning piteously and rubbing his hand over the gaping wound from which his brains were oozing. How we pitied the poor wounded man – ten minutes ago a foe, now a helpless comrade needing our care! One of our boys, with tears in his eyes, put his gum blanket under the sufferer's head, and said, in a choked voice. 'There, my poor fellow, that will make you rest easier,' and other comrades moistened the feverish lips with water from the pump."[90]

Howard could not rid himself of the piteous nighttime sounds. "The ground was covered with the groanings and moanings of the wounded. While the soldiers were

88 Southerton, "What We Did There," 12.

89 Rich, *Cape Cod Echoes*, 44.

90 Conklin, "History of the 134th N.Y."

sleeping, the medical men with their ambulances, their lanterns, and their stretchers, aided here and there by a chaplain or a member of the Christian Commission, were going from point to point to do what little they could for the multitude of sufferers." It is so difficult, he thought, "to see our comrades there upon the ground with their darkened faces and swollen forms; another thing to watch the countenances of friends and companions but lately in the bloom of health, now disfigured, torn, and writhing in death; and not less affecting to a sensitive heart to behold the multitude of strangers prone and weak, pierced with wounds, or showing broken limbs and every sign of suppressed suffering, waiting for hours and hours for a relief which is long coming—the relief of the surgeon's knife or of death.[91]

Back in town Michael Jacobs, professor of mathematics at Gettysburg College, wrote in his diary: "The rebels returned to our street at ten p.m., and prepared their supper; and soon we began to hope that all was not lost. Some of them expressed their most earnest indignation at the foreigners—the Dutchmen—for having shot down so many of their men. This led us to believe that the Eleventh Corps, of whom many were foreign Germans, and whom, on the previous evening, they tauntingly told us they met at Chancellorsville—had done their duty and had nobly redeemed their character."[92]

At the base of Cemetery Hill the same thought passed through John Ryder's mind that no doubt occurred to survivors on both sides of the battle lines. "In the quiet hours of the beautiful moonlight night we asked ourselves the question: 'What will tomorrow bring forth?'"[93]

91 Howard, *Autobiography*, I, 431, 441.

92 Miers and Brown, *Gettysburg*, 183.

93 Ryder, *Reminiscences*, 35.

Chapter 15

"Our Boys All Fought Well"

July 3-16, 1863

FRIDAY, JULY 3, PROMISED TO BE another hot, muggy day. By 7:00 am the temperature was already 73 degrees and it would rise to 87 by 2:00 pm. Humidity was exceptionally high, but although there were thunderstorms reported in the vicinity none seemed to pass close enough to the battlefield to merit notice. Lt. Lucian Smith watched as "The sun came up over the eastern hills like a great ball of fire; the stillness was oppressive and ominous."[1]

Sharpshooters were in action early, popping away at anything that moved. About 6:00 am Capt. Emil Koenig received orders to move his 58th New York from its reserve position in the cemetery to a stone fence to the left of Wiedrich's battery. They were to replace troops who were being withdrawn for a rest and to replenish their ammunition. Bending low, hastening along as quickly as possible to give the rebels as little target as possible, they reached the wall and some degree of relative safety. Koenig next ordered Lt. Carl Schwartz to take his company over the wall and into the next row of houses so the regiment covered the approaches along both sides of Baltimore Street. All of this Koenig accomplished without loss; however, "The enemy's sharpshooters kept up a brisk fire at these houses, and killed a girl who was living in one of them." The dead woman was twenty-year old Jenny Wade, shot in her sister's kitchen as she baked bread. She is believed to be the only civilian killed during the battle. Although Koenig attributed her death to rebel sharpshooters, Lt. M. H. Daniels of the 17th Connecticut

1 Nofi, *Gettysburg Campaign*, 168; Smith, "Gettysburg," 302.

later wrote that "The enemy were firing on us from the houses of the town. Out of one house came two shots in quick succession. We returned the fire, but soon after learned we had killed a young woman in that house, while she was kneading bread."[2]

As the sun rose and the heat of its direct rays reached the men, thirsts became intense. In the 107th Ohio Frederick Nussbaum determined to reach a small spring near the base of East Cemetery Hill to obtain water. What he met along the way was sobering. "The lane was covered with dead men from both sides, also a number of horses, cows and mules, so that it was impossible for me to get to the spring without stepping on the dead. In the middle of the lane I stopped to pick up a rifle and exchange it for mine, when a bullet passed close by my ears; I dropped the gun and a few steps further on another ball went whizzing above my head, and so on until seven shots were fired at me by a Rebel sharp shooter from one of the windows of the Reformed church. The sixth shot struck a gate post directly in front of my head, while the seventh touched the sole of my right shoe as I alighted on the ground, leaping over a gate to reach the regimental line. I succeeded in bringing eleven canteens full of water; these I left near the gate, telling the boys to go after them themselves. I had a very narrow escape."[3]

On Cemetery Hill Capt. Michael Wiedrich was in action again, but not as consistently or intensely as the previous afternoon. "[W]e had several artillery duels during the forenoon, but of short duration, as we silenced their batteries after a few rounds as often as they brought them against us." In the relative calm that descended before noon, the troops in and around the cemetery took advantage of the opportunity to relax. Looking at the scene, Schurz observed that "Some sat silently on the ground munching their hard-tack, while others stretched themselves out seeking sleep, which they probably would have found more readily had the cannon been thundering at a distance. The officers stood together in little groups discussing with evident concern what this long-continued calm might mean."[4]

Speculation came to an end around 1:00 pm—estimates vary widely—when Col. E. Porter Alexander ordered a signal fired that loosed some 150 Confederate guns on the Union positions in a furious bombardment designed to suppress the artillery and drive off the infantry in preparation for a major assault on the federal center. "Then came a storm of shot and shell," reported newspaper correspondent Charles Carleton Coffin, "marble slabs were broken, iron fences shattered, horses disemboweled. The

2 *OR* 27, pt. 1, 740-41; Warren journal.

3 Baumgartner, *Buckeye Blood*, 141-42.

4 *OR* 27, pt. 1, 752; Schurz, *Reminiscences*, III, 27.

air was full of wild, hideous noises—the low buzz of round shot, the whizzing of elongated balls and the stunning explosion of shells overhead and all around."[5]

When the barrage began Howard was "sitting in front of my batteries on the slope of Cemetery Hill. Feeling that my greatest danger came from the strippings of the shells as they flew over my head, I had cracker boxes piled behind us—affording protection from our own cannon." Immediately after the signal gun, Confederate batteries "filled the whole region of mountain, hill, and valley with one continuous roar, instantly varied by sudden bolts at each lightening flash from the cannon's mouth, and by the peculiar, shrill screech of the breaking shells. Then the crash of destruction, the breaking of carriages, the killing and wounding of men—in one of my regiments twenty-seven fell at a single shot." Howard recalled that "every part of that field was visited. Men were killed while straightening their teams; while carrying orders; on horseback; on foot; while talking, eating, or lying down. The lowest ground in our rear was quickly cleared of noncombatants, camp followers, and overcurious civilians. No orders were needed after the first bombshell exploded there. The air was so full of terror and death-dealing fragments that every man at first must have doubted if he should ever see the light of another day."[6]

"[P]andemonium seemed to break loose as thousands of shells passed over the place where our Regiment lay," Henry Henny in the 55th Ohio recorded. "Mainly the boys were hugging the stone fences for the little protection they offered from the flying fragments of exploding shells. The shots from both sides screamed overhead, some close to the ground and others high up in the air. Most of the shells were aimed at the guns on the hill back of where we lay, and passed far to the rear of their aim. Others fell short, striking in the water between our regiment and the cemetery, blowing great furrows in the rain soaked earth. The suspense was very trying on those who had to lie still and take anything in the encounter, simply hugging the stone walls, not knowing what moment a shell would strike short and plunge through the slight barricade on it's motion of death and destruction."[7]

William Southerton in the 75th Ohio was staggered by the "violent concussion as our artillery replied." It "was the most appalling I had ever heard. The duel was relentless! No one could describe it! Terrific heat, and no breeze to lift the dense clouds of smoke and fumes." A short distance away lay the 136th New York. Lt. Lucian Smith hugged the ground as federal counter battery fire streaked over his head. "The pieces of

5 Crumb, *Eleventh*, 66.

6 Howard, *Autobiography*, I, 436-38.

7 Henny diary, July 3, 1863.

Lt. Lucian Smith, 136th New York
John DuBois

wood that helped keep the flannel bag that held the powder attached to the ball, would fly down upon us, and often struck us with such force as to produce great pain. Occasionally a shell would prematurely burst before it reached us, and our own troops would suffer the consequences." Aaron Walker was seriously wounded in the left arm by a fragment from one such premature detonation. "As we lay on our backs, looking up into the clear sky, we could at intervals of about 30 seconds apart, see a black speck suddenly appear about a mile up in the air. It at first seemed to be stationary. In an instant it would begin to fall and for a little ways the eye could follow it and then it was lost, and soon came tearing thro' the air sounding like a sky-rocket only ten thousand times louder. . . . It would hit the ground, tear out a dozen bushels of earth, and then go bounding thro' the fields, something after a run, hop, skip and jump fashion. It frightened the whole regiment every time it came, for no live man could tell where it would hit next."[8]

Lt. John W. Hand in the 136th New York recalled that "For two savage hours the air above and about us was filled with hissing, shrieking, howling messengers of death; a roaring, raging, withering hell of missiles, a pandemonium of unearthly sounds." There seemed to be no position in which one could feel secure. "In spite of the soldier's ingenuity in adjusting himself to the situation there was no relief," Smith recalled, "the last condition was always worse than the preceding. If you laid down on the ground and put your fingers in your ears you got, in addition to the crash in the air, the full effect of the earth's tremor and its additional force as a conductor. . . . If you rolled over on your back and looked up at the heavens, fairly black with missiles exploding continually and sending their broken fragments in every direction, the situation was not more assuring. If you sat with your back to the stone wall and looked over into the Cemetery, you saw long, fiery tongues leaping toward you, thick clouds of sulphurous smoke settle down

8 Southerton, "What We Did There"; Smith, "Gettysburg," 302.

around you, blackening the countenance almost beyond recognition. If you turned around and looked over the wall toward the enemy each cannon ball seemed directed toward that particular spot. . . . All this time our nerves were strung to the highest pitch, water ran from every pore in the skin like squeezing a wet sponge, and our clothes were wringing wet. It was nature's provision for our safety, as it prevented a total collapse of the nervous system, and the mind from going out in darkness." Smith thought it would go on forever. "It seemed an age to us; it was an age if you count time, not by minutes and seconds, but by the amount of nervous suffering and mental agony that can be condensed into a given period."[9]

Lt. Hand was struck by the picture about him as the smoke from guns and exploding shells soon blanketed the fields. "The sun no longer glares fiercely down with a blistering heat, but gleams redly through the smoky air." His gaze went from man to man, observing how they appeared to feel, the various emotional stages they went through. "Human courage has its limitations. The concentrated fire of a hundred cannons affects the mind in much the same manner as do the destructive forces of nature—the lightening, the tornado, the earthquake—all dangers to be avoided, not resisted. Men may meet death bravely, when nerved to supreme effort by a gallant charge; they must await it in fear when unnerved by inaction. But fear also has its limit. If one may survive that withering fire for a moment, why not for an hour? Philosophy comes to the rescue. The missile that is seen or heard has already passed by on its cruel errand. Why shrink in terror from an unseen danger? What can one do but sit with his back to the wall against which the fragments of shell are striking, and watch with such composure as he may command the curious flights of the different projectiles, while awaiting the time and the order for personal action? . . . Drowsiness and, in a few cases, sleep ensues."[10]

Much of the Confederate fire overshot its mark along Cemetery Ridge, falling behind the Union lines. Surgeon Henry Van Aernam at the XI Corps hospital on the property of George Spangler along the Baltimore Pike remarked that the shells "fell very thickly about our hospital, especially on the third day. For a while, from 1 to 3 or 4 o'clock it was a perfect shower." One of those hit was Assistant Surgeon William S. Moore of the 61st Ohio who was overseeing the removal of the more lightly wounded when a shell fragment mangled his left thigh. He died three days later.[11]

9 Hand, "A Graphic Account"; Smith, "Gettysburg," 303-04.

10 Hand, "A Graphic Account."

11 Van Aernam letter to "My Dearest Lis," July 30, 1863; Baumgartner, *Buckeye Blood*, 151.

Maj. Thomas Osborn commanded the batteries in and around the Evergreen Cemetery. Lt. Christopher Schmitt's section of Weidrich's battery engaged in counter-battery fire across the fields at the rebel guns. Then, when the Southern infantry began its march toward Cemetery Ridge, Schmitt changed to shells to disrupt the long lines moving toward him. At one point when the bombardment was at its peak, Meade suddenly approached Osborn and asked whether he could stay on the hill. "I assured him we would do so. He said the result of the fight depended on our holding the hill. I replied that the enemy also seemed to have the same idea." Meade offered no advice or orders, he appeared to Osborn "to be much concerned as to the possibility of holding the men up to the work under the fire then going on. He remained only two or three minutes, but repeated the question: 'Can you stay here?' and 'Are your men thoroughly in hand?' I replied: 'The officers and men are in good condition and we would stay.'"[12]

Some of the men attempted to keep their minds off the cacophony about them by "cleaning their gun-locks, others by polishing the buttons of their uniforms, still others by sewing up rents in their clothes." The chaplain in the 33rd Massachusetts went through the ranks asking "If any of you want to write a letter I will take it and after the battle mail it for you." One of those who did was John Ryder. The letter made it home safely to his mother who kept it. Fifty years later Ryder was attending the reunion of the Blue and Gray in 1913. At the exact hour he wrote the original letter, he "lay down on that identical spot of ground and re-read the letter."[13]

As time passed, Carl Schurz became "desperately hungry." Turning to his adjutant, Capt. Fritz Tiedemann, lying next to him, Schurz asked the aide if he would try to find him a cracker. The Tiedemanns were long-time friends of Schurz stretching back to their time in Europe. Gustav Nikolaus Tiedemann was commander fortress Rastatt and had been executed for siding with the revolutionaries in 1848. His brother Heinrich, Fritz's father, had married a sister of Friedrich Hecker and escaped to the United States with Hecker in 1848. Heinrich settled in Philadelphia where he practiced medicine. It was there that Schurz learned English when he first arrived in America, and it was there that he and his wife Margarethe had their first child, Agathe. The captain obliged Schurz's request for a cracker, standing up and walking off to see what he could find. No sooner had he left than a large shell fragment buried itself deep into the ground exactly where the officer had been reclining. Schurz's hunger saved

12 Remington, *Wiedrich's Battery*, 21, 28; Crumb, *Eleventh*, 72-73.

13 Schurz, *Reminiscences*, III, 29; Ryder, *Reminiscences*, 36.

Capt. Fritz Tiedemann, 75th Pennsylvania, on the staff of Gen. Schurz.
U.S. Army Heritage and Education Center

Tiedemann's life. Thirty years later the captain's daughter would marry one of Schurz's sons.[14]

The lengthy bombardment was a trying experience because the men had no opportunity to retaliate for the punishment they received. Schurz was clearly awestruck. "All that I had ever read in battle-stories of the booming of heavy guns out-thundering the thunders of heaven, and making the earth tremble, and almost stopping one's breath by the concussions of the air—was here made real, in terrific effect. The roar was so incessant and at times so deafening that when I wished to give an order to one of my officers I had to put my hands to my mouth as a speaking trumpet and shout my orders into his ear." Most of the rebel fire went high and missed their position, but "enough of them struck the ground on the cemetery and exploded there, to scatter death and destruction among the men immediately around, and to shatter gravestones and blow up ammunition caissons. But as most of them flew over us, rushing, screaming, whirring, and as they burst above, and sent down their deadly fragments, they added to the hellish din a peculiarly malicious noise of their own. ... As a matter of course we ordered the troops to lie down flat on the ground, so as to present the smallest possible target. But when I observed the effect of the dropping of a shell right into the midst of a regiment which caused some uneasy commotion, I though it my duty to get upon my feet and look after it. I found that it had a very steadying and cheering effect upon the men to see me quietly walking up and down in front smoking a cigar. I could not speak to them, for the incessant roar of the cannonade would not let them hear me. But I noticed that many of them returned my smile in a sort of confidential way when I happened to catch their eyes." Noticing the good effect that he was having on the men,

14 Schurz, *Reminiscences*, III, 29-30; Trefousse, *Carl Schurz*, 46; Zucker, *Forty-Eighters*, 348.

he "invited, by gesture, some of the regimental officers to do likewise. They promptly obeyed, although, I suppose, they liked the stroll no more than I did."[15]

The bombardment seemed as if it would go on forever. No sooner had Meade departed from his conversation with Maj. Osborn than Gen. Henry Hunt, chief of the army's artillery, arrived. As he inspected the placement of the batteries and their condition, Howard and Schurz approached. All four of the officers agreed that the bombardment must be a preparation for an infantry attack and that Lee was no doubt trying to drive away the federal guns before launching the assault. Osborn, perhaps fearing that he would not have enough ammunition left to counter the infantry if the exchange of fire lasted too long, said that he "believed that if we should stop firing along our entire line suddenly and as though the artillery on Cemetery Hill was driven off the field, Lee would at once develop his plans." Howard and Hunt both liked the idea, but Hunt expressed concern whether the men could be controlled if no longer serving their guns but simply withstanding the bombardment. Osborn replied that his "men were under perfect control by their officers and nothing was to be feared from the order." After a few more moments of conversation Hunt left to issue the appropriate orders. Osborn went to Wiedrich's battery nearby, "ordered him to cease firing and for every officer and man to lie flat upon the ground covering themselves as best they could by the unevenness of the ground, and to remain there until further orders." He then moved on to each battery on the hill issuing in turn the same directives.[16]

The artillery fire began to slacken, then nearly cease. During the artillery duel Howard was "watching the event. In the lull I suddenly observed beautiful lines of regiments as on parade emerging from the woods in rear of the enemy's cannon." Lt. John Hand rose "somewhat cautiously" to see what was happening. "We see a gleam of gun-barrels as the indistinct gray lines emerge from the opposite woods, their line of march directed on the brigade next to our own on the left. They move out rapidly in good form, a second line following at supporting distance, and a moment later a third, followed by artillery. . . . Occasionally a well directed shot makes a gap in the approaching ranks. They lose the touch of elbows, but press gallantly forward. The advance reaches a stout board fence. They are now within musket-range. They climb the fence; many fall, some forward, some backward. The wounded in great numbers are seen passing to the rear. The alignment is lost; the different lines are merging into a seething, struggling mass, that surges onward like the waves of an angry ocean. . . .

15 Schurz, "Battle of Gettysburg," 282; Schurz, *Reminiscences*, III, 28-29.

16 Crumb, *Eleventh*, 36, 39, 40, 75.

What a moment of suspense! Soldiers turn to their comrades and read in their pale faces only the reflection of their own fears."[17]

Across the rolling fields came line after line of determined Confederates, over 12,000 resolute veteran troops intent upon breaking the center of the Union line, destroying the Army of the Potomac, and winning the war. Major Osborn quickly began redirecting whatever batteries he could to meet the threat. Along the front line, the 136th New York and 27th Pennsylvania redeployed some of their men taking advantage of their position beyond the flank of the rebel assault to deliver a destructive enfilade fire into the advancing ranks. Martin Graham, color sergeant in the 136th, was struck three times, twice by shell fragments and once by a minie ball to the stomach, but survived. His hometown newspaper commented that "he still carries [the ball] in the pit of his stomach, probably unable to digest it," noting that the sergeant had been "temporarily hauled off for repairs."[18]

Sergt. Charles Link's 45th New York sharpshooters also had a view of the charge and were able to shoot into the rebel flank. John McMahon in the 136th estimated he was in the fight for half an hour. He was "hit by a ball that tore my pants and went down into my boot; without doing me any more harm." McMahon claimed in his diary that his regiment lost three killed and one wounded during the repulse of Pickett's Charge, while taking three rebel flags and "one whole brigade" of prisoners.[19]

With the rebel assault aiming at Cemetery Ridge, Osborn received an order from Hunt to send a battery as quickly as possible to reinforce Gen. Alexander Webb in the II Corps. Osborn dispatched Wheeler's 13th New York Independent Battery. Wheeler moved his battery out immediately, reported to Gen. Hancock, and was ordered into position to the left of Capt. James Rorty's Battery B, 1st New York Light Artillery, located just south of the famous copse of trees on Cemetery Ridge. Wheeler arrived to find the rebels already within 400 yards. "[A] battery of theirs opened very fiercely upon us, and made things very hot; but we paid no attention to their battery, and just kept the canister going into them. Once a double round of canister struck close to their flag, and I saw a dozen of them drop, and the whole column wavered and halted; but the standard-bearer waved his flag and they moved on again, but in a weary and spiritless manner. Just at this moment what should the infantry in front of us do but get up and

17 Howard, *Autobiography*, I, 437-38; Hand, "A Graphic Account."

18 *OR* 27, pt. 1, 756; Daily Log of 11th Corps, July 3, 2:25 pm; Priest, *McMahon's Diary*, 53; unidentified newspaper clipping on 136th New York, New York State Division of Military and Naval Affairs.

19 *OR* 27, pt. 1, 736; Priest, *McMahon's Diary*, 53.

leave! The Battery seemed lost, but I got hold of some of them, told them not to let the Eleventh Corps' boys laugh at them, and in this way, first a squad, and then the whole regiment, was rallied and got back to the fence again, and about every reb who came up on to that hill was either killed, wounded, or captured."[20]

Before returning to his corps Wheeler took the time to assist with the wounded. "Utterly as I detest a living active rebel, as soon as he becomes wounded and a prisoner I don't perceive any difference in my feelings towards him and towards one of our own wounded heroes. I suppose this is very heterodox, but I can't help it. I found a Colonel of a Mississippi Regiment shot through the breast, a man of stately bearing, and a soldier of his regiment told me that he was judge of the Supreme Court of that State. Now here was a man, evidently one of the real old original Secesh; but I forgot that, took him into a barn, made him a straw bed, fixed a pillow for him, got him a cup of coffee, and ignored the fact that he gave me no word of thanks or farewell when I left him."[21] The unfortunate Confederate was most likely Col. Hugh R. Miller of the 42nd Mississippi.

John Ryder in the 33rd Massachusetts was appalled by the appearance of the battlefield. "The most sorrowful of all sights was the wounded—so many of them. The whole neighborhood in the rear of the lines for miles in extent was one vast hospital. At every house and barn and shed, at cooling stream or shady grove or hillside, the red flags were surrounded by torn and mangled men, wounded by shot and shell in every conceivable way—thousands of them." He consoled himself with the thought that "Our Boys in Blue" had "counted not their lives in defense of the union cause, but had by their heroic efforts contributed to the final victory."[22]

The setting sun mercifully brought a cloak of darkness over the devastation of the day, yet it could not muffle the piteous lamentations of the wounded lying without succor between the lines. Lt. Lucian Smith would "never forget that night. It made its memory fixed for all time to come. Words are useless things, and imagination cannot be vivid enough to compass its horrors. The night was black with darkness. A rainstorm was gathering in the west. Before us were ten thousand men writhing in the agonies of death. The air was filled with groans, moans, shrieks and yells. Prayers were offered and curses pronounced. Piteous appeals were made for water, for help, for

20 Letter of William Wheeler to grandfather and aunt, July 26, 1863, in Bershears, *Loyal Till Death*, 189.

21 Letter of William Wheeler to grandfather and aunt, July 26, 1863, in Bershears, *Loyal Till Death*, 190.

22 Ryder, *Reminiscences*, 37-38.

death. The sounds came from everywhere, distinctly heard from those near by, and growing fainter and more indistinct, until lost in one constant, low, far-away moaning sound. Occasionally, by the flashing of the lightening, you could see a dark form rise from the ground as some poor wretch by a superhuman effort would attempt to rise and then it would disappear. These spectacles covered acres and acres of ground. I see them now when my eyes are shut, and hear the sounds I cannot describe, whenever I let my mind dwell upon that night of all nights. . . . As the long night wore away, and it seemed morning would never come, there came a drenching rain. . . . When the storm of the elements had abated, I found that the life-spark had gone out of many of those to whom death was a most welcome visitor. The battle field was quieter now."[23]

☽ ☽ ☽

Saturday, July 4, had barely begun when the noise of movement came to the attention of Gen. Adelbert Ames. Curious, he ordered Col. William H. Noble, who had just returned to the 17th Connecticut on the evening of July 3 following his wounding at Chancellorsville, to send out a patrol to ascertain what was happening. Noble dispatched Lt. Milton H. Daniels and Sergt. Patrick Wade with ten men about 3:45 am with strict orders not to cause any noise as they advanced across the meadows separating their position from town. Given the deadly skirmishing of the past three days, Sergt. Wade was apprehensive. "There were some white faces in the squad when we started, and it was the first time in my army experience that I felt as though the odds were greatly against us." After suitable instructions on the use of hand commands, the group moved out. "The meadows being low, damp ground, and the days being very hot, a heavy fog had risen during the night and had settled over everything, making it almost impossible to see 300 feet ahead. We kept close together, for the fog was too thick for the usual distance between the skirmishers." Cautiously they advanced until they reached the forward rebel positions, expecting explosions of fire at any moment. They did not come. Instead, they found the line vacant. They moved on to the second line and found no one. The only rebels they met were a few they found sleeping in barns or nearby. With eighteen prisoners, they retraced their steps to Cemetery Hill to report the news that the rebels appeared to be abandoning the town.[24]

23 Smith, "Recollections of Gettysburg."

24 "Squad of the 17th Conn. First Learned of Lee's Retreat at Gettysburg," *National Tribune*, October 8, 1896.

Dawn soon broke, revealing what promised to be another uncomfortably hot day with the temperature reaching 69 degrees as early as 7:00 am, but by 2:00 pm it peaked at only 72 degrees, a welcome relief from the stifling heat of the previous day. Nonetheless, the oppressive humidity continued with some isolated showers in the morning and heavier rains in the afternoon. In the immediate hours after daybreak a strange silence hung over the battlefield. In the 58th New York Capt. Emil Koenig was "astonished not to hear any firing recommenced."[25]

With the belief spreading that the Confederates might have withdrawn from Gettysburg, the captain sent Lt. Carl Schwartz with "a patrol of 10 men into the town, to ascertain whether the enemy had retreated." No shots rang out. The men looked into barns and outbuildings, and behind rail fences and stone walls. They found nothing. "The citizens gave them signs, and showed them the houses which were occupied by the enemy. Our men entered them, and took most of the sharpshooters prisoners while asleep." When word came back that the rebels indeed seemed to have pulled back, Koenig sent Lt. Friedrich Lauber and twenty more men "into town, and these two squads took about 200 prisoners." Another regiment in Krzyzanowski's brigade, the 26th Wisconsin, also sent a patrol into the streets of Gettysburg with similar results—47 prisoners and no enemy resistance. Altogether Krzyzanowski's patrols took 280 prisoners. More importantly, they brought the welcome confirmation that Gettysburg lay devoid of hostile Southern troops. By the end of the day Assistant Adjutant General Meysenburg would record that the XI Corps took some 500 prisoners during the day.[26]

Alexander Schimmelfennig had been in hiding since the afternoon of July 1. The German general was exhausted, cramped, hungry, thirsty, and above all concerned about the outcome of the fighting that his ears told him had raged violently over the intervening days. When it finally became apparent that federal troops were now back in control of the buildings in the outskirts of town near Cemetery Hill, he emerged from his hiding place to the amazement and relief of his comrades. "He was a brave German, spare, sinewey form, a splendid horseman and a popular officer, whose men received him back with glad shouts of welcome," observed Howard. "He was as one risen from the dead."[27]

25 Nofi, *Gettysburg Campaign*, 168; Henny diary, July 3, 1863; *OR* 27, pt. 1, 741.

26 *OR* 27, pt. 1, 741; *Annual Report of the Adjutant General of the State of Wisconsin*, 404; Karsten diary, July 4, 1863; Miers and Brown, *Gettysburg*, 183; Meysenburg journal, July 4, 1863.

27 Rowland Howard, "The Story of Gettysburg."

No one was happier than Carl Schurz. Of all the losses on July 1, that of Schimmelfennig had been "nearest to my heart. He had not only been an officer of exceptional ability, but my military instructor in the old German days, and a dear personal friend." He had been missing since July 1, last seen "in the thickest of the fight" and "in the rear of his command." As he entered town on July 4, Schurz suddenly spotted his friend "in the door of one of the houses on the main street." Not only was he alive, but waving his hat to Schurz he invited him to breakfast! "I knew you would come. I have been preparing for you. You must be hungry. I found some eggs in this house and saved them for you. We shall have them fried in a few minutes. Get off your horse and let us take breakfast together." It was a most improbable and joyous reunion. "A happy moment it was to me," Schurz wrote, "when I could telegraph Mrs. Schimmelfennig, who was with my family at Bethlehem, Pennsylvania, that her husband . . . had been found, sound and safe!"[28]

☽ ☽ ☽

Capt. von Fritsch ventured into town to the field hospital of the XI Corps that had, with the rebel withdrawal, only been recaptured that day. "When our forces took possession of the town the inhabitants opened their houses and acted as though just released from prison." In the hospital he found Dr. Franz Hübschmann and the other surgeons still operating. "Piles of legs and arms lay near the operating stone, and still the surgeons cut away." He later rode over to the XI Corps hospital on the Baltimore Pike. "The stench on Cemetery Hill was terrible. The rain and sun had decomposed men and horses quickly, and the General and myself kept as far away as possible." Located in a barn and a farm house, the sheer number of wounded meant that many of them still lay on the ground in the several acres surrounding the buildings. The now frequent and heavy rain was "distressing for many of the wounded who have lain on the wet ground without any shelter."[29]

One of those suffering within the Spangler house was Confederate Gen. Lewis Armistead. Brought to the makeshift hospital "at dusk of July 3" with serious wounds to his breast and leg, he was treated by Surgeon Henry Van Aernam of the 154th New York assisted by Surgeon Bleecker L. Hovey of the 136th New York. Armistead shared a small bedroom in the Spangler house with Capt. Fred W. Stowe, assistant adjutant general of von Steinwehr's division who was suffering from a serious head wound from

28 Schurz, "Battle of Gettysburg," 284-85.

29 Butts, *Gallant Captain*, 43, 44, 88-89.

a shell fragment. The general received all of the care that circumstances allowed, but his injuries soon proved mortal.[30]

It troubled Corp. John McMahon that "In the night you could hear the wounded groan on the battlefield; some have been there for 36 hours: some of the poor fellows cried out for some one to kill them; they were in such pain. . . . This is the first battle field I ever went over and never want to see another. I pray God that this wicked rebellion will soon end." Lt. Lucian Smith in the same regiment passed over the field on a reconnaissance toward Seminary Ridge. "The slaughter here had been fearful, and the stench was sickening. The dead were swollen until their strained and torn clothing could hardly contain their bodies; some were very giants in size." Capt. von Fritsch noted that the tremendous slaughter quickly spawned a new industry in the small town, "an extensive coffin mart & embalmers harvest field. The coffins were stacked on the streets blockading the sidewalks. These coffin speculators make an enormous profit."[31]

With the town and the area east of Seminar Ridge now back in federal control, Schurz "at once rode with some staff-officers and orderlies to satisfy myself whether there were any wounded men left in the houses or on the fields beyond, where my troops had been engaged on the first day of the battle." After his reunion with Schimmelfennig, Schurz visited the battlefield and then went to the corps hospital to visit with the men. "No contrast could have been gloomier than that between the light-hearted hilarity of our breakfast and my visit to the battlefield." The Confederates had removed most of their own dead, "but ours lay still in ghastly array on the ground where they had fallen. There can be no more hideous sight than that of the corpses on a battlefield after they have been exposed a day or more to the sun in warm weather — the bodies swollen to monstrous size, the faces bloated and black, the eyes bulging out with a dead stare, all their features puffed out almost beyond recognition, some lying singly or in rows, others in heaps, having fallen over one another, some attitudes of peaceful repose, others with arms raised, others in a sitting posture, others on their knees, others clawing the earth, many horribly distorted by what must have been a frightful death-struggle."[32]

30 Mark H. Dunkelman, "Additional Notes on the 154th New York at Gettysburg," *Gettysburg Magazine*, 29 (July 2003), 79. Writing in the Atlanta Constitution on Oct. 13, 1896, Surgeon Jay Kling of the 55th Ohio, who also examined Armistead, wrote: "a rifle ball had entered his body in the right lumbar region, passing through the kidney and bowels, making its exit in front. He died the next morning, July 4th, about 1:20 o'clock. His body was buried in the rear of the garden connected with the cottage."

31 Priest, *McMahon's Diary*, 54; Smith, "Gettysburg," 307; Butts, *Gallant Captain*, 45.

32 Schurz, *Reminiscences*, III, 34, 37.

From the battlefields Schurz made the rounds of the makeshift hospitals and as many barns, houses, and other places he could find where the Union wounded had been taken. He found them "crowded with moaning and wailing human beings, and still an unceasing procession of stretchers and ambulances was coming in. A heavy rain set in during the day—the usual rain after a battle—and large numbers had to remain unprotected in the open, there being no room left under roof. I saw long rows of men lying under the eaves of the buildings, the water pouring down upon their bodies in streams. Most of the operating-tables were placed in the open, where the light was best, some of them partially protected against the rain by tarpaulins or blankets stretched upon poles. There stood the surgeons, their sleeves rolled up to the elbows, their bare arms as well as their linen aprons smeared with blood, their knives not seldom held between their teeth while they were helping a patient on or off the table, or had their hands otherwise occupied; around them pools of blood and amputated arms or legs in heaps, sometimes more than man-high." The stream of wounded lifted onto the tables seemed never-ending. "As a wounded man was lifted on the table, often shrieking with pain as the attendants handled him, the surgeon quickly examined the wound and resolved upon cutting off the injured limb. Some ether was administered, and the body put in position in a moment. The surgeon snatched his knife from between his teeth, where it had been while his hands were busy, wiped it rapidly once or twice across the blood-stained apron, and the cutting began. The operation accomplished, the surgeon would look around with a deep sigh, and then—'next!' And so it went on, hour after hour." Schurz was stunned by the misery and the reactions of the wounded, which ranged from grim humor to heartrending despair. "Some cried for their mothers or fathers, some screamed out in pain, some remained eerily quiet, while still others wished only for death to put them out of their misery."[33] Schurz would never forget these scenes.

That evening Robert Hubbard, surgeon of the 17th Connecticut, managed to find time to write home. "This is a glorious 4th of July to us & a sad & mortifying one to the rebels & Copperheads generally." His regiment "has covered itself with glory," he wrote with obvious pride. "The whole army has acquitted itself splendidly. The Eleventh Corps has redeemed its reputation. It maintained its position unfalteringly to the end." In the following days, others would voice similar sentiments. John McMahon wrote in his diary that "The 11th Corps has got a good name this time. Our boys all fought well this time."[34]

33 Schurz, *Reminiscences*, III, 37.

34 Hubbard letters to Nellie, July 4, 1863; Priest, *McMahon's Diary*, 54.

☽ ☽ ☽

Dawn on July 5 found the Confederate army in full retreat. When it became apparent the rebels were gone, orders arrived for the XI Corps to move out. Elements of the corps took to the road about 5:00 pm. John McMahon "was glad to leave for the stench was getting so very bad, enough to make one sick." Struggling over roads turned "horribly muddy" by the rain and the thousands of feet that preceded them, the troops labored along, halting at midnight to camp about "five or six miles from Cemetery Hill." On the following day the XI Corps moved south through cloudy, stormy weather to Emmitsburg, camping near the spot it occupied the night before the battle began.[35]

The corps was on the road at 4:00 am on July 6. Up the muddy inclining roads they struggled, then down equally taxing declines, to Emmitsburg and then onward, laboring across the rough Catoctin Mountains to Middletown thirty miles away. Intense, stifling July heat took its toll on the men. Drenched in their own perspiration, they pushed on through the heat, the mud, and the occasional rain showers. The march did not end until July 7 when it finally halted amid "a furious rain that drenched us to the skin." Capt. Frederick Winkler felt lucky to find a loyal Union family who treated him very well. That night he "Had a nice, clean, white bed to sleep in" which he considered a great "luxury." Lt. Col. Meysenburg recorded that "A great number of men are without shoes. Nothing can prevent straggling."[36]

On the 8th the march continued to Boonsboro where the rebels attacked Gen. Judson Kilpatrick's cavalry. The 58th New York fought a brief skirmish with marauding rebel cavalry, driving them off but losing Private N. M. Ahlers captive and Private John Hoffenback wounded. Rushing forward, Winkler hoped they would "have another battle this side of the river" where "we can concentrate a large force and, if their retreat is cut off, we can give the rebels a blow which will go far to end the war."[37] But when they arrived at the scene of the action west of town the rebels had already vanished. The column halted to settle into camp for the night.

Relieved by a division of the V Corps on July 9, the XI Corps concentrated in an area at the foot of South Mountain. That day Maj. Charles Howard wrote to his mother that nearly half of the corps was forced to march barefooted "or suffering from poor shoes." The previous day Gen. Ames had reported to Meysenburg on the number of

35 Priest, *McMahon's Diary*, July 5, 1863; Keeler diary, July 6, 1963, USMHI.

36 Winkler, *Letters*, 72; Meysenburg journal, July 7, 1863.

37 Winkler, *Letters*, 72.

troops in his division who were shoeless and sockless. The First Brigade reported 142 men without shoes, while in the Second Brigade 428 had no shoes and 752 no socks. Ames added that the First Brigade had only one day of rations on hand with no sugar and only two days in the supply train. The Second Brigade had a total of only three days of rations, and these consisting only of coffee and hardtack.[38]

Capt. Benjamin Stone on the staff of Orland Smith's brigade found "everyone was in high spirits & bodily misery. When we reached Md line over 300 of our soldiers were absolutely barefooted & many more as good as shoeless. We had no time to stop & get up supplies from the depots." Lt. Jacob Mader of the 61st Ohio wrote home to tell his fiancée that he "had no change of clothing since this campaign commenced. I made one days march entirely bare footed. We could not get shoes or boots for love or money." George Metcalf found "Scattered along our entire line of march and under every meeting-house shed and every shade tree were the state militia with their new, Bright guns and clean uniforms. They made a wonderful contrast to us. We were ragged, smoky, grimy and dirty. We had not seen water enough (except rain) in five days to wash our faces even once. I had on only one shoe, the other foot was bare. My pantaloons were minus one leg below the knee, leaving the leg without any covering from there down."[39]

Despite the hardships, the troops pushed forward. The sound of artillery fire could be heard in the distance throughout the day and into the next morning, but nothing further developed. On the 10th they marched to within about three miles of Hagerstown, expecting a fight at any time, but again nothing developed and there appeared to be some confusion about the whereabouts and intentions of Lee's army. "We have no knowledge of the movement of the enemy at our headquarters," Capt. Winker reported, "but from the quiet that prevails infer his retreat across the Potomac." Continuing on, Gen. Kilpatrick's cavalry in the advance, a force of eight regiments, numbering only about 1,200 men, was hurried forward in advance of the rest of the corps to provide support should the mounted troops run into trouble as they neared Hagerstown. "This traveling at the heels of cavalrymen was rather novel to us, and the rapid marching was not very pleasant," noted a soldier in the 17th Connecticut. "However, we surprised the enemy, dashed upon his lines, took about one hundred

38 Charles H. Howard letter to mother, July 9, 1863, Howard Papers Bowdoin; Ames letter to Meysenburg, July 8, 1863, RG 393, Pt. 2, 11th Army Corps, Letters Received, 1863-1864. Box 2, NARA.

39 As quoted in Baumgartner, *Buckeye Blood*, 188-89.

prisoners, drove them in disorder through the town to their strong entrenchments in the rear of it, which constituted the left defenses of their main front line."[40]

That same day, July 10, Howard took the opportunity to issue General Orders No. 18 to express his appreciation to the troops for their recent efforts. "The General again thanks his Command for what has been done during the last month. You have now met the enemy and feel conscious that you have done your duty. On the first day of July with the First Corps and Buford's Division of Cavalry you held double your numbers in check from 12 M until night and thus opened the way for the victory that followed. On the Second you held an important position during the cannonade and repulsed the enemy when already within your Batteries and breaking through your lines. On the third the same post was strongly held under the severest cannonade of the war. Our Batteries aided by our infantry contributed a full share to the repulse of the enemy's last attempt to drive the Army from its position. The Eleventh Corps, as a Corps, has done well—well in marching, well in fighting; the sacrifices it has made shall not be forgotten. In the retrospect your General feels satisfied. Now we must make one more effort. Let there be no wavering, no doubt. Our cause is right and our success sure."[41]

The XI Corps passed through Hagerstown on July 11 to the approval of enthusiastic "hurrahs" from the local emergency militia. Citizens lined the streets, showering the men with an ovation of cheers that heartened them beyond words. "I think it is a wonder that any one will cheer us," marveled John McMahon, "or look at us, for the dirtiest man that ever walked the street of Lima is no comparison to us soldiers. We are dirty from head to foot. . . . However the people seem to appreciate what we are doing for them and show it in waving their hats & flags."[42]

The army finally caught up with the Confederates the next day between Hagerstown and Funkstown. Andrew Boies in the 33rd Massachusetts took time to confide to his diary the good news that had arrived from the west. "Well, we have given them a sound thrashing upon 'loyal soil,' and now to cap what we have done, Vicksburg is ours also. It seems that the tide has turned in our favor. Oh! Jeff, where are you now? Where is your Stone-wall, and your Long-street, and your Barks-dale, with your 'legion,' who came upon the Northern soil to whip the 'cursed Yanks?' But the Army of the Potomac met them, gave them battle, and is now in full pursuit of the retreating foe, and echo answers, their 'Stonewall' has tumbled down, their 'Longstreet' has become a

40 Winkler, *Letters*, 75; "Seventeenth Regiment," *The Connecticut War Record*, Vol. I, No. 2, 36-37, in Unpublished MOLLUS Papers, Box No. 41, USAMHI.

41 O. O. Howard, General Orders No. 18, July 10, 1863, RG 393, Pt. 2, 5321 & 5348, NARA.

42 Reid, *Ohio in the War*, 474; Priest, *McMahon's Diary*, 57.

short one, and their 'Barksdale' has found that he barked up the wrong tree, while many of their 'legion' are prisoners and many are lying dead upon the blood-stained field of Gettysburg."[43]

That night a group of officers of the XI Corps, seeking some momentary relaxation, visited the Hagerstown Female Seminary. In the presence of the women the small group of men affected their best manners. Col. von Gilsa played waltzes on the seminary's piano while his fellow officers enjoyed the evening dancing with obliging young ladies. Von Fritsch recorded that "we young fellows danced with the girls, to the very amusing disgust and horror of the old lady principal." As they danced, the corps commanders met in a council of war to decide upon the advisability of attacking Lee's army as it tried to cross the Potomac River. On behalf of the I and XI Corps, the two units that had suffered the most at Gettysburg, Gens. Wadsworth and Howard voted to attack the rebels before they could cross the Potomac into the relative safety of Virginia. All of the others, citing losses and the fatigue of their troops as excuses for not engaging the Confederates, voted "no."[44] The battered remnants of the Army of Northern Virginia completed their escape across the Potomac River into Virginia on July 13-14.

☽ ☽ ☽

Capt. Frederick Winkler expressed concern that the public, its expectations heightened by sensational news stories of the Northern victory, would be disappointed by Lee's escape, but he was content to see an end to the campaign. He thought an attack by the greatly weakened Northern regiments on the "strong defensive position of the enemy" would have been problematic. The army "needs more men and re-organization before it will be reliably effective." Few outside the army agreed with him. Both the public and the president were disappointed the Southern army had escaped back to Virginia. Nor did many of Winkler's own comrades share his opinion. Adj. Augustus Horstmann believed "The failure produced a great drooping in the spirits of the soldiers & great discontent showed itself everywhere." Quartermaster William G. Le Duc was more pointed, and not a little sarcastic: "The Army of the Potomac followed up in a leisurely way, and camped, and fortified their camp, waiting for Lee to escape across the Potomac. The soldiers were anxious to go in and make an

43 Boies, *Thirty-third Massachusetts*, 35.

44 Butts, *Gallant Captain*, 90; Howard, "Gettysburg Campaign," 708-09; *Meade, With Meade at Gettysburg*, 187.

end of the war, and go home. They could not understand such generalship, and became very impatient."[45]

Surgeon Henry Van Aernam summed up the feelings of many in the XI Corps in a letter to his wife. "There has never been such a blunder in the army as allowing them to escape. They were completely within our grasp and with energy, boldness and promptness that army and the rebellion could have been crushed at a blow! We were at Boonsboro on the morning of the 8th and could easily have reached Williamsport on the morning of the 9th. We should have then met a defeated and divided (a portion over the river) enemy—and what is more all that day they were without ammunition! We came here as I said on the 8th and unaccountably let day after day go by without striking a blow! Put a Generals shoulder straps upon a man and he loses all common sense at once. He seems giddy with his elevation. Every private in the army knew that every moments delay was disastrous to us as it gave time for the rebs to escape—to entrench themselves likewise. . . . When we were chasing the rebs, the boys, although barefooted and ragged and half fed, were cheerful on their forced marches, but today they feel chagrined and humbugged. They are silent and morose and what little they do say is damning the foolishness and shortsightedness of the officers. They are right for they have endured everything, braved everything for the sake of success, and success bountiful and lasting was within our grasp—but lost by the imbecility of commandry. Our army is an anomoly—it is an army of Lions commanded by jackasses! . . . am heartsick and discouraged and thoroughly disgusted with such folly and humbugging."[46]

45 Horstmann, Battle of Gettysburg, GNMP; William G. Le Duc, *Recollections of a Civil War Quartermaster: The Autobiography of William G. Le Duc* (St. Paul, MN: North Central Publishing Company, 1963), 99.

46 Van Aernam Papers, letter July 15, 1863, USMHI.

Chapter 16

"I Saw No Running, No Undue Haste"

Reflecting on the Eleventh Corps at Gettysburg

THE BATTLE OF GETTYSBURG MARKED a milestone in the history of the Army of the Potomac. For the first time the Federal army in the East won an unmistakable victory in a major battle with the Army of Northern Virginia. Receiving the news of the battle's outcome, Joseph Hooker wrote to Howard to congratulate him on the conduct of the XI Corps. "I am rejoiced that yourself and command acquired so much fame at Gettysburg. It must be a great satisfaction to you especially." On July 4, even the *New York Times*, previously a bastion of anti-foreign criticism, reported that the XI Corps had redeemed the disgrace of Chancellorsville.[1] Yet, the good will engendered by the triumph did not long survive the echo of the guns. It was only a matter of time until the initial jubilation ceased. Subsequent stories saw the journalistic chameleons change their attitude with correspondents pointing accusing fingers at the despised "Dutchmen" for "running away" on the first day of the battle. Soon, the stories returned the familiar anti-foreign sentiment so prevalent after Chancellorsville.

Regrettably, it is this stereotype that has continued to be endorsed by most historians. Since Edwin Coddington's *The Gettysburg Campaign: A Study in Command* has long been regarded as the "bible" of Gettysburg studies, it is perhaps best that we begin our analysis with that influential work. While Coddington's study has many positive attributes to recommend it, his examination of theXI Corps is not one of them. To begin with, if one looks at the sources listed in the book's bibliography, the only

1 Hooker to Howard, July 3, 1863, Bowdoin College; *New York Times*, July 4, 1863, 1.

manuscript collections of officers or men in the XI Corps that Coddington used were those of Howard, Schurz and Barlow. Of all the published regimental or other unit histories that he consulted, the only one from the XI Corps was a history of a nine-month regiment. The only other published sources used from the corps were the memoirs of Howard and Schurz and an article by Charles H. Howard. Compared with other corps that were heavily engaged this is a very sparse source base and is also heavily weighted toward the two Howards and Barlow, the latter of whom clearly disliked his men, especially the Germans, and wished only to vindicate himself from culpability. This is a familiar pattern with most early historians, and even many of more recent vintage.

Coddington begins his assessment of the XI Corps by quoting a letter that Barlow wrote to his mother in which he disingenuously claimed that "we ought to have held the place easily" but the Rebel "skirmishers had hardly attacked us before my men began to run. No fight at all was made." The historian appears to accept this self-serving nonsense as established fact. "The old hue and cry about 'heavy masses' of the enemy overwhelming the thin lines of the two small divisions of the XI Corps," Coddington wrote, "makes better rhetoric than historical truth."[2] As shown in previous chapters, von Gilsa's brigade, which bore the immediate impact of the Rebel assault, was, in fact, greatly outnumbered, as was Barlow's entire division. Nor does Coddington account for the numerical superiority of the Confederate artillery, which also enjoyed positions allowing it to direct a converging fire on the outnumbered XI Corps batteries, or the terrible disadvantage in position that the corps occupied because of Barlow's own disobedience of orders. Any military officer or serious historian of military affairs is well aware of the inherent weakness of a salient for defense, but it appears to have escaped Coddington. Likewise, he seems to have paid no attention to the other inherent weaknesses of the position Barlow occupied or the fact that because of his unauthorized move the Confederates enjoyed such an advantage in numbers at the point of attack that they could reprise their accomplishment at Chancellorsville by enveloping both Federal flanks at once. All of this eluded Coddington's shallow attempt at analysis.

Coddington goes on to an equally unsophisticated attempt to relate casualties suffered and inflicted to the quality of the fighting done by the I and XI Corps. He says that for a loss of about 40 percent of his own men, Schurz "inflicted losses on the enemy of about 14 percent. Ninety percent of the Confederate casualties were listed as killed or wounded, and only 10 percent as captured or missing, whereas 50 percent of

2 Coddington, *Gettysburg Campaign*, 304-05.

the Union losses were counted in the latter category."[3] Aside from not providing any comparable data for the I Corps, there are several flaws in this argument. First, it does not take into account the relative positions of the I and XI Corps. The latter was positioned on an open plain of softly undulating ground with the almshouse complex as the only real barrier to an enemy advance, and that was easily turned. The corps was subject to a converging crossfire of artillery from Rodes's and Early's guns, the former of which were also in position to inflict a plunging fire. Finally, the troops available were not sufficient to both protect the I Corps flank and successfully dispute the arrival of an entire new Confederate division on and beyond its own right flank. On the other hand, the I Corps defended an area with several woods, railroad cuts, and other obstructions that could be used for defense, as well as holding a position that required the Confederates on most occasions to advance on an upgrade. Then too, the I Corps was under no obligation to protect the left of the XI Corps or to hold back a new division arriving on its exposed left flank. Since it was not ordered to hold a specific position, and since Doubleday had orders to hold as long as possible and then retire, the I Corps had the flexibility to extend or contract its line to conform to defensive terrain and the number of men it had available. Interestingly, as soon as it *did* become outflanked on its left by Pender's division it began a hasty retreat. This was of course no different than what happened to the XI Corps when its right was turned.

Coddington asserts that any advantage the I Corps might have had in position was offset by "the loss of its commanding general at the beginning of the engagement."[4] Yet, could not the same be said of the XI Corps? With the death of Reynolds, Howard assumed command of the field which left Schurz to act as corps commander. It was the first time he had led the corps in a combat situation. Further, with Schurz's elevation, Schimmelfenning now led a division in combat for the first time and von Amsberg likewise had his first experience in brigade command in combat. One could certainly argue that Schimmelfennig did a much better job than Brig. Gen. Thomas A. Rowley who replaced Doubleday in division command and was later court-martialed for drunkenness at Gettysburg, but the point is that both of the corps experienced command changes as they went into action so there is no reason to cite this as something being detrimental to the I Corps but not to the XI.

Then there is also the question of Coddington's numbers. Comparing the percentage of captured and missing among XI Corps casualties with that among the Confederates is hardly valid since the Rebels held the field at the end of the day. They

3 Coddington, *Gettysburg Campaign*, 305.

4 Coddington, *Gettysburg Campaign*, 307.

had an opportunity to identify those "missing" who might be killed or wounded and to remove their wounded so they did not become prisoners. The XI Corps enjoyed neither of these advantages. If one of its soldiers was killed and no one noticed him fall he was listed as "missing." If one was wounded and could not move from the battlefield, he might be recorded as either "captured" or simply "missing." It would be more valid, if any such attempt at numerical comparison must be made, that it be between the I and XI Corps, both of which retired from the field where their losses occurred. If we do this, then the most detailed exploration of the question, John Busey and David Martin's *Regimental Strengths and Losses at Gettysburg*, reveals that the I Corps lost 49.6 percent during the entire battle and the XI Corps lost 41.2 percent, respectively the highest and second highest proportion of losses by any Union corps. For the I Corps the great majority occurred on July 1, while the XI also incurred significant losses on July 2.[5]

Similarly, the two corps ranked in the same order when it came to "captured and missing"—the I losing 17.7 percent and the XI 16.4 percent.[6] It was the I Corps that lost the higher percentage of captured and missing, *not* the XI. It is also interesting that most listings of colors lost suggest that the I Corps also lost more than the XI on July 1. The I Corps lost six: 104th New York (Perrin's South Carolina brigade), 149th New York national colors (55th Virginia), 149th New York state colors (42nd Mississippi), 56th Pennsylvania (2nd Mississippi), 150th Pennsylvania (14th North Carolina), and I Corps Headquarters flag (Perrin's South Carolina brigade). The XI lost only three: 119th New York (13th Georgia), 157th New York (possibly by 12th Georgia), 26th Wisconsin state colors (possibly by 12th Georgia or 44th Georgia).

Coddington maintains that the XI Corps inflicted only 14 percent losses on the attacking Confederates. Southern losses are difficult to determine and always problematic because of lost records, incomplete returns, and different ways of recording losses. A. T. Cowell, for one, noted that Confederate records admit the loss of 5,150 captives while documents in the Union adjutant general's office record the names of 12,227 Rebel prisoners. He also cites the example of Lane's North Carolina brigade which reported 660 losses, but was listed as losing 389 in the *Official Records*. Recognizing these difficulties, if we accept the work of Busey and Martin, Gordon's brigade is a good test of this myth because he was not seriously engaged following the first day except for sharpshooting in the town. So, the great majority of his losses were suffered on July 1. Gordon himself wrote in a letter to his wife that he had "lost about

5 Busey and Martin, *Regimental Strengths*, 458.

6 Busey and Martin, *Regimental Strengths*, 461.

350 men."[7] That would be a loss just short of twenty percent—hardly "inconsequential." Busey and Martin place his loss at 537, which they calculated at 29.6 percent. Only one of the regiments in the brigade lost less than 14 percent, all of the rest were more and four of the six lost more than a quarter of their men. This is quite a different picture than that presented by Coddington. And it includes the 26th Georgia which was held back to support the artillery. Eliminating it would increase Gordon's percentage of losses even more. When one deletes the 26th Georgia, the effect of the XI Corps resistance becomes all the more apparent. Casualties for the remaining regiments in his brigade numbered 505 of 1,498 or 33.7 percent.

Similarly, Coddington, after claiming that the XI Corps lines below Cemetery Hill on July 2 were all protected by stone walls, asserts that von Gilsa and Harris offered "feeble resistance," claiming that they fired only "a few scattered shots" and then "ran away almost to a man."[8] For this he does not cite a single XI Corps source but instead relies upon two I Corps sources. Coddington goes on to say that Howard and Ames had so little confidence in their troops that they required Carroll's brigade from the II Corps to remain with them in case of another attack and that Howard impressed other troops as well. Of course, given the depleted ranks of the XI Corps, and especially Ames's division, it was quite reasonable that Howard and Ames would seek support because they simply did not have enough men left to form a solid defensive line with appropriate reserves. The same scenario took place, for example, when Greene called for reinforcements on the evening of July 2 and held onto them until the balance of the XII Corps returned to its position on Culp's Hill. And it occurred on many other occasions when officers from various corps called for reinforcements. These instances in no way indicated a loss of confidence in their own troops, only recognition that their strength was insufficient to hold their assigned positions.

Although Coddington claimed not to blame the officers or men of the XI Corps, his comments and conclusions about their conduct on July 1 and July 2 leave it clear that he considered them to be less reliable than the balance of the Army of the Potomac. Yet, as we have seen, his analysis was based largely on sources from outside the corps, from people who had never considered the XI Corps to be a real part of the army, and on faulty data and reasoning. Having disposed of the most sacred of Gettysburg sources, it is time to move on to look at July 1, July 2, and the aftermath.

7 Cowell, *Tactics at Gettysburg*, 182; Gordon to wife, July 7, 1863, Gordon Family Papers, University of Georgia Special Collections.

8 Coddington, *Gettysburg Campaign*, 436.

☽ ☽ ☽

On the morning of July 1 Buford's cavalry division and Reynolds's I Corps were heavily engaged with a larger Confederate force on the outskirts of Gettysburg. Using the data in Busey and Martin's *Regimental Strengths and Losses at Gettysburg*, there were 16,293 Union troops on hand—12,220 infantry and 4,073 cavalry[9]—to oppose, initially, A. P. Hill's corps of 21,948 infantry. Ordered by Reynolds to move as quickly as possible to his aid, the XI Corps marched some thirteen miles over rough roads through warm, humid weather, through a drenching rain, then on over muddy rutted roads, their pace increasing to the quick step and the last two to three miles at the double-quick. By the time they arrived they were exhausted, but they had covered the distance in only about four hours and they arrived in time to prevent the I Corps right from being turned by Rodes's newly arriving division that was coming in directly on that exposed flank.

Engaging the Confederates, the XI Corps skirmishers pushed back those of Doles's and O'Neal's Rebel brigades, including Maj. Eugene Blackford's select sharpshooters, an exceptionally skillful feat for a force initially numbering less than 200 men on its skirmish line. Col. Josephus Hall of the 5th Alabama, on the flank of O'Neal's brigade facing the XI Corps confirmed that the fire he received from the Federals caused "a very severe loss." Then, when O'Neal attempted to attack the flank of the I Corps, the enfilade fire delivered by the 45th New York and Dilger's battery caught the Confederates in a deadly crossfire. Col. Samuel Pickens of the 12th Alabama stated that "the regiment on our left gave way, being flanked in [*sic*] a large force." The brigade commander, Col. O'Neal, likewise asserted that "We were compelled to fall back as the regiment on the extreme left, being flanked by a superior force of the enemy, gave way."[10] An estimated 300 Confederates fell into XI Corps hands as prisoners. The so-called "superior force" was a portion of the 45th New York. The XI Corps performed its responsibility well in protecting the I Corps flank.

Throughout the early afternoon, Dilger's and Wheeler's batteries, despite being out-gunned by Confederate artillery that enjoyed superior positions on the slopes of Oak Hill, dealt out considerable punishment. William Carter of the King William Artillery wrote that they "were pretty hotly engaged," certainly an understatement. Dilger pummeled Capt. R. C. M. Page's Morris Artillery. The battery loss was described as "heavy"—four killed, 26 wounded, including Capt. Page, and 17 horses. Under what

9 Busey and Martin, *Regimental Strengths*, 16, 103.

10 Bachelder, *History*, 259, 261, 312; *OR* 27, pt. 2, 592.

Lt. Col. Thomas Carter, commanding the Rebel artillery battalion, characterized as "a very destructive" fire, Page's battery had to be withdrawn over the crest of the hill to escape further punishment.[11] Both the infantry and artillery engaged against O'Neal, Doles, and Carter's artillery battalion acquitted themselves admirably.

When Krzyzanowski arrived, his skirmishers from the 119th New York drove back Doles's and Blackford's skirmishers and took possession of the Crawford barn and home and portions of the almshouse complex. With the arrival of Barlow's division, von Gilsa's skirmishers also drove back the Rebels in their front, then pushed forward to seize Blocher's Knoll. Certainly the latter was an error in judgment by Barlow, but his troops executed the orders promptly and successfully. In fact, the aggressiveness of the XI Corps skirmishers and Barlow's movement forward greatly worried the Confederates who, before Early's arrival, feared that their own flank might be turned.[12] Thus far, the corps had been quite successful, only the critical portion of the day was but minutes away with the arrival of heavy Confederate reinforcements on both the Union left and its right. The veteran division under Gen. Jubal Early was about to pounce on the right flank of the XI Corps which was in the air and separated from any direct infantry support by Barlow's ill-advised disobedience of orders.

One of the early historians of Gettysburg whose works have been widely used by others was Glenn Tucker. In his *High Tide at Gettysburg: The Campaign in Pennsylvania* he asserts that on July1 the battle north of town was "fought by two divisions of the XI Corps mainly against two Georgia brigades, the Confederates were heavily outnumbered, even after Hays and Avery had brought their brigades into the attack."[13] This was patently false. First, Confederate brigades and divisions were on average larger than their Union counterparts. Second, the XI Corps was also in action against O'Neal's brigade, not just the "two Georgia brigades," as well as Hays and Avery. Third, Tucker does not mention the great numerical superiority the Confederates enjoyed in artillery. Fourth, he does not take into consideration the relative positions of the opposing forces. Fifth, even his basic comparison of infantry forces is flawed. Using the numbers from Busey and Martin reveals that the brigades of Doles, Gordon, Hays, Avery and O'Neal and the Rebel artillery brought into action numbered 8,019 men and 32 guns. The Union brigades of von Amsberg, Krzyzanowski, Ames, von Gilsa and Coster with their supporting batteries counted 6,476 men and 20 guns. These figures make it clear that the XI Corps was outnumbered by the Confederates it faced

11 Carter to "dear Col." in the King William Artillery File, GNMP; *OR* 27, pt. 2, 603.

12 Pfanz, *First Day*, 220; Gordon, *Reminiscences*, 151.

13 Tucker, *High Tide*, 160.

and had available to it over a third fewer artillery pieces. If one looks at the critical portion of the battlefield where the assault on the Union right flank took place, von Gilsa's infantry was outnumbered 3.4 to 1. Including Ames, the Federals were still outnumbered by 1.4 to 1, and if one includes Hays and Avery who took part in the struggle that afternoon then it becomes 2.5 to 1. The most important factor, aside from the untenable position assumed by Gen. Barlow, was that the superiority of numbers enjoyed by the Confederates at the point of attack allowed them, as it had at Chancellorsville, to easily outflank the Union lines and attack them from the flank and rear.

Tucker goes on to claim pejoratively that "Von Gilsa's German New Yorkers broke. They had not expected such internecine fury in New World fighting. . . . The situation on the Federal front was rendered critical by the flight of Von Gilsa's brigade." Aside from the fact that over half of von Gilsa's men were from Pennsylvania—not New York—as we have seen earlier in this text these men did not run away. They, together with Barlow's other brigade under Ames, fought. Their casualty rates prove it. But so do the comments of their opponents. There were, as there always are, grandiose statements about sweeping the enemy from the field, of valiant charges that left the enemy panic stricken, and other such boasting. But of those veterans who wrote serious descriptions of what they saw this was portrayed as no cakewalk. Gen. Richard Ewell, commanding the corps to which most of the attackers belonged, described it as an "obstinate contest." Gen. Jubal Early leading the attacking division portrayed it as a "hot contest." Gen. John B. Gordon, leading the assault, recalled meeting "a most obstinate resistance." In a letter home on July 7 he wrote of "a desperate fight."[14]

They were not the only ones who believed the conflict to be desperate. Sidney Richardson Jackson, Company I, 21st Georgia, called it "a hard fight. . . . our loss was very heavy . . . I think they fight harder in their our Country, then they do in Virginia." To Joseph Hilton, 26th Georgia, it was "a stubborn fight." Marcus Hefner, Company H, 57th North Carolina, asserted "I can inform you that the army met there it was the hardest fite [*sic*] I ever was in." George W. O'Neal, Company G, 31st Georgia, met "stubborn resistance." Michael O'Connor, Company F, 6th Louisiana, experienced "a heavy fire of artillery and infantry . . . a stubborn resistance." William J. Seymour, Hays's brigade staff, encountered "a heavy fire. . . . The musketry was very severe and we feared that Gordon would be borne back." Patrick McGee, Company E, 9th

14 *OR* 27, pt. 2, 445, 469, 492; Gordon to wife, July 7, 1863, Gordon Family Papers.

Louisiana, recalled "The fighting was fast and furious."[15] And this is only a sampling, there were more.

Glenn Tucker continued his comments about July 1 by claiming that "Gordon's losses were inconsequential, so were those of Hays and Hoke."[16] This myth has also been perpetuated by a host of writers, and not only those influenced by a Southern perspective. It is evident from the casualties discussed earlier in this chapter that Gordon's brigade did not have an easy time on July 1. There were obviously quite a few men in the XI Corps who did not "run away." These men were defeated, but they rallied around the almshouse, they rallied again at the edge of town, they fought in the town, and then they rallied on Cemetery Hill. It was a fighting withdrawal, not a panicked rout.

In his *They Met at Gettysburg*, Edward J. Stackpole ascribed the loss of the forward positions of the First and XI Corps to the latter. "The retreat of the XI Corps, first to break, uncovered the right flank and rear of the First Corps, which might otherwise have held for a longer period. The latter well-disciplined organization, however, effected its withdrawal in reasonably good order and what remained of it was placed on the left of Steinwehr's reserve brigade."[17] This is another conclusion frequently encountered in books on the battle. The First Corps could have held out if only the XI Corps had not broken. This argument ignores the repeated pleas of Doubleday for reinforcements and his own admission that he ordered a retreat when he was no longer able to hold his position. In fact, in the same manner in which the XI Corps was forced to retire when its right was turned by Early's division, the left of the First Corps was turned by Pender's division, placing Doubleday in the same untenable position that caused the retreat of the XI Corps. He reacted the same way, he ordered a retreat.

Even the most novice student of military history knows that being outflanked is a serious matter that usually causes a defending force to retire. This is exactly what happened to *both* the First and XI Corps on July 1. They both held out until flanked by a larger force of enemy troops. In a speech given in 1896, Confederate Gen. John Gordon explained that Early was able to throw his division "squarely on the right flank" of the Federals. "Every man who was in that war on either side knows exactly

15 Jackson to parents, July 8, 1863, 21st Georgia File, GNMP; Hilton to Cousin, n.d., 26th Georgia File, GNMP; Hefner to wife, July 10, 1863, 57th North Carolina File, GNMP; O'Neal, reminiscences, 31st Georgia File, GNMP; Gannon, "The 6th Louisiana," 90; Jones, "A Louisiana Tiger," manuscript, Hays Brigade File, GNMP; letter of Patrick McGee in *Confederate Veteran*, November 1906, 499.

16 Tucker, *High Tide*, 173.

17 Stackpole, *They Met at Gettysburg*, 141.

what that meant—squarely on the flank—and the fact that that portion of Meade's army melted was no disparagement of his courage, for the Old Guard of Napoleon himself would have been as surely and swiftly shattered." In his memoirs Gordon asserted that "Any troops that were ever marshalled would, under like conditions, have been as surely and swiftly shattered. There was no alternative for Howard's men except to break and fly, or to throw down their arms and surrender. Under the concentrated fire from front and flank, the marvel is that any escaped."[18]

It is generally accepted that the XI Corps broke first, but there is some interesting evidence which at least provides a more nuanced scenario. There are numerous observations by members of the First Corps who claimed to see the XI Corps break before their own corps retired. These are well-known, having been published in accounts of the battle. Less well known are some of the observations of participants from the XI Corps. Shortly before the retreat began, Doubleday sent a request for reinforcements to Schurz who at that time was completely engaged and had no one to send. In his memoirs, Schurz adds some detail to Doubleday's request, explaining that "the right wing of the First Corps, which had fought heroically all day, had been pressed back." Notice that he says it was the right wing of the First Corps that was "pressed back." Later in his memoirs, Schurz comments that "When Schimmelfennig saw the First Corps retreating from Oak Ridge, he ordered the 45th [New York] to the rear," leaving the impression that the right of the First Corps retired *before* Schimmelfennig who was in command of the left of the XI Corps line. In fact, Doubleday himself confirmed this, explaining that he thought "the retreat would have been a very successful one if it had not been unfortunately the case that a portion of the XI Corps, which had held out very well on the extreme right, had been surrounded and had fallen back *at the same time that my right flank fell back*" [italics added].[19] This seems to confirm that Doubleday's right was driven in about the same time that Barlow's division was retreating on the XI Corps right, and thus *before* Schimmelfennig ordered von Amsberg to retire.

In his official report of the engagement, Doubleday described his actions when his corps retired. "I remained at the seminary superintending the final movement until thousands of hostile bayonets made their appearance around the sides of the building. I then rode back and rejoined my command, nearly all of whom were filing through the

18 Speech given by Gordon at Keystone State Normal School in Kutztown, October 24, 1896; Gordon, *Reminiscences*, 151.

19 Schurz, *Reminiscences*, III, 11, 257; Howard, *Autobiography*, 416-17; Howard, "Howard's Reminiscences," *National Tribune*, November 20, 1884.

town. As we passed through the streets, the pale and frightened inhabitants came out of their houses, offering us food and drink and the expression of their deep sorrow and sympathy."[20] Note that he says "nearly all" of his men were filing through town and that citizens were offering them food and drink. Citizens would certainly not be in the streets if fighting was taking place and there was imminent danger, suggesting that when Doubleday retired the Confederates had not yet invested the city and were not yet sweeping its streets with musketry.

Captain George Warren of the 157th New York, leading Schimmelfennig's provost guard, retired from the field riding with Capt. Dilger. "Before we left we saw troops retreating over the hill toward the town, which proved to be the First Corps, as I saw members of the 76th N. Y. with whom I was acquainted." Warren asserted that "When the rear of the Eleventh Corps passed through the village the Rebels were entering from both east and west."[21] This appears to have been exactly the case since the men toward the rear of the retreat took fire from both directions and either fought their way through or were cut off and surrounded. It seems that in whatever order the various regiments retreated, it was the rear guard of the XI Corps that entered town last since it took fire from the east where Hays and Avery were outflanking the right of the XI Corps and the west where the First Corps had likewise withdrawn.

There were other remarks that supported this. Lt. Col. Dobke in the 45th New York wrote that "the First Corps on our left gave way and exposed our left flank." Major Benjamin Willis of the 119th New York claimed his troops "stood firmly until the First Division Second Corps [no doubt he meant Second Division I Corps] had fallen back toward the town." Confederate Gen. George Doles declared that as his men advanced the I Corps on Seminary Ridge retired toward the railroad. Gen. Jubal Early contended that he saw the I Corps retiring as he moved forward to continue his attack after defeating Barlow.[22] This would place the I Corps retreat either at the time that Early engaged the almshouse line or when that line fell back to the outskirts of town, probably the latter. Clearly Barlow fell back first, but all of these sources seem to indicate that the I Corps fell back closely following the time that the XI Corps right was turned and its retreat through town began.

There is an interesting letter from former Corp. A. F. Sweetland of the 55th Ohio that appeared in the *National Tribune* in response to an earlier letter by a correspondent

20 *OR* 27, pt. 1, 248; Doubleday, *Chancellorsville and Gettysburg*, 149.

21 Warren, "Exceptions to Gen. John C. Robinson's Statements," *National Tribune*, July 21, 1887.

22 Beale, *Statements of Time*, 69-72.

named McConnell criticizing the XI Corps for retreating, causing the I Corps to have to withdraw from Seminary Ridge. Sweetland quotes the author of the original letter as saying that the I Corps "passed thru the town without molestation by the enemy." According to McConnell's account, Sweetland explained, the XI Corps supposedly left the field first but had to fight its way into and through town while the I Corps, which supposedly retreated later, moved "leisurely" through town. "If the first statement be true," Sweetland asked, "how can the second statement be true?" Sarcastically he opined that "Perhaps the enemy, having spent their wrath upon the Eleventh Corps, felt peaceably inclined toward the First Corps, and stacked arms and held up their hands in token of a temporary armistice, that the First Corps might 'go thru without molestation.'" He continued: "No writer has attempted to explain away the antagonistic impossibility of harmony of statements in this matter, and the reader must accept such 'stuff' for history. . . . The old adage, that, 'All history is an agreed-upon lie,' is especially true of much that has been written about the fighting and action of the XI Corps on the first and second days of the battle of Gettysburg."[23]

Most likely what happened is that Barlow's division was driven back and while Krzyzanowski's brigade was engaged in trying to halt the Confederate advance on the right, Pender's division was flanking the I Corps on its left and Ramseur's brigade, supported by other units, was beginning to drive in the I Corps right. With the troops on both his right and left in retreat, Schimmelfennig ordered the regiments of von Amsberg's brigade, which were not being as hard pressed at the time, to retire since they were in danger of encirclement. But how was this retreat conducted?

One of the sources used by a great number of historians examining Gettysburg is a lengthy letter written by Frank Haskell to his brother in the aftermath of the battle. Haskell was an aide on the staff of Gen. John Gibbon commanding a division in the II Corps. No less a figure than Bruce Catton proclaimed the work "One of the genuine classics of Civil War literature." Writing about the XI Corps on July 1, he described it as "making but feeble opposition to the advancing enemy" and "in disorganized masses they fled into the town, hotly pursued, and in lanes, in barns, in yards and cellars, throwing away their arms, they sought to hide like rabbits, and were there captured, unresisting, by hundreds. . . . I suppose our losses during the day would exceed four

23 Sweetland, "Some Criticisms," *National Tribune*, November 2, 1916. Maj. Thomas Osborn wrote that "After the First corps was in position on the hill the XI Corps was withdrawn through the city to the hill." No doubt he did not mean this literally, but that the I Corps arrived at Cemetery Hill first, followed by the XI Corps. See Thomas W. Osborn, "Annals of the War/Chapters of Unwritten History/The Artillery at Gettysburg/An Account of the Operations at Cemetery Hill/General Howard's Position/The Work of the Batteries Described by an Artillery Chief," *Weekly Times* (Philadelphia), May 31, 1879, 62.

thousand, of whom a large number were prisoners. Such usually is the kind of loss sustained by the Eleventh Corps."[24]

The main problem with Haskell's observations, as a historical source, is that he was not there. He did not arrive at Gettysburg at all until July 2, long after the first day's fighting had concluded. Nevertheless his baseless statements have been used by many historians as "eyewitness" proof of the utter XI Corps rout north of and through the town on July 1. The truth was quite different. John W. Frazier replied to these allegations in a 32-page document he titled "Reply of the Philadelphia Brigade to the Foolish and Absurd Narrative of Lieutenant Frank A. Haskell." In addition to defending the reputation of his own brigade, Frazier also noted that Haskell had "maligned the brave men of the XI Corps." Warming to his subject, Frazier included in his essay a copy of a letter from Gen. Alexander Webb, commanding his brigade, to the New York State Monuments Commission in which the general charged that "What Haskell wrote he wrote in ignorance. He paraded with the stragglers and prisoners behind a fighting Brigade and thought he was leading a Division."[25]

Capt. Frederick Winkler also penned a lengthy response to Haskell, though more temperate in tone. "Mr. Frank Haskell, whom I knew well, was a very accomplished gentleman, a very brave officer. He wrote a very graphic description of the battle of Gettysburg from the field shortly after the battle in the form of a letter to his brother. His story is thrilling and in so far as it relates to what he personally saw and did is entitled to full credit. In other respects it can make no claim to historical accuracy. It was not written for publication and without either opportunity or so far as appears any attempt to gain reliable information on subjects referred to. His references to and insinuations against the 11th Corps are without justification. They are a reflex of the prejudice against that corps which at that time prevailed in the Army of the Potomac by reason of the disastrous defeat it had sustained at Chancellorsville two months before, the causes of which were not then fully understood. No operation of any part of the 11th Corps came under Col. Haskell's personal observation on the first day when the chief engagement of this corps occurred and when its very heavy losses were sustained. Col. Haskell was miles away from the field of battle." Winkler then proceeded to review the events of the day before he introduced what is probably a very fair and reasonable conclusion: "Of course I do not claim that every man of the corps was a hero, that many in their distress did not seek the shelter of houses and hide there as they passed

24 Haskell, *Battle of Gettysburg*, vii; Haskell's letter is taken from *The Harvard Classics*, Volume 43.

25 Frazier, "Reply of the Philadelphia Brigade," unpublished manuscript, MOLLUS Papers, Box 41, USMHI, 6-7.

through that town. There was more or less of that in both corps. There always will be under similar circumstances. There are Skulkers in every battle and they are found in every military organization. But there is no warrant whatever for Col. Haskell's slurs upon the 11th Corps for its conduct on that day."[26]

Another comparison that could be made is the treatment of Alexander Schimmelfennig with that of Thomas Rowley. The familiar story of Schimmelfennig hiding in town is related in nearly every history of the battle, usually in humorous fashion with him supposedly cowering in a pig sty and often with the obvious connotation of cowardice. But is it not true that the German did exactly what he should have done under the circumstances? Is it not the duty of soldiers to avoid capture? Compare this to Rowley, leading a division in the I Corps, who eyewitnesses claim was nearly incoherent, behaving in an irrational manner. He was later court-martialed and dismissed for being drunk during the engagement. Unlike Schimmelfennig, his case has rarely been referred to except in some recent works. So Schimmelfennig is made into a laughing stock for doing his duty, while Rowley is given a pass for being drunk on duty.

Was the retreat through town really a rout? Schurz provided a candid assessment in his memoirs: "It has been represented by some writers, Southerners, that the Union forces on the first day of the battle of Gettysburg were utterly routed and fled pell-mell into the town. This is far from the truth. That there were a good many stragglers hurrying to the rear in a disorderly fashion, as is always the case during and after a hot fight, will not be denied. Neither will it be denied that it was a retreat after a lost battle with the enemy in hot pursuit. But there was no element of dissolution in it. The retreat through the town was of course more or less disorderly, the streets being crowded with vehicles of every description, which offered to the passing troops exceedingly troublesome obstructions."[27] Naturally, what one observed depended on the stage of the retreat one encountered. A person on Baltimore Street near Cemetery Hill would first have seen some walking wounded, then probably ambulances and perhaps some skulkers feigning injury. Once the retreat began, ammunition wagons, caissons, and other vehicles would have crowded the streets. The first regiments into town would most likely have retreated through the streets in more or less orderly fashion, followed by those at the end of the columns who were fighting as they retired, some being caught in dead-end alleyways while others turned now and then to fire aimed volleys at their pursuers. Eyewitness accounts vary, but seem to fit into this scenario when one

26 Winkler's account is in the Frederick C. Winkler Papers.

27 Schurz, *Reminiscences*, III, 12.

correlates them with the regiments involved and the likely order in which they retreated.

Doubleday described the retreat as the troops passing "through the town quietly and calmly; I saw no running, no undue haste." Schurz portrayed it as "effected as well as could be expected under such circumstances, the streets being filled with vehicles of every description and overrun with men of the First Corps." Of course both had a vested interest in making the retreat seem orderly. Col. Charles Wainwright in charge of the I Corps artillery was also on the scene. He saw "troops of both corps in the streets, the men of the First Corps tending to one side, those of the Eleventh Corps on the other. Units mixed, but he saw no panic; instead, most of the men seemed to be talking and joking as they passed along." Capt. Edward Culp on the staff of Gen. Ames also reported men of both corps walking hurriedly along the streets, but no panic.[28]

Schurz wrote: "the fact remains that in whatever shape the troops issued from the town, they were promptly reorganized, each was under the colors of his regiment, and in as good a fighting trim as before, save that their ranks were fearfully thinned by the enormous losses suffered during the day." Gen. Henry Hunt, chief of artillery for the Army of the Potomac, confirmed this: "It is very true that our men arrived in disorder, but that they were 'panic' stricken or 'demoralized' so that they couldn't fight is all stuff." When the retreating troops reached the position of von Steinwehr's reserve on Cemetery Hill, Hunt testified, "the troops of both 1st and 11th Corps rallied, *not* from a panic nor from a desperation to retreat further, although there were doubtless as always, in every battle, some who did go to the rear, and had to be brought back."[29]

Regarding the withdrawal, Hunt offered the following judgment: "The retreat was effected in tolerably good order the rear guard repeatedly halting and renewing the combat and took post as directed although in the *disorder of such a retreat*, *not* in the disorder of panic. The 11th Corps was badly handled, was altogether too weak for the ground it covered, was taken in flank and rear but did some pretty good fighting for all of that. Getting entangled in the town it lost many prisoners and got broken up a great deal but it formed on its reserve division, the troops immediately occupied their positions, the stone walls and the houses selected for them. Injustice has been done to that Corps. It is not a question with me between Howard and Hancock, or any body else, but between Hancock, Howard, Warren, *et al* and the *troops*." His comment about being badly handled no doubt referred to Barlow, but his assessment of the troops'

28 Barthel, *Abner Doubleday*, 153; *OR* 27, pt. 1, 729; Pfanz, *Gettysburg: Culp's Hill & Cemetery Hill*, 47-48.

29 Schurz, *Reminiscences*, III, 12; Hunt to Gault, Mar. 20, 1886, Box B-11, GNMP.

fighting was positive. John Vautier of the 88th Pennsylvania in the First Corps offered more support when he wrote that "fragments of *both* Corps did their level best to breast the storm and repulse the graybacks. Amidst all this excitement, the 17th Connecticut deployed in the streets, firing several rounds before it was compelled to fall back; the 119th New York made a plucky stand at the foot of Washington Street, holding the enemy in check a little while and then retreating in good order to the hill."[30] Both of the regiments he specifically identified were from the XI Corps.

George Meade, the son of the commanding general, served on the staff of his father at Gettysburg. In his postwar *With Meade at Gettysburg* he evaluated the performance of the XI Corps on July 1. "[I]t would be unfair not to take into consideration the many disadvantages under which it labored. Most unfavorably situated as to position, with the greater portion of its troops stretched across an open plain, with little or no advantage for defence from the character of the ground, it was hurried into action before its lines were thoroughly formed. Under these circumstances it was not capable of making the organized resistance which, otherwise, it might, under more favorable auspices, have opposed to the advance of the enemy."[31]

Both the I and XI Corps were badly hurt, but neither had broken. Both came off the field in some confusion, compounded by the difficulty of negotiating the streets of town, but they continued to resist until they rallied on Cemetery Hill. During the afternoon crisis Carl Schurz and his two XI Corps divisions performed as well as could be expected. Placed in a position with no natural obstacles upon which to anchor a defensive line, with an inadequate number of troops, Schurz deployed the available manpower skillfully to protect the flank of the I Corps and to face the anticipated arrival of Early's division from the north. The critical error came from Francis Barlow whose unauthorized movement forward created an untenable salient while at the same time presenting completely exposed flanks to the enemy. Despite the failure in Barlow's generalship, the troops fought well in an impossible position as the accounts of their opponents attest. Overwhelmed on Blocher's Knoll, with Krzyzanowski's reinforcements caught in a killing crossfire, all three brigades rallied much of their commands at the almshouse to continue the fight. When that position was flanked, they fell back to the outskirts of town where Coster's brigade, arriving too late with too few men, was also flanked by the numerically stronger Confederate assault. When Schurz ordered the final retreat to Cemetery Hill the corps performed the very difficult task of retiring from a closely fought, active battlefield. The 17th Connecticut, several

30 Hunt to Gault, Mar. 20, 1886, Box B-11, GNMP; Bellah, *Soldiers' Battle*, 63.

31 Meade, *With Meade at Gettysburg*, 90-91.

guns, and some regiments from Krzyzanowski's brigade and von Amsberg's brigade fought rear guard actions along the various streets of town, fighting all the way to Cemetery Hill. Those who were cut off around the Eagle Hotel fought until they were out of ammunition and there was no hope of relief. The retreating troops of both corps rallied relatively quickly once they reached the reserve position on Cemetery Hill.

Nor was the defeat of the XI Corps on July 1 the only forced retreat of Union forces during the battle. A quick comparison with the experience of Gen. Daniel Sickles's III on July 2 is revealing. As is well known, Sickles did not like the position he was assigned along the southern end of Cemetery Ridge and Little Round Top so he unilaterally moved his entire corps forward without even bothering to inform his commanding officer. This mirrors almost exactly what Barlow did the previous day, only with a much larger force. The result was the same. Sickles's 10,674 men were left with their flanks in the air, although they had a much better position to defend than Barlow since there were some woods and broken ground that could be used for defense, as well as Little Round Top where a flank could be securely anchored. Nevertheless, when Gen. James Longstreet attacked with two divisions numbering about 14,533 men[32] he drove the corps from the field. Portions of Gen. A. P. Hill's corps joined in the attack, but on the Union side reinforcements from the II, V, and XII Corps were all fed into the fight to repel the assault and stabilize the line. The III Corps was defeated and forced from the field, much as Barlow, and by extension the two divisions of the XI Corps, were the previous day, despite the fact that it fought under less disadvantages than had the XI Corps. Has anyone suggested cowardice on the part of the III Corps? Of course the charge should not be made, but neither ought it be made in the case of the XI Corps.

The XI Corps was defeated on July 1, as was the First, but there is no doubt that both fought. The casualty lists of both prove this, as do the comments of their foes that attested to the tenaciousness of the contest. The two corps paid for precious time with their blood, saving the position that Howard had chosen to fight the battle until the rest of the army could come up. As Schurz observed, "Would not the enemy, if we had retreated two hours, or even one hour earlier, have been in better condition, and therefore more encouraged to make a determined attack upon the cemetery that afternoon,—and with better chance of success?"[33]

☽ ☽ ☽

32 Busey and Martin, *Regimental Strengths*, 16, 170.

33 Schurz, *Reminiscence's*, 18.

By dawn on July 2 the XI Corps could count only about 5,500 men present and fit for duty. Duels between opposing sharpshooters flared from dawn until dark with the corps acquitting itself well. Its men not only suppressed the most deadly of Southern fire during the day, but actually gained ground by taking control of a barn and some other buildings that had previously been occupied by Confederates or been in "no man's land." Proof of its effectiveness came from a number of Rebel sources including a soldier in Avery's brigade who asserted that "a man could not show himself along the line without being shot at." An officer in the 8th Louisiana testified that "If any one showed themselves a volley was poured into us." An aide to Gen. Harry Hays observed that "It was almost certain death for a man to stand upright, and we lost during the day, forty-five men in killed and wounded from the fire of the enemy's sharpshooters."[34] All of these, and others, testify to the marksmanship and zeal of the XI Corps.

During the afternoon the corps withstood a concentrated Southern artillery barrage on Cemetery Hill and its environs, taking casualties without any reports of anyone, much less any units, abandoning their positions. The accuracy of the artillery engaged in counter battery fire under Major Osborn against a battalion of Confederate artillery on Benner Hill commanded by Major Joseph Latimer was extremely effective. Federal fire killed Latimer and inflicted heavy losses on his batteries. The Alleghany Artillery of Virginia reported 26.4 percent losses, fourth highest of any Southern battery for the campaign. The 4th Maryland Battery lost 22.4 percent, the eighth highest loss. His other two batteries, somewhat more protected a distance away, recorded 5.6 percent loss in the 1st Maryland Battery and 4.4 percent in the Lynchburg (Virginia) Artillery. As a battalion, Latimer's command suffered 14.3 percent casualties, the second highest of any Rebel artillery battalion in the battle.[35] Chasing the Confederate artillery off Benner Hill with such losses was a significant achievement that reduced the amount and accuracy of the artillery fire reaching Union positions on both July 2 and 3.

In the evening, as darkness descended and Confederates launched a division-size assault on the lone brigade holding Culp's Hill, Gen. George Greene quickly asked for assistance. Both the First and XI Corps responded swiftly with Howard dispatching one of his decimated brigades—the 45th New York, 61st Ohio, 82nd Illinois and 157th New York—under Lt. Col. August Otto from Schurz's staff. The troops arrived in position just in time as some of Greene's units were running out of ammunition. The

34 McPherson to Avery, Aug. 3, 1863, 6th North Carolina File, GNMP; Jones, "Going Back," 55-60; Fuerschbach, *Wiedrich's Battery*, 23; Jones, *Memoirs of Captain William J. Seymour*, 73.

35 Busey and Martin, *Regimental Strengths*, 553-55, 595.

45th New York and 82nd Illinois helped to stabilize Greene's left, and even managed to retake some of the trenches already occupied by the attackers. The other two regiments moved to Greene's right where they helped to support the endangered flank of the 137th New York. All four regiments remained until released by Greene to return to their corps which, of course, meant that they were *not* available as a reserve to counter the attack of Hays and Avery on Cemetery Hill later that night. After the attacks finally ended, Greene and Slocum made it a point to thank Howard for his timely and effective assistance and the "good service" his regiments provided. Compare this conduct to that of the 71st Pennsylvania from the II Corps. Sent to the same right flank of Greene's position it retired as soon as it took fire and, in the words of its commanding officer, "returned to camp against orders."[36]

Certainly the most serious crisis faced by the XI Corps on July 2 was the unexpected late evening attack directly on Cemetery Hill by two brigades of Early's division. Despite its overall positive performance during July 2, it was this attack that once again called into question the fighting ability of the corps. One of the more blatant attacks on the honor of the corps appeared in *Last Chance for Victory: Robert E. Lee and the Gettysburg Campaign* by Scott Bowden and Bill Ward.[37] Since this is such a pointed smear, it may serve well to begin with it. Following a number of disparaging comments about the XI Corps and its men, all offered with no supporting evidence, Bowden and Ward assert that Ames's two brigades were "decisively beaten by two brigades under Harry Hays and Isaac Avery. This despite the fact that the Federals had more than 24 hours to rest and fortify their position, were fighting on the defensive with supporting artillery, and had the advantage of terrain." The authors do not seem to realize that all brigades are not equal. Actually, Ames reported only 1,150 men fit for duty on July 2 compared to an estimated strength of Hays and Avery of 2,100. The authors also point to the "supporting artillery" without understanding that the XI Corps artillery was placed for long-range fire, not to protect the front lines from attack. Placed behind the crest of the hill, it could not be brought to bear on the Confederate attack against the base of the hill; only Stevens's battery from the I Corps was placed to sweep the area in front of the XI Corps line. And the authors also fail to understand that the parallel ridges and valleys running perpendicular to Ames's position effectively concealed much of the Rebel assault from Stevens's fire, as did the darkness of the hour.

Bowden and Ward go on to claim that the Confederates "fought their way up and over stone walls and abatis, lunettes and other earthworks, and defeated them

36 Bachelder, *History*, 586.

37 Bowden and Ward, *Last Chance for Victory*.

capturing numerous artillery pieces in the process." Most of Ames's men were located behind a fence of piled stones, but it varied in height from only about two to three feet. It was low enough for some Rebels to step on top and vault over. There was no abatis and there were no earthworks for the simple reason that being on the front line subject to Confederate sharpshooters the defenders had no opportunity to construct them. They certainly were not resting as the authors claim, but were actively engaged in skirmishing and withstanding artillery fire all day. The only lunettes were those atop Cemetery Hill where the attack was halted, and of course the attackers did not capture "numerous artillery pieces," they in fact captured none since the gunners stood and defended their pieces while XI Corps infantry defeated and pushed back the assault. Then too, as we have seen, much of the Federal line at the base of Cemetery Hill in fact held. The 33rd Massachusetts and most of the 41st New York held their position on the right. The 54th New York and 68th New York, with barely 200 men or less in line, retired back up the hill where they rallied on the batteries. Proof that the first two held and the others rallied is that the batteries in position on the hill above the 33rd Massachusetts and 41st New York did *not* report being attacked by Confederate infantry. Some of the 153rd Pennsylvania seems to have retired but rallied at Ricketts's guns, while part of it maintained its position, as did the two regiments to its left, the 75th Ohio and 17th Connecticut. Both of these regiments held firm. Among the handful of men remaining in the 25th Ohio some stayed to fight with the 75th, while others retired up the hill along with the 107th Ohio which apparently received an order from someone to fall back. Regardless, these units rallied at Wiedrich's guns where they captured the colors of the 8th Louisiana. Of the nine infantry regiments, five held and four retired, one of the latter under orders. Of those who retreated there is evidence that most rallied either at the guns or close behind them.

Further, if we look at the various Confederate reports and the diaries and memoirs written by Southern survivors, one consistent point they make is the small number of attackers who made it to the guns. Major Samuel Tate of the 6th North Carolina claimed that only 75 men from Avery's brigade and 12 from Hays's brigade, a total of 87 Confederates, reached the guns. How he managed to count them in the darkness and confusion is most unlikely, but in any case he testified to the small number. Col. Archibald Godwin of the 57th North Carolina who wrote the report for Avery's command stated that upon crossing the stone wall that "it was not found possible to concentrate more than 40 or 50 men at any point for a farther advance." A report on file in the Gettysburg National Military Park says that "less than a platoon" of the 7th Louisiana reached the hilltop position. Samuel W. Eaton of the 57th North Carolina wrote in his diary that "We were under a desperate fire, only a few got to the batteries and could not hold them. . . . There was harder fighting today than ever I knew of

This photograph by Timothy O'Sullivan shows the cemetery gatehouse. In the foreground are temporary revetments where Wiedrich's battery was located. Note the broken windows in the gatehouse. *Library of Congress*

before."[38] Being generous, if we say that 100 Confederates made it to the guns, and if we use Harry Pfanz's estimate of 2,100 men in the two attacking brigades, then only 4.8 percent of the attackers managed to penetrate to the top of Cemetery Hill. This was hardly a major breakthrough.

Bowden and Ward continue on to claim that when Howard and Schurz attempted to organize a counterattack "few responded and the burden was carried by Carroll's 'Gibraltar' Brigade."[39] Most authors join Bowden and Ward in crediting Carroll with stopping the Confederate attack and driving it back down the hill. This is completely erroneous since there is a multitude of documented evidence that it was elements of Ames's division and the artillerymen who stopped the Confederate assault at the crest of the hill and it was Krzyzanowski's counterattack, aided by some other Eleventh Corps regiments, that drove the attackers out of Wiedrich's battery and back down the hill. To be sure, Carroll did move quickly and did arrive at the end of the engagement,

38 *OR* 27, pt. 2, 484-85; Tate to Governor of North Carolina, July 8, 1863, 6th North Carolina File, GNMP; Battlefield Commission Papers, Position of Troops, Box B-12, GNMP; Eaton W. Eaton, Diary, Co. B, 57th North Carolina, GNMP.

39 Bowden and Ward, *Last Chance*, 382.

but by that time the attack had already been defeated and most of the attackers, the few that actually made it to the top of the hill, were either casualties of in retreat. Questions like this were the source of endless post-war debates.

A. F. Sweetland made a very interesting point in a letter to the *National Tribune* in 1909. He argued that "Howard's and Hancock's headquarters were nearly a mile distant from each other at this time. It must have taken five minutes' hard riding to reach Hancock, two or three more to reach Carroll with the order, and 15 minutes for Carroll to reach Cemetery Hill. Here are nearly 25 minutes consumed from time of attack to arrival of Carroll to take part in an attack that did not exceed 15 to 20 minutes by the accounts of many of those present."[40] The point, of course, is that given the time it would take for Carroll to be ordered to Cemetery Hill, for the troops to form, and for them to reach their destination, they could not possibly have arrived until the attack was already winding down. While it has been stated that Hancock dispatched Carroll on his own before Howard's request arrived, it still would have taken time for Carroll to form and march to the scene meaning that he would have arrived toward the end of the engagement.

There was no doubt that Wiedrich's German gunners fought with exceptional courage and determination that evening, standing by their pieces and defending them with everything from sponge staffs to rocks and their own bare hands. Col. Charles Wainwright of the I Corps, who had been very critical of the XI Corps and especially of its German element, wrote that "the men of 'I' Company . . . fought splendidly, sticking to their guns, and finally driving the rebs out . . . the Germans have got fight in them." But what about the XI Corps infantry. We have already seen that the Confederates who made the assault did not consider it easy. The few who made it up the hill were largely those that came through the gap left in the line by the last-minute movement of the 17th Connecticut just before the assault. A few others followed the retreat of the 107th Ohio on the left and a handful were probably those who vaulted over the low wall in front of the Ohioans or followed the 54th and 68th New York to the top of the hill. Yet, it is clear from these and other recollections that only 100 or less of the attacking force reached the crest of Cemetery Hill—more than 95 percent did not. Far from an easy attack on men who ran away, the assaulting Confederate units suffered serious loss. Avery's brigade alone reported 412 casualties in the attack. The diary of Capt. William J. Seymour of Hays's brigade recorded a loss of 332 in killed and wounded alone.[41] If these figures are correct, then the attackers lost 35.4 percent of their total

40 Sweetland, "Repulsing the 'Tigers'," *National Tribune*, Oct. 21, 1909.

41 Nevins, *A Diary of Battle*, 245-46; Archer, "The Hour Was," 77; Seymour diary, July 2, 1863.

force. It appears that the penetration was not nearly as serious as is usually believed, and that many more of the XI Corps held firm or rallied to the guns than heretofore acknowledged.

☽ ☽ ☽

Finally, a word about numbers. Stephen Sears, in his *Gettysburg*, is only one of the more recent historians to use the argument that the number of men captured in the XI Corps was evidence that it had not fought well: "The Eleventh put five of its six brigades, 7,000 men, into a mere hour's action that Wednesday afternoon and lost 3,200 of them. Almost half that number were prisoners."[42] Of course, the XI Corps fight lasted much longer than an hour on July 1. The first units arrived in position about 12:30 and did not begin arriving back at Cemetery Hill at the end of the retreat until around 5:00 pm, nearly five hours later. Of course some units were under fire longer than others for the simple reason that some arrived earlier than others. But from the time that the lead unit of the XI Corps arrived on the field it was under fire from sharpshooters, infantry, and artillery culminating in an intense engagement with troops from Rodes's and Early's divisions that lasted upward of two hours.

If we look at the basis of the argument, the number of men captured, the facts do not support Sears's conclusion. According to the detailed calculations of Busey and Martin, the XI Corps brought 9,242 men into action at Gettysburg. It lost a total of 3,807 casualties of whom 1,514 were captured and missing. Note that the number 1,514 is *not* the number of "prisoners" as Sears, and many other authors, claimed. It is the number of men who were captured *and* missing. In addition to those who were captured, it included people who were dead on the field and people who were wounded. Since the XI Corps did not hold the field following the engagement of July 1 it was not possible to accurately determine the fate of those men. Weeks or months later, or in some cases after the war, when additional information became available the actual number of prisoners was revised down as it became known that many of the missing had actually been killed or mortally wounded.

In Krzyzanowski's brigade, for example, postwar independent researchers found that it had not suffered 75 killed, but actually 155, more than twice the initial reported loss. Many of these were first reported as missing since their fate was then unknown. And of course the captured included many who were wounded and thus could not escape. Then too, if we look at those who were captured it appears from the

42 Sears, *Gettysburg*, 244.

fragmentary existing sources that at least 300 men were captured along with Capt. Irsch after holding out in and around the Eagle Hotel. They only surrendered later that evening when surrounded, virtually out of ammunition, and with no hope of relief. Capt. Irsch was awarded the Medal of Honor. Clearly these were not people who simply gave up. Nor were other pockets of men like the 12 skirmishers of the 55th Ohio who were surrounded in a barn[43] north of town or others of the 82nd Illinois and 26th Wisconsin who, among the last to retreat, were likewise cut off and only surrendered when further resistance became impossible. Aside from the deductions which must be made for those who it was later found had perished, if we deduct upward of 500 men who surrendered honorably under impossible conditions after holding out as long as possible, then the figure Sears gives does not look so bad after all.

The numbers also do not look so bad if we compare them to the I Corps which brought 12,220 men onto the field, losing 2,162 men captured and missing, *more* than the XI Corps.[44] Much of the I Corps was able to retire through the fields south of the village or through the fringes of the town, thus reducing the possibility of its men being cut off and surrounded like those in the XI Corps. Since the I Corps was larger than the Eleventh, if we look at the number captured and missing as a percentage we find that the XI Corps lost 16.4 percent and the I Corps 17.7 percent, a *higher* percentage than the Eleventh. No one has suggested that the I Corps ran away or did not fight well, nor should they as it performed valiantly, but the use of the data on captured and missing to try to argue against the courage of the XI Corps is clearly not supported by either the evidence or by logic.

Only the First and XI Corps were engaged all three days. If we again look at the Busey and Martin figures, it is evident that only the I Corps suffered a higher percentage of casualties than the XI Corps. The smallest corps on the field suffered the second highest percentage of losses. The data was as follows: First (49.6), Eleventh (41.2), Third (39.5), Second (38.9), Fifth (20.0), Twelfth (11.1), and Sixth (1.7). Barlow (52.6) and Schurz (47.4) ranked third and fourth in the percentage of losses among divisions, behind only Robinson (56.4) and Wadsworth (55.9) of the I Corps. If we look at the Union brigades that were engaged during the battle, on a percentage basis the five from the XI Corps engaged on July 1 ranked fifth, eighth, tenth, twelfth, and fourteenth of the total of 58 brigades engaged at Gettysburg. Reviewing the strengths and losses of individual regiments, again based on percentages, of the top six three are

43 Busey and Martin, *Regimental Strengths*, 16, 139. See also Pula, *Sigel Regiment*; Pula, *For Liberty and Justice*. Report of the Gettysburg Memorial Commission, 33.

44 Busey and Martin, *Regimental Strengths*, 16, 125.

from the I Corps and three from the Eleventh, with the latter in first, second, and sixth position. Fifty-five Union regiments lost fifty percent or more, twelve of these were from the XI Corps, surpassed only by those of the I Corps.[45]

In 1890 J. W. Hand, a former captain in the XI Corps, wrote to the *National Tribune* to comment on the habit of equating losses with the quality of a unit's service. "The losses of a regiment in action are the measure of its sacrifices, not of its services. The man who was wounded and recovered is as likely to have been a fighting man as he who died of his wounds. A brigade may charge an opposing line boldly, and carry the position with little loss. Another may attack feebly and be repulsed with great slaughter. Then there is the element of luck or fate or Providence, which is always worthy of consideration. Finally, it must be the living and not the dead who in the end achieve the victories."[46] He was, of course, correct. Losses do not necessarily denote the efficiency or steadfastness of a unit. Yet, regiments, brigades, divisions, and corps do not lose these high percentages of casualties when they run away. The men in the XI Corps without a doubt stood and fought as long as they possibly could, their "butcher's bill" providing ample evidence.

45 Busey and Martin, *Regimental Strengths*, 125, 127, 131, 133, 136, 139, 141, 392, 463, 472.

46 Hand, "A Graphic Account," *National Tribune*, July 24, 1890.

Chapter 17

"A Hard Ride in Cattle Cars"

From Virginia to Tennessee

THE END OF THE GETTYSBURG campaign left the XI Corps in appalling condition. Of the seven infantry corps that engaged in the battle, only the I lost a higher percentage of casualties. On July 18 Assistant Adjutant General Theodore Meysenburg noted in his journal the roll call returns for the various regiments. The news was not good. Some entire regiments numbered less than a standard company—the 54th New York reported 96 men on duty, the 25th Ohio 97, and the 75th Ohio only 88. Eight other regiments reported less than 200 men. At the beginning of August Carl Schurz reported to Meysenburg that his division needed 5,973 men to bring it to full strength, while Adolph von Steinwehr reported a need for 3,835 men to fill his ranks. Of course, Civil War regiments were never up to full strength, but the reports nevertheless indicate the severe nature of the casualties. The artillery reported corresponding needs. During the campaign it lost 187 horses from "exhaustion, lameness, disease, death on the march, and included 98 lost in battle" along with 22 mules. In addition, Osborn needed 185 men to bring his batteries up to strength. On July 30 Howard reported an XI Corps need for fifty artillery, two cavalry and twenty ambulance horses. In Dilger's battery alone, eleven of the remaining horses were judged unfit for service while fifteen halters and thirteen traces were damaged or worn out and in need of replacement.[1]

1 Meysenburg journal, July 18, 1863; Schurz to Meysenburg, Aug. 3, 1863, RG 393, Pt. 2, Vol. 4, NARA; Steinwehr to Meysenburg, Aug. 4, 1863, RG 393, Pt. 2, Vol. 4, NARA; Cole, *Artillery at Gettysburg*, 118-19; Report of Gen. Howard, July 30, 1863, RG 393, Pt. 2, Vol. 16, II-5314, 5437.

Aside from shortages in manpower, another problem was missing, damaged, or worn out equipment. Ames's brigade, for example, reported missing or unserviceable bayonets, cartridge boxes without coverings, and about 25 percent of the muskets without tompions. Another report dated July 12 noted the astounding need in the XI Corps for ten jackets, 1,222 blouses, 2,390 pairs of pants, 3,228 shirts, 1,650 drawers, 2,772 socks, ten boots, 894 shoes, 342 gun belts, 1,839 haversacks, 240 S. tents, 343 caps, 947 canteens, five axes, and two drums. Some of the equipment was lost during the campaign—the large number of haversacks, for example, resulted from regiments being ordered to stack them before going into action and then not returning to reclaim them during the retreat of July 1—but much of it was simply old and worn out. Von Steinwehr reported on July 9 the need for some 700 new pairs of shoes in his First Brigade alone. Yet even when some attempt at resupply was made it was not always successful. An inspection report dated July 27 complained that the shoes provided to the corps were "of an inferior quality, not lasting more than two or three weeks."[2]

To strengthen the depleted corps, the War Department once again reshuffled its regiments. Throughout July new troops arrived to fill some of the gaps. Some of the assignments were only temporary as the units moved on to other commands, but some were badly needed permanent additions. Among the latter were four infantry regiments —33rd New Jersey, 141st New York, 143rd New York, and 168th New York—along with two batteries of light artillery, Battery G, 4th U. S., and the 12th Ohio Independent Battery. Special Order No. 129 assigned Brig. Gen. George H. Gordon, a new arrival in the corps, to command of the 1st Division, relieving Schimmelfennig who resumed command of his old brigade. He was not happy, nor were many in the corps, especially the German element who perceived this as yet another slight to the troops who had fought so hard and endured so much. Clearly Gordon was not happy either. No sooner had he arrived than he wrote a scathing letter to Howard complaining of his situation. "The reputation of this corps in the army is so bad that good troops are demoralized and rendered worthless while they wear its badge and form part of its organization. That its reputation is bad is patent to all. It is so from its disgraceful record at Chancellorsville, and not a clean reputation at Gettysburg; from its lack of discipline; from its unsoldierly education; from its great number of poor and worthless officers. The great number of skeleton regiments that form part of the corps is large enough to

2 Cooper to Meysenburg, July 27, 1863, RG 393, Pt. 2, Vol. 18: Box 1, NARA (This report was confirmed by Capt. Smith, Acting Assistant Inspector General of the 2nd Brigade during an inspection on July 26.); McAloon to Schriver, July 12, 1863, RG 393, Pt. 2, Vol. 4, NARA; Steinwehr report, July 9, 1863, RG 393, #5406, NARA; quote from McAloon to Schriver, July 27, 1863, RG 393, Pt. 2, Vol. 4, NARA.

demoralize the conscripts that enter it, but not good enough to make them soldiers. The stigma of the corps attached to all. New men enter it with reluctance, and remain in it from compulsion, with dejection and indifference; it is a fate which they must bear, but under which they break. These facts can be abundantly proved. I see no remedy for the salvation of the 'matériel' of this corps, but the breaking up of the organization, its name and symbol cast into oblivion, the consolidation of its regiments into other corps, and pretty general dismissal of officers now or hereafter, as they shall, under other influences, prove themselves still worthless. My own command is already affected, and I desire to remove them."[3]

Reorganization also required determining which officers would be assigned to command and which would be demoted to their previous positions. Adelbert Ames, who distinguished himself through coolness and bravery under fire at Gettysburg, was assigned to a brigade containing Ohio and Connecticut regiments, none of them "German." Never any friend of the Germans, the general was quite happy with the change. Howard reported that in a conversation on July 21 Ames told him that "he has a good brigade now. He has one or two new regiments & has exchanged his Germans."[4]

Another change brought Brig. Gen. Hector Tyndale to Schurz's Third Division as leader of the First Brigade. Although he had excellent credentials as an ardent abolitionist who had accompanied John Brown's wife to Virginia to retrieve his body, nevertheless he seems to have made less than a favorable impression. He assumed command at Funkstown, Maryland, on July 13 and no sooner arrived than he ran afoul of his troops. Lt. Col. David Thomson in the 82nd Ohio wrote to his wounded commanding officer, Col. James S. Robinson, on August 22 to apprise him of what was transpiring. "Our Brig. Gen'l. Tyndale was the cause of the trouble. He is a D—d Jackass & no mistake. His Adjutant was at my quarters today & said he is the meanest cusshound. Krzyzanowski is the one we all desire to be under now." The Polish colonel also received a vote of confidence from Schurz who recommended his promotion to brigadier general, noting that at Gettysburg he "did not only his duty, but more than his duty; he exposed himself to the bullets of the enemy as freely as if he had been

3 Special Orders No. 129, July 17, 1863, RG 393, Pt. 2, 5322, NARA; Gordon to Howard, July 29, 1863, *OR* 27, pt. 3, 778-79.

4 Howard to Dearest, July 22, 1863, Howard Papers, Bowdoin College.

Brig. Gen. Hector Tyndale
National Archive

accustomed to see every one of them bring him honor. . . ."[5] Yet in this case, as with others, the "foreign" officers went unrewarded.

☽ ☽ ☽

The XI Corps crossed the Potomac River back into Virginia in "hot and sultry" weather on July 19. Capt. Charles A. Currier of the 40th Massachusetts, temporarily assigned to the corps during the recent reorganization, commented on his new assignment and the river crossing:

> We found the new command to which we were attached composed largely of German troops who proved during the short time we were with them to be pleasant companions. To one Brigade of our Division was attached 'dot little Getman Band' who regaled us morning, noon and night, while on the march, with 'Rally round the flag boys.' As a 'street band' they were not an unqualified success, but for serenade or quadrille music were second to none. In the second Division of our corps we were pleased to find the 33rd. Mass. Regiment, which had an excellent band. . . . Soon after the completion of the pontoons, orders for a forward movement were received and on a most delightful Sunday morning it was commenced. The movement was in three columns, and for two hours before the 11 corps started, our men stood upon the hill watching them as they moved down to the river to cross. It was a sight that can never be forgotten by those who witnesses it. As they approached the pontoons, the bands of men of the various commands struck up and made the valley echo, with the melody of 'Carry me back to old Virginny,' which was sung with more gusto than heart, for if left to their own choice, Virginia was the last direction in which they would have gone, but the crossing was made, and from this date until the early days of August, we were constantly on the move, promenading in one direction one day, and seemingly retracing our steps the next, the only apparent purpose being to test the endurance of the men.[6]

5 *OR* 27, pt. 1, 732; Thomson to Robinson, Aug. 23, 1863, Robinson Papers, Ohio Historical Society, MSS 29, Box 1; Schurz to Howard, Aug. 21, 1863, RG 393, NARA.

6 Keeler diary; Currier, "Recollections of Service," unpublished regimental history dated 1886 in the USMHI, 49-50.

Once back in the Old Dominion State, civilian attitudes changed dramatically. "The inborn secesh were sullen and hid themselves," noted Col. Adin Underwood. "Where a town was found with blinds all closed and curtains down, it was stirred up with 'Yankee Doodle' and 'John Brown' from the band." Marching through Middleburg, Corp. William Paynton noticed "a woman, residing in one of the best looking houses of the village, was sitting by a front window." As Paynton watched, "the music of our drum corps attracted her attention. She looked out to see what was passing, and as she saw the 'Stars and Stripes' instead of the 'Stars and Bars,' she deliberately arose and turned her back to the window, and remained in that position until we had passed, thus showing her contempt for the flag under which she was born. But for her being a woman, I could have shot her with a good will."[7]

In Virginia the Army of the Potomac was under constant threat of guerillas who made life hazardous, necessitating continuous vigilance. Confederate raiders attacked isolated patrols, captured supply wagons, and on one occasion came dangerously close to carrying off Gen. Schurz. As the army continued on, pursuing Lee's forces at a respectable distance, its critical supply lines along the Orange and Alexandria Railroad came under repeated attacks. Clearly Meade could not ignore these assaults upon his vital supply line. The XI Corps was assigned the mission of protecting the railroads and supply lines.[8] It was a pleasant change from the difficult campaigning of the previous months.

Late July and early August were unseasonably mild in Virginia in 1863. Regardless, the troops did not always find it so. "You never saw such hot weather as we have here," commented Lt. Col. David Thomson. "I cannot keep cool, although I take a bath every day. The woods are shady but no air can circulate and so they are about as warm as the plains."[9]

With their camps now somewhat more permanent, the men could use off-duty hours to write home, visit friends, engage in regimental contests, or join an occasional hunting party. Food supplies were in most cases now plentiful. Chefs and self-proclaimed connoisseurs from many European groups prepared the delightful delicacies of their native lands. Their skill in culinary arts gained such universal fame that officers from other corps, including Meade himself, were known to find excuses for visiting their camps around suppertime. Foragers brought in chickens, pigs,

7 Underwood, *Three Years' Service*, 14; Dreese, *Old Flag*, 44.

8 Circular, Aug. 8, 1863, RG 393, Pt. 2, 5322, NARA; Circular, Aug. 17, 1863, NA-RG 393, Pt. 2, 5322, NARA; Circular, Aug. 28, 1863, NA-RG 393, Pt. 2, 5322, NARA.

9 Thomson to Mary, Aug. 11, 1863, Thomson Papers in the possession of Ms. Mary Geiger.

vegetables, and anything else they could purchase, beg, or steal. Col. Krzyzanowski attended one affair for which Capt. Fritz Tiedemann donated several wild turkeys that he bagged on a safari into the surrounding countryside. Captain Friedrich Otto von Fritsch of the 68th New York returned from leave that same day with a large barrel of lager beer to add to the festivities. Juicy helpings of fresh-roasted turkey, followed by bubbling cups of ever-popular lager succeeded in taking minds off the immediacy of the war. Many in the army poked fun at the Germans, stereotyping them due to their fondness for onions, sauerkraut and lager beer. Doctors later discovered that these ethnic staples proved to be excellent antidotes for dysentery, a disease which usually affected the XI Corps less than the other army corps. In this case, the proverbial last laugh bore a distinctly "foreign" accent.[10]

Chaplains preached to large audiences. Howard took as many opportunities as possible to attend religious services, but on one occasion the minister preached the entire service in German so he understood only a few words. Corp. John McMahon, a particularly religious soldier in the 136th New York, attended services whenever they were available. In his diary he critiqued the chaplains and their sermons. August 9 he wrote: "Today we had preaching. The man was about 6 feet high and well built but nothing extra on a sermon. His text was 'Come unto me, all ye that are weary, and heavy laden, and I will give you rest." On August 16 he listened to the chaplain of the 33rd Massachusetts speak on the effect of Christianity on a Christian government. The entire service lasted only fifteen minutes. McMahon concluded that "our Chaplains are a class of men that could not get employment at home and by underhanded work have got to be Chaplains. At any rate I never heard a good sermon from a Chaplain yet."[11]

Near Warrenton Junction Capt. Charles A. Curries attended a service when the 40th Massachusetts spent a few days camped in the area. "We tarried over a Sunday, and hearing the sonorous voice of a Chaplain holding forth a short distance away, the writer went over to listen to him. On one side and very near the preacher, our German Band was playing some most delightful waltz music, while on the other hand, the Officers and men of a western regiment were gambling, some with sweat cloths, and others with cards, a not altogether uncommon sight in the army, though one not conducive to proper Sunday meditation or pious thought." German musicians found themselves much in demand throughout the army. Surgeon Hubbard reported that the 33rd Massachusetts had the best band he had heard in the service and that "About half the Staff are singers and Col. [Charles W.] Assmussen is an accomplished pianist and

10 Butts, *Gallant Captain*, 91-92; Howard, *Autobiography*, 448-49.

11 Howard to "My dear guy," Sept. 7, 1863, Bowdoin College; Priest, *McMahon Diary*, 60.

organist so we have great musical treats." Maj. George Benson Fox of the 75th Ohio believed his own regimental band took second place to no one. "I would just say that our Band is considered ahead of anything in the Corps, and much pride is being taken by the members of it to keep ahead, they are learning all the new pieces of the day."[12]

Despite the abnormally mild weather, diseases flourished throughout August and September. A severe epidemic of typhoid fever swept through the camps disabling scores of men. Several fatalities occurred. Occasional raids by Rebel cavalry punctuated the relative calm of the corps' new assignment, but by late summer the battlefields of political strife stirred the feelings of many. Some followed the news of the draft riots in New York City, all with disgust. "We were very sorry to hear of the riot in New York," one soldier wrote from Point of Rocks, Maryland, on July 17. "It does excite the soldiers awfully some that came from that vicinity say that [if] they could only have been there, there might have been a different result if they had. It seems to[o] bad that while the soldiers are doing so well in the field that there should be a division at home. It will never shorten the war but may be the means of lengthening it. All men that cry Peace! had better beware, as they may get a price that they did not call for."[13]

The upcoming fall elections also began to command notice, especially following the disturbances caused by the draft. Most of the troops categorically rejected the Northern peace movement led by Ohio politician Clement Vallandigham, none more so than troops from his own home state. "I am severely affected with what I would term Anti-Vallandighamiracy," confided Alva Howe of the 55th Ohio in a letter home. "It gives me an unpleasant information on the brain. Union meetings are all the go now & Val gets it on all sides. If I know the feelings of the soldiers they are all sound on the opposition to Val." A. W. Ross of the 73rd Ohio waited "patiently for the close of this war which wont be long if valandingham is defeated in Ohio which I think is certain for I know that no one but a damd Traitor will vote for him. The last hope of the Sesesh is in his ellection if he is badly defeated I think the war will be over by the first of January."[14]

☽ ☽ ☽

12 Currier, "Recollections of Service," 50; Hubbard to wife, July 20, 1863; Hubbard to wife, Aug. 4, 1863; Fox to father, July 29, 1863.

13 Letter to parents, July 17, 1863, USMHI.

14 Howe to "Coz," Aug. 23, 1863, VFM 1797A, OHS; Ross to Sarah, Sept. 13, 1863, VFM 1904, OHS.

In the immediate wake of Gettysburg, most of the troops believed they had performed well, redeeming their collective reputation. Major Osborn, previously critical of his new artillery command, confessed in a letter home to his brother that "My command fights well." Gen. Ames, no friend of the Germans, wrote that "no troops fought better." "I believe that the Corps successfully executed every order of the Commanding General of the Army," Howard wrote home. "Sometimes the marches were long and tedious, but they were always performed with cheerfulness, and very little straggling can be laid to our charge. I feel grateful to the officers and men of this Corps, for the part they have borne in this eventful Campaign, and whatever misrepresentation or prejudice may have set against them, they nevertheless deserve the gratitude of their Country."[15]

Col. Orland Smith was even more effusive in a general order he published to his troops, congratulating them "on the part which they have borne in the great conflict just terminated and the magnificent victory which is its result. He has witnessed with admiration not unmingled with astonishment the unmurmuring patience with which they have endured long and weary marches bearing heavy burdens, suffering excessive fatigue and exposure, with insufficient food & rest until they reached the scene of final triumph. . . . Still more does he admire the behavior of the troops when in the presence of the enemy. Assigned to a most difficult position, yet one of vital relation to the final result (the defense of the center of our line of battle) they were called upon to exhibit the utmost coolness and steadiness in the face of a constant fire from the trained sharpshooters of our foes. Most nobly have they discharged their trust. Not for a moment did they falter, though the long list of casualties tells the great price of their valor and fidelity. The older troops have added to their laurels. Younger ones have proved themselves worthy of the name of veterans. Nobly have they wiped out the stain on their fame which the failures of others had put upon it."[16]

Unfortunately, the good-will engendered by the triumph did not long survive the echo of the guns. Subsequent stories in many newspapers completely neglected the crucial parts played by the XI Corps, while before long journalists returned to proffering accusations of cowardice. It is not surprising that the men took these stories as an offense to their honor and to the memory of their departed comrades. For many, the continuing allegations were the proverbial "last straw." While few enlisted men

15 Osborn to Abraham, July 8, 1863, in Crumb and Dhalle, *No Middle Ground*, 146; Ames to Headquarters, July 13, 1863, RG 393, NARA; Howard report Aug. 31, 1863.

16 General Orders No. 7, Barlow's division, order by Col. Orland Smith commanding, July 5, 1863, RG 393, Pt. 2, 5353, 5354, 5357, 6530, NARA.

deserted, many wrote scathing letters home and vowed never to re-enlist once their terms of service expired. Gen. Schimmelfennig requested an immediate transfer to a different theater of operations where his talents might better be appreciated. Some of the officers, who had an opportunity to resign that the enlisted men did not enjoy, requested immediate discharge. Major Henry Baetz of the 26th Wisconsin submitted a particularly detailed letter of resignation in which he criticized the absence of any official denunciation of the fictitious accusations circulating in the "news" stories. In his case the fury which drove his pen must have been extreme for he had no immediate need to write the letter. He would receive a discharge anyway since he lost a leg at Gettysburg.

Amid the recriminations, Howard became aware of the publication of the speeches and proceedings of the meeting of Germans in New York's Cooper Union following Chancellorsville. Major Charles Howard, clearly offended and disgusted by the revelation, wrote that "A pamphlet has been published on the battle of Chancellorsville—meant to be in justification of the 11th Corps at the expense of its Commanding Officer. It consists chiefly of certain speeches made at a German meeting in N. Y. and translated into English. It contains many downright falsehoods and is full of misrepresentation of facts. There was also an article appeared in Wilkes' Spirit of the Times (No. for Aug. 29th I think) in which both Otis and his staff are shamelessly slandered." Referring to a planned history of the war that he believed was in preparation, the major concluded that "I think of writing an account of the battle of Chancellorsville and sending it to J. L. C. Abbott so that he may have some reliable material for writing the history (if he has not already passed that point in his history of the Rebellion.)"[17]

☽ ☽ ☽

The woeful condition of the XI Corps following Gettysburg and the resurfacing of ugly recriminations were not the only crises that faced it that August. Well aware of the army prejudice directed toward the XI Corps, Meade proposed to solve the situation by officially disbanding Howard's corps. On July 29 Meade confided his thoughts to Halleck. "Much feeling exists in this army in regard to the Eleventh Corps. This consideration, in addition to my own judgment that the other corps should be increased, induces me to submit to you for approval the propriety of breaking up the organization of this corps by sending General Howard with one division to the Second

17 C. Howard to brother, Sept. 4, 1863, Howard Bowdoin College.

Corps, which he will then command, another division to the Twelfth Corps and leaving the third division, under General Schurz, with a brigade of cavalry, to guard my rear from the Rappahannock to Manassas Junction. Please reply as soon as convenient." Under this plan, Schurz's division, containing the bulk of the despised "foreigners," was to be used to provide personnel for permanent guard posts along the Orange and Alexandria Railroad.[18]

On the same day Howard wrote to Halleck about his impressions of the plan and of Schurz. "I wish to say that the General [Schurz] has been prompt and energetic and able during the operations in which I have been associated with him. Should you see fit to occupy the Shenandoah valley with a small force, so as to cooperate with this army & prevent its occupancy by the Rebels, I believe I do not flatter him when I say, that General Schurz will not fail to give complete satisfaction. As to the changes proposed merging the two divisions of this Corps into the 2nd & 12th respectively, they have my approval as also that of the division commanders concerned. We feel sensitive under false accusations but considering the existing prejudices in this army against the 11th Corps and the great difficulty of overcoming them we regard it better for the service to make these changes. The different Corps are now so small that a consolidation is advisable. General Steinwehr desires to go with the 2nd Corps. General Gordon with his division to the 12th. Personally it will be gratifying to me to return to the Second Corps, but I do not feel dissatisfied with the Eleventh during the present campaign, and hope the changes referred to will not be regarded as a reflection upon the officers and soldiers of this command who have worked so hard and done so much to carry out every order."[19]

Word of the proposed changes naturally leaked out. Surgeon Robert Hubbard wrote to his wife about the proposed realignment only one day after Howard's communication to Halleck. "I should, aside from my personal interest in the matter be sorry to have the old 11th annihilated and its associations destroyed, but the duty of the true soldier is to serve wherever he may be placed and I shall give myself no trouble about the matter."[20]

Others were less accepting, convinced that the proposal reflected on their soldierly qualities. In a letter to his wife, Howard reflected on the impending change, noting, improbably, that "The Germans begin to be attached to me." Schurz was particularly sensitive to the criticism of the corps and especially its German element. On the same

18 Meade to Halleck, July 29, 1863, *OR* 27, pt.1, 105; Howard, *Autobiography*, 448.

19 Howard to Halleck, July 29, 1863, Bowdoin College.

20 Hubbard to wife, July 30, 1863.

day that Meade sent his telegram to Halleck, Schurz went to see Meade to argue his case. Meade responded with the following communication to Halleck: "Since my dispatch of this morning, I have had a consultation with Major-General Schurz, who has presented views to me which may in some measure modify your action. I have, therefore, authorized General Schurz to see you on the manner of effecting the change proposed in such way as to be least offensive to the officers and men concerned, and I shall be very glad if the propositions of General Schurz should meet with your approval, as it is my desire to render this change as agreeable to this officer and those under his command as the interests of the public service will permit."[21]

The War Department gave the proposal serious consideration, but in the end the corps survived intact, but only briefly. On August 5 the War Department ordered Meade to send Gordon's division to the Department of the South where it was attached to the Tenth Corps to participate in its operations against Charleston, South Carolina. With it went Gens. Alexander Schimmelfennig and Adelbert Ames along with some of the XI Corps' veteran regiments—17th Connecticut, 41st New York, 54th New York, 157th New York, 25th Ohio, 75th Ohio, 107th Ohio, and 74th Pennsylvania. Howard complained bitterly about the reduction of his corps but to no avail. Some writers have suggested that the corps was broken up because of a lack of confidence in its abilities, but more likely it was caused by the high percentage of loss it suffered at Chancellorsville and Gettysburg. The dismemberment of corps formations was not unique. The Fourth Corps was broken up following the Peninsula Campaign in 1862. There were seven corps in the Army of the Potomac in 1863, but the First and Third, which suffered heavy losses at Gettysburg, were eliminated and their composite units distributed among the other corps. Over the next two years the regiments who went south with Gordon's command established positive records of success in coastal operations in South Carolina and Florida. Schimmelfennig's command was credited with the capture of five Confederate colors and the general had the honor of accepting the surrender of the city of Charleston, South Carolina. Henry Finkenbiner of the 107th Ohio was awarded the Medal of Honor at Dingel's Mill, South Carolina, when he crossed a burning bridge under artillery fire to scout enemy positions.[22]

☽ ☽ ☽

21 Howard to Dearest, July 31, 1863; George G. Meade to Henry Halleck, July 29, 1863.

22 *OR* 27, pt. 2, 7-8; These included the garrison flags at Secessionville on James Island, and Fort Moultrie, Fort Ripley, The Citadel and Castle Pinckney, the latter four all in Charleston.

During the late summer and early fall of 1863 Northern and Southern armies vied for position in an intricate series of maneuvers near Chattanooga, Tennessee. The campaign culminated on September 19-20 when Gen. Braxton Bragg's Confederates defeated the Union forces in a bloody battle along Chickamauga Creek in northwest Georgia. Gen. William S. Rosecrans' vanquished army retreated to Chattanooga where he determined to hold the city at all costs. While Bragg settled down to conduct a siege, Rosecrans telegraphed urgent appeals for help to the War Department.

In the capitol, Secretary of War Edwin Stanton was not only receiving official reports from Rosecrans, but accounts from Charles Dana, a journalist who Stanton named his assistant and sent west to act as his personal intelligence agent—essentially his spy. After a series of dire descriptions of the aftermath of Chickamauga, on September 23 Dana implored Stanton to send reinforcements as quickly as possible if Chattanooga were to be saved. With this urging, Stanton called an emergency meeting with the president, Maj. Gen. Henry W. Halleck, and various other officials. The Secretary of War proposed to meet the crisis in the west by dispatching troops from the Army of the Potomac since, in his estimation, the conflict in the east was at an ebb with no major fighting anticipated in the near future. Stanton estimated that upwards of 30,000 troops could be dispatched west in five days. A disbelieving president, all too often disappointed by the snail-like pace of the Army of the Potomac, remarked "I will bet that if the order is given tonight, the troops can not be got to Washington in five days." Stanton replied that he proposed to effectively seize control of the railroads to reserve them for the movement to the exclusion of other business while the troops were being transported. Halleck remained unconvinced, estimating that it would take forty days to make the move. Stanton called in Col. David C. McCallum, superintendent of military railroads, as the person with the most relevant expertise. McCallum assured the gathering that "The transfer can be begun and fully completed within ten days." After some additional questioning by the president, Lincoln turned to Stanton and said "Mr. Secretary, you are the captain. Give the necessary orders and I will approve them."[23]

The move began with the troops marching to the nearest United States Military Railroad in Virginia for transport to Washington. There the men would be transferred via the Baltimore & Ohio Railroad west through Maryland to Benwood on the Ohio River near Wheeling. After crossing the river smaller railroads would move the men across Ohio to Indianapolis where the command would take the Jeffersonville Railroad south to the Ohio River. Once over the waterway, the Louisville & Nashville Railroad

23 Pickenpaugh, *Rescue by Rail*, 3-6.

would carry them further south, connecting with the Nashville & Chattanooga which would move them to their final destination at Bridgeport, Alabama. Once completed, the relief force would be within thirty miles of Chattanooga.[24]

At 2:30 am the following morning Halleck wired Meade to ascertain whether he contemplated any move in the near future and apprise him of the intended plan. At 9:00 am he sent another message ordering the implementation of the transfer, followed by a third wire explaining more precisely what he meant: "[T]he Eleventh and Twelfth Corps are positively to be sent here with the least possible delay. Every effort must be made to have them ready to-morrow morning." Meade responded with alacrity, immediately dispatching orders to Howard and Slocum to prepare their corps and begin the movement as soon as possible. The XI Corps, already guarding the railroads that would transport it north, had the shortest distance to travel, while the XII Corps would have to be relieved from its picket positions by the I Corps and then march to Brandy Station to be loaded onto the United States Military Railroad for the trip to Washington.[25]

The War Department's decision to take Gen. Joseph Hooker off the shelf to lead the two corps west provided him with a chance to revive his dormant career following his poor performance at Chancellorsville and subsequent resignation on the eve of Gettysburg. In the XI and XII Corps, few had any confidence in "Fighting Joe's" abilities, and this included their commanders. Howard was upset to be once again serving under Hooker. In addition, he felt slighted at not receiving the command himself. He offered his resignation, but the president refused to accept it. Howard was ordered to report to Hooker forthwith. Slocum, who also harbored ill feeling toward Hooker since Chancellorsville, was less circumspect. Upon hearing of his new assignment he dashed off a letter to the president tendering his resignation. "My opinion of General Hooker both as an officer and a gentleman is too well known to make it necessary for me to refer to it in this communication," he began. Because of these strong feelings "it would be degrading in me to accept any position under him." To reinforce his view, Slocum even visited the White House to meet with the president in person. Lincoln rejected the resignation, but apparently promised Slocum that upon arrival in Chattanooga he would not have to serve under Hooker. The president then wrote to Rosecrans informing him of the problem and asking him, when the troops

24 Pickenpaugh, *Rescue by Rail*, 52, 101.

25 Pickenpaugh, *Rescue by Rail*, 53-54.

arrived, to remove Slocum from under Hooker's command and compensate Hooker with "some other equal force."[26]

The mismatched command began its Odyssey west.

☽ ☽ ☽

Marching orders arrived at the XI Corps headquarters on September 24. The troops were to rendezvous at Alexandria where they would board trains for their trip. This required the scattered units to assemble and march to the nearest railhead from which they could be transported north. Steinwehr and Schurz ordered the troops to prepare cooked rations to last five days and be ready to board trains. Throughout the camps rumors abounded. What was happening? Where were they going? Was a new campaign beginning? Speculation flourished. Ernst Damkoehler in the 26th Wisconsin told his wife that some believed they would be following the First Division to South Carolina while others anticipated a movement west to reinforce Rosecrans. Frank Smrcek and the 26th Wisconsin left camp on the evening of the 24th, marching all night until he reached Catlett's Station. After a three-hour rest, the march continued until the tired command arrived at Manassas Junction about 5:00 p.m. the next day. Within four hours the men of the entire brigade "were packed into the dirty baggage cars and started" for the trip to Alexandria, across the river from Washington. Remarkably, all but 1,700 of the XI Corps troops left for the west by the end of the day, September 25, with the rest following beginning at 6:00 am the next morning.[27]

When it finally became apparent to everyone that the two corps were being transferred west the rank and file generally reacted positively. The men in the XI Corps felt just as happy to leave Virginia as the Army of the Potomac did to see them go. And it was not only the XI Corps that felt relief at the reassignment. In the XII Corps Sergt. David Nichol spoke for many in a letter he sent home announcing the move. "This news was hailed with delight by all. Any place but Virginia. It will just be the making of this Army, this change will put new life in the men & I think in this new field of operation everything will go on better."[28]

26 Daily Log of 11th Corps, Sept. 25, 1863; Pickenpaugh, *Rescue by Rail*, 69-70.

27 Daily Log of 11th Corps, Sept. 25, 1863; Circular, Sept. 24, 1863, RG 393, Pt. 2, 5321, 5348 and 5407, NARA; Keeler diary; Henny diary, Sept. 24,1863; Damkoehler to Mathilde, Nov. 8, 1863; Daily Log of 11th Corps, Sept. 24, 1863; Smrcek diary, Sept. 25, 1863; Butts, *Gallant Captain*, 96; Bates, *History*, II, 920; Karsten diary, Sept. 24, 1863; Pickenpaugh, *Rescue by Rail*, 73.

28 Nichol to father, Sept. 27, 1863, in Brady, *Hurrah for the Artillery*, 291-92.

Shortly, a long line of Baltimore & Ohio Railroad boxcars appeared. The men clamored aboard, forty to sixty bodies shoving into each of the cramped cars. The pungent smell of manure greeted them, but speed was of the essence. No time could be wasted cleaning out the wastes of the freight cars' recent occupants. Capt. Frederick Winkler found "The cars were so crowded, it was almost impossible to live in them." Ernst Damkoehler, in the same regiment, told his wife that he "could write pages if I wanted to give you a good description of our oppressions on the train where we were packed together like herrings." He found the whole movement "a terrible fatigue for animals and humans." Hartwell Osborn noted that "one passenger coach to each train provided partial quarters for the officers, and the impedimenta were loaded in such cars as chance provided."[29]

Yet, it appears that some commands fared better than others. Capt. von Fritsch, appointed transportation officer for Schurz's division, described the situation: "Forty to sixty men were packed into each cattle car, still smelling of manure, and very poor accommodations were offered to the General and the other officers. As I could not kick, I tried 'soft soap,' and sometimes improved the first arrangements by getting a few cars more, and a passenger car for officers. How we got the two Corps alive to Nashville in seven days it is difficult to explain, as our men were so crowded, had so little chance to obtain water or food, and, locked up in the cars, had neither fresh air enough nor even the ordinary necessities of life."[30]

Rumbling through western Maryland on the morning of September 26, the leading elements reached Cumberland by mid-afternoon. Lt. Karl Karsten noted the 26th Wisconsin reached Harper's Ferry, which it found "almost all burnt down," at 2:00 pm, and arrived at Martinsburg at 6:00 pm where the men received coffee and bread. "We passed some fine scenery yesterday between Washington and here," Capt. Winkler wrote as the train paused at New Creek, a town in western Virginia. "We were at Harper's Ferry at about sunset." Still uncertain of their destination, the captain believed the prevailing rumor they were destined to reinforce Rosecrans in Chattanooga. It was obviously an emergency move, "and that, to my judgment, can be nothing but Rosecrans need of reinforcements."[31]

Surgeon Robert Hubbard found the scenery compelling. "We have passed and are still passing through a most romantically wild mountainous region." The weather was

29 Winkler, *Letters*, 88-89; Damkoehler to Mathilde, Nov. 8, 1863; Osborn, "The XI Corps in East Tennessee," 350.

30 Butts, *Gallant Captain*, 96.

31 Karsten diary, Sept. 26, 1863; Winkler, *Letters*, 88.

Crowded troop trains passing through Harper's Ferry.
United States Military Academy

"delightful" during the day, but there was frost the previous night. In search of better air, Henry Henny "passed the night on the top of the cars, and nearly froze to death in doing so."[32]

All appeared to go well until September 27 when Schurz, at the trailing end of the corps, sent a message ahead to the station at Grafton ordering them to halt cars carrying his division until he arrived. William P. Smith, responsible for transportation in that area, instructed the local agent to disregard the order and telegraphed Secretary of War Stanton to apprise him of the situation. When Schurz finally arrived in Grafton he embroiled himself in an argument with the stationmaster, demanding to know why his orders had not been obeyed. His humor was not improved by a message he received from Gen. Daniel Butterfield, Hooker's chief of staff, directing that he should "under no circumstances order any trains of troops stopped or delayed for a moment."

On the heels of this apparent reprimand, a telegram arrived from Secretary Stanton informing him that "Major-General Hooker has the orders of this Department

32 Henny diary, Sept. 28, 1863; Hubbard to wife, Sept. 26, 1863; Henny diary, Sept. 28, 1863.

to relieve you from command and put under arrest any officer who undertakes to delay or interfere with the orders and regulations of the railroad officers in charge of the transportation of the troops."

Schurz was shocked. He was also uncertain what the communication meant. Was he relieved? To clarify the issue he telegraphed Stanton: "Am I to understand from your dispatch that I am relieved from command?" He also explained that his only motive was to try to bring order to a confusing situation and therefore expedite the movement. Stanton bluntly responded that "General Hooker is authorized to relieve from command any officer that interferes with or hinders the transportation of troops in the present movement. Whether you have done so, and whether he has relieved you from command, ought to be known to yourself. The order will certainly be enforced against any officer, whatever his rank may be, who delays or endangers transportation of troops."

Duly chastised, Schurz would not let the matter drop. Instead, he sent a lengthy explanation to Stanton. Howard supported him, but Hooker was plainly unhappy with his argumentative subordinate.[33] Schurz was obviously wrong to attempt to halt the movement until he could reach the front of his division and the incident only served to further erode the relationship between him and Hooker that had already been seriously compromised over the Chancellorsville controversy.

☽ ☽ ☽

At Benwood, on the Ohio River, the trains halted to deposit their load of human cargo. Grateful for the opportunity to get some fresh air, the men boarded ferries that carried them to Bellaire on the Ohio side of the river. Maj. Samuel Hurst and the 73rd Ohio "greeted with hearty cheers the hills of our own native State." Once again racing across the countryside, the air within the cars became hot and foul smelling. There was no opportunity to obtain food, water, or fresh air. Men found it impossible even to tend to the natural necessities of life. Sickened by the crowded conditions in the acrid cars, some soldiers chose to climb outside in search of relief. Perched precariously atop the boxcars, they enjoyed the fresh air and open scenery of southern Ohio. Unfortunately the urge to avoid the stifling atmosphere below placed the men in grave jeopardy when the speeding train passed under low bridges or entered darkened tunnels. Ernst Schaubhut, a drummer in the 58th New York, met his death when he fell

33 Pickenpaugh, *Rescue by Rail*, 89-90.

from the roof of a car as his train crossed a river near Zanesville At least seven others met a similar fate.[34]

While waiting for the next train to load and move out of Zanesville, the band of the 55th Ohio played several lively tunes for the local populace and their fellow soldiers. Wherever a momentary halt occurred the citizens offered refreshments to the huddled mass of humanity within the boxcars. Travel through the North proved quite different than marching along hostile Virginia roads, but was tiring nonetheless. "This mode of traveling is so fatiguing," Capt. Winkler complained. "We have seen little of papers for some days, and the account of the Battle of Chattanooga was very meager. It seems unquestionable that Rosecrans suffered very severely and was pretty badly defeated, but he seems to hold and maintain a strong position."[35]

Surgeon Hubbard marveled at the prosperous countryside. "We are now only 40 miles from Columbus on the Ohio Central R.R. and emphatically in the land of grape, the finest & most luscious specimens of the catawba being offered to us at all the Depots at marvelously low prices. We pass round the hat for resources and our car is at present abundantly supplied with apples peaches and grapes. We have a large water pailful of the latter standing in the center of the car by the stove. . . . The day is beautiful and the fruitful fields & comfortable dwellings and evidences of general prosperity are in pleasing contrast with the desolate regions we have but recently occupied. The farther we get from the blighting influences of the accursed system of slavery the most evident are the smiles of Providence on human industry."[36]

The troops' ingenuity for conjuring up pranks found new ways in which to discomfort their comrades. George Warner explained that "In those railroad days the water tanks standing by the side of the track were manipulated by pulling a rope when the fireman wished to replenish his boiler. Through a desire for revenge on their comrades sheltered within the car and for mischief generally, the 'roosters' were not slow to discover an admirable plan to gratify their wishes by pulling the rope as the train passed a tank, and thus sending a six inch stream of water against the side and into the open doors of the cars. No record has been left as to the precise form of language used by those sitting opposite those doorways."[37]

34 Hurst, *Journal-History*, 82; Howard, *Autobiography*, 435; Regimental Descriptive Book, Cos. A-D, 58th New York Infantry.

35 Henny diary, Sept. 28, 1863; Winkler, *Letters*, 88; Karsten diary, Sept. 28, 1863.

36 Hubbard to wife, Sept. 29, 1863.

37 Conklin, *Crescent and Star*, 131.

Luther Mesnard had been released from the hospital just in time to catch one of the last trains. He was lucky to be in a car with only about twenty men "rather than the usual 40 due to a trick of some kind." His group "had a violin and good singers, dancers and story tellers in the crowd, and the previous trains of soldiers had so advertised the movements, that especially as we moved through Ohio every crossroad and station seemed to be lined with good things to eat, and our car became well stocked with luxuries. The loyal citizens were out in force, especially pretty girls, and we enjoyed the trip greatly, and crowded more fun and amusement into that week than I ever had known before, this with a lot of boys I had known but a few days and never saw afterwards."[38]

In Xenia the train stopped for an hour and a half. "[W]e had a perfect ovation. Ladies[,] Gentlemen & children through the train its whole length of some 30 cars and loaded down the soldiers with all kinds of eatables. When they found Gen. Howard was on board the Ladies all came along in succession to shake hands with him as he stood on the platform of the rear car. They heaped upon us their gifts of pies, cakes, bread & butter, sandwiches, apples, peaches and most abundantly grapes" with some "seeking autographs." Still vivid after more than four decades, Howard described the experience in his memoirs: "All the way along through Indiana and Ohio we received an enthusiastic welcome. Multitudes—men, women, and children—filled the streets of the towns as we passed and gave us refreshments and hearty words and other demonstrations of their appreciation. At Xenia, for example, little girls, gaily attired, came in flocks and handed up bouquets of flowers to the soldiers; the children and the ladies, too, were the bearers of little housekeeper bags, needlebooks, and bright flags, each bringing some small thing for use. Nothing ever inspired our men more."[39]

Dayton was the hometown of the notorious Copperhead Clement Vallandigham who was just then running for election. Major Charles Howard reported that as the train approached groups of people gathered in the small towns of southwestern Ohio "[A]ll the boys were hurrahing for [John] Brough . . . who is the Republican candidate for Governor in opposition to Valandingham." Gen. Howard also noted that there were some people who, for political reasons, were "always unfriendly to President Lincoln and his administration. . . . We heard from these in every crowd; they called us cutthroats, Lincoln hirelings, nigger savers, or by some other characteristic epithets.

38 Mesnard, 55th and 25th Ohio, CW Misc Coll., USMHI, 42.

39 C. Howard to mother, Oct. 4, 1863, Bowdoin College; Howard, *Autobiography*, I, 453-54.

Our loyal soldiers denominated them 'copperheads,' and when there was opportunity for a more forceful rejoinder it was quick to come."[40]

The politics of this election season did indeed provide opportunities for "more forceful rejoinder," which led to one of the most serious incidents that occurred during the movement. When the trains stopped briefly in Cambridge, Ohio, some members of Dilger's battery took the opportunity to refresh themselves at a local saloon. One of the artillerymen raised a political toast to which the proprietor took exception. When he complained, the offending soldier and several comrades raised an even louder cheer for their candidate. An argument ensued in which the owner stabbed the offending soldier in the neck with a cheese knife. Additional soldiers came to their wounded friend's aid and the proprietor fled out the back door, but a bullet sliced through his thigh as he escaped. The troops then ransacked the saloon and an attached grocery store, carting off anything they could use and much they could not. During the same stop unidentified soldiers are reported to have fired their rifles at a group of civilians cheering for Vallandigham, although the muskets were reportedly loaded only with blanks to scare the Copperheads.[41]

At Richmond, Indiana, Lt. William Wheeler marveled that "great crowds of ladies came to the cars, with baskets of bread and cake and pie, cold meats and chickens, sourkraut for the Dutchmen, and doughnuts for the Yankees, and pressed it upon the men, without distinction of rank, in the most charming manner."[42]

From Indianapolis the tracks turned south to Jeffersonville on the Ohio River which the leading cars reached shortly before midnight on September 28. Ferries carried men and equipment to Louisville. The band of the 55th Ohio played as it crossed, continuing on as it marched through the Kentucky city. Henry Henny and some of his friends found time to have a good breakfast, but where he did not say. Capt. Winkler enjoyed the opportunity for a hearty breakfast at the Louisville Hotel before again boarding trains for Nashville. "It is tiresome and wearisome on the cars," Winkler complained, "I feel the fatigue, but we have to take them again." Capt. Franz Lackner characterized it only as "a hard ride in Cattle cars."[43]

Howard took advantage of the brief halt to write to his wife from the Galt House in Louisville. "I had no idea of this beauty & fertility of Ohio & Indiana till I came

40 C. Howard to mother, Oct. 4, 1863, Bowdoin College; Howard, *Autobiography*, I, 451.

41 C. Howard to mother, Oct. 4, 1863, Bowdoin College; Pickenpaugh, *Rescue by Rail*, 104-05.

42 Wheeler to mother, Oct. 8, 1863, in Bershears, *Loyal Till Death*, 254.

43 Henny diary, Sept. 29, 1863; Winkler, *Letters*, 89; Lackner diary, Dec. 22, 1863; Karsten diary, Sept. 29 and 30, 1863.

through. . . . I feel that I am sent out here for some wise and good purpose. I believe my Corps will be better appreciated. Already the good conduct of the soldiers excites wonder."[44]

☽ ☽ ☽

The XI Corps began arriving at Bridgeport, Alabama, on September 30. "How we got the two Corps alive to Nashville in seven days it is difficult to explain," marveled Capt. von Fritsch. Maj. Thomas Osborn found diminutive Bridgeport "only a place in name but at present of considerable military importance. There was once a house and a sawmill here, but the house has been burned and the mill torn down. It is on the bank of the Tennessee River, which the Nashville and Chattanooga Railroad crosses at this point. . . . Much rain has fallen since we arrived here. The days are too hot and the nights too cold. Along the river the fogs are very dense and do not rise until nine o'clock in the morning." Lt. William Wheeler was struck by the abject poverty. "The people of this region are, many of them, on the very border of starvation, and swarms are fleeing from it to the happier North, their children in their hand or following in a mournful train behind, their few household effects in a broken wagon, drawn by a miserable horse, and upon their faces a strong, fixed look of despair, which it makes me sick to think of. And indeed I do not allow myself to reflect upon the necessary and collateral accompaniments of this war, as it would make me too miserable."[45]

Surgeon Hubbard wrote home comparing Bridgeport with the city by the same name in his home state of Connecticut. "The saying that 'a rose by any other name's as sweet' does not make it true that a place is attractive merely on account of its name. Altho I am writing from a Bridgeport it is a very different Bridgeport from the one in which center so many attractions for me. . . . It is difficult to discover any good reason for christening it Bridgeport as the only evidence of its ever having been inhabited are less than half a dozen dilapidated shanties tenantless except by some ambitious Sutler or Qr. master. Genl Schurz remarked facetiously at dinner today that the only apology for the christening was a saw mill & a steamboat landing—but that no steamboats ever came up here." If Hubbard was not complimentary about Bridgeport, he was brutal in his estimation of the local inhabitants. "The natives living about here are the most ignorant abject people it has ever been my misfortune to see. . . . It is almost impossible

44 Howard to Dearest, Oct. 1, 1863, Bowdoin College.

45 Butts, *Gallant Captain*, 96; Osborn to Spencer, Oct. 20, 1863, Crumb and Dhalle, *No Middle Ground*, 166; Wheeler to mother, Nov. 8, 1863, in *Bershears, Loyal Till Death*, 260.

to find one of the common class of society able to read or spell even his own name & this is often the case with owners of hundreds of acres of land. . . . I am not surprised that such a people can be made to believe the secession lies that they may be politically damned."[46]

☽ ☽ ☽

Gen. Howard arrived at Stevenson, Alabama, at 9:00 pm on October 3. He found it "a poor town with some half dozen miserable houses" and a makeshift supply base where stores had been accumulating for the relief of Rosecrans' army in Chattanooga. "It was a singularly rough country—nothing but abrupt hills and mountains, nothing except the broad river and the crooked railway! Though early in October, the air was very chilly; and the old camps left by the Confederates as they withdrew to the south shore were, as old camps mostly are, very uninviting." Within the next few days the remainder of the Eleventh and XII Corps arrived, their historic trek complete. Howard established his headquarters in Bridgeport inside a small abandoned Confederate fort.[47]

The movement of the XI and XII Corps from Virginia to reinforce the defense of Chattanooga, Tennessee, was an amazing feat. In only eleven and one-half days two entire army corps numbering 17,500 men rested on the banks of the Tennessee River. In that short space of time ten batteries of artillery with forty-five guns, 717 wagons and ambulances, over 4,400 horses and mules, and all of the two corps' baggage traveled over some 1,192 miles of track.[48] It was the largest, most successful movement by rail in the history of warfare. The troops were now in place to attempt the relief of the besieged city. The campaign could begin.

46 Hubbard to wife, Oct. 5 and 16, 1863.

47 Howard to Dearest, Oct. 5, 1863, Bowdoin College; Howard, *Autobiography*, I, 457; C. Howard to mother, Oct. 11, 1863, Bowdoin College.

48 Osborn, "The Eleventh Corps in East Tennessee," 350; *OR* 31, pt.1, 111.

Chapter 18

"We Were Received With Hearty Cheers"

The Relief of Chattanooga

THE SUMMER OF 1863 WAS brutally hot and dry in the Chattanooga area. Rain had been very sparse since the beginning of July allowing a scorching sun to harden the ground until it cracked. Nature chose to remedy this oversight with a vengeance shortly after the XI Corps arrived. A torrential downpour turned parched, blistered earth into deep, clinging mud that entombed everything with wheels. Roads became impassable. Supply routes were cut off. When men opened barrels of crackers they were greeted by waves of glutted worms. Improperly packaged salt-pork rotted into contaminated refuse. For several days, until the deluge abated, the men subsisted on half-rations. "Where is the boasted magnificence of the south," Capt. George Turnbull of the 134th New York asked. "I have yet to see it. . . . We are encamped on the banks of the Tennessee River and a most dreary looking place it is."[1]

Temperatures varied almost as much as the moisture, although perhaps on a more predictable schedule. By mid-October the weather began to turn cold, alternating between warm days and cold nights as the onset of winter neared. On October 19 Surgeon Hubbard told his wife that "It is a most delightful day worthy of Indian Summer but more in this climate like one of Spring's most genial days than like our October. The birds are singing and I suppose here they remain, many kinds all winter. The location is infested nights and until late in the day by a dense fog so that it seems

1 Fullerton, "Army of the Cumberland at Chattanooga," 719; Winkler Papers; Howard, *Autobiography*, 457; Butts, *Gallant Captain*, 96; Wickesberg to family, Oct. 17, 1863; Conklin, "History of the 134th N.Y."

morning until 10 to 11 oclk A.M." While temperatures during the days could be quite pleasant, the mercury dropped significantly as night set in. Henry Henny wrote that "The day is very pleasant but the nights are uncomfortably cold and it requires all of our limited supply of clothing to keep warm." Capt. Frederick Winkler found "such a scarcity of blankets" that he slept "in full-dress uniform, lacking only boots and spurs," but nevertheless had "to tremble with cold all night."[2]

Rebel raids on supply lines, including the destruction of crucial railroad bridges, also affected the availability of provisions. Surgeon Hubbard reported having "very poor tough beef of which I have not eaten 2 oz. in a week, and villainous coffee which I cannot swallow. . . . The deprivation of vegetables is a great one as well as prolific of disease." Ernst Damkoehler's impressions were similar: "Here we have the same rations which are crackers, sugar and coffee and one half pound of meat. No rice or beans. Our troops are half-starved and work day and night digging trenches." Winkler found the plight of the animals especially severe. The "mules and horses look wretched and are almost wholly without forage." Sutlers scalped food and other supplies at outrageous prices in blatant profiteering. Nevertheless, there was one very positive aspect to their new surroundings. "I am out of the Army of the Potomac," Andrew Boies noted in this journal, "and am glad of it."[3]

The constant dampness, fluctuating temperatures, inadequate clothing and tents, along with the insufficient diet led to outbreaks of illness and disease that ravaged the camps. "Since we have came to this department," Ephraim Hutchinson in the 82nd Ohio observed, "the men have been dying off very rapid by disease. The change of climate I suppose is the cause principally of so much sickness, and the fatigue and exposure." Surgeon Hubbard reported that "The whole valley of the Tennessee is infested with Fever and ague and if we lie here long I anticipate plenty of business for Surgeons." By mid-October Howard was listed among the sick. He was "not very well having had a severe cold ever since we arrived here. Still he is actively engaged with his duties."[4]

Sickness arrived, but mail did not. "There is no mail communication," Winkler lamented, "no communication at all." Many soldiers followed Sergt. Wickesberg's lead by writing home for "pectoral tea," leather boots, foodstuffs, and new clothing, but the letters could not begin their journeys until mail delivery was restored. By the second

2 Hubbard to wife, Oct. 19, 1863; Henry Henny diary, Oct. 8, 1863; Winkler, *Letters*, 94.

3 Hubbard to wife, Oct. 18, 1863; Damkoehler to Mathilde, November 8, 1863; Winkler, *Letters*, 89; Boies, *Thirty-third Massachusetts*, 45.

4 Hutchinson to "Friend John," Feb. 8, 1864; Hubbard to wife, Oct. 19, 1863.

half of October the XI Corps had not received any mail since leaving its camps in Virginia. "I am so disappointed that I almost wish Lee's Army would get into Washington and capture some of the Hds of Department for I think half of them could be spared with benefit. There is no excuse for their keeping back our mail nearly a month—it makes soldiers discontented and homesick and therefore the influence is pernicious."[5]

But if life was difficult in the XI Corps, it was much worse in Chattanooga where Gen. William Rosecrans' besieged army slowly starved. Gen. Ulysses S. Grant later described the conditions in his *Memoirs*: "The country afforded but little food for his animals, nearly ten thousand of which has already starved, and not enough were left to draw a single piece of artillery or even the ambulances to convey the sick. The men had been on half rations of hard bread for a considerable time, with but few other supplies except beef driven from Nashville across the country. The region along the road became so exhausted of food for the cattle that by the time they reached Chattanooga they were much in the condition of the few animals left alive there—'on the lift.' Indeed, the beef was so poor that the soldiers were in the habit of saying, with a faint facetiousness, that they were living on 'half rations of hard bread and *beef dried on the hoof*.' Nothing could be transported but food, and the troops were without sufficient shoes or other clothing suitable for the advancing season. What they had was well worn. The fuel within the Federal lines was exhausted, even to the stumps of trees."[6] In short, Rosecrans' army was on the verge of being destroyed by starvation, disease, and exhaustion.

Albert R. Greene, an officer in the XII Corps, explained the problem facing the relieving columns. There was "a good wagon road from Wauhatchie, a railroad junction in Lookout Valley, along the river to Brown's Ferry. The railroad, the river and the wagon road on the left bank of the river are the only ways of communication between Bridgeport and Chattanooga that were then at all practicable; and these were all in the hands of the enemy. The only other roads were little better than mule paths, and lay on the south of the river from Jasper over Walden's Ridge into Chattanooga, the shortest at least fifty miles, and passable only in good seasons of the weather."[7]

For more than a month, the only supplies getting into Chattanooga were brought by a few mules winding along broken muddy paths that were not intercepted by Rebel cavalry patrols in the area. Although occasional deliveries such as these made it through

5 Winkler, *Letters*, 90; Wickesberg to parents, Oct. 17, 1863; Hubbard to wife, Oct. 19, 1863.

6 Grant, *Personal Memoirs*, 234, 236.

7 Greene, "From Bridgeport to Ringgold," Vol. 6.

to the city, they were not nearly enough to sustain the beleaguered garrison. By October 20, most of the animals in Chattanooga were dead, having been eaten by the starving troops. "[T]here were absolutely not a day's rations in Chattanooga. Half rations and lesser quantities had been issued for weeks, and on that day the last pound of food had been given out." Gen. George H. Thomas, among the beleaguered forces in Chattanooga, upon assuming control had issued a defiant message promising that "I will hold the town till we starve."[8] He and his troops were about to do just that.

Twenty-eight miles separated Chattanooga from the salvation being stockpiled for its relief in Bridgeport. Those twenty-eight miles represented a significant obstacle in early October 1863. "It was raining cats and dogs," Lt. Karl Karsten of the 26th Wisconsin wrote in his diary. "It rained nearly all the time," Major Winkler agreed. "As we retired at half past eight o'clock last night," Winkler wrote on October 16, "the sky was brilliant with its thousands of stars. It was a cheering sight for us, somewhat as the rainbow must have been to Noah, for even if it did not tell us that the days of deluge were past forever, it did seem to promise that to-day's sun should rise unobscured; but in this land of treason, signs are false, the first peer through the opening of my tent this morning showed lowering skies."[9]

Surgeon Hubbard also noted the frequently changing weather patterns: "It is now raining altho a few hours since the sky was clear & promised a pleasant day, but the clouds soon gathered around our limited horizon and in a short time a most terrific thunderstorm was upon us. I have never heard such a grand demonstration of heavens artillery—it reminded me of descriptions of thunderstorms in the Alps."[10] Constant rain during the first three weeks of October turned the dirt roads into muddy quagmires, halting almost any serious military movement. Nonetheless, a plan for breaking the siege of Chattanooga was in the works. But first some changes were in order.

☽ ☽ ☽

On October 16 the War Department issued General Orders No. 337 announcing a major reorganization of the western commands. The order created a new military division by combining the Departments of the Cumberland, Ohio, and Tennessee under the command of Maj. Gen. Ulysses S. Grant. Due in no small part to Secretary of

8 Greene, "From Bridgeport to Ringgold"; Raum, "Hazen's Night Expedition," 278.

9 Karsten diary, Oct. 23, 1863; Winkler, *Letters*, 92, 95; Winkler to Gaylord, Aug. 25, 1864.

10 Hubbard to wife, Oct. 21, 1863.

War Stanton's dislike for Rosecrans, Grant was given the option of relieving him from command of the Army of the Cumberland and replacing him with Maj. Gen. George H. Thomas who had won considerable laurels for his firm stand at Chickamauga against repeated Confederate assaults. Grant quickly chose to exercise that option. Word of the changes reached the XI Corps on October 18.[11]

Grant arrived in Stevenson three days later to assume personal command of the Union efforts. Howard happened to be in Stevenson when Grant appeared and was introduced to him, along with Brig. Gen. John A. Rawlins, and a handful of Grant's staff. Howard had never met Grant before. "I had heard so much about the general that I was very anxious to see him. I found him only a little taller than I, thin, and very pale. I had heard so much of his toughness, and seen so much in the papers concerning his drinking habits, that I had expected to witness a different sort of man altogether. As he looked upon my approach, the clearness of his complexion and the pleasant expression of his eyes told me at once a different story. He rose, extended his hand to me as I gave him my name, and said gently, 'I am glad to see you, General Howard.' Then he waited, as he was wont to do, for me to continue the conversation or to retire."[12]

While Grant and Howard conversed, a messenger from Hooker arrived "extending also an invitation to [Grant] to stay and partake of Hooker's hospitality." Howard was surprised when Grant bluntly responded "If General Hooker wishes to see *me* he will find me on the train!" Howard quickly understood that "it was Grant's way of maintaining his ascendancy where a subordinate was likely to question it." Hooker apparently also understood because he soon arrived in person.[13]

Later that day Grant continued on to Bridgeport where he spent the night with Howard in his tent. During their evening conversations Grant spotted a whiskey flask. Seeing that Grant was looking at the flask, Howard quickly informed him that the "flask in not mine. It was left there by an officer to be returned to Chattanooga; I never drink." Grant replied in an even voice "Neither do I." Howard, who was favorably impressed with Grant, believed him, attributing the rumors of Grant's drinking habit to "a thousand falsehoods which ambition and envy had industriously circulated against him." Howard later wrote "I liked his appearance better than that of any Major general I have seen. He is modest, quiet and thoughtful. He looks the picture of firmness. He does not drink liquor and never swears. A member of his staff told me he never had

11 Meysenburg journal, Oct. 18, 1863.

12 Howard, "Grant at Chattanooga," 375; Meysenburg journal, Oct. 21, 1863.

13 Howard, *Autobiography*, 460; Sword, *Mountains Touched with Fire*, 52-53.

used a profane oath. How differently from what we had imagined when those stories of Shiloh were being circulated." Surgeon Hubbard, who always seemed to be nearby when important events were unfolding, also believed Grant did not look like someone addicted to drink. "His thin, slightly compressed lips tell of firmness and perseverance in whatever he undertakes." His demeanor was "quiet, self-possessed and not communicative, evidently avoiding all effort to impress any idea of greatness upon those around him."[14]

While Hooker and Howard were meeting with their new commanding officer, Gen. Braxton Bragg's Confederate army occupied the heights to the east and south of Chattanooga, with its cavalry operating north of the city. This left only a long, circuitous wagon route of some sixty miles as the lifeline connecting the city to Federal supply bases. With the onset of the rainy days of October, this route often became impassable. A shorter route via Kelley's and Brown's Ferries existed, but Confederate forces in Lookout Valley and on Raccoon Mountain made this route inaccessible. Grant assigned Hooker's newly-arrived troops the important task of opening this vital supply line into the city. The plan called for the XI and XII Corps to cross to the southern side of the Tennessee River at Bridgeport then move into Lookout Valley via Shellmound, Whitesides, and Wauhatchie to Brown's Ferry. This would open the river to steamboat traffic that could then bring cargo to a point where it could be offloaded and transported overland into Chattanooga.[15]

It sounded simple. It would not be. The weather and Bragg's army, reinforced by the Federals' old nemesis from the east, Gen. James Longstreet with his corps from the Army of Northern Virginia, promised to make the attempt problematic.

☽ ☽ ☽

While the XI Corps waited for the weather to clear Howard attempted to get his units ready for the forthcoming campaign. He requested 200,000 rounds of various caliber ammunition to bring the corps supply up to eighty rounds per man, ordered the inspection of all arms, and solicited information from division leaders on the status of their troops. The brief respite also allowed time for some alterations in the corps command structure. Under Special Orders No. 209 dated October 19 Howard announced a number of changes. Aside from an independent infantry company from

14 Pickenpaugh, *Rescue by Rail*, 162; Howard to Dearest, Oct. 24, 1863, Bowdoin College; Hubbard to wife, Oct. 23, 1863.

15 Boatner, *Civil War Dictionary*, 142-43; Greene, "From Bridgeport to Ringgold."

the 8th New York under Capt. Anton Bruhn acting as the XI Corps headquarters guard, Howard still commanded two division which continued to be referred to as the Second and Third Divisions long after the First Division had been transferred to South Carolina. Both continued under their long-time leaders, Brig. Gen. Adolph von Steinwehr and Maj. Gen. Carl Schurz respectively.[16]

Col. Adolphus Buschbeck led von Steinwehr's First Brigade composed of four veteran regiments—the 27th Pennsylvania (Maj. Peter A. McAloon), 73rd Pennsylvania (Lieut. Col. Joseph B. Taft), 134th New York (Lt. Col. Allan H. Jackson), 154th New York (Col. Patrick H. Jones)—and the relative newcomer 33rd New Jersey (Col. George W. Mindil). The New Jersey regiment was recruited in the Newark area, its colonel already a celebrity. Born near Frankfort, Germany, he enlisted in the 61st Pennsylvania in 1861, rose to the rank of captain, and while on the Peninsula under McClellan his bravery in leading an assault was recognized with a Medal of Honor. Promoted to colonel of the 27th New Jersey, he recruited the 33rd when its term of service expired. Although a new regiment, nearly all of the officers and some three quarters of the men were veterans of previous service. Commanded by Col. Orland Smith, the Second Brigade was an all-veteran group—33rd Massachusetts (Lt. Col. Godfrey Rider, Jr.), 55th Ohio (Col. Charles B. Gambee), 73rd Ohio (Maj. Samuel H. Hurst), and 136th New York (Col. James Wood, Jr.).[17]

In the Third Division Carl Schurz reorganized his command into three brigades, replacing the previous two brigade structure. One reason for this was certainly to give the division more flexibility when it became engaged, the three-brigade structure being the norm for a division, but it appears that personal issues relating to seniority among the officers in his command played a primary role in the shifting of regiments so as to reward Col. Friedrich Hecker with brigade command without displacing Col. Krzyzanowski, who was his junior in seniority. As a result, command of the First Brigade went to Brig. Gen. Hector Tyndale. Included along with a trio of XI Corps veteran regiments—the 45th New York (Major Charles Koch), 61st Ohio (Col. Stephen J. McGroarty), and 82d Ohio (Lt. Col. David Thomson)—were the 101st Illinois under Col. Charles H. Fox and the 143rd New York led by Col. Horace Boughton.[18]

16 Howard letter, October 9, 1863, RG 393, Pt. 2, Vol. 16, II-5314; Keeler diary, USMHI.

17 Powles, "New Jersey's Western Warriors," 47; Hunt and Brown, *Brevet Brigadier Generals in Blue*, 416; *OR* 31, pt. 2, 17.

18 *OR* 31, pt. 2, 17.

Col. Adolphus Buschbeck commanded a brigade in the Tennessee campaigns.
MOLLUS Collection, Philadelphia

Organized at Camp Duncan in Jacksonville, the 101st had seen limited service with the Army of the Tennessee in 1862-63, much of it being captured and paroled at Holly Springs in December 1862. Col. Boughton was an attorney born in Rush, New York, who had prior service as an officer in the 13th New York. His command, known as the Sullivan County Regiment, organized at Monticello in the hills west of the Hudson Valley in October 1862, serving first at the Siege of Suffolk and in skirmishes at Providence Church Road and Bottom's Bridge, all in Virginia and all without loss. It joined the XI Corps in the wake of the Gettysburg Campaign.[19]

Col. Wlodzimierz Krzyzanowski retained the Second Brigade with his own 58th New York (Capt. Michael Esembaux) along with the 26th Wisconsin (Capt. Frederick C. Winkler), 119th New York (Col. John T. Lockman) and 141st New York (Col. William K. Logie). Col. Logie's regiment was organized at Elmira in the Southern Tier's 27th Senatorial District. The regiment left the state on September 15, 1862, and was assigned to the defenses of Washington, followed by a stint in the Middle Department with the VIII Corps. It spent the first half of 1863 moving from one assignment to another assignment, serving at the Siege of Suffolk, Bottom's Bridge, and Diascund Bridge in Virginia, losing its only combat fatality at the latter combat. Logie was a native in Louisiana and had attended Hobart College in western New York's picturesque Finger Lakes region. He graduated from Union College in Schenectady and soon thereafter began the study of law in 1858, and the following year was admitted to the bar. Thereafter Logie moved to Corning, where he was practicing when the Civil War broke out in 1861.[20]

19 Hunt and Brown, *Brevet Brigadier Generals in Blue*, 416.

20 *OR* 31, pt. 1, 111, 804, and Part 2, 17; Dyer, *War of the Rebellion*, 456; *OR* 31, pt 1, 804; Fenton, *Fifth Annual Report*, 362-71.

Col. George W. Mindil, 33rd New Jersey
U.S. Army Heritage and Education Center

The new Third Brigade was given to Col. Hecker, who inherited the veteran 68th New York (Lt. Col. Albert von Steinhausen), 75th Pennsylvania (Major August Ledig) and 82nd Illinois (Lt. Col. Edward S. Salomon). The 80th Illinois (Capt. James Neville) was added to these three veteran commands. An Illinois native, Neville attended McKendree College. His regiment was organized in Centralia, drawing its men from the southern counties of the state. It had seen hard service at Perryville with the Army of the Ohio and took part in Col. Abel D. Streight's disastrous raid into northern Alabama where the regiment seemed to have performed well but was captured by Confederates under Gen. Nathan Bedford Forrest. As a result, its officers were confined to Libby Prison in Richmond while most of the enlisted men were soon exchanged for Confederate prisoners. Remaining unattached to individual brigades, the XI Corps artillery batteries under Major Thomas Osborn were all veteran outfits: Battery I, 1st New York (Capt. Michael Wiedrich); 13th Independent New York Battery (Capt. William Wheeler); Battery I, 1st Ohio (Capt. Hubert Dilger); Battery K, 1st Ohio (Lt. Nicholas Sahm); and Battery G, 4th United States (Lt. Christopher F. Merkle.[21]

The weather-induced lull afforded the easterners their first noteworthy contact with western soldiers. Although Howard was impressed with Grant, few others—east or west—shared those feelings about each other. "The Army of the Cumberland doesn't like the Army of the Potomac very much," Henry Henny recorded matter-of-factly in his diary. Surgeon Hubbard thought that "The Western Department is so far as my observation goes less efficient, more disorderly & more corrupt than the

21 Krzyzanowski, Knoxville campaign, 111; Dyer, 456; *OR* 31, pt. 1, 804; "80th Illinois Volunteer Infantry Regiment," http://en.wikipedia.org/wiki/80th_Illinois_Volunteer_Infantry_Regiment; *OR* 31, pt. 2, 18.

Col. William K. Logie, 141st New York
U.S. Army Heritage and Education Center

Eastern and I am disposed much to doubt the superior fighting qualities with which they are credited so readily by many." With their defeat at Chickamauga, "The disposition among Western Officers to speak contemptuously of the Army of the Potomac has sensibly diminished since the recent battle in which they had to contend with the skill and mettle of the Army of Northern Virginia. The fact is that Generalship in a great measure makes or unmakes an army and the Confederacy have had their best Generals and consequently their best disciplined and most effective troops in Virginia. . . . Western officers have frankly admitted to me that they have never encountered any such obstinate fighting material as the reinforcements sent from Lee's Army to Bragg in the fight near Chattanooga."[22]

Differences between eastern and western troops were not the only frictions that emerged as the relief force awaited orders to move toward Chattanooga. The simmering tensions between Howard and Schurz burst forth. Schurz apparently took offense with the nature of the orders emanating from corps headquarters that he felt unduly tied his hands. In a letter addressed directly to Howard, Schurz expressed concern about the orders being so detailed that they were usurping his authority, hindering his ability to command his division. Schurz was careful to state that he meant no disrespect to Howard, but felt the corps commander might not be aware of the orders being given in his name, orders that Schurz believed were much too specific, leaving him no discretion. This, he opined, might result in "removing every stimulant to action and independent activity."[23]

22 Henny diary, Oct. 22, 1863; Hubbard to wife, Oct. 5, 1863.

23 Schurz to Howard, Oct. 22, 1863, RG 393, Pt. 2, 11th Army Corps, Letters Received, 1863-1864. BOX 1, NARA.

Lt. Col. Albert von Steinhausen, 68th New York
U.S. Army Heritage and Education Center

Howard was in no mood for criticism, much less from Schurz. In his response he chastised Schurz for addressing his letter directly to him rather than going through the corps adjutant general which would have been proper procedure. Howard took issue with all of the assertions in the original letter and accused Schurz of attempting to "weaken" the commanding general's authority. He closed: "The General trusts that no such impertinance will ever again be offered himself or his staff as the implication in this letter."[24]

Schurz, believing that his initial letter had intended no offense, was only roused to anger by Howard's reply. "[T]he undersigned must consider himself unjustly treated," Schurz began. He then proceeded to rebut in order every point contained in Howard's letter, arguing in the process that he had a perfect right to raise any issues about which he believed he had a legitimate complaint. Warming to his task as he wrote, Schurz next had the effrontery to lecture Howard on what his proper course of action should have been upon receiving Schurz's initial letter, which Schurz instructed his commanding officer ought to have been to investigate the legitimacy of the complaint before prematurely issuing a reprimand. Contending that he meant "no imputation of a disrespectful nature," he challenged Howard to withdraw any statements implying that Schurz had done so.[25]

Before the war of words escalated further, and also before it could be resolved or time provided for tensions to dissipate, the shooting war intervened. Orders arrived for the new campaign to relieve the siege of Chattanooga.

24 Howard to Schurz Oct. 23, 1863, RG 393, Pt. 2, 11th Army Corps, Letters Received, 1863-1864. BOX 1, NARA.

25 Schurz to Howard, Oct. 23, 1863, RG 393, Pt. 2, 11th Army Corps, Letters Received, 1863-1864. BOX 1, NARA.

☽ ☽ ☽

With Grant's obvious approval, Gen. George H. Thomas issued orders for the campaign to relieve Chattanooga to begin. Hooker issued orders on October 26 for the movement to commence at sunrise the next morning. The infantry were to carry sixty rounds of ammunition each, and the XI Corps would take 200 artillery rounds, three days' rations, three days' forage, and a full inventory of entrenching tools. The corps was to proceed along the road to Shellmound, then on to Rankins' Ferry.[26] To accomplish his mission of opening a supply line to Chattanooga, Hooker needed to secure possession of a rail and water route into the city. With this objective in mind the eastern infantrymen crossed the Tennessee River on a pontoon bridge on the night of October 26, the XI Corps in the advance, to begin the campaign.

Von Steinwehr's division led the march, followed by the XI Corps artillery, Schurz's division, and a division of the XII Corps under Brig. Gen. John W. Geary. A company from the 5th Tennessee Cavalry and a portion of a company from the 1st Alabama Cavalry, two Union units, screened the movement and acted as scouts. One regiment was left to defend the crossing and take possession of the passes through Raccoon Mountain to prevent any Confederate raids. Since Geary's wagon train and ambulances had not yet arrived, causing "some embarrassment upon us," the "necessary transportation" was "kindly furnished by Major-General Howard."[27]

Hooker's route led east along the railroad following the base of Raccoon Mountain to Running Waters, then followed that stream into Lookout Valley along its gorge. Leading the march, von Steinwehr stepped off at 6:00 am with Buschbeck's brigade in the lead followed by Orland Smith. Howard noted that the morning "found my command full of exhilaration and in rapid motion." His men recalled it somewhat differently. Lt. Karl Karsten in the 26th Wisconsin noted in his diary that the road was "mountainous" and in "very bad" condition, with the men struggling through constant "mire" resulting in a "very disagreeable" march. "You can hardly imagine a rougher country, rocks, hills and mountains with deep valleys," Howard wrote to his wife.[28]

Surgeon Hubbard was even more descriptive. "There is really no level country here except a very little at places along the river. The whole country is divided into valleys and narrow defile by ranges of mountains running at various angles to each

26 Oct. 26, RG 393, Pt. 2, Vol. 16, II-5318, NARA.

27 *OR* 31, pt. 1, 92, 112; Circular, Oct. 26, 1863, RG 393, Pt. 2, 5321 & 5348, NARA.

28 *OR* 31, pt. 1, 92, 101, 112; Howard, *Autobiography*, 459; Karsten diary, Oct. 27, 1863; Howard to Dearest, Oct. 30, 1863, Howard Papers Bowdoin.

Capt. Hartwell Osborn, 55th Ohio, in a postwar photograph. Following the war he penned the history of his regiment.
Osborn, Trials and Triumphs: The Record of the Fifty-Fifth Ohio Volunteer Infantry

other and not infrequently for a long distance parallel. Our road was along these valleys and defiles or along the river bank underneath overhanging ledges & cliffs of limestone towering hundreds of feet and apparently threatening to topple from their insecure bases upon our devoted heads. The roads, it is superfluous to add, through such a country are exceedingly difficult. Many of these defiles at the bottom are not over 50 yards wide."[29]

The marching was laborious. "[T]he roads were full of rocks and still more it was continually up hill and down. The leading regiment was moved as slowly as possible, not faster than two miles an hour, and yet the rear of the column struggled along with great effort." Albert R. Greene, marching in the XII Corps with Geary, was surprised to find the "mud was as bad as in the east, yes, worse, deeper and stickier and meaner." The artillery in line ahead of them "was often stuck, and the infantry helped by hauling with ropes through the worst places. Halts for a few minutes were frequently made to let the men breathe, and altogether it was toilsome and tedious enough."[30]

Von Steinwehr's leading division began arriving at Whitesides, about sixteen rocky, muddy, mountainous miles from Bridgeport, around 5:00 pm and commenced going into camp for the night. The artillery and Schurz's division followed, the entire command in camp by about 8:00 pm. John Geary's division of the XII Corps, bringing up the rear, arrived at Shellmound around 2:00 pm where it set up camp for the night. Dawn on October 28 found the troops once more in motion. Leading the advance, von Steinwehr's division was delayed somewhat when some of the wheels in the artillery batteries were broken trying to negotiate the rock-strewn road, requiring a brief halt as the column entered Lookout Valley. Hartwell Osborn estimated the valley at "about

29 Hubbard letter to wife, Oct. 28, 1863.

30 Greene, "From Bridgeport to Ringgold."

two miles in width" and could not help but notice that it was "completely overlooked by the lofty crests of Lookout and Raccoon mountains on either side. A range of hills some 300 feet in height, broken with narrow wooded crests, divides the valley for some three miles." Ominously, as his eyes scanned the scene he could clearly see that "from the lofty palisades of Lookout a Rebel flag waved defiance to the column and advised [the Confederates] of our numbers."[31]

Upon reaching the road to Trenton Col. Adolphus Buschbeck temporarily detached the 27th Pennsylvania to occupy a hill commanding the road. The rest of his regiments continued the advance, but almost immediately encountered the first instance of Rebel resistance when skirmishers fired into the brigade from a small, but steep wooded hill. Buschbeck deployed the 73rd Pennsylvania into a skirmish line and pushed it forward. He sent the 134th New York to the right of the hill and the 154th New York to the left to outflank the Confederate position. When they were in place, Buschbeck ordered an advance. As he watched, the Rebels "retreated in great disorder across Lookout Creek." Federal losses were two wounded. It was a small affair, but the men rejoiced in the success of the initial contact. "Our boys are in good spirits and quite jubilant over this afternoons performance," noted Maj. Lewis Warner of the 154th New York. "This is the first time that they have had a chance to make the Rebs run, and the way they made the woods ring with their cheers was really amusing."[32]

Howard advanced with prudent caution, flankers in place to guard against any ambush. The troops trudged along, warily watching the surrounding hills and woods. Occasionally sudden bursts of skirmish fire announced the continuing presence of watching eyes. In one such incident Rebels fired into Schurz's skirmishers from a woods bordering the road as his Second Brigade passed. Col. Krzyzanowski rushed reinforcements forward, outflanking the woods and turning it into a trap for its occupants. With the proficiency of veterans who gained their experience in the hard campaigning in Virginia, the men methodically cleared the hostile area at a cost of one man dead and one wounded. The Rebel loss in this small affair was four killed and at least eight wounded.[33]

Advancing closer to Lookout Creek, the column came within easy range of Confederate batteries placed along the slopes of Lookout Mountain and the adjoining ridges. The deadly artillery was plainly visible. Howard noted that "From the crest of

31 *OR* 31, pt. 1, 92, 101, 112; Meysenburg journal, Oct. 27, 1863; Osborn, "East Tennessee," 357.

32 *OR* 31, pt. 1, 101-02; Dunkelman, *Brothers One and All*, 134.

33 Schurz, *Reminiscences*, III, 59-60; Winkler Papers; Butts, *Gallant Captain*, 98.

the high mountain Longstreet and his men were taking a good view of us. Just above the perpendicular rocks which crown the highest part of the range we could discover the Confederate signal officer waving and dipping his small ensign of Stars and Bars in a most lively manner, and then we saw a flash and a volume of smoke, which was soon followed by a double explosion."[34]

Surgeon Hubbard was surprised at the sight: "[W]e were obliged to pass directly beneath their frowning muzzles which was an exciting experiment the valley being too narrow for us to give them a wide berth. They were so near that we could see the guns with a glass distinctly and clearly discern the Rebel signal officer on a jutting cliff waving his flag by the motions of which he was giving information of our approach, strength and disposition. Part of the way we were shielded from view—not protected—by woods but they knew exactly how the road ran and threw over their shell as fast as possible."[35]

The woods thinned somewhat approaching Brown's Ferry leaving the infantry to negotiate occasional open fields with no hope of being screened from Confederate view or artillery fire. Surgeon Hubbard watched as the column "halted under cover of a piece of wood and then 'ran the blockade' at 'double quick' . . . . All the loss we suffered was two men killed, five or six wounded and two horses killed. . . . Although a battery firing directly at you makes you a little nervous at first, still a little experience teaches that there are so many more chances that you will not be hit than that you will be that you soon cease to think much about it."[36]

Col. James Wood of the 136th New York was impressed that as he "passed the point most exposed to the fire I found Major-General Hooker stationed beside the road notifying the men as they passed that there was no danger from the artillery firing, and testifying by his presence and position that he believed what he said. It is unnecessary for me to say that this conduct of our commanding general had the most inspiriting influence on the officers and men of my command."[37]

Col. Adin Underwood, leading the 33rd Massachusetts, reached "an open space, where the line was ordered to halt, a brisk fire of solid shot and shell was opened upon it from a battery of heavy guns upon the top of Lookout Mountain. The men were ordered to lie down." After about half an hour, he received orders to follow the 73rd

34 Howard, *Autobiography*, 463-64.

35 Hubbard to wife, Oct. 28, 1863.

36 Hubbard to wife, Oct. 28, 1863.

37 *OR* 31, pt. 1, 104; McMahon, Diary, 67.

Col. James Wood, Jr., 136th New York
John DuBois

Ohio off to the right, backtracking through the woods to a point where they could follow the wood line a little longer, reducing the time they had to spend crossing the open space. "This movement was executed in good order and without hurry, the men marching steadily, regardless of the shot and shell which the enemy continued to shower upon the column, until it was beyond the reach of his guns." Underwood's regiment lost one man killed and one wounded.[38]

Despite the constant shelling, only minor occasional delays occurred and there were fewer casualties from the artillery than from the sporadic skirmishing. By mid-afternoon von Steinwehr's advance reached its destination at Brown's Ferry, covering a distance of some twelve miles, affecting a junction with some of Gen. William B. Hazen's brigade from the Chattanooga garrison who had successfully laid a pontoon bridge over the river and were holding the elevated south bank protecting the passageway. At Brown's Ferry, the approaching troops were not immediately identified until "Suddenly, from the head of the column 'Old Glory' spread its folds to the breeze."[39]

Maj. Samuel Hurst of the 73rd Ohio eyed the scene. "As our column marched along the valley, greeted and greeting, the shout was passing from hill-top to hill-top—the bands played, flags waved, and the very heavens rang with shouts such as are only heard in the army; and their shouts were answered back by our men with real soldierly enthusiasm." Sergt. Andrew W. Kelly wrote proudly that his 134th New York "had the honor of being the first troops of the Army of the Potomac, to form a junction with our comrades of the Cumberland, by whom we were received with hearty cheers."[40]

38 *OR* 31, pt. 1, 103.

39 *OR* 31, pt. 1, 92; Meysenburg journal, Oct. 28, 1863; Sword, *Mountains Touched with Fire*, 127.

40 Hurst, *Journal-History*, 85-86; Conklin, "History of the 134th N.Y."

In the 154th New York, Edgar Shannon recalled racing forward with their knapsacks and accoutrements in an effort to make the junction. "Our faces were red enough when we stopped for we went nearly a mile on a dog trot with heavy loads. We soon formed a junction with the [besieged] men. They cheered us & we them till this old valley fairly rung. I tell you if the old flag did not look good as they waved it & welcomed us to their aid & if they were not pleased I never saw men that were."[41]

Gen. Howard described it thusly: "Hazen's men who, excited by the cannonading, had left their brigade camp and had come out to meet us. As we neared them and could catch their accents, we took in the memorable words: "Hurrah! hurrah! you have opened up our bread line!" It was a glad meeting; glad for us, who felt that we had accomplished the difficult march; glad for them, who had for some time been growing thin on supplies; for at times they were living only on parched corn, and not enough of that. It is always hard for a soldier or sailor in active service, who is put on half rations and is forced to resist hunger by shortening his waist belt, to continue this weakening operation too long. The slow starvation of a siege is properly more dreaded by them than the exposure in campaign and in battle."[42]

Tenuous as it might be at the moment, the XI Corps had opened the first line of supply into the besieged city.

☽ ☽ ☽

The Confederate command besieging Chattanooga was every bit as fractious and more as the conflicts between the officers and men in the XI Corps and their leaders Gens. Hooker and Howard. In the wake of the decisive Confederate tactical victory at Chickamauga in September, recriminations flew as thickly within the Confederate high command as musket balls on that deadly battlefield. First, Braxton Bragg, commander of the Army of Tennessee, was unhappy with the earlier conduct of Gen. Thomas C. Hindman and suspended him from command. Bragg also asked Gen. Leonidas Polk for an explanation of his allegedly slow movement during the battle and, unsatisfied with Polk's response, suspended him as well. When Polk blamed Gen. Daniel Harvey Hill for his problems, Bragg determined that he, too, should be relieved of command and sacked him. The three generals in question began bombarding friends and officials in Richmond with letters demanding Bragg be removed from army command, this at

41 Dunkelman, *Brothers One and All*, 134.

42 Howard, *Autobiography*, 418.

the same time Bragg was moving behind the scenes to besmirch Hindman, Polk, and Hill.[43]

While letters flew back and forth, Polk and Hill met with Gens. Simon Buckner and James Longstreet, the latter newly arrived with reinforcements from the Army of Northern Virginia, to plot Bragg's downfall. Following a meeting on September 26 Longstreet sent a letter to Secretary of War James Sedden criticizing Bragg's planning and the general himself in no uncertain terms. Longstreet urged that Bragg be replaced by Lee, and Polk wrote directly to Lee asking him to come west. All of the conspirators wrote to whatever influential people they knew, all condemning Bragg and urging his removal from command. Matters seemingly escalated on October 4 when Longstreet met with several corps and division commanders during which those in attendance drew up a petition to President Jefferson Davis that twelve general officers signed asking for Bragg's removal. At one point, during a heated argument, Gen. Nathan Bedford Forrest apparently even threatened Bragg with bodily harm.[44]

Greatly concerned with matters in the west, President Jefferson Davis arrived on October 9 to try to sooth things over, but, in the presence of Bragg, Longstreet told Davis that Bragg was "incompetent to manage an army or put men into a fight." This opinion was seconded by Gens. Simon B. Buckner, Benjamin Cheatham and Daniel Harvey Hill, and possibly others. Despite the near unanimous disapproval of Bragg by his senior officers, Davis decided to keep Bragg in command and the vindictive general wasted no time retaliating by sacking Hill, demoting Buckner, and reducing the size of Longstreet's command to only those troops he brought from Virginia. Relations between Bragg and Longstreet came to a virtual standstill, with only the exchange of occasional written correspondence.[45]

Longstreet and his veterans from the Army of Northern Virginia were assigned to defend the approaches to Chattanooga from the west including the area in Lookout Valley through which the XI Corps had to pass. The icy relationship between Bragg and Longstreet clearly impaired any planning for a coordinated defense against the Federal threat posed by Hooker's advance since Bragg deigned only rarely to communicate with Longstreet, and then with barely disguised contempt. Longstreet replied in kind. One result seems to be a snit in which Longstreet was amazingly

43 McDonough, *Chattanooga*, 28; Tucker, "The Battles for Chattanooga," 13-14; Sword, *Mountains Touched with Fire*, 30-31.

44 McDonough, *Chattanooga*, 28-30, 34.

45 Pickenpaugh, *Rescue by Rail*, 172; Tucker, "Battles for Chattanooga," 15-16; McDonough, *Chattanooga*, 36; Sword, *Mountains Touched with Fire*, 32-33.

negligent in covering the obvious possibility that the Federals might move into Lookout Valley. The impasse between the two finally culminated in Bragg meeting with Longstreet on Lookout Mountain on October 28 to ascertain for himself what was happening. Looking out over the valley, the two could clearly see long lines of blue infantry moving steadily toward Chattanooga. With the realization finally before their own eyes that Federals were indeed approaching, Bragg ordered an attack. Longstreet seemingly agreed.[46]

On the evening of October 28, while the XI Corps pitched camp about Brown's Ferry and Geary's division of the XII Corps did likewise at Wauhatchie, Longstreet completed his planning for a strike on the separated commands. He ordered a division under the command of Gen. Micah Jenkins to move into Lookout Valley and assume a position from which it could attack Geary's isolated command. Jenkins, with his own brigade and that of Brig. Gen. Henry L. Benning in reserve, was to attack Geary directly. He ordered the brigades of Brig. Gen. Evander Law and Brig. Gen. Jerome B. Robertson to establish a blocking position between Geary and Howard to ensure that no troops from the XI Corps could be speedily dispatched to Geary's aid.[47]

As Jenkins prepared to launch his assault, Law and Robertson maneuvered their brigades into the desired blocking location. Taking position on a wooded hill overlooking the road connecting Brown's Ferry with Wauhatchie, Law placed his men so as to command the road and the approaches from Brown's Ferry from where any attempted relief of Geary must come. Robertson's brigade arrived some time after Law and Jenkins ordered a portion of it into a position in line with Law. One regiment from Robertson's command was placed in reserve on a road to the left while another was detailed to guard the bridge to Law's rear.[48] When his dispositions were completed, Law had some 1,700 of his own men plus an unknown number in Robertson's Brigade, but certainly in excess of 1,000, in position to prevent Howard from sending any relief to Geary. Jenkins was now ready to advance.

At Wauhatchie, some three to four miles distant from Hooker's headquarters, Gen. John Geary ordered his command to "bivouac upon their arms, with cartridge boxes on." He placed his guns on an elevation to command the approaches to his position and made sure that his outposts were alert and placed correctly. "The utmost vigilance was enjoined upon all." Ernst Damkoehler of the 26th Wisconsin moved slowly forward with the XI Corps supply trains. The hour was already late and there

46 Pickenpaugh, *Rescue by Rail,* 172-73, 177; Sword, *Mountains Touched with Fire,* 128-29.

47 *OR* 31, pt. 1, 223.

48 *OR* 31, pt. 1, 226.

remained four miles of unsafe roads between them and their own corps, so the quartermaster halted the supply train to spend the night with Geary's troops. Damkoehler and his comrades "started a fire and covered ourselves with our saddle blankets and after we got a cup of coffee from some soldiers, we believed ourselves very comfortable." They were not. About 11:00 pm sudden firing broke out along Geary's picket lines. Startled by the unexpected commotion, Damkoehler "got up and saddled the horses," but still "did not believe they would attack."[49]

Brown's Ferry was just out of range of the Confederate guns on Lookout Mountain. The XI Corps camp on the evening of October 28 lay with its left resting on the Tennessee River, its right stretching to the base of the Raccoon Mountain. While Jenkins maneuvered his forces for the attack, Hooker, repeating his earlier errors at Chancellorsville, congratulated himself upon the success of his movement but took no further action to guarantee the safety of his command. In the twilight hours of October 28 he remained inactive, allowing his troops to cook supper, relax, and retire for the evening. As darkness enveloped Lookout Valley, firing occasionally broke out along the picket lines. Around 11:15 pm Maj. Charles H. Clanharty leading a 150-man patrol from the 141st New York in Krzyzanowski's brigade ran into Confederate skirmishers of the 48th Alabama from Law's brigade on the road to Wauhatchie prompting a brief fire-fight. Once again, as had been done nearly six months before, both Howard and Hooker took little notice of it.[50]

"We got into camp at night in quite a pleasant valley," Major Frederick Winkler reported, "pitched our tents and went to sleep at an early hour." Surgeon Hubbard took advantage of the evening halt to begin writing a letter to his wife, but becoming tired he decided to go to sleep and complete the missive in the morning. Major Charles Howard also began a letter before retiring for the night, a message to his sweetheart. His brother, Gen. Howard, too, noted that by midnight "our weary men were in their soundest sleep, undisturbed by the friendly moon, which was shining brightly that night, and free from apprehensions—for our march had been completed and we had a good, strong position."[51]

☽ ☽ ☽

49 *OR* 31, pt. 1, 112; Damkoehler to Mathilde, Nov. 8, 1863.

50 Hubbard to wife, Oct. 28, 1863; OR 31, pt. 1, 98, 111; Sword, *Mountains Touched with Fire*, 134; Cubbison, "Midnight Engagement," 82.

51 Winkler, *Letters*, 96; Hubbard to wife, Oct. 30, 1863; Howard, *Autobiography*, 466; Osborn, "East Tennessee," 359.

The dull thuds of artillery fire and crackle of heavy musketry echoed down the valley, reaching the XI Corps encampment about 1:00 am. It was clear to everyone that there was fighting in the direction of Geary's position at Wauhatchie. Aroused from his sleep, Hooker acted quickly. He sent an aide, Lt. Paul A. Oliver, to Howard to order a brigade sent to occupy a hill on the road to Wauhatchie in the event the firing was a prelude to an attack on the Brown's Ferry position and to order Steinwehr's division to rush to Geary's support. Howard, acting "in accordance with General Hooker's instructions," sent Major Howard with an order to Steinwehr to send a brigade "to the position of the skirmish of the day before, and another to the assistance of General Geary." Steinwehr sent Smith's brigade in the advance followed by Buschbeck. John Ryder recalled that he was hardly asleep when "the long roll was sounded and we were quickly formed in column and started back to the assistance of the 12th corps."[52]

Orland Smith advanced at the double quick, the 73rd Ohio in advance followed by the 33rd Massachusetts and 136th New York. Though illuminated by a bright moon, the shadows of surrounding hills and woods produced an eerily ominous scene. After only a few minutes, firing erupted. Maj. Samuel Hurst in the 73rd Ohio was surprised when "the enemy began to fire from the hill right down our line of battle, completely enfilading it."[53]

Howard was pleased that "The troops were quickly on foot. Schurz's men were that night especially alert and the first under arms." Seeing that part of Schurz's division was already formed, Howard sent an order via Lt. Oliver directing Schurz to "push his leading brigade as fast as possible to the relief of General Geary." Schurz rode over to Howard where he received verbal orders confirming what Lt. Oliver told him. Howard and Schurz then rode over to confer with Brig. Gen. Hector Tyndale, whose brigade was at the front of Schurz's division. By 1:10 am Tyndale had his men in motion with Schurz accompanying him forward.[54]

"Schurz was ordered to go on to Geary's relief," Howard later wrote, "but he had hardly set out over the rocks and through the thickets, feeling his way to the west and north of the wagon road in the uncertain light, probably not very clear in his own mind just how to get to that heavy and continuous firing, when a skirmish fire began, coming upon his advance troops from those low hills which skirted Lookout Creek."[55]

52 Daily Log of 11th Corps, Oct. 29, 1:00 am; Meysenburg journal, Oct. 29, 1863; *OR* 31, pt. 1, 101; Osborn, "East Tennessee," 359; Ryder, *Reminiscences*, 42.

53 *OR* 31, pt. 1, 106; Hurst, *Journal-History*, 85-86.

54 Howard, *Autobiography*, 466-67; *OR* 31, pt. 1, 110; Sword, *Mountains Touched with Fire*, 138.

55 Howard, *Autobiography*, 466.

About this time Howard joined Hooker and his chief of staff, Daniel Butterfield, "on the side of a knoll, where a fire had been started; for the night was cold. He was evidently disturbed, but not impatient. He thought my command was not pressing on fast enough, but agreed with me that the first thing to do was to clear those low hills along Lookout Creek." Hooker ordered Howard to send the nearest troops to Geary's support, but at the same time, to meet the unexpected firing in front, sent Steinwehr, who was in the lead, an order to take the hill from which the Confederates were firing. Steinwehr placed Buschbeck's brigade in reserve along with his artillery, then, in response to an order from Howard carried by his brother the major, ordered Col. Orland Smith to seize the heights with his brigade. In the moonlight, it was difficult to see exactly what was happening. Events unfolded quickly in these opening minutes, further confusing the situation. Schurz's lead brigade under Brig. Gen. Hector Tyndale moved out to the relief of Geary as ordered, but was fired into and deployed skirmishers to protect its flank. Unaware of what force he might be facing, Howard ordered Schurz to send a brigade "to occupy the hill in the angle formed by the road to Wauhatchie and the Chattanooga Railroad" to protect against any attempt by the Confederates to attack the corps' exposed flank. Whether Howard specified Tyndale's brigade or phrased his order to require immediate compliance is difficult to determine, but Schurz, with Howard's personal approval, rushed over to Tyndale's brigade since it was first in line of march. Ordering him forward as quickly as possible he placed himself at its head and rushed off to comply with his orders.[56]

At this point, with the battle in progress, Howard suddenly turned to Hooker and said: "With your approval, I will take the two companies of cavalry and push through to Wauhatchie." Hooker replied "All right, Howard; I shall be here to attend to this part of the field." Howard then, "immediately, with my small squadron, I set out, moving toward our right till beyond range of the enemy's shots. I picked my way along the foothills of the Raccoon Mountain."[57] Why Howard would choose to dash off into the unknown on a dark night when Confederate troops were not only in the area but already engaged with his men remains known only to the general. His absence at this important juncture no doubt led to some confusion since he apparently did not tell

56 Howard, *Autobiography*, 466; Daily Log of 11th Corps, Oct. 29, 1:00 am; Osborn, "East Tennessee," 360.

57 Howard, *Autobiography*, 466-67. In his autobiography Howard claimed that he rode right through the Confederate army with these two companies of Federal cavalry. "The Confederate soldiers were evidently surprised at this bold movement, and as soon as they saw in the moonlight the shimmer of bayonets they gave way at every point." See Howard, *Autobiography*, 467-68.

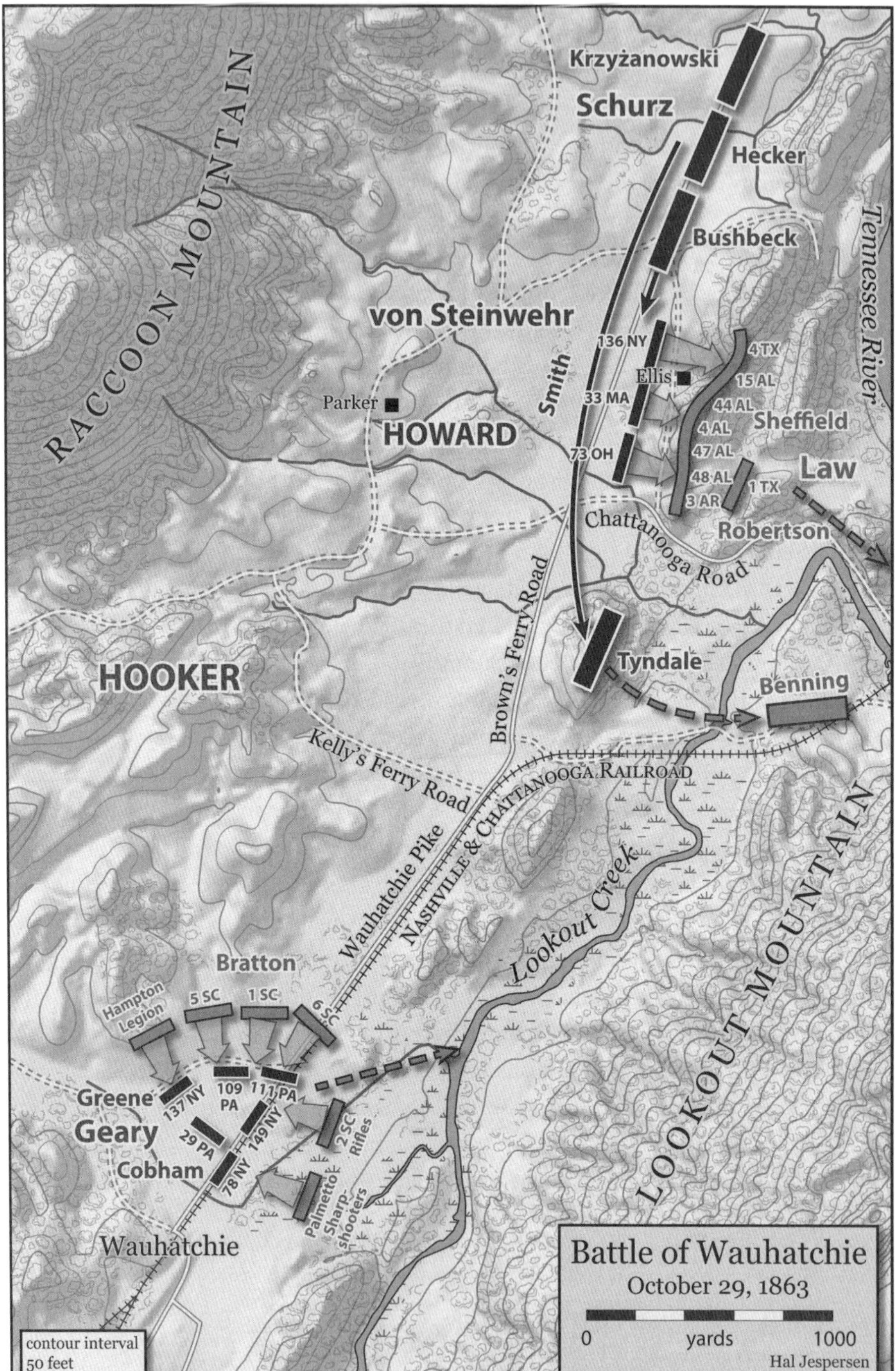
RACCOON MOUNTAIN
Krzyżanowski
Schurz
Hecker
Bushbeck
Tennessee River
von Steinwehr
Smith
136 NY
33 MA
73 OH
Ellis
4 TX
15 AL
44 AL
4 AL
47 AL
48 AL
3 AR
1 TX
Sheffield
Law
Robertson
Parker
HOWARD
Chattanooga Road
Brown's Ferry Road
Tyndale
Benning
HOOKER
Kelly's Ferry Road
Nashville & Chattanooga Railroad
Wauhatchie Pike
Lookout Creek
LOOKOUT MOUNTAIN
Bratton
Hampton Legion
5 SC
1 SC
6 SC
Greene
137 NY
109 PA
111 PA
Geary
29 PA
149 NY
2 SC Rifles
Cobham
78 NY
Palmetto Sharp-shooters
Wauhatchie
contour interval 50 feet
Battle of Wauhatchie
October 29, 1863
0 yards 1000
Hal Jespersen

Schurz that he was yielding temporary command of the corps to him and it was now left to Hooker, whether he realized it or not, to personally command the XI Corps.

Although there was a "bright moonlight," the ground was rough preventing a rapid movement. "About one-half mile from our camp," Schurz later told Howard, "while moving through the fields, in order to cut off the angles of the road, according to your direction, the flankers on my left were attacked by a Rebel force concealed in the woods on a hill on my left, and my leading regiment received a full volley, which wounded 1 of my staff officers, Captain [Robert] Lender, and several men. This Rebel force was, however, immediately afterward attacked by regiments of the Second Division, and we continued our march toward the hill General Tyndale was to occupy." Moving forward, Tyndale's brigade fought a brief skirmish against Gen. Henry Benning's brigade of Georgians in which "the enemy was speedily dislodged." Tyndale "established himself in the position assigned to him" and Schurz immediately reported the success and the positioning of Tyndale's brigade to Hooker.[58]

While Schurz and Tyndale were attending to the perceived threat they faced, von Steinwehr ordered Col. Orland Smith's brigade to seize the Confederate position atop the steep wooded hill to the left of the road to Wauhatchie. According to Steinwehr, "I ordered Col. O. Smith to advance upon the hill with the Seventy-third Ohio and Thirty-third Massachusetts in line of battle, and directed the One hundred and Thirty-sixth New York to ascend the hill on the left of the other two regiments. The troops were ordered not to fire, but to use the bayonet." Opposed to Smith were the Confederate brigades of Evander Law—4th, 15th, 44th, and 47th Alabama—under the command of Col. James L. Sheffield since Law was commanding the combined force, and Jerome B. Robertson—1st, 4th and 5th Texas and 3rd Arkansas. Law had arrived some time before and ordered his men to fell trees and dig entrenchments to strengthen their position. By the time Smith was ready to launch his assault, Law was in position, ready and waiting for the Federals.[59]

The place to be assaulted was daunting. "The face of the hill is covered by a forest and a thick coating of leaves, broken by gullies or ravines, and obstructed by brush and upturned trees." Given the size of the force facing him, and their well-prepared defensive position, Smith's brigade was not nearly strong enough for the task. Since the 55th Ohio had earlier been assigned to picket duty, Smith had only three regiments at his disposal, but the Bay State regiment had only seven companies present as companies A, B, and G had been assigned to picket duty and could not be brought in

58 *OR* 31, pt. 1, 110.

59 *OR* 31, pt. 1, 101-02, 224, 229.

before the regiment marched off. His total force numbered no more than 700 men while the defenders mustered an estimated 1,700 in Law's brigade alone, with some 1,000 in Robertson's brigade nearby in support.[60] Since it was generally considered at the time that a force about five times the size of the defense was required for a successful assault on prepared works, Smith undertook an almost impossible task.

Col. Adin Underwood led his 33rd Massachusetts up the steep slope in near pitch darkness. Despite the difficulties, they retained fairly good order until they came upon a "crooked ravine some 20 feet deep running parallel with the hill-side, the sides of which were almost perpendicular, slippery with leaves and clay, and covered with brush, and its appearance rendered still more formidable by the deceptive moonlight." This major obstacle disrupted the regiment's lines as it was only possible to move forward individually with each man grasping branches and otherwise finding means to pull himself forward. Rebel fire began to make the ascent more difficult as the regiment "gallantly plunged into it—the dead and living rolling down together—climbed the opposite side, and halted in some disorder." While trying to reform after negotiating the ravine, the men began to hear shouts of "Don't fire" in front of them. Since they had lost all contact with the other assaulting regiments in the dark and tangled terrain, some thought they might have overlapped the 73rd Ohio. Adj. William P. Mudge, determined to find out exactly who was ahead, yelled out "Who is it?" The reply was a noncommittal "Who are you?" that should have been a tipoff. Mudge quickly answered "The 33rd Massachusetts," which brought an immediate volley in response.[61] Mudge received his answer the hard way.

Gasping for breath, the Massachusetts men somehow reached a small crest in the hill about sixty yards from the main Confederate position. "It took about all our breath to get up the hill," John Ryder explained, "and here was where the Rebels had the advantage, for as soon as we came into their view we were only 20 yards from their rifle pits. Their first volley put over 60 of our regiment on the ground, half of whom were killed outright. Our color bearer fell with one foot over the rifle pits. Col. Underwood was preparing to order the final charge when a musket ball shattered his thigh bone. Adj. Mudge, seeing his commander fall, rushed over. "Good God, colonel, are you wounded?" Underwood replied only with an order to lead the men forward. "Here the enemy opened a deadly fire from the whole length of their line upon our front flank and rear." The men returned fire for a few minutes, but with their ranks disordered, their

60 *OR* 31, pt. 1, 107; Underwood, *Three Years' Service*, 157.

61 *OR* 31, pt. 1, 104; Underwood, *Three Years' Service*, 157.

colonel out of action, and without any idea if the rest of the brigade was advancing or not, the 33rd Massachusetts retired to regroup.[62]

Maj. Samuel Hurst encountered the same "irregularities of the ground, the dense growth of underbrush, and the fallen timber" that plagued the advance of Underwood's command. "The hill-side was covered with heavy timber and underbrush, and, in many places we could only advance by holding on to or pulling ourselves up by the underbrush." At first, the Rebel musketry generally went high, a frequent occurrence when troops were firing downhill. As they advanced further the fire became more accurate, taking them in front and enfilading their ranks from the left. A runner brought an order to move left to connect with the 33rd Massachusetts, but Hurst could not find the other regiment and the more he moved left the stronger the enemy fire became. He ordered the regiment to halt for a moment and lie down to escape the fire and rest before the final push. "We had yet another hundred paces to climb before we could use our bayonets, and we rose up and moved forward again to the charge, cheering as we went." Nearing the top of the hill "we were confronted by the enemy's whole line of battle, sheltered behind formidable breastworks on the crest of the hill. As we came in sight of them in the clear moonlight they lowered their guns and poured into our ranks a most deadly fire. Our boys began to fall rapidly."[63]

Within two or three rods of the Confederate works William Hughey and his comrades were swept by "an enfilading volley which mowed our brave boys down like chaff before the wind." Maj. Hurst called for the men to be steady, "yet we were met by volley after volley and each was answered by as prompt as could be, for it was almost impossible for us to load and move forward at the same time as it was very dark, being by this time [past] midnight, and the mountain was thick with bushes, trees, and tree tops making [it] almost impossible to get along." Hurst "knew we had no support on our right, and we had not held communication with the Thirty-third Massachusetts at any time during the engagement."[64]

At this point Hurst began to hear off to his left shouts of "Don't fire into your own men!" "Cease Firing!" "You are killing your own friends!" Perhaps emanating from the same Rebels that caused uncertainty among the Massachusetts men, the cries created the same doubt among the Ohioans. Under the circumstances, Hurst "deemed it rash to advance father until I knew that one, at least, of my flanks was protected." Hurst ordered his command to "retire a few rods, which they did in perfect order, and lay

62 *OR* 31, pr. 1, 104; Underwood, *Three Years' Service*, 160; Ryder, *Reminiscences*, 42.

63 *OR* 31, pt. 1, 107-09; Hurst, *Journal-History*, 87.

64 Hughey diary; *OR* 31, pt. 1, 109.

Adjutant William P. Mudge (left) and Lt. Caleb Blood, 33rd Massachusetts. Note the XII Corps crescent on Blood's hat.

U.S. Army Heritage and Education Center

down again, while I sent Captain Higgins to ascertain the position and movements of the Thirty-third Massachusetts."[65]

Col. Orland Smith met Lt. Col. Godfrey Rider of the 33rd Massachusetts as his regiment was reforming. "We must take that hill at any cost," he half-explained and half-ordered. "Now, when you reach the top again don't stop to fire but rush for them with the bayonet and yell for all you are worth at the same time. It will make them think you have had a reinforcement." Steinwehr ordered Col. James Wood's 136th New York from its reserve position to advance on the left of the Bay State regiment, with similar orders to charge with the bayonet. If you fire, he cautioned, "that will give them the range to shoot you."[66]

Clawing and scrambling forward, the second assault began. Adj. Mudge, apparently not learning his lesson from his earlier experience, rushed to the front rank, stood up, and yelled "Forward, boys, and avenge our colonel." The words no sooner left his mouth than a ball entered his heart, killing him instantly. The regiment surged back up the daunting slope until "within a few yards of the breastworks," annoyed but not stopped by a poorly directed fire. "As by a mighty impulse every man started up the hill and without halting to fire a shot dashed themselves like a living wall of steel on and over those rifle pits," recounted John Ryder. Near the top of the hill, as the regiment formed for the final assault, a volley swept through its ranks. Led by Lt. Col. Rider, "with a cheer" the line swept forward, bayonets fixed, "turned by the right flank, gained the crest, crossed the rifle-pits, and charged upon the enemy's flank with the bayonet, at the same time pouring a volley into his retreating ranks." Ryder reported the capture of

65 Hurst, *Journal-History*, 88; *OR* 31, pt. 1, 109.

66 *OR* 31, pt. 1, 104; Cozzens, *Shipwreck of Their Hopes*, 96.

two officers, 39 privates, "together with a large number of muskets and all the enemy's intrenching tools." The regiment brought about 230 men into the action and lost three officers and 22 men killed, along with five officers and 56 men wounded, a total of about "one-third of the whole number engaged."[67]

Led by Maj. Hurst, the rest of the 73rd "immediately charged forward again [and] took and occupied the works and hill in our own front, from which the enemy rapidly fled." But the cost of the success was "fearful." Hurst reported half of his officers and a third of his men killed or wounded in the "brief but desperate struggle." One of them was William Hughey. "Men were falling in every direction, screaming and crying with pain. The Maj. gave the order to fix bayonet and charge, and we did charge, and we did charge with a zeal worthy of the cheers, moving forward amid cheers and yells, firing and falling by scores. We were getting in very close quarters, almost within reach of the points of our bayonets, and feeling as though we were certain of victory and thinking of nothing but victory. When alas my hopes were all blasted, and that very suddenly, for all of a sudden I was struck in the face, as I thought by a cannonball, and for a moment thought my whole head was shot away." Hughey's jaw had been broken, his mouth "cut about 4 inches longer than its usual length," his right wrist, right hand, and left shoulder hit by Minié balls. He survived, but had to grow a beard to hide his disfigured face.[68]

Col. James Wood formed his 136th New York at the base of the hill in accordance with Steinwehr's orders. "My center was opposite the highest crest of the hill. Although it was a bright moonlight night, neither the height of the hill nor the obstacles to be encountered could be seen. I was ordered to charge in line of battle to the top of the hill, drive off the enemy, and form a junction with the Thirty-third Massachusetts on my right." Advancing steadily uphill under a desultory fire, the regiment reached a point only a few yards from main Rebel positions. "We gave out a most unearthly yell," reported George Metcalf. "If the Rebels were not frightened, I was. We ran toward them with our bayonets. They never stopped to ask who we were, or how we got there, or how long we had come to stay, or how many there were of us, or to bid us good-by. They just ran."[69]

Col. Wood reported that his men did not fire until they let loose with a single well-timed volley "at the retreating enemy." With the Confederate works in his possession, and the Rebels in retreat, Wood moved his command to the right until he

67 Ryder, *Reminiscences*, 42; *OR* 31, pt. 1, 104.

68 *OR* 31, pt. 1, 109; Hughey diary.

69 *OR* 31, pt. 1, 106; Metcalf, "Reminiscences," 127-28.

was able to link up with the 33rd Massachusetts. "The victory was complete," he later wrote. "The crest of the hill is not more than 6 yards in width, from which there is a rapid descent into a valley on the other side. Down this declivity the enemy precipitately fled in the utmost confusion. . . . The ground over which he retreated was strewn with rifles, swords, hats, caps, and haversacks. As daylight opened upon us, we were all astonished at the audacity of our charge and astounded at our success. The hill is over 200 feet perpendicular height, and the distance from the road where I formed line of battle to the crest of the hill is 180 yards." Miraculously, the 136th New York suffered only two killed and four wounded.[70]

"The Inspector General of this army," Surgeon Hubbard reported, believed "that the charge of Smith's Brigade is one of the most gallant feats of the kind of the war." The doctor was not the only one impressed. The Confederate defenders were stunned at what the enemy was able to accomplish. Capt. A. B. Waddell in the 15th Alabama reflected that he "had fought the same troops in Virginia, but I never saw them behave so well as they did that night." Lt. Richard C. Jones of the 44th Alabama declared that he "never saw more gallantry exhibited by Federals or Confederates than was done in the Lookout Valley fight."[71]

Schurz and Steinwehr had both accomplished their tasks. Schurz personally led Tyndale's brigade forward, supervised its assault, and took the position assigned to it. Steinwehr likewise led his division forward and when fired into he deployed Smith's brigade which surprisingly took a heavily fortified hill from a superior number of veteran Confederates. Major Hurst's comment about his regiment might well apply to the whole brigade: "With daring, dauntless spirits, they attacked an enemy vastly superior in numbers and holding a fortified and almost impregnable position, and drove them from that position by the most heroic and desperate effort. It was an achievement worthy of the best men of a veteran army, and must add new luster to our already honorable names."[72]

Nor was it only the immediate commanders who reveled in the achievements. Quartermaster General Montgomery C. Meigs wired Secretary of War Edwin M. Stanton on the following day calling Smith's assault "one of the most brilliant feats of the campaign. Only after walking over the ground to-day do I fully appreciate the

70 *OR* 31, pt. 1, 106-07.

71 Hubbard to wife, Oct. 31, 1863; *Report on the New York Monuments at Chattanooga*, 123.

72 *OR* 31, pt. 1, 109.

exploit. The whole affair is most creditable to those troops from the Army of the Potomac."[73]

But who was rushing to support Geary?

☽ ☽ ☽

When the firing from Wauhatchie first became audible at Hooker's headquarters he ordered Howard into action. Howard ordered von Steinwehr to Geary's assistance, but he ran into Law's Confederates and received orders to halt and take the hill containing the Rebel positions. Following next in line, Howard ordered Schurz to send Tyndale's brigade through to Geary, but Tyndale received fire from Benning's Georgians and was ordered to clear them from their positions. That left only two brigades available that could have been moved to Geary's immediate relief.

Following in the wake of Tyndale's brigade was Col. Wlodzimierz Krzyzanowski's command containing the 58th, 119th, and 141st New York along with the 26th Wisconsin. When the Confederates fired into Tyndale's lead brigade, Schurz sent an aide, Lt. Eugene Weigel, with an order for Krzyzanowski to halt to await the outcome of the fight. It was a sound move. For all Schurz knew at that moment the murky shadows ahead might conceal an entire army.[74] On receipt of the order, the Polish colonel stopped his advance, moved his brigade off the roadway to make room for the following troops, and formed his regiments in an open field facing the firing.

While they deployed, Col. Friedrich Hecker, receiving no order to halt, continued along the road until he passed Krzyzanowski's stationary brigade. At that point Hecker met Major Charles Howard who delivered an order from Gen. Howard for him to "halt at the crossroads ahead of us, and bring my men into position, as there was firing on the hills on our left." As he was moving into position, Hooker arrived. "What troops are these?" the commanding general inquired. "Third Brigade, Third Division, XII Corps, sir," Hecker replied. Hooker asked where Schurz was and Hecker told him that the division commander was at the front with Tyndale. Hooker asked why he had stopped and Hecker answered that he had done so under orders from Howard. Hooker then pointed to the position where Krzyzanowski's brigade was halted some 100 to 150 yards away, asking Hecker whose command it was. The Illinois colonel answered that it

73 Telegraph message, Meigs to Stanton, Oct. 29, 1863, quoted in Osborn, "East Tennessee," 362.

74 Schurz, *Reminiscences*, III, 61, 65; Winkler, *Papers*; Osborn, "East Tennessee," 360.

was Krzyzanowski's brigade. "You stay here," Hooker ordered, then spurred his horse over to the Second Brigade.[75]

Looking for Howard, Lt. Col. Meysenburg encountered Hooker a few moments later. The general was in front of Krzyzanowski's brigade peering into the night to catch a glimpse of the distant muzzle flashes. At some point, a number of prisoners were brought in from the fighting. Surgeon Hubbard reported that "The prisoners were greatly mortified to find that they had been routed from a strong position by only two regiments." They estimated their own strength at 2,000, about three times the number of men in Smith's three attacking regiments.[76]

Gen. Daniel Butterfield, Hooker's chief of staff, briefly questioned the Rebels, then turned to Capt. Robert H. Hall, Hooker's aide-de-camp, who was standing a short distance away. "Tell the commanding officer of the brigade to send them to Chattanooga," Butterfield commanded, pointing to Krzyzanowski's command. Hall immediately spurred his horse over to the colonel and delivered the order for him to move his brigade to Chattanooga—in the opposite direction of the firing at Wauhatchie. The colonel got his brigade underway, but apparently either he questioned the order or the aide soon realized he had made a mistake, or Hooker or Butterfield realized the error when they saw the brigade begin to head to the rear. The brigade had only marched a short distance when Capt. Hall returned with the correct order which was to send the prisoners under guard to Chattanooga and to "bring his brigade back to its original position." Krzyzanowski reversed his march, then, in accordance with the new orders, redeployed his troops in the position they had only just vacated.[77]

Krzyzanowski sent Capt. Louis Orlemann to Schurz to inform him that his Second Brigade was halted under orders from Gen. Hooker. Major Charles Howard soon arrived, informing Schurz that Hecker's brigade had likewise been stopped under the orders of Hooker. When Tyndale's attack successfully concluded, Schurz rode back along the road looking for Hooker to find out why his other brigades had been halted and what orders Hooker now had for him. He found the commanding general near a farm house at the foot of the hill where Smith's brigade was engaged. According to Lt. Weigel, who witnessed the meeting, Hooker "asked Schurz why he had not pushed

75 Hebert, *Fighting Joe Hooker*, 260; Schurz to parents, Feb. 20, 1864; "Proceedings of the Court of Inquiry at the XI and XII Headquarters in regard to the Wauhatchie Affair," *OR* 32, pt. 1, 137-216 [hereafter cited as "Proceedings"].

76 "Proceedings," 151, 165-66, 170, 183; Butts, *Gallant Captain*, 98-99; Hubbard to wife, Oct. 31, 1863.

77 "Proceedings."

through with that brigade to General Geary." Taken aback, Schurz "told him that one of General Hooker's aides had given him the order to take the Tyndale Hill, and that he had no other troops with him." Hooker ignored Schurz's comment, saying only that "he had given him the order in person to march through." Krzyzanowski, who apparently accompanied Schurz, stood only a few feet away when Schurz "then asked General Hooker if he could now have his two brigades." Hooker replied that he wanted Schurz to move quickly to Geary's aid. Schurz turned, ordered Krzyzanowski to place his brigade in position to fill the gap between the hills assaulted by Smith and Tyndale, then ordered Hecker, reinforced by the 141st New York from Krzyzanowski's brigade, to march immediately to the relief of Geary. The XI Corps diary places this at 4:30 am, by which time the fighting at Wauhatchie had long since ceased.[78]

Gen. Geary reported that Hecker's brigade arrived at 5:30 am and Krzyzanowski's, sent some time later, at 7:00 am or 7:15 am. He "furnished them with intrenching tools and they worked industriously and cheerfully in constructing extensive breastworks with numerous traverses advantageously formed, to which I gave personal attention." Capt. Frederick Winkler of the 26th Wisconsin noted that they "stayed there on the right through rain and mud without tents, and very short of provisions . . . without sleeping at all, watching the guns on the mountains right opposite, expecting every moment that they would open upon us." They were finally relieved about 5:00 pm on October 31.[79]

☽ ☽ ☽

Once the sounds of battle receded it became apparent to all that the Confederate attempt to prevent the relief of Chattanooga had failed. The city was saved, and with it Gen. George Thomas's Army of the Cumberland that had been trapped inside on the verge of starvation. Unlike its experience with the Army of the Potomac, here heartfelt compliments arrived at XI Corps headquarters quickly from all quarters. One of the

78 "Proceedings," 151, 165-166, 170, 183; Butts, *Gallant Captain*, 98-99; Osborn, "East Tennessee," 361; Howard, *Autobiography*, 467; Hooker, *OR* 31, pt. 1, 110, 584, 587; Schurz, *Reminiscences*, III, 62-64; Winkler to Gaylord, August 25, 1864; Daily Log of 11th Corps, Oct. 29, 1863, 4:30 am. The Daily Log also indicated that Krzyzanowski's brigade was not ordered to Geary until later that morning. Meysenburg journal, Oct. 29, 1863, says that Hecker's brigade was ordered to Geary at 4:30 am and Krzyzanowski's brigade was not ordered to Geary until 7:00 am.

79 Geary to Howard, Oct. 31, 1863, 11th Army Corps, Letters Received, 1863-1864, RG 393, Pt. 2, Box 2, NARA; *OR* 31, pt. 1, 11, 110-11, 114, 118; Winkler, *Letters*, 97.

first was a letter from Gen. Thomas to Hooker dated October 30: "I most heartily congratulate you and the troops under your command at the brilliant success you gained over your old adversary (Longstreet) on the night of the 28th Inst."[80]

In a wire to General-in-Chief Henry W. Halleck in Washington, Thomas wrote: "In the fight of last night the enemy attacked Geary's division, posted at Wauhatchie, on three sides, and broke into his camp at one point, but was driven back in most gallant style by part of his force, the remainder being held in reserve. Howard, while marching to Geary's relief, was attacked in the flank, the enemy occupying in force two commanding hills on the left of the road. He immediately threw forward two of his regiments and took both at the point of the bayonet, driving the enemy from his breastworks and across Lookout Creek. In this brilliant success over their old adversary, the conduct of the officers and men of the XI and XII Corps is entitled to the highest praise."[81]

Thomas followed the personal letter and official wire to Washington with an official proclamation. "The column under Major-General Hooker, which took possession of the line from Bridgeport to the foot of Lookout Mountain, deserve great credit for their brilliant success in driving the enemy from every position which they attacked. The bayonet charge, made by the troops of General Howard, up a steep and difficult hill, over 200 feet high, completely routing the enemy and driving him from his barricades on its top, and the repulse, by General Geary's command of greatly superior numbers, who attempted to surprise him, will rank among the most distinguished feats of arms of this war."[82]

Hooker passed the praise along to his troops in General Orders No. 5 issued from his headquarters on November 1: "It is with extreme pleasure that the major-general commanding communicates to the troops composing the XII Corps, and to the Second Division of the Twelfth Corps, the subjoined letter from the major-general commanding the Army of the Cumberland, expressive of his appreciation of your distinguished services on the night of the 28th instant. It is a noble tribute to your good conduct from a brave and devoted soldier. The general hopes that it will inspire as much satisfaction in the breasts of his officers and men as it has in his own, and that we may all be stimulated by it to renewed efforts to secure the good opinion of our

80 Thomas to Hooker, October 30, 1862, RG 393, Pt. 2, Vol. 16, II-5318, NARA.

81 *OR* 31, pt. 1, 41.

82 *OR* 31, pt. 1, 68.

commander while we also emulate the courage and valor of our companions in arms."[83]

Oliver Otis Howard also took the opportunity to offer his congratulations his corps in General Orders No. 29 issued on November 4: "The Commanding General takes this occasion to thank the Officers and Men of his command for their uniform good conduct during the extreme fatigue, continuous hard work and exposure from the time of leaving the Rappahannock to the present and especially for the boldness and energy displayed during the skirmish and night engagement of the 29th ult. It is with a feeling of sorrow that we mention the names of Capt. Buckwalter, Capt. McGroarty, Lieut. Mudge, Lieut. Burrage and Lieut. Hill and the rest who have given their lives for their country. Our sympathy for Col. Underwood 33d Mass Vols and the other wounded is unfeigned. Let the consciousness that they are suffering in a righteous cause cheer them on to a speedy recovery. Let every new engagement and every success gained unite us in thanksgiving to Him who has given us his blessing."[84]

The Battle of Wauhatchie was a disorganized affair that spawned differing accounts among the various after-action reports. Neither Confederate nor Union losses approached the terrible tolls exacted by Chancellorsville or Gettysburg, yet the result was impressive. The gateway to Chattanooga stood open and the Union army in that besieged city received a new lease on life. And for once, the services and sacrifices of the maligned XI Corps were recognized.

83 Hooker, General Orders No. 5, November 1, 1863, RG 393, Pt. 2, Vol. 16, II-5318, NARA.

84 Howard, General Orders No. 29, November 4, 1863, RG 393, Pt. 2, 5321 & 5348, NARA.

Chapter 19

"One Mighty Chorus of Victory"

November, 1863

ONCE THE VITAL SUPPLY LINE to Chattanooga was opened it had to be protected. For the first three weeks in November Grant assigned the task of defending this "Cracker Line" to Hooker's command. This assignment was essential to the success of the Chattanooga campaign. During the relative lull that followed Wauhatchie, Grant ordered Gen. William T. Sherman to join him with all of his troops and began planning for the next move against Bragg's Confederates. Howard had ample opportunity to interact with the commanding general and was "very much pleased. . . . He doesn't play the great man at all, but goes straight forward about his business." Howard later professed to appreciate Grant's quiet take-command attitude, as well as his plans for the coming movements. "Of course, many croakers found fault with this and prophesied disaster; yet the most of us were inspired by Grant's quiet confidence and plans." Schurz was also impressed with Grant's demeanor. "There was absolutely nothing of the fuss-and-feathers style, nothing of the stage or picture general about him. His head was covered with the regulation black felt hat. He wore a major-general's coat, but it was unbuttoned and unbelted. He carried no sword. . . . He smoked a large black cigar with great energy, and looked about him in a business-like way with an impassable face."[1]

1 Howard to Dearest, Nov. 4, 1863, Bowdoin College; Howard, *Autobiography*, 472; Schurz, *Reminiscences*, III, 68-69.

Luther Mesnard, 55th Ohio
Ohio Genealogical Society

The Lookout Valley position was not entirely secure. Confederate artillery on the summit of Lookout Mountain, 1,464 feet above the valley below, dominated the landscape for miles around. Luther Mesnard in the 55th Ohio recalled "the rebs throwing shells at us about an hour each day. We kept a man on the watch all the time and when a shell was coming our way we took cover. We could tell by the smoke of the gun whether the shell was meant for us or not. In fact if it was aimed say twenty rods to the left no alarm would be given, but when we saw a plain round puff—no elongation—then lookout."[2]

The constant booming of Rebel guns became so much a part of the soldiers' daily lives they fashioned a game out of it. Eager eyes scanned Lookout Mountain for the puff of smoke that invariably identified the firing of a gun. When one was detected the soldiers quickly placed bets on where the deadly projectile would hit. Yet, the seemingly random firing was not without effect. As the 26th Wisconsin hugged the ground in its exposed rifle pits, shells from Lookout Mountain wounded two men. On another occasion, a shell landed between Maj. Frederick Winkler's tent and the cook's tent next to it, burrowing several feet into the ground without exploding. Mesnard also had a close call. "One day I was cooking some coffee in a tin just back of the breastworks when the alarm was given and I jumped behind the works. A piece of the shell hit my coffee dish." Another shell penetrated Schurz's mess tent while he was having dinner with his staff, causing "a momentary sensation and a rapid scattering of the diners. But as the shell did not explode, confidence was soon restored."[3]

Daily life was unpleasant, rain continued to fall at frequent intervals and supplies were slow to arrive, often necessitating a reduction to three-quarter rations for days at a

2 Mesnard, "Reminiscence," 44.

3 *OR* 32, pt. 3, 4; Lackner diary, Dec. 22, 1863; Schurz, *Reminiscences*, III, 69, 71; Howard, *Autobiography*, 472; Mesnard, "Reminiscence," 44.

time. Maj. Osborn complained in a letter home that "When we left Bridgeport, we brought as little with us as would support us for three days. Unfortunately, we could get no supplies for seven or eight days and have been living on as small an allowance as mortal man could well stand up under." Winkler complained "We have lived such a comfortless life ever since we left Bridgeport; we have not been in camp since; we have been always moving about, digging rifle pits in every position we occupied, and been constantly on the watch for an attack from the enemy. We have nothing with us but shelter tents and often we were not allowed to put them up, and crackers and coffee with bacon and occasionally a little fresh beef is all we have to subsist on."[4]

Luther Mesnard and his comrades "were very short of rations. During the next ten days drew but ten crackers or one days ration. I never was so hungry before or since. After fasting all day I remember I dreamed all night about mothers cupboard, and all the good things to eat I had ever had. . . . I got up at break of day and looked down into my haversack. Now the worst thing a hungry soldier can look at is the bottom of an empty haversack. I just broke down as the tears came I thought 'This will not do' and tried to brace up." With hardtack selling for the incredible price of one dollar per cracker, one day a "forager from the regiment brought in half a bushel of corn and it seemed like a feast."[5]

Andrew Boies described his usual fare. "I have just finished my dinner, and for the benefit of all whom it may concern, I would like to have them know what a good dinner is. Recipe: 1st—Take a quart dipper and put in one spoonful of coffee, one spoonful of sugar, fill to the brim with water; put it on the fire and boil; this is coffee. 2nd—Take a frying-pan, cut three slices of fat pork, fry to a crisp. 3rd—Take five 'hard-tack,' soak them in cold water 10 minutes, place them in the pan with your pork, fry 10 minutes; having done this, your dinner is ready; then sit down upon the ground, take your knife —your fingers will serve as a fork—then eat hearty. This is what may be called a good dinner and a cheap one, and this recipe should be carefully preserved."[6]

As the month progressed, rations became increasingly scarce. For a week, chilling rains fell almost daily. Intensified by the cool and damp climate, sickness spread rapidly through the ranks. Expecting at any moment to be moved about, as had become the practice in the valley, the men forsook the usual practice of making their camp more

4 Osborn to Spencer, Nov. 5, 1863, Crumb and Dhalle, *No Middle Ground*, 168; Winkler, *Letters*, 97; Winkler to Gaylord, Aug. 25, 1864; *OR* 31, pt. 2, 383.

5 New York State Monument on Lookout Mountain; Phisterer, *New York*, 2518; *OR* 31, pt. 2, 17; Howard, *Autobiography*, 479; Mesnard, *Reminiscence*, 44-45.

6 Boies, *Thirty-third Massachusetts*, 51-52.

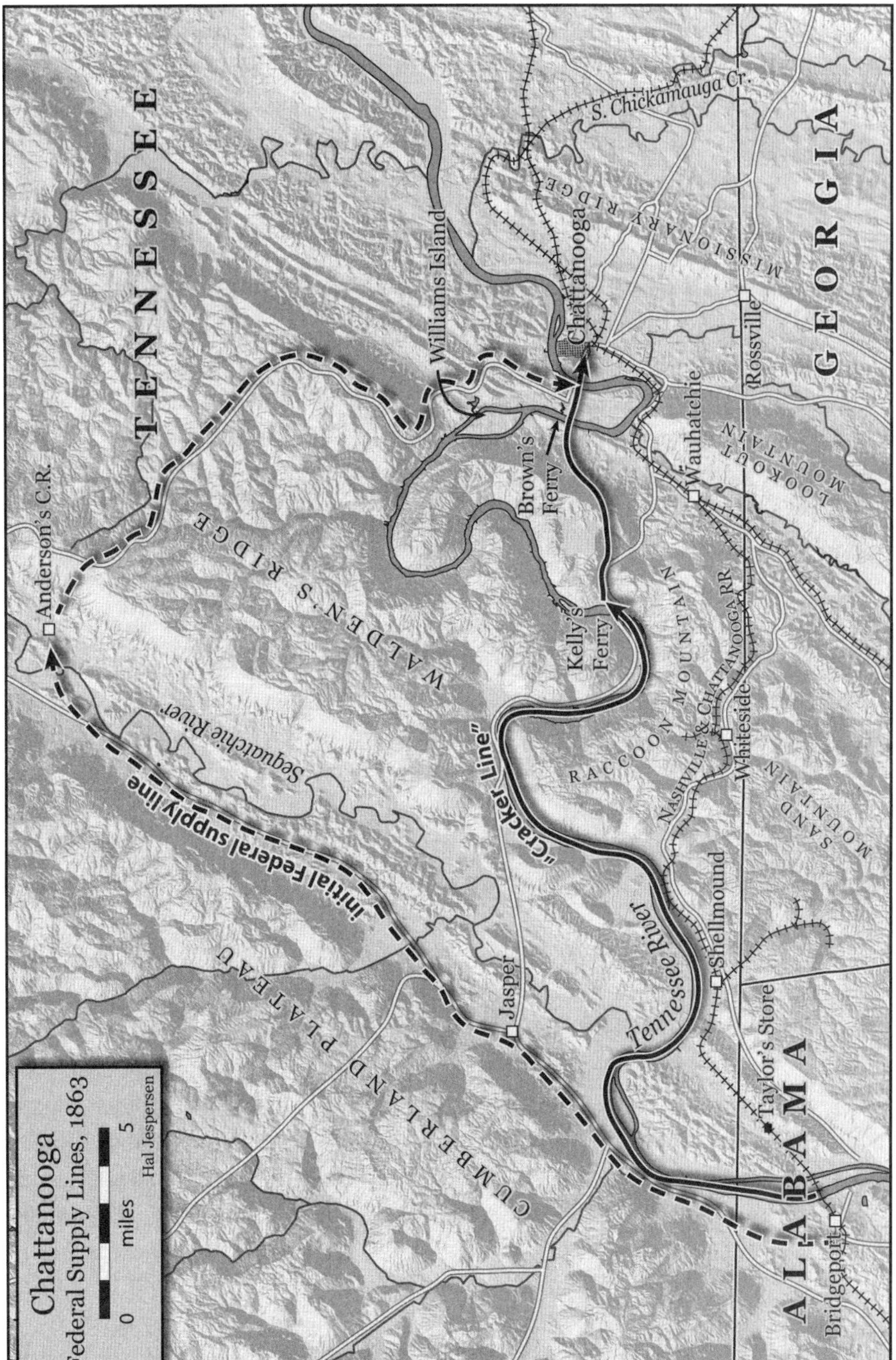
Chattanooga
Federal Supply Lines, 1863
0
miles
5
Hal Jespersen
TENNESSEE
GEORGIA
ALABAMA
Anderson's C.R.
WALDEN'S RIDGE
Sequatchie River
Initial Federal supply line
CUMBERLAND PLATEAU
Jasper
"Cracker Line"
Tennessee River
Kelly's Ferry
Brown's Ferry
Williams Island
Chattanooga
S. Chickamauga Cr.
MISSIONARY RIDGE
Rossville
Wauhatchie
LOOKOUT MOUNTAIN
RACCOON MOUNTAIN
NASHVILLE & CHATTANOOGA RR
Whiteside
SAND MOUNTAIN
Shellmound
Taylor's Store
Bridgeport

comfortable. When the weather turned, however, they paid the price for their collective decision. "It is very cold," Winkler recorded, "and my fingers are too numb for writing." Since they thought their stay would be only temporary, they "had not deemed it worth while to go to such extravagance as to build fire-places. As I went shivering to bed last night, I made up my mind that I would have a fire-place if it were only for one day's use."[7]

Occasionally, when a train or a supply wagon would stop on its way into the besieged city, the troops would enjoy a holiday from the hardtack and coffee that became so repetitive. To further relieve the monotonous diet, foraging expeditions took to the countryside. Lt. Karl Karsten reported marching forty miles on one of these excursions during which he "arrested" one goose. On other occasions individual enterprise yielded rewards. One day Henry Peiper in the 26th Wisconsin acquired a small amount of flour and other delicacies he prepared for the regimental commander's mess. By "taxing his culinary talents to the utmost, we had biscuits to take the place of hard tack at breakfast this morning," Winkler reported. "The judgment of the mess was that they were excellent; yes, tough biscuits, without butter, and coffee without milk, constitute an excellent breakfast. Today too, for the first time, except once at Bridgeport, since we came to this department we have had potatoes for dinner. Ah, you don't know what a luxury a potato is."[8]

The cold damp weather and inadequate diet, along with those wounded in action, sent a constant stream of men to the corps hospital. "It is a terrible thing to be wounded and lie as I have seen thousands of brave fellows, through long weeks of agony with so little to palliate their sufferings," observed Surgeon Hubbard. On Sunday, November 15, Howard, accompanied by a number of officers including Hubbard, visited the XI Corps hospital in Lookout Valley, something he did whenever possible. "We found the religious services in progress on our arrival. The poor sick ones who could leave their beds had gathered near the largest hospital and kept their hats off reverently while the chaplain was praying. The sick inside the different tents could hear everything, as canvas obstructs the sound but slightly. We sang a hymn and then the chaplain preached a sermon about giving our bodies and spirits a living sacrifice. He made many earnest appeals, and I think left a good impression on the men and officers who were present. While he was speaking the Confederates made themselves heard by an occasional shell from Lookout Mountain. The Thirty-third

7 Winkler, *Letters*, 98.

8 Winkler, *Letters*, 100; Winkler to Gaylord, Aug. 25, 1864; Karsten diary, Nov. 12, 1863.

Massachusetts band came near and, as soon as the service was over, struck up some familiar hymns and airs that were sweet and cheering."[9]

Despite the shortages, the weather, and the general misery, Henry Van Aernam thought "The army are in good spirit, generally healthy and confident of success when the fight comes on. The Rebel army are fearfully demoralized. It would average as many as 100 deserters a day that come into the 11th and 12th Corps not privates only but Captains, Lieutenants, and even Majors and Colonels." Schurz explained that "they came over in great numbers. They were mostly from some Alabama regiments which were camped opposite us on the other side of Lookout Creek. They would during the night crawl over a big tree which had fallen across the creek, and then surrender to our pickets. There were so many of them that I sometimes, when I rose in the early morning, found the space between my headquarter tents filled with a dense crowd. They were a sorry lot; ragged, dirty, and emaciated." Schurz believed most of them came over for food and were "relieved by the subsequent distribution of rations among them, and the avidity and relish with which those rations were devoured spoke volumes of the lean days when they had had nothing to live upon but roasted ears of corn."[10]

Lt. William Wheeler commanding the 13th New York Independent Battery pondered what it must be like in the Confederate lines. "Bragg's army must be in a deplorable condition; deserters are coming into out lines continually, by squads, and even by companies, who declare that they could not stand it any longer, with no blankets to cover them and with nothing but a small ration to eat. They also say that if it were not supposed by most of their troops that they would be forced into our ranks if they should come over, the army could not be held together. Then nights lately have been intensely cold, so that under several blankets my feet have been like ice. If we suffer this with our complete clothing and equipage, what must be the state of the thinly-clad Rebels."[11]

☽ ☽ ☽

Camp in Lookout Valley ended abruptly on November 22. With the arrival of Gen. William T. Sherman's Army of the Tennessee, Grant directed him to cross the

9 Hubbard to wife, Nov. 5, 1863; Howard, *Autobiography*, 472-73.

10 Van Aernam letter, November 18, 1863, Henry Van Aernam Papers in USMHI; Schurz, *Reminiscences*, III, 69-70.

11 Wheeler to mother, Nov. 8, 1863, in Bershears, *Loyal Till Death*, 260.

Tennessee River at Brown's Ferry, march northeast beyond Chattanooga, then re-cross the Tennessee to place his force on the far Union left directly west of Tunnel Hill. The XI Corps would follow in Sherman's wake, crossing the Tennessee and moving into place near Citico Creek. This would place Howard's command between Sherman and Gen. George H. Thomas's troops in Chattanooga, creating a relatively contiguous Union line from the city north along the river to Tunnel Hill and South Chickamauga Creek.[12]

The XI Corps began its march at 1:00 pm that afternoon. The men were instructed to leave their knapsacks behind, but to bring their shelter tents and blankets, rations for three days, and 100 rounds of ammunition (counting those in wagons). Wiedrich's and Heckman's batteries were to be left behind because, as Maj. Osborn reported, "the horses were greatly reduced, both by the long passage from Virginia to this place and by starvation in the valley. I could then only horse three batteries indifferently. The roads over which we marched were very bad; much of the time we could get no forage either from the depots or in the country. The horses were continually giving out from exhaustion and want of food." Wiedrich and Heckman eventually supported a movement in the direction of Lookout Mountain to be led by Hooker, who would also remain behind. The corps crossed the Tennessee River some 6,000 strong and moved into its new position northwest of Orchard Knob. As the men marched, Union officers could clearly see Confederate signal flags waving a message that "a large force, apparently a corps, had passed into Chattanooga."[13]

The 27th Pennsylvania, 33rd Massachusetts, and 33rd New Jersey provided skirmishers to screen the move, but they met little opposition. In the Bay State regiment Earle Rich had a close call when a Rebel sharpshooter fired at him. "[T]hat damn bullet hit the stock of my musket and ricocheted off the fore end, nicking the lobe of my ear when it went past my head; that was a close one." By late afternoon the 33rd New Jersey reported that "it halted and bivouacked for the night, throwing up breastworks on its line of battle front, the Twenty-seventh Pennsylvania on its left and the Seventy-third [Pennsylvania] on its right." Stretched out behind them along the line of march, the rest of the corps gradually arrived. Schurz's division completed its move "after dark," camping "on the right of General Wood's division in front of Chattanooga" with the last units going into place a little after 8:00 pm.[14]

12 McDonough, *Chattanooga*, 110.

13 Circular, Nov. 22, 1863, RG 393, Pt. 2, 5321 & 5348, NARA; Meysenburg journal, Nov. 22, 1863; *OR* 31, pt. 2, 346-47, 386.

14 Rich, *Cape Cod Echoes*, 44; *OR* 31, pt. 2, 363, 368, 382-83.

Early on the morning of November 23 Confederate deserters arriving within the Union lines reported that Bragg's army "intended to retreat." From Fort Wood, officers with field glasses verified that some of the Rebel camps appeared to be deserted, reinforcing the belief that perhaps a withdrawal was already in progress. To ascertain the truth, Grant ordered Thomas to make a reconnaissance in force, an order Thomas took the opportunity to turn into a real attack on the Confederate advanced posts a mile and a half away, about half the distance between Thomas's position outside Chattanooga and Gen. Braxton Bragg's Rebel entrenchments atop Missionary Ridge. Running just east of the Western and Atlantic Railroad, the forward Confederate line was anchored on one hundred foot high Orchard Knob.[15]

Thomas assigned Maj. Gen. Gordon Granger's IV Corps to lead the attack, with Brig. Gen. Thomas J. Wood's division in the lead and Maj. Gen. Philip H. Sheridan's division to its right and slightly behind. The XI Corps was to be held in reserve should support be needed. About 1:00 pm, while Howard watched, Granger's troops "moved briskly forward, driving in the enemy's outposts and taking Orchard Knob, a small hill little more than half way to the ridge, and 1 mile south from the Tennessee." When Granger requested artillery support, Howard ordered Lt. Christopher Merkle forward with Battery G. 4th U.S. Artillery, which was later "highly complimented for good firing."[16]

Once Granger took Orchard Knob, Grant, also observing the progress of the assault from the vicinity of Fort Wood, moved to make sure that the new position was held. To cover Granger's left flank, Grant ordered Howard to advance the XI Corps along Citico Creek, a partially wooded stream bending around the hill. About 2:00 pm Howard ordered Schurz's division to form on the right, with Steinwehr on the left, and to seize the woods between Orchard Knob and the Tennessee River. With skirmishers forward, the corps "deployed with great promptitude."[17]

Under some fire from a Rebel battery, Steinwehr ordered two regiments from each of his brigades to form line of battle with skirmishers ahead, while the "remaining five regiments formed the second line" in support. Schurz deployed his division with Hecker's brigade in front and the remaining brigades following. Leading Steinwehr's advance, Buschbecks's brigade moved forward with the 134th New York on the right and 33rd New Jersey on the left, each regiment "in deployed order, with skirmishers about 150 paces in advance." Behind the leading regiments Buschbeck placed a second

15 *OR* 31, pt. 2, 346; McDonough, *Chattanooga*, 110-11.

16 McDonough, *Chattanooga*, 110-11; *OR* 31, pt. 2, 346-47.

17 *OR* 31, pt. 2, 347-48, 382.

Lt. John Toffey, 33rd New Jersey, received the Medal of Honor for his heroism during the Chattanooga Campaign.

U.S. Army Heritage and Education Center

supporting line consisting of the 27th and 73rd Pennsylvania and the 154th New York. The left flank was protected somewhat by a railroad embankment, but "Hardly had the line of skirmishers gained 10 paces ere it was fired upon from the woods skirting the creek, from behind the railroad bridge and from under cover of several buildings."[18]

In its first fight, the rookie 33rd New Jersey under Col. George W. Mindil advanced briskly toward the woods before Citico Creek and suffered accordingly, meeting a destructive fire which wounded Capt. William Boggs who was leading the regiment's skirmishers. Mindil ordered Lt. John Toffey out to replace Boggs, not knowing that he was in no condition for the assignment. Toffey had been sick with a serious fever for a week, but when his company was called into line before the action he dutifully fell in. Surgeon James Reiley spotted him and told the lieutenant to report to the hospital. Toffey declined. "You know you are not able," Surgeon Reiley replied, "so come and go with me to the hospital." Toffey refused and took his place in line. Now, feverish and exhausted, barely able to keep up as the regiment moved, Toffey did not hesitate. Dodging "bullets [that] flew as hailstones," he made it to the skirmish line, but no sooner arrived than a musket ball slashed through his thigh. The resilient officer stayed there for another hour, directing the skirmishers despite the pain, loss of blood, and high fever, until finally carried off to the hospital. His heroism would later be recognized with the Medal of Honor.[19]

Following Toffey's exploits, Col. Mindil dispatched Capt. Thomas O'Connor to reinforce the skirmish line with his Company F. Pushing forward through the woods to

18 *OR* 31, pt. 2, 359, 362, 383.

19 *OR* 31, pt. 2, 362; Zinn, *Mutinous Regiment*, 41-42; Powles, "Western Warriors," 48.

the banks of the stream, a steady firing commenced from skirmishers hidden behind the trees, sometimes only ten yards apart. To continue the advance, Mindil ordered Capt. Charles J. Field's Company E to reinforce the skirmish line, and led the balance of the regiment forward under a "heavy fire" to clear the banks of Rebels and move beyond toward the walls of a bridge hiding Rebels whose fire proved especially bothering. Mindil sent Major David A. Peloubet back to Buschbeck for further instructions. He returned with orders to halt the advance and hold the creek bank to prevent the Rebels from regaining a hold on Citico Creek. Mindil, justly proud of his men, wrote that "For a regiment but of three months' creation, without much drill and discipline, the Thirty-third did remarkably well. I feel confident that the regiment can now be relied upon for any emergency, as the men will perform their whole duty."[20]

Under Col. Patrick H. Jones, the 154th New York followed behind the left flank of the New Jersey regiment as a reserve, but as the skirmishing developed and the front widened Col. Buschbeck ordered it to seize a railroad bank. Lt. James L. Harding led about thirty skirmishers to the creek with no opposition, but came under heavy skirmish fire attempting to cross the stream that cost them six wounded. Jones held his position the rest of the day, digging rifle pits and throwing up breastworks to provide cover.[21]

To the right of the New Jersey regiment Col. Allan H. Jackson led the 134th New York forward, also advancing until the regiment was struck by a "sharp fire" from Confederates hidden in the woods. Jackson ordered Companies B and C forward under Lts. Edwin Forrest and Benjamin Sheldon. Together the two cleaned out the woods allowing the regiment to occupy an abandoned Rebel breastwork. "We disturbed them before they had finished their breakfast," William Levey mused, "and in their hurry they left food and cooking utensils scattered over the ground in their camp. It seemed a pity to deprive them of their breakfast, but such are some of the discomforts and deprivations of war."[22]

To the right of Orland Smith's brigade, Krzyzanowski's brigade of Schurz's division advanced at the same time as Steinwehr's command, with the 26th Wisconsin fighting a sharp skirmish at Citico Creek that enabled the brigade to move into position to cover the otherwise exposed flank of the Northern army. By that evening, the fighting had diminished to little more than an occasional greeting from a sharpshooter. In the 55th Ohio, Luther B. Mesnard and Lt. Frederick Boalt sat conversing in a room

20 *OR* 31, pt. 2, 362-63.

21 *OR* 31, pt. 2, 366.

22 *OR* 31, pt. 2, 364; Conklin, *Crescent and Star*, 141.

about three-quarters of a mile behind the front lines when a lead ball zipped right between the two men and lodged in the wall on the opposite side of the room. Another round from a sharpshooter passed through Lt. Edward Bromely's heart, killing him instantly.[23]

It had been a busy day, but nightfall on November 23 found Orchard Knob and the surrounding landscape firmly in Union hands. Tunnell Hill, the last Rebel defensive position protecting the northern portion of Missionary Ridge from attack, now lay open to assault.

☽ ☽ ☽

Grant's plan for November 24 called for the XI Corps to support Sherman's push against the approaches to the Confederate right. Grant also decided to change his original orders to Hooker in Lookout Valley which had only called for him to make a "demonstration" toward Lookout Mountain while Sherman launched the main assault on the other end of the extended Union position. However, the continual rains had raised the Tennessee River so much that the pontoon bridge across Brown's Ferry was carried away preventing Brig. Gen. Peter J. Osterhaus's division of Sherman's command from crossing the river. With this unanticipated increase in the strength of the troops south of the river, Grant changed Hooker's orders, authorizing him, as Hooker explained, "to take the point of Lookout Mountain if my demonstration should develop its practicability."[24]

At first light a spirited fire broke out between Rebel skirmishers and those of Schurz's division along Citico Creek. Howard commenced the movement of the XI Corps at 9:00 am by ordering Steinwehr to advance until he made contact with Sherman's troops. Steinwehr placed three regiments under Col. Buschbeck in line of battle, skirmishers forward, with orders to cross Citico Creek and move along the Tennessee River until the desired juncture was affected. Orland Smith's brigade was held back to guard the line along Citico Creek. In preparation for the advance, the 73rd Ohio crossed the creek to root out sharpshooters between there and the East Tennessee Railroad. With Howard watching, the Ohioans "swept the front beyond the creek of all Confederate sharpshooters who were inclined to loiter in that region." Cut

23 *OR* 31, pt. 2, 373, 378, 382; Schurz, *Reminiscences*, III, 72; Winkler report, Aug. 25, 1864; *Annual Report of the Adjutant General of the State of Wisconsin*, 404; Wickesberg to parents, Dec. 19, 1863; Winkler to Gaylord, Aug. 25, 1864; Mesnard, *Reminiscence*, 45.

24 *OR* 31, pt. 2, 314.

off from their own lines, about fifteen men from the 7th Mississippi surrendered themselves to Major August Riedt's 27th Pennsylvania.[25]

With the sharpshooters cleared out, Buschbeck's brigade advanced quickly, accompanied by Howard who went in person to supervise the linkup. When firing erupted off to the right, Howard ordered Schurz to send forward a brigade. About 3:00 pm Schurz ordered his reserve brigade under Col. Krzyzanowski to accomplish the task. With "very little opposition being made," Howard completed the roughly four mile move and made a junction with Brig. Gen. Hugh Ewing's division of Sherman's command. About a mile and a half separated him from Missionary Ridge upon which Sherman was moving. Pointing to a hill he wanted to occupy, Sherman asked Howard if he would agree to leave Buschbeck's brigade with him to guard his right when his own troops moved forward. Howard agreed and Buschbeck went into position near the Sanderson farm. With his orders for the day accomplished, Howard returned to the XI Corps over the same route he had come, stopping briefly to order Krzyzanowski to remain in his position protecting the flank. For the next two days that brigade exchanged picket fire with the Confederates, capturing several deserters and some 80 to 100 prisoners.[26]

Howard was quite pleased with the day's events. "In truth, we of the Eleventh Corps were soon ahead of our neighbors and proud of it. . . . It was, indeed, a successful reconnaissance, and, though not much of a contest, served with its small losses and its real gain to inspirit the whole command." While Howard was returning to his corps "heavy cannonading was heard in the direction of Lookout Mountain" indicating that Hooker's offensive was underway. The western face of Lookout Mountain was steep, even perpendicular in places, with less than a handful of trails to the top that were easily guarded. But on the Chattanooga side, which Hooker found "less precipitous, a road of easy grade has been made communicating with the summit by zig-zag lines running diagonally up the mountain side, and it was believed that before our troops should gain possession of this, the enemy on the top would evacuate his position, to avoid being cut off from his main body." It would be a very difficult assignment. To any observer, despite the narrow zig-zag road, the "steep, rugged, rocky, and deeply-furrowed slopes, presented an imposing barrier" made even stronger by "well-planned, and well-constructed defenses." Despite the near-impossibility of the assignment, Geary's

25 *OR* 31, pt. 2, 348, 359, 368; *Report on the New York Monuments at Chattanooga*, 75; Howard, *Autobiography*, 479.

26 *OR* 31, pt. 2, 348, 359, 368, 382; *Report on the New York Monuments at Chattanooga*, 75; Wickesberg to parents, Dec. 19, 1863. Ewing was also Sherman's brother-in-law.

division drove across Lookout Creek, "marched directly up the mountain" to a crest along the side, then pushed on down the valley separating Lookout Mountain from Chattanooga.[27]

Heckman's battery was particularly effective enfilading the Rebel defensive positions as the blue-clad soldiers reached the base of the mountain near the zig-zag road. By 2:00 pm, heavy clouds that had been obscuring the view of the top of the mountain began to descend into the valley increasingly obscuring the fighting, which could only be followed by the flash of muskets as they were discharged.[28] With the rest of the army looking on in disbelief, Hooker's troops battled their way up the formidable mountain nearly everyone presumed impregnable. On they went, climbing, clawing, and battling to the top, evicting the Rebel defenders and seizing the dominant heights commanding the city and the valley through which flowed its lifeline of supplies. It was a pivotal event in the campaign, by taking the seemingly impregnable mountain the improvised Federal force under Hooker's command had assured control of the vital river and railway lines into Chattanooga and uncovered the Confederate flank of Missionary Ridge which was now exposed to direct artillery fire and possible assault.

Ernst Damkoehler could not wait to write home about the event. "Must tell you the good news. Lookout Mountain is ours. We are in the midst of the battle. The capture of Lookout was a sensational sight. Our boys started at the right time and drove the Rebels like wild rabbits out of their holes. The 'Hurrah' calls of our boys lasted to late in the evening when the hill was in our permanent positive possession." On the other side of Chattanooga, Maj. Samuel Hurst joined in as the 73rd Ohio "wakened the grandest echoes among the hills of Old Chickamauga. Regiment after regiment, and brigade succeeding brigade, took up the shout, until it became one mighty chorus of victory of forty thousand voices." Dahmkoehler's comrades in Krzyzanowski's front lines could hear the sounds of battle echoing up to them from the valley behind. The noise "lasted long after dark," and it was not until late at night that word arrived of their comrades' success. When it did, the men were beside themselves with joy, cheering and huzzahing well into the night. To Sergt. Karl Wickesberg "It seemed that the hurrah-calling did not want to end."[29]

27 Howard, *Autobiography*, 479-80; *OR* 31, pt. 2, 315, 348.

28 *OR* 31, pt. 2, 316-17, 348, 387.

29 Damkoehler to Mathilde, Nov. 25, 1863; Hurst, *Journal-History*, 95; Wickesberg, Dec. 19, 1863.

"That night," Maj. Hurst enthused, "we slept sweetly by the blazing piles of rails. Our hearts which had, but a few hours before, been sad with the thought of failure and defeat, now leaped with the joy and thrilled with the pride of victory. That night our hardtack and coffee were better than a prince's feast, and out earthly bed was a couch for kings."[30]

☽ ☽ ☽

When November 25 dawned the Union forces were in a much better position than they were the previous morning. Lookout Mountain was in Union hands, eliminating the strong geographical feature that anchored the Confederate left while at the same time providing Hooker's Federals with the real possibility of attacking the Rebel flank on Missionary Ridge. Thomas was entrenched in and around Chattanooga, his lifeline now firmly in Northern hands and providing all the sustenance and supplies his men needed. To the north of the city, Sherman and Howard had pushed the Confederates back and stood poised facing the main Rebel positions on Tunnel Hill and Missionary Ridge.

Grant's plan for the day called for Sherman to initiate the action with a major assault on Bragg's right held by troops under Maj. Gen. Patrick R. Cleburne, one of the best Confederate commanders in the west. Howard was to conform to Sherman's movements in support. Hooker was to march to Rossville Gap so as to outflank Bragg's left. Thomas, facing what appeared to Grant and the other Union officers to be the strongest part of the Confederate defenses, was simply to throw forward his command to seize the Confederate rifle pits below the ridge, more as a feint to support the assaults on the flanks than anything else. Grant never contemplated a major assault on the center of the main Confederate lines since they appeared so formidable.[31]

Sherman began his assault on Tunnel Hill at dawn with Ewing's division in the lead. About 9:45 am Howard received an order to move to Sherman's support, a directive that was soon repeated by one of Grant's aides who told Howard to hurry since Sherman was involved in a tough fight and needed reinforcement right away. Col. Alan Jackson's 134th New York crossed Citico Creek, cleared out a number of remaining Rebel skirmishers in front of von Steinwehr's division, and the move began. At the same time, Schurz assigned a similar task to Col. Friedrich Hecker who accomplished it "without serious resistance on the part of the Rebels." Then Schurz

30 Hurst, *Journal-History*, 95.

31 McDonough, *Chattanooga*, 143, 150, 159; Meysenburg journal, Nov. 25, 1863.

advanced his division across Citico Creek. Howard rode ahead to report in person to Sherman who he found heavily engaged. When the XI Corps arrived Howard directed them to form near Boyce's Station. From there they were to "push forward," protecting Sherman's flank as the assault progressed.[32]

While von Steinwehr's leading troops went into position, on Sherman's right Col. John M. Loomis found his brigade's flank uncovered as he advanced toward a contested ridge. Loomis called for help, an appeal Howard answered by dispatching Col. Buschbeck with a portion of his brigade to Loomis's support. On his arrival Buschbeck was directed into a woods adjoining an open plain. He deployed Lt. Col. Joseph B. Taft's 73rd Pennsylvania as skirmishers to drive Rebel sharpshooters out of a barn and some outhouses. Taft led the assault at the double-quick, his men enduring artillery and musketry sweeping the field. Rushing across the open area, they quickly gained the buildings, flushing out the Rebel sharpshooters. Seeing the ferociousness of the fight, Buschbeck ordered Maj. Peter A. McAloon's 27th Pennsylvania across the field to support Taft.[33]

There were Confederate guns atop the ridge to McAloon's front located in a position from which they could enfilade Ewing's lines as they advanced. About 1:00 pm, Buschbeck ordered McAloon to silence the guns. The colonel led his 27th Pennsylvania, reinforced by Company B of the 73rd under Lt. Samuel D. Miller, in a charge "across the open field and up the ridge under a heavy fire of musketry and canister, and opened fire upon the enemy, who was in strong force and well intrenched just beyond the summit of the hill." Up the ridge they went as musketry and canister sliced through their ranks. In the face of this intense fire the regiment drove the Rebels back to within a few yards of their main works where the Pennsylvanians, exhausted and nearly out of ammunition, hugged the ground while they continued exchanging fire with the defenders. Casualties were high, but Buschbeck's men "at last succeeded in silencing the artillery by their well-directed and steady fire." "McAloon actually led his regiment up that steep acclivity, 500 or 600 feet high, under a terrific fire of grape and musketry," Howard reported with obvious astonishment. Col. Loomis called it "a spirited and gallant attack."[34]

Both of the Pennsylvania regiments accomplished their missions, but once in possession of their objectives staying there was another issue. "The regiment held its position for over two hours," Major August Riedt reported. "The 60 rounds of every

32 *OR* 31, pt. 2, 349, 364, 382, 384; Schurz, *Reminiscences*, III, 74; Howard, *Autobiography*, 482-83.

33 *OR* 31, pt. 2, 359-60, 364, 367.

34 *OR* 31, pt. 2, 349, 359-60; McDonough, *Chattanooga*, 151; McDonough, *Chattanooga*, 152.

man were already exhausted, and they had to supply themselves from the cartridge-boxes of the killed and wounded." Lt. Col. Taft was killed. Major McAloon, wounded five times, refused to leave the field. His wounds proved mortal. At one point a Rebel counterattack cut off a portion of the 73rd Pennsylvania including Color Sergt. Charles Wendler. Fearing capture, he tore the state colors from their staff and handed them to Capt. John Kennedy. But it was too late, both men were captured. Wendler died in Andersonville prison. In the confusion, Kennedy managed to hide the colors under his uniform. Marched off to Libby prison, he survived and was exchanged in March 1864. Somehow the Rebels never discovered the hidden treasure which was joyfully returned to its rightful owners with Kennedy's release.[35]

As casualties rose, Buschbeck had no one to send to the aid of his embattled men since a portion of his troops had been retained by von Steinwehr and his 33rd New Jersey had been ordered off by higher authority to provide a reserve for Col. Loomis's brigade where it stood in formation under heavy shell fire all afternoon. Eventually, after what seemed like an eternity to the beleaguered command, two regiments finally arrived to relieve them and the Pennsylvanians, exhausted and virtually out of ammunition, fell back.[36]

While Sherman and his XI Corps supports battled against Cleburne's stubborn defense of the Confederate right, Gen. Thomas began his movement to capture the Rebel rifle pits below the center of Missionary Ridge. Looking to Confederate observers almost like preparation for a dress parade, the regiments formed in line of battle and moved forward. Without much difficulty they easily secured their objective then, without orders to do so, surged up the steep slope of the ridge itself. With Northern generals looking on in utter disbelief the Southern troops on Missionary Ridge broke, fleeing from the scene in abject rout. Cheering Union infantry followed the retreating Confederates into their trenches, their victorious banners waving above the captured works.[37]

35 *OR* 31, pt. 2, 359-61, 363, 367; Bates, *History of Pennsylvania Volunteers*, 393; *Report on the New York Monuments at Chattanooga*, 77; Sauers, *Advance the Colors!*, I, 198.

36 *OR* 31, pt. 2, 363; Bates, *History of Pennsylvania Volunteers*, 393.

37 *Union Army*, 136; Schurz, *Reminiscences*, III, 74; *Annual Report of the Adjutant General of the State of Wisconsin*, 404; *Soldiers' and Citizens' Album*, 324.

When "news arrived in the evening that General Thomas had carried Mission Ridge by direct assault, that General Hooker had moved to Rossville and got upon the enemy's left flank, and that the enemy were in full retreat," Howard could not help but think that the day-long fight by Sherman and the XI Corps, which siphoned off Rebel reinforcements from other portions of the line all day, had played a part in the victory. "[T]hese vigorous assaults served to accumulate against us a heavy force, and thus weakened other portions of the enemy's line. It is due to the true-hearted men who nobly sacrificed their lives at this point, or who are now suffering with painful wounds, that their names and their regiments should not be overlooked. They contributed all they could to the grand result."[38]

That evening the men sensed victory, although the extent was not immediately clear. Nevertheless, most believed the day had gone well for the Union. Schurz was eating a supper of coffee, hardtack, and a slice of bacon with his staff when his division surgeon arrived to join them bringing the news that Missionary Ridge was in Federal hands and the Rebels were in full retreat. "The rest of us jumped up without finishing our supper and hurriedly ran out for more news. Then we heard from afar a swelling wave of cheers rolling along our lines toward us, and in a few minutes we had the whole glorious story." Maj. Frederick Winkler found everyone "jubilant." Howard reported that "The news flew like wildfire, and the Chickamauga hills echoed with our soldiers' victorious cheer." In the 134th New York, William Levey recorded that "After the noise and strife had ceased, we began to hear in the distance the loud hurrahs and joyous shouts of victory come ringing down the line, until it reached the ears of all our mighty host and reverberated over those picturesque hills and dales of 'Sunny Tennessee.'"[39]

☽ ☽ ☽

Chattanooga was saved, Bragg was defeated, but the war continued. By 4:00 am the XI Corps was in motion pursuing the retreating Rebels. "[W]e started in the dark," Maj. Winkler recalled, "and it was very foggy." Howard found the fog "so dense that you could not discern a horse at 100 yards." Feeling their way, the troops moved back toward Chattanooga and crossed the pontoon bridge near the mouth of Chickamauga Creek. As the 26th Wisconsin negotiated the undulating pontoons, a staff officer

38 *OR* 31, pt. 2, 349-50.

39 Schurz, *Reminiscences*, III, 76-77; Winkler, *Letters*, 103; *OR* 31, pt. 2, 350; Conklin, *Crescent and Star*, 146.

arrived from XI Corps headquarters with the welcome news they were "in pursuit of the fleeing foe." Immediately "there was rejoicing, every heart was glad. I never knew the column to march so rapidly," Winkler marveled. "We halted for a time; some one suggested this was Thanksgiving Day in Wisconsin; I thought of the holiday at home; remarks were passed, how the people were spending it in a social circle; yes, they were spending it festively, but this army was enjoying it and there was not a man who would have exchanged his proud place for a seat at the festive board." John Ryder in the 33rd Massachusetts celebrated a memorable Thanksgiving dinner. "[W]ith half a canteen which I used for a frying pan, I cooked a dish of fried hardtack beside a log on the side of the road, and then sitting on the log ate it with a good appetite."[40]

The column "pushed forward carefully till the fog cleared," the advance reaching Chickamauga Station at noon. Sergt. Karl Wickesberg marveled that the Rebels "had destroyed everything. He had burned everything at the railroad stations. They left their ammunition and everything and ran away as fast as they could. 60 to 70 prisoners fell into our hands. We had the good fortune not to get into any battle." In the 55th Ohio, Alonzo Keeler wrote in his diary that his regiment captured four artillery pieces and 200 men. Others reported similar seizures. In his official campaign report, Howard enumerated "two siege guns, about 1,000 bushels of corn, 10 pontoons, and considerable flour were captured here [Chickamauga Station]. Large quantities of flour and corn were burning when we arrived." Maj. Samuel Hurst and his 73rd Ohio had the good fortune to capture a large amount of corn meal and flour which somehow survived among what the Rebels had destroyed. "That night we feasted on corn cakes made of Rebel meal, to which the men had helped themselves as they passed the station, and though we had never envied the Rebel soldiers their rations of corn bread, the cakes were a real luxury to our cracker-worn palates."[41]

The corps pushed on to Graysville where it finally halted to encamp about an "hour after sundown." Maj. Samuel Hurst of the 73rd Ohio was struck by the pro-Union sentiment in the area. "There were unmistakable evidences of joy at our coming from many who had sons, brothers, or friends fighting under the flag and for the cause of the Union. One gray-haired woman came from the door of her humble cottage, as our column marched along, and asked our color-sergeant to unroll the 'old flag,' 'for,' said she, with tears of joy in her eyes, 'I want to see the stars again.'"[42]

40 *OR* 31, pt. 2, 350, 359; Winkler, *Letters*, 103, 108; Ryder, *Reminiscences*, 44.

41 Wickesberg to parents, Dec. 19, 1863; Keeler diary, Nov. 26, 1863; *OR* 31, pt. 2, 350; Hurst, *Journal-History*, 95-96.

42 *OR* 31, pt. 2, 382, 384; Hurst, *Journal-History*, 97.

☽ ☽ ☽

After another short night the men were on the road again early the following morning. Howard directed the corps through Parker's Gap, his objective for the day being the railroad between Dalton and Cleveland. He dispatched two brigades under Col. Orland Smith to destroy the railroad at Red Clay. They arrived in the town "just at sunrise" according to Andrew Boies, "and then you ought to have seen the 11th corps walk in. We tore up five miles of railroad, burning the ties, and twisting the rails in the form of a letter S. We burned all the public buildings. This was on the Knoxville and Atlanta railroad, where Longstreet got his supplies, but we 'Yanks' shortened the street for him." Along the way the troops captured some prisoners, among them a Confederate officer carrying dispatches to Bragg. Howard explained that "This operation prevented, for the present, the possibility of Longstreet joining Bragg by railroad, and it equally prevented the passage of any re-enforcements from Bragg to Longstreet." By the time the day's work was completed some in the corps had marched as much as 27 miles.[43]

On the morning of November 28, Grant suspended the pursuit. Howard received orders that the corps should rest for the day before returning to Chattanooga. Yet not everyone was able to rest. Howard explained that "Wagons belonging to the different brigades were on the road, many of them stuck in the mud, all the way from Parker's Gap to the mouth of the Chickamauga. As the command was short of rations the wagons had to be brought up before the next morning. By extraordinary exertions this was done, and three days' rations distributed. One battery and all of the wagons, except the ammunition, were sent back to Chattanooga."[44]

With the siege of Chattanooga ended, Bragg's army thoroughly defeated, the surviving Rebels in full flight, and the pursuit now suspended, everyone in the XI Corps looked forward to a well-deserved rest, time to recuperate and resupply from the lengthy campaign. But it was not to be.

43 *OR* 31, pt. 2, 351, 382; Boies, *Thirty-third Massachusetts*, 54.

44 *OR* 31, pt. 2, 351; Meysenburg journal, Nov. 28, 1863.

Chapter 20

"A Victory Achieved by the Soldiers' Legs"

The Relief of Knoxville

AFTER FAILING TO PREVENT THE opening of the "Cracker Line" Bragg ordered Longstreet's infantry and Gen. Joseph Wheeler's cavalry north to assist Gen. Samuel Jones's troops operating against Federal forces under Maj. Gen. Ambrose P. Burnside in northeastern Tennessee. Bragg hoped the threat to Burnside would ease pressure on his own forces and help him reestablish the siege of Chattanooga or force Grant to abandon the city. The move succeeded in forcing Burnside inside the defensive works around Knoxville, to the great consternation of the authorities in Washington, but Grant correctly chose to ignore the threat and concentrate on defeating Bragg's army. This accomplished, under growing pressure to help Burnside, who issued repeated calls for assistance, and prevent the fall of Knoxville, Grant ordered Sherman to march his command rapidly to Burnside's aid.[1]

The most important factor in the relief of Knoxville was time. A delay, even of a day or two, could spell doom. Sherman met Howard on the afternoon of November 28 to apprise him of the new orders. Howard recalled that "General Sherman made known to me that General Grant had instructed him to move to the Hiwassee to operate against Longstreet. He wanted his entire column, and issued orders to me accordingly, designating the route I should take. The rest of the day and night was, therefore, spent in preparation." Major Charles Howard noted "They did not wait for supplies to come from Chattanooga. The troops were without knapsacks and the 11th

1 Schurz, *Reminiscences*, III, 78; *OR* 31, pt. 2, 350.

Capt. George Turnbull, 134th New York
U.S. Army Heritage and Education Center

Corps had already been absent from Camp an entire week. Some brigades had left even their blankets behind on going into battle in front of Chattanooga and had not yet been able to return to get them. There was no supply train and no hope of having any as we were to move directly away from our base not attempting to keep connection with the same."[2] With their shoes falling apart or entirely lacking, the cold, damp December weather promised only future suffering.

The corps took to the roads by 6:00 am on November 29 marching steadily through cool, damp air with von Steinwehr's division in the lead. Schurz reckoned the distance to Knoxville at 120 miles. The line of march roughly followed the East Tennessee and Georgia Railroad some twenty miles to Cleveland where the men camped for the evening. Capt. Franz Lackner, now serving on Schurz's staff, found the surrounding countryside "charming, the cities neat, the people respectable, the girls pretty and friendly, and the chickens not too timid," the last phrase no doubt alluding to the availability of livestock along the way to supplement the troops' diet. Major Howard was gratified to see that "All along this day's march we met with earnest Union people who came sometimes a mile or two to convey information and they turned out all along that road seemingly gratified at a sight of 'the Yankees' as is the habit of the country to denominate the Federal forces. Secesh stays sullenly within doors, scowling through the windows or not deigning to look out at all." That first night Maj. Samuel Hurst of the 73rd Ohio found "bitter cold; but in the absence of blankets, the men built large fires, and made the best of the situation." Capt. George Turnbull in the 134th New York "did not have any blankets nothing but an overcoat, and it froze ice thick enough

2 *OR* 31, pt. 2, 351; Meysenburg journal, Nov. 28, 1863; C. Howard to Mr. Gilmore, Dec. 11, 1863, William E. Brooks Collection, Library of Congress.

to slide on in the morning, so you can calculate it was patriotism that kept me from freezing that night."[3]

Schurz thought the men "were in fine spirits after the great victory, and bore the fatigue of the forced march with excellent cheer." He had obviously not spoken to John Ryder or his friends in the 33rd Massachusetts: "As we had left all our tents, overcoats and blankets in our camp in Lookout Valley before entering the previous battle, we suffered terribly from the cold nights. It was impossible to sleep but very little. The only way to even do that was to stand before a hot fire and get as warm as possible, then lie down and quickly fall asleep. We would sometimes get a few hours sleep before the cold would awaken us, and then we would repeat the process. Then we were out of rations, except for flour, which we had only time to cook by mixing it with water and baking it on a board before the fire. The ground was frozen and numbers of the men's shoes were wholly worn out . . . we literally tracked blood on the frozen ground."[4]

Early marches continued on November 30, the columns being in motion about 7:00 am with Schurz's division leading. In Charleston, a company of Rebel cavalry, backed by about 300 infantry, retreated from town before the Union advance, heading toward Athens with several wagons. Before leaving, they did everything they could to inhibit the Federal advance by destroying any means of crossing the Hiwassee River. Arriving at the stream, Howard "found the pontoon bridge broken, swung around, and many of the boats stove and others rapidly floating down stream, the railroad bridge partially destroyed, the stringers having been sawed off, and two of the trestles thrown down. A detachment of Rebels on the opposite bank were trying to destroy three cars loaded with stores."[5]

Howard ordered Capt. William Wheeler to move a section of guns forward into battery and in minutes the Rebels were dispersed, fleeing out of range of the exploding Hotchkiss percussion shells. With resistance ended, Major Ernst Hoffman's engineers worked overnight without stop to construct a floating bridge over 200 feet long using timbers taken from nearby sheds and outhouses. While the engineers began their toils, Major Howard watched as skirmishers from two companies of the 55th Ohio crossed

3 *OR* 31, pt. 2, 382, 433; Circular, Nov. 29, 1863, RG 393, Pt. 2, 5321 & 5348, NARA; Schurz, *Reminiscences*, III, 78; Meysenburg journal, Nov. 29, 1863; Lackner, "Toward a History of the Twenty-Sixth," unpublished manuscript written in the summer of 1865, in the possession of Alexander G. Morehouse; C. Howard to Mr. Gilman, Dec. 13, 1863, Bowdoin College; Hurst, *Journal-History*, 98; Cosgrove, *History of the 134th New York*, 122.

4 Schurz, *Reminiscences*, III, 78; Ryder, *Reminiscences*, 44-45.

5 *OR* 31, pt. 2, 351, 382; Osborn, "East Tennessee," 368.

the river "in such rough boats as could be collected" and "rushed forward into town and we saw the Rebels running like rats upon the other side of the river." The Ohioans also captured a train loaded with supplies that the fleeing owners did not have time to destroy. Obviously overjoyed, Howard reported that "From these cars we subsequently obtained some two days' rations of flour and seven or eight days' of salt, and a quantity of spikes, which came in play in repairing the bridge. . . . During the rest of the day and the following night the railroad bridge was repaired, planked over, and rendered passable for artillery and wagons."[6]

With the bridge completed, the corps began crossing around 4:00 am on December 1 with Schurz's division again in front. Before reaching Riceville each regiment in turn stopped briefly to receive its share of the captured Rebel flour and salt, then pushed on toward where they found windows decorated with United States flags. Colby Bryant's 154th New York "marched through the village with our banners waving unfolded and keeping step to the martial music, we were welcomed by women waving handkerchiefs and in one or two instances our flags, which had evidently been kept secreted since the war [began]. Most all seemed pleased at the sight of a Union army." Capt. Lackner thought they "marched through good Country & neat villages." Major Winkler found "the days very pleasant," but worried that the nights were "very cold" and the marches "strenuous." Arriving at Athens around supper time, Andrew Boies reported the marching column "entered this town, our band playing 'The Star Spangled Banner.' The women waved their handkerchiefs; the sight of our army was a new birth to them." In town a cheering report reached Howard that "Longstreet had attacked Burnside at Knoxville and been repulsed on Sunday, November 29," but he cautiously wondered whether it was true or just another camp rumor.[7]

The troops were roused from sleep at 3:00 am on December 2 and on the road an hour later, Dilger's battery marching with Schurz in the van and Wheeler' battery with von Steinwehr. The muddy, rutted roads were difficult going for the guns, especially since their horses were largely broken down. "I had much trouble in moving my battery toward Cleveland," reported Capt. Wheeler, "as my horses were extremely exhausted; I

6 *OR* 31, pt. 2, 351, 371, 388; Howard, *Autobiography*, 491; C. Howard to Gilmore, Dec. 11, 1863, William E. Brooks Collection, Library of Congress; Keeler diary, Nov. 30, 1863; Meysenburg journal, Nov. 30, 1863.

7 Circular, Dec. 1, 1863: RG 393, Pt. 2, 5321 & 5348, NARA; Schurz, *Reminiscences*, III, 78; Winkler report, Aug. 25, 1864, Winkler Papers; Wickesberg to family, Dec. 19, 1863; C. Howard to Gilmore, Dec. 11, 1863, Brooks Collection, Library of Congress; Dunkelman, *Brothers One and All*, 197; Lackner diary, Dec. 22, 1863; Winkler, *Letters*, 103; Boies, *Thirty-third Massachusetts*, 55; *OR* 31, pt. 2, 351, 367, 382-83, 433.

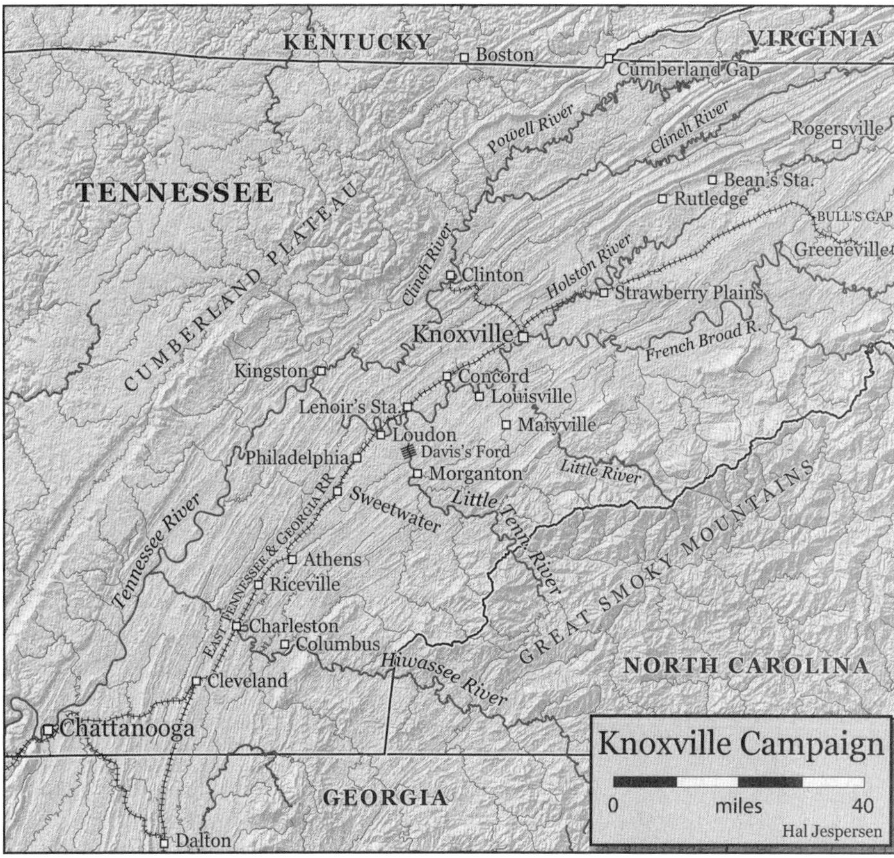

was consequently compelled to press horses from the country, giving conditional receipts for the same; and this course I was obliged to pursue more or less upon the whole march; sometimes taking mules as well as horses. I have memoranda of all animals taken and receipted for in this manner, and am prepared to account for them." Both batteries, Major Osborn reported, "were unable to move with the column to and from Knoxville without impressing a considerable number of horses and mules in the country."[8] At some point infantry were detailed to help move the guns by human muscle power.

Most of the men marched with protesting stomachs, the supply of rations having given out with the only replenishment being the captured flour and whatever they could forage along the way. "[W]e had to survive through food that farmers gave us or

8 Circular, Dec. 2, 1863, RG 393, Pt. 2, 5321 & 5348, NARA; *OR* 31, pt. 2, 367, 386, 388.

that which we took from the enemy," Sergt. Karl Wickesberg reported. Major Winkler pronounced the land "a fine agricultural country, but it is very much exhausted. It was with difficulty that we could get a cow and ox and [a] few sheep or hogs from a farmer as we passed along, but we had to take them to subsist our column."[9]

One "frosty morning" Schurz happened upon a house from which a "blue cloud of smoke curled up." Thinking there might be officers inside and food to be had, he entered to find Gens. Sherman and Jefferson C. Davis warming themselves by the fire. Schurz joined them at Sherman's invitation. Soon Howard arrived. "General Sherman greeted him in his brusque way, exclaiming: 'Glad to see you, Howard! Sit down by the fire! Damned cold this morning!' Howard, who especially abhorred the use of 'swear words,' answered demurely: 'Yes, General, it is *quite* cold this morning.' Sherman might have noticed a slight touch of reproof in this answer. At any rate, I observed a wink he gave General Davis with his left eye, while a sarcastic smile flitted across his features." Encouraged thus by Sherman, Davis launched into a spirited conversation liberally laced with "a profusion of 'damns' and the like," which made Howard increasingly uncomfortable. "Encouraged by repeated winks and also a few sympathetic remarks from Sherman, Davis inexorably continued the lurid flow of infernalisms, until finally Howard, with distress painted all over his face, got up and left."[10] While Schurz may have enjoyed the fire and Sherman's joke at Howard's expense, the troops were left to contend with the cold, the mud, and the hunger.

Once again the tired men were up early, on the road by 4:00 am. One advantage they enjoyed was no lack of accurate information from the local populace and Confederate deserters. "Along the entire route," Howard observed, "we were cheered by the most lively demonstrations of loyalty on the part of inhabitants. Therefore we never lacked for information as to roads, bridges, fords, location of the enemy, &c." As they approached Loudon a former Confederate major, who had apparently recently resigned his commission, came into the Union lines. Brought to Howard, the man "without laying any claim to loyalty, stated that he had drifted with the current, but since our recent victory was satisfied that Tennessee would resume her place in the Union. He gave me information so accurate that I was able to sketch the works at Knoxville and the enemy's position. He also gave me the enemy's strength, with the

9 *Annual Report of the Adjutant General of the State of Wisconsin*, 404; *OR* 31, pt. 2, 382-383; Quiner, *Military History of Wisconsin*, 752; Wickesberg to parents, Dec. 19, 1863, quote from Jan. 17, 1864; Winkler, *Letters*, 103-104.

10 Schurz, *Reminiscences*, III, 78-79.

names of the officers commanding at different points, all of which proved to be substantially correct."[11]

There were sizable Rebel works guarding Loudon that made it the most formidable obstacle the Federal advance faced since beginning the march. "There were two redoubts upon the heights on the west side of Loudon, one of which was located upon a position of natural strength, and made to face southward: the other was nearer the river and facing toward it. . . . Off against the redoubts the river makes a sudden bend, forming a peninsula. The road leading to the Rebel pontoon bridge passes across this peninsula, making the bridge about three-fourths of a mile from town by land and 6 by water." The defenders included a brigade of Tennessee infantry under Gen. John C. Vaughn, some artillery and "a detachment of cavalry." Col. Long's cavalry screening the infantry came under Confederate artillery fire from Loudon as they approached the town the previous evening. Once daylight returned on the morning of the 3rd, Howard brought Wheeler's battery forward to fire on the Rebel positions. As he explained, in addition to paving the way for the infantry advance this had a secondary purpose. "Considerable artillery firing was allowed in accordance with instructions, in the hope that the guns might be heard by General Burnside at Knoxville, and he thus be made aware of the approach of re-enforcements."[12]

The infantry arrived with Krzyzanowski's brigade in the advance. The Polish colonel deployed the 26th Wisconsin, the recently-promoted Major Frederick Winkler commanding, in skirmish order, with an appropriate reserve and orders to move quickly into town. Winkler's rapid advance swept into the outskirts of the town so quickly the Rebels were forced to abandon huge quantities of stores in order to make their escape. Howard reported that the Rebels "destroyed from 60 to 75 cars containing supplies of commissary stores, clothing, and ammunition, 3 locomotives, and, finally, their pontoon bridge." The stone piers upon which the destroyed railroad bridge had stood were still in place, but the main channel of the Tennessee River was "completely filled with the rubbish of locomotives, cars and their contents, which had been set on fire before being run into the river." The Confederate hospital contained a large number of sick who could not be moved, along with about 75 wounded soldiers from Longstreet's command. The wounded men reported the failure of the Rebel assault on Knoxville, yet still no official word came from Burnside so the news remained unconfirmed. Despite the destruction, Howard's troops recovered enough

11 Keeler diary, Dec. 3, 1863; *OR* 31, pt. 2, 351-52, 383, 433.

12 *OR* 31, pt. 2, 352, 386, 388; Meysenburg journal, Dec. 3, 1863.

food to supply the corps for three days and to provide for the Rebel sick and wounded in the hospital.[13]

The large quantities of supplies temporarily eased much of the men's shortage of rations. Andrew Kelly in the 134th New York described how the hungry men attacked the precious supplies. "Some would be down upon their knees scraping a flour barrel, while others above them were filling canteens with molasses, from which would flow a steady stream of the sweet fluid, which dropped on the heads and flowed down the backs of those beneath." When they marched off, "from every gun hung a bag of flour, the owners of which were white with it, and on the majority of them the molasses had run in all directions through the flour, so that at a small distance they looked like traveling maps of the countries of the globe, with the principal rivers thereon." The men had a good chuckle describing themselves as "the flour of the army."[14]

Tyndale's brigade pitched in to provide the labor while the engineers' directed the construction of a makeshift bridge across the Little Tennessee River. One of those who worked on the bridge was Andrew Boies. "[W]e had no tools except axes, spades and picks. We gathered all the wagons that we could find from the citizens, besides the unoccupied buildings of the place. We sank them in the river, about 10 feet apart; upon these we laid plank, boards, fence rails, etc., and then made wooden 'hosses' and sank them for a quarter of a mile." He found the river "quite deep and the water freezing." He had an excellent perspective to judge since he was among those who volunteered to go into the freezing waters "to sink those 'hosses.' It was a bitter cold night, snow on the ground, and the current was running at the rate of nine miles an hour. A rope was put under my arms and I was lowered into the water; could only stay about 10 minutes at a time, (stark naked at that); after being pulled out would run to a fire built of rails to be well rubbed, and then try the same over again. Three times in succession this was done, in order that our army could pass over. . . . We worked all night, until 3 o'clock in the morning, and at 5 o'clock all of our cavalry, artillery and infantry crossed over in safety and were moving rapidly on to the assistance of Burnside, who must have aid, and have it in a few hours."[15]

After a brief but welcome halt to allow the bridge to be built and the column to close up, the advance continued. Roused at midnight, the column was on the road by 1:00 am on December 4. In the advance, the 82nd Illinois of Col. Friedrich Hecker's brigade crossed the river in a flatboat and skirmished briefly with cavalry covering the

13 *OR* 31, pt. 2, 352-53, 383; Keeler diary, Dec. 3, 1863; Howard, *Autobiography*, 491.

14 Cosgrove, *134th New York*, 123-24; Kelly, *134th Regiment, N.Y.S. Vol.*, 28.

15 Howard, *Autobiography*, 491; OR 31, pt. 2, 353; Boies, *Thirty-third Massachusetts*, 55-56.

Rebel retreat. Hecker's men captured four abandoned rifled artillery pieces and a stand of colors. Continuing on, the corps made remarkable speed over the muddy roadways. Major Winkler was well-pleased with his men's performance. "[T]he regiment never marched better, with fewer stragglers; we have been in positions that tried them too."[16]

That night, Surgeon Henry Van Aernam found time to write home. "We have all been two weeks to the front—ordered to go out 'light,' consequently left everything behind except the clothes upon our backs and turned immediately from the battlefield of this campaign and long march and have suffered from hunger, cold and fatigue—but we are all happy and cheerful." His mood buoyed by the victories around Chattanooga and the pursuit of a quickly retreating foe, Van Aernam was optimistic despite the corps' condition. "For my own part, I don't know whether I am sick or well and don't much care for I feel well and I am happy. Hunger and cold and the fatigue of long wearisome marches and ill health are all forgotten in the proud satisfaction of seeing the Rebel army crushed and fleeing before us. . . . Our record since here is a proud one. We opened up Lookout Valley and fed the starving Army. Hooker charged and took Lookout Mountain and we were a part of the Grand Army that drove Bragg from Missionary Ridge and are now turning upon Longstreet."[17]

Schurz's division took the lead early on the morning of December 5, marching to Little River near Louisville, less than fifteen miles from their ultimate goal of Knoxville. Howard was conferring with Sherman near Unitia when a courier arrived from Burnside with the welcome news that Longstreet was in retreat, the first direct confirmation the two had received that Knoxville was safe. The two generals immediately rode forward with their escorts to the relieved city to meet its commander. Howard found "Burnside was delighted to see us, and gave us a turkey dinner."[18]

Following the joyous meeting, Burnside took the time to formally thank Sherman and his troops. "General, I desire to express to you and your command my most hearty thanks and gratitude for your promptness in coming to our relief during the siege of Knoxville and I am satisfied that your approach served to raise the siege." Major Charles Howard wrote to inform his sister that "We went as you will have learned to visit Mr. Longstreet but found him out. He went away bag and baggage, journeying

16 Circular, Dec. 4, 1863, RG 393, Pt. 2, 5321 & 5348, NARA; *OR* 31, pt. 2, 353, 383, 433 (The colors captured by the 82nd Illinois was described as a having a "Southern Cross" pattern.); Meysenburg journal, Dec. 4, 1863; *Annual Report of the Adjutant General of the State of Wisconsin*, 404; Winkler, *Letters*, 104-05.

17 Van Aernam, Dec. 4, 1863, Papers in USMHI.

18 Circular, Dec. 5, 1863, RG 393, Pt. 2, 5321 & 5348, NARA; Howard, *Autobiography*, 492; *OR*, 31, pt. 2, 353.

'back to Old Virginny,' on Friday night." It was, Schurz appropriately concluded, "a victory achieved by the soldiers' legs."[19] He might also have added by their fortitude in the face of exceptional suffering.

☽ ☽ ☽

December 6 brought welcome relief to the exhausted troops who enjoyed a day of rest now that the danger to Knoxville had passed. Because of the destitute condition of the XI Corps, Sherman ordered it to "return as soon as possible to our camps" in Lookout Valley, the march to begin the following day. Howard would later report that "On the march back the commissaries generally preceded the corps, and seizing the mills notified the inhabitants to bring in wheat and corn, which they purchased and ground in readiness for distribution on the arrival of their respective brigades. The mills were kept running night and day. The salt captured at Charleston on the way up lasted till our return to the same place. By means of this we were able to make use of the cattle and sheep of the country, which were sufficient for our purpose. The region of our march also abounded in sorghum or home-made molasses, which was purchased in quantity and issued to the troops. This was found a suitable substitute for sugar. For coffee, wheat in the grain was issued. No complaint of want of food came to my ears."[20] It seems few would have agreed with him.

The weary troops moved out at 7:00 am on December 7 bound for Sweetwater with Schurz's division in the lead. "After one day's rest we started back over the same road with all of its added discomforts included," reported John Ryder. "While we did not need to hurry back for other reasons, yet our necessity for food and clothing made it imperative for us to reach some place where we could obtain a supply. The weather for that part of the country was unusually cold, and not only were our feet shoeless but our trousers were almost indescribable with many of us. We had no sewing material for repairing the rents made by the bushes and briars through which we had been fighting the recent battles. The only way we could keep them together from the waist down was by using thorns for pins, the thorn bushes furnishing an abundant supply." "A portion of us were barefoot," William Levey recalled, "our shoes being worn out, and the railroad torn up, no supplies could reach us; the best we could do was tie rags and handkerchiefs around our feet to protect them from the frosty earth and small pebbles." Sergt. Karl Wickesberg saw that "many men had no shoes anymore and had

19 *OR* 31, pt. 2, 36; C. Howard to sister Ella, Dec. 9, 1863; Schurz, *Reminiscences*, III, 80.

20 *OR* 31, pt. 2, 354.

to walk barefooted and many got sick." Maj. David Peloubet in the 33rd New Jersey witnessed ambulances and wagons full of "barefooted and sore footed men unable to march."[21]

By the 9th the corps was passing through Athens. Frequent rains covered the cold and rocky roads with a slippery mud. One man in four lacked shoes, while blankets were viewed as a luxury. Threadbare clothing proved inadequate against the brutally cold winds that brought with them freezing sleet. Perpetually damp clothing froze to men's bodies as they slept. Equipment parked overnight had to be pried free in the morning before it could be moved. Even the supply of coffee gave out, forcing the men to roast corn or wheat kernels as a substitute. While the officers generally managed to save some food and coffee, and thereby fared better, the men fared worse. One cold morning Schurz watched as "The men rose and tossed and swung their limbs to get their blood into circulation. The feet of not a few were frozen fast in the soil, and when they pulled them up, they left the soles of such shoes as they had, sticking in the hardened mud." It was, Col. Krzyzanowski wrote with dramatic understatement, a "terrible ordeal."[22]

In the 45th New York Leonhard Schlumpf commented that "Most of us are without shoes for the last 8 days. We are hungry, exhausted, cold, wet and want to go home. No roads or bridges to walk on, only mud, rivers and swamp. It rains most of the time and our clothes never get dry. It does not matter anymore, whether we have to wade through water 1 foot deep or 3 feet deep. We are all wet down to our skin. We had to march on all last night, barefoot and wet. Every so often soldiers cried out in agony as they stepped on thorns or sharp stones in the dark night. They collapsed and fell and were left behind." "Blood could be traced along the line of march," reported George Warner, "and for three or four days the return to Chattanooga began to compare with the historical 'Retreat from Moscow.' At about forty miles from Chattanooga, and after the troops had apparently been taxed to the utmost, General Howard ordered a halt, and a detail of all shoemakers. These men were set to work to make a substitute for shoes from the green hides of cattle, which proved a failure. They were 'too slippery.' After spending a day or two on the experiment, and seeing that the men would starve before they could be shod, the march resumed and the men ordered to get to

21 Circular, Dec. 7, 1863: RG 393, Pt. 2, 5321 & 5348; *OR* 31, pt. 2, 433; Ryder, *Reminiscences*, 45; Cosgrove, 134th New York, 124; Wickesberg, Jan. 17, 1864; Zinn, *Mutinous Regiment*, 54.

22 Lackner diary, Dec. 22, 1863; Winkler, *Letters*, 105; Schurz, *Reminiscences*, III, 80-83; Quiner, *Military History of Wisconsin*, 752; Cavins to wife, Dec. 19, 1863; *History of Milwaukee*, 800; Love, *Wisconsin in the War of the Rebellion*, 999; Krzyzanowski, *Wspomnienia*, 80; *Annual Report of the Adjutant General of the State of Wisconsin*, 404.

Chattanooga as best they could."[23] Many of the men developed colds, bronchitis, or pneumonia, some of whom would pay with their lives.

On they plodded, reaching Cleveland on December 13. The cold, inclement weather continued. William Lambert in the 33rd New Jersey portrayed it as "a storm which exceeds all that have gone before it . . . we sleep in mud, which nearly engulfs us." Maj. David Peloubet pronounced the night "the most miserable of the whole march." Leonhard Schlumpf in the 45th New York described the conditions in his diary: "We are at the foot of Lookout mountain at our old camping place. Nothing to eat all day. It is terribly cold. We were told from now on we would only get 1/2 rations of food." "When we got back," Capt. George Turnbull wrote, we "were the sorriest looking lot of soldiers you ever saw." Milton Griswold in the 154th New York was more descriptive: "We saw some tough times on this march. We have marched about 250 miles, and the boys are hard up for shoes and boots. I have seen the boys march, when the ground was frozen hard, with nothing on their feet but some old rags wrapped round, and I have seen them march through the mud with nothing on their feet all day, and that looks tough, especially in the month of December. I have marched when my boots were so poor and feet so sore you could track me for miles from the blood that ran from the sores on my feet, and when I pulled my boots and pieces of socks off, the skin came off my feet with the socks."[24]

Capt. Friedrich von Fritsch looked about him on their return. "We were in rags, boots and shoes torn or burned to pieces, everybody more or less sick, terribly worn out and starved. We found very little to eat, as the Commissary had not expected us so soon. Old hardtacks, covered with mould, a little bacon, and, fortunately, some coffee were distributed in ridiculously small rations. The weather was beastly. It rained all the time, and a cold wind blew down the valley day and night."[25] At least the severe marching was over, they would now have an opportunity for a well-deserved rest.

☽ ☽ ☽

The Confederate siege of Knoxville failed because of the rapid marching and willing sacrifices of thousands of Union infantrymen. In his official report of the

23 Schlumpf diary, Dec. 16, 1863; Cosgrove, *134th New York*, 124; Warner, *Military Records of Schoharie County Veterans*, 28.

24 *OR* 31, pt. 2, 433; Zinn, *Mutinous Regiment*, 57; Schlumpf diary, Dec. 17, 1863; Conklin, "History of the 134th N.Y."; Dunkelman, *Brothers One and All*, 106.

25 Butts, *Gallant Captain*, 102.

activities of the 33rd New Jersey in the Knoxville Campaign, Col. George W. Mindil asserted that "Considering the severity of the weather, often exceedingly cold and stormy, the absence of blankets and tents, the miserable condition of the shoes of a large portion of the command, scores being barefooted, and the insufficient and poor rations furnished, the troops have withstood the hardships of this severe but glorious campaign with firm determination and remarkably good cheer." Howard's thoughts were similar: "The corps had endured the extreme fatigue of a three days' battle, engaged in the pursuit for two days, effectively destroyed the railroad communication between Longstreet and Bragg, and then turned northward, and made a march of 120 miles, to the relief of Burnside, and then immediately returned to its old camp; and when we consider that this was accomplished under such unfavorable circumstances as wretched roads, no transportation, few blankets and tents, with rivers to cross without bridge trains, and supplies to be collected from the country, why may we not speak of our soldiers, with pride, as equal to any in the world?"[26]

To his troops, Howard issued grateful thanks in General Orders No. 32 dated December 17, the same day the corps returned to its Lookout Valley camps: "Words cannot express the gratitude and praise due to a command that has so cheerfully suffered every hardship in order to perform its part and secure to our country and to our cause, results more glorious and more valuable than any of the war. But it will be better than praise to clothe you and cover your bleeding feet so that the General now will only tender you his warmest congratulations and hearty thanks for the good name which you have won and secured in this eventful campaign. We will not soon forget a battle which has cost us such precious lives as those of Lt. Col. Taft and Major McAloon and the other dead. These true and noble soldiers have with their blood enhanced the price of victory. Let God in his wisdom temper our rejoicing by care for the wounded and sympathies with the friends that have been afflicted."[27]

That Howard's praise was sincere can be seen in a letter he sent to his wife on December 20 in which he again recited the travails facing his soldiers and their achievements. The men of the XI Corps could well be proud of their accomplishments. No doubt they received the words of praise from their commander with appreciation, but more importantly they once again received commendation from outside the corps, something that never happened in the Army of the Potomac. In General Orders No. 6, Gen. Sherman wrote: "The Gen Comd'g hereby thanks all Officers and men for the promptness with which all orders were obeyed, more especially for the cheerfulness

26 *OR* 31, pt. 2, 355, 362. The march was approximately 120 each way, or 240 miles round trip.

27 General Orders No. 32, Dec. 17, 1863, NARA.

exhibited under privations of the severest kind, without tents, without rations, with insufficient clothing, almost without shoes in midwinter, this Army sprang with a generous impulse and marched to Knoxville, a distance of one hundred and twenty miles over the worst of roads, and relieved from danger twelve thousand of our fellow soldiers, besieged by a dangerous enemy and returned only after Gen Burnside had asked for partial reinforcements and that the remainder should return to the more important strategic field of Chattanooga. That all Officers and soldiers who have participated in the hardships of the march may feel that their labors have been appreciated, the Gen Comd'g hereby makes public the letter he received at Knoxville at the hands of Gen Burnside and he takes this method of conveying to this Army the thanks which Gen. Burnside so manfully tendered on the part of himself and his brave garrison."[28]

In a personal letter to Howard the following day, Sherman reiterated his appreciation for the eastern troops he had commanded for the first time. "I have deemed it my duty to express to Genl Grant and others in whom I confide not only the satisfaction but the great pleasure I experienced in being associated with you in our late short but most fruitful campaign. Not only did you do all that circumstances required, but you did it in a spirit of cheerfulness that was reflected in the conduct and behavior of your whole command. I beg you will convey to Genl Schurz, Col. Buschbeck and all your officers the assurance of my personal & official respect. Should fortune bring us together again in any capacity, I will deem myself most fortunate, and should it ever be in my person to serve you, that you will unhesitatingly call on me as a Friend." The letter was signed "With great respect."[29]

Among the troops, perhaps Andrew Boies of the 33rd Massachusetts best captured the mood of those whose efforts led to the success. "I have been thinking of our last campaign and what we accomplished in the space of four weeks for our country and its cause; and having done our duty, we have a reason to rejoice over a victory that belongs to us. We have borne the fatigue without a murmur, we have travelled 250 miles and fought the enemy one-half of the time, have bivouacked upon the ground, endured both storm and sunshine, and we are still in good spirits. … The future is unknown to me, but to judge from the past. I know that we have gained the summit of the mountain and made our descent into the valley below, and if I judge the present by what we have experienced in the past, it is a surety upon which rests a good

28 Howard to Dearest, Dec. 20, 1863; General Orders No. 6, Army of Tennessee, Dec. 16, 1863, NARA.

29 Sherman letter to Howard, Dec. 18, 1863, GNMP.

hold. A defeat has befallen our enemies, while we have been crowned with success. The 'Star of Hope' still beams bright to cheer us on our way with more courage than before. Lookout mountain, a few weeks ago, bade us defiance, and from its top would be hurled shot and shell into our ranks, but to-day it is ours, and over it floats the 'Stars and Stripes,' and all is calm and serene."[30]

The campaign may have been short by most standards, and it may have been relatively bloodless in terms of direct military confrontations, but it was nonetheless deadly. In the place of bullets and exploding shells, the wet, freezing weather combined with the lack of adequate winter clothing and poor diet to greatly increase the rate of sickness—and with it death. Sherman recognized this, as did Grant and the other officers in command, and for once so did the *New York Times*, which had been a critic of the corps when it was attached to the Army of the Potomac. "The possession of Tennessee is no longer a dream," a correspondent reported, "the brave Western troops, who, aided by the two corps from the old Army of the Potomac, chased Bragg into Georgia, and the Eleventh corps, who, with a portion of Sherman's men, sent Longstreet fleeing into North Carolina, have made it a stirring reality. The battle and our pursuit of the enemy to Ringgold is already matter of history, but the last achievement can scarcely have become so save in telegraphic outline. Having shared the fortunes of their march, I can glory in its results," he continued. "Heroically have they retrieved the reputation periled at Chancellorsville under the watchful eyes of the Generals of the West."[31]

30 Boies, *Thirty-third Massachusetts*, 58-59.

31 "Eleventh Army Corps Their March to Knoxville and Back," *New York Times*, Jan. 13, 1864 (the story was dated Dec. 25, 1863).

Chapter 21

"At Last Officially Appreciated"

To Victory and Beyond

WITH THE HARD CAMPAIGNING OVER for the year the XI Corps settled into its winter encampments. Howard was pleased with the way his corps performed in Tennessee. They had fought in three engagements, marched over 250 miles, often with many of them barefoot, and established a record that brought praise from the western generals they served under. Yet, he also worried about the men's condition, informing his wife that "my Corps is so poorly provided with clothing and supplies. It is too bad, when there is such abundance in the country, that our men can't have pants to cover them and proper food to eat. The trouble is the want of transportation."[1]

In the 33rd Massachusetts John Ryder found "The ground was frozen so hard we could not put up our fly tents, as we always had to cut pins from the woods." He had to sleep on the frozen ground with no bushes or anything for bedding. "During my two hours sleep in the early morning my hair became frozen to the wet ground so I was unable to rise when my time came to go on post. I had to lose a goodly portion of my back hair by the use of a jackknife to separate me from my contact with the base of Lookout Mountain." By the end of the month some six inches of snow blanketed the camps. "[W]e are living in our Pup tents as the boys call them," wrote William Defoy of the 73rd Ohio, "about fit for a dog but too good for a soldier as the saying is." Some of the men were sent out to work on constructing more blockhouses on Christmas Eve, but Leonhard Schlumpf reported he "don't have to work today because I don't have

1 Howard to Dearest, Jan. 13 and 20, 1864, Bowdoin College.

shoes and it is too painful without shoes in this rainy cold weather. Our 1/2 ration consists of 5 crackers a day with a little bacon and morning and evening 1/2 cup of coffee." His only notation the following day was "The sadest Christmas."[2]

Although prosecution of the war with the Rebels would have to wait for better weather, the war of words between Schurz and his superiors continued unabated. The day after Christmas Hooker sent a message to Howard complaining that camps in Schurz's division were not in proper military order and that dead animals littered the fields. Howard forwarded the complaint to Schurz who responded the same day that some regiments were unable to pitch tents due to the frozen condition of the ground and that some animals had not been buried because he had received orders to use all of the tools available to repair the roads, thus there were no tools available for animal burials. Nor had Schurz forgotten a simmering slight at Hooker's hand. Although most observers heaped praise upon the eastern infantrymen for their conduct at Wauhatchie, Hooker refused to credit Schurz's division with its share in the fighting. Instead, he blamed Schurz for arriving too late to aid Geary. In his official report on the action he also condemned Col. Hecker for his failure to march to Geary's relief sooner. With the campaigning over, Schurz demanded a court of inquiry. Charles Howard was not sure if that was a good decision. He opined that "Schurz is going to have not so easy a victory with Hooker I think."[3]

The sharp retort of a gavel brought the first session of the Court of Inquiry to order at 11:00 am on January 29, 1864. The composition of the Court about to consider the testimony of the various witnesses was unusual. Col. Adolphus Buschbeck, commanding a brigade of the XI Corps, served as presiding officer. Seated about him as colleagues were Col. James Wood, commanding a brigade in the corps; Col. Patrick H. Jones of the 154th New York; and Capt. William H. Lambert of the 33rd New Jersey. Schurz immediately noted the uniqueness of the arrangements. In a breach of usual procedures, not a single member of the tribunal ranked as a peer of the man upon whom the primary charges fell. With these procedural questions settled, albeit in irregular fashion, the Court continued with the business of formally entering the offending portion of Hooker's report into the record: "I regret my duty constrains me to except any portion of my command in my commendation of their courage and valor. The brigade dispatched to the relief of Geary by orders delivered in person to its

2 Ryder, *Reminiscences*, 45-46; Defoy to aunt, Jan. 2, 1864, VFM 1904, Ohio Historical Society; Schlumpf diary, Dec. 24 and 25, 1863.

3 Hooker to Howard, and Schurz to Howard, Dec. 26, 1863, RG 393, Pt. 2, Vol. 18, NARA; Hooker, Wauhatchie report, 584; Howard to brother, Jan. 24, 1864, Bowdoin College.

division commander, never reached him until long after the fight had ended. It is alleged that it lost its way, when it had a terrific infantry fire to guide it all the way, and also that it became involved in a swamp, where there was no swamp or other obstacle between it and Geary which should have delayed it a moment in marching to the relief of its imperiled companions."[4]

Schurz prepared his case well. The testimony of the witnesses he called made it clear that he acted under orders first in moving forward with one brigade, then in using that brigade to capture Tyndale Hill. From the testimony given by Schurz, Lt. Eugene Weigel and Lt. Paul Oliver there remained no doubt that Schurz was ordered to take Tyndale Hill with the brigade that later gave the knoll its name. It was also evident that Schurz instructed his other two brigades under Hecker and Krzyzanowski to continue toward Wauhatchie. Testimony indicated that subsequent to this Major Howard ordered Col. Hecker, in the general's name, to halt his brigade to await the outcome of the fighting along the roadway, while Capt. Robert Hall of Hooker's staff first erroneously ordered Krzyzanowski to Chattanooga, then countermanded that by ordering him back to his original position. Hooker may have been betrayed by faulty staff work, but the testimony made it obvious that Schurz's two remaining brigades were held back by direct orders of Howard or Hooker or their staff officers acting in their name. Thus, Schurz could not be held culpable since his brigade commanders followed the direct orders of the commanding general. The Court vindicated Schurz, but it would not be the last act in this ongoing dispute.[5]

With the approach of spring, rumors swirled about the camps. Some had the XI and XII Corps being sent back to the Army of the Potomac. Others had them being attached to one command or another, still others that the two corps would be combined. On April 5 Howard visited army headquarters in Chattanooga where he was informed unofficially that the decision had been made to merge the two corps into a single unit under Hooker. Given the reduced size of the two corps, it was a reasonable decision, one that should probably have been made much earlier. Official word arrived at XI Corps headquarters on April 7.[6]

"There is a good deal of a fluttering among the disturbed brood at these Head quarters," commented Charles Howard. "We feel somewhat sad at thoughts of leaving

4 Proceedings of the Court of Inquiry at the XI and XII Headquarters in regard to the Wauhatchie Affair, *OR* 31, pt. 1, 137-38. This source contains the testimony of the principals involved in the case and will be cited hereafter as Proceedings.

5 Proceedings, 165, 209-10.

6 Daily Log of 11th Corps, Apr. 5 and 7, 1864; Meysenburg journal, Apr. 5 and 7, 1864.

old associations here and attached friends." His brother the general seemed almost nostalgic, writing to his wife that "after a year and four days of trial with the 11th it goes out and I begin again. . . . The new house always breaks up the pleasant associations of the old one." Surgeon Henry Van Aernam spoke for many in the corps when he wrote the following on the back of Howard's farewell to his troops: "The 11th Corps accepts the change in their status without a single regret. Knowing as we do that our new Commander in a military point of view is every way superior to Gen. Howard. In fact, as a 'fighting' man to lead a single corps in battle, I think 'Old Joe' has no superior in the Army." Yet, at the same time, "it is a sad thing to see an organization with all its Sad & pleasing association of nearly two years so cruely be [swept] away and the old 'Crescent' go down to rise no more!"[7]

☽ ☽ ☽

The new unit created by the consolidation of the XI and XII Corps was to be called the XX Corps, Army of the Cumberland. Although a seemingly simple fusing of the two former organizations, the reality was quite different. Since Hooker was designated the commanding officer of the new corps, what would happen to Howard and Slocum? Howard emerged well. He left a corps in which he was not held in great esteem to be assigned as commanding officer of the IV Corps, Army of the Cumberland, replacing Maj. Gen. Gordon Granger. For him, it was an opportunity to start over. Slocum was not as fortunate, being reassigned to a backwater position in Vicksburg. He would eventually return to lead the XX Corps following Hooker's resignation later that year. But what to do with Schurz? The initial plan was for the XX Corps to contain four divisions. Hooker immediately recognized the problem. On April 10 he wrote to Brig. Gen. William D. Whipple, the Assistant Adjutant General: "In the event of the 20th Corps being organized into four Divisions as is proposed, the rank of Major General Schurz will entitle him to the command of one of them, and as this would not be satisfactory to me, and should not be to him, I respectfully request that he may be removed from the Corps." Gen. George H. Thomas endorsed the letter: "It is necessary for the promotion of the efficiency and harmony of the service, that Major General Carl Schurz, should be removed from command in the Department of the Cumberland. I would therefore respectfully ask that such disposition be made of him." The feisty German was assigned to the Camp of Instruction in Nashville. He

7 C. Howard to brother, Apr. 6, 1864, Bowdoin College; Howard to Dearest, Apr. 6, 1864, Bowdoin College; Henry van Aernam, Apr. 11, 1864; Dunkelman, *Brothers One and All*, 190.

would return as chief of staff of the Army of Georgia, but only on April 14, 1865, when the war was all but over.[8]

In the wholesale overhaul, most of the division and brigade commanders of the XII Corps kept their positions because of seniority and the XX Corps adopted the star emblem of the former XII Corps. Von Steinwehr, who had for so long capably led a division as a brigadier general without being promoted, found himself on the bottom of the seniority list for division command in the new corps. He was offered a brigade, but resigned in protest. The same circumstances acted against other veteran XI Corps leaders who had labored long without promotion. Aside from seniority, another consideration was size. The smallest regiments that were unable to recruit up to strength were reassigned to garrison duty in towns or guarding railroads, bridges, and blockhouses. Only the larger regiments were retained for active field service and there was an attempt to equalize the size of the various brigades, as well as to fill out the standard three brigade structure for each division. Additionally, several of the regiments that had originally served in the east were completing their terms of service. Some went home permanently, while others who reenlisted as Veteran Volunteers enjoyed a thirty-day furlough. In either case, these were unavailable. The ones that later returned from furlough were assigned to guard railroads, supply lines, and other important rear-echelon positions.

The First Division, led by Brig. Gen. Alpheus Williams from the XII Corps, contained three brigades. The first two were comprised of regiments transferred in from the XII Corps with the third being Brig. Gen. Hector Tyndale's brigade from the XI Corps—61st Ohio, 82nd Ohio, 45th New York, 143rd New York, 82nd Illinois, 101st Illinois—supplemented with the 31st Wisconsin. The Second Division went to Brig. Gen. John Geary of the XII Corps, two of the brigades made up of XII Corps regiments and the third under Col. Adolphus Buschbeck of XI Corps units—27th Pennsylvania, 73rd Pennsylvania, 33rd New Jersey, 119th New York, 134th New York, 154th New York—plus the 109th Pennsylvania from the XII Corps. The Third Division went to Maj. Gen. Daniel Butterfield, a Hooker favorite who had been his chief of staff when he commanded the Army of the Potomac. Most of the troops were new to the organization, coming from neither of the two original corps, except for Col. James Wood of the XI Corps who led a brigade comprised mostly of XI Corps troops—33rd Massachusetts, 136th New York, 55th Ohio, 73rd Ohio, 26th Wisconsin—supplemented with the 20th Connecticut. There was also a Fourth

8 Hooker to Brig. Gen. Whipple, Ass't. Adj. Gen., Apr. 10, 1864, Carl Schurz Generals File, NARA.

Division under Maj. Gen. Lovell H. Rousseau, but this unit was assigned to various garrison posts and did not serve in the field with the XX Corps during the coming campaigns. The 45th New York was reassigned to this division before the beginning of the spring campaign. Other XI Corps units included the 58th New York, 68th New York, and 75th Pennsylvania, all of which had departed on furlough after reenlisting as Veteran Volunteers.[9]

☽ ☽ ☽

Following the consolidation the resulting XX Corps was much stronger than either of its parental components. Structurally, each of the three divisions contained three brigades totaling 21,280 men.[10] It was indeed a potent force. The XX Corps formed the backbone of Gen. William Tecumseh Sherman's army that fought its way south, captured Atlanta, marched across Georgia to the sea, captured Savannah, then moved north through the Carolinas to the Bennett farm near Durham, North Carolina, where Sherman accepted the surrender of Gen. Joseph E. Johnston's army on April 26, 1865, effectively ending large-scale military operations during the war. In all of these campaigns the XX Corps won laurels. Once the men of the maligned XI Corps were away from the Army of the Potomac they were appreciated and praised for their efforts during the campaigns in Tennessee. As part of the new XX Corps they continued to win their share of the plaudits.

Sherman led his army south to begin the march on Atlanta during the first week in May, 1864. On May 8 he pushed forward two brigades of Gen. John Geary's division against Confederate positions at Dug Gap and Rocky Face Ridge, Georgia. One of those was Buschbeck's brigade containing formerly XI Corps troops who attacked up an 800-foot slope held by the 1st and 2nd Arkansas regiments of Gen. Patrick Cleburne's corps and a Kentucky cavalry brigade. These were later reinforced with Gen. Hiram Granbury's Texas brigade. Watching them claw their way up the hill, Geary commented that the "attack was a most gallant one." Buschbeck was particularly impressed with the "heroic behavior" of the 134th New York. The 134th and 154th New York planted their colors atop the crest despite the obstacles and incessant enemy fire. During the firefight Charles W. McKay and Sergt. Stephen Welch of the 154th voluntarily went forward under fire to rescue a wounded comrade between the lines.

9 Dyer, *Compendium*, 458-60.

10 Fox, *Regimental Losses*, 104.

Both were awarded the Medal of Honor for their heroism.[11] It had never been intended, nor had it been thought possible, for such a small force to actually gain the crest of the hill since it was not supposed to be the main assault, only a diversion. Yet these XI Corps veterans did it, only retiring when no supports were available to hold their gains in the face of two brigades of enemy reinforcements.

Moving south to Resaca, it was the turn of Col. James Wood's former XI Corps brigade to gain honors. In a gallant charge, the 26th Wisconsin and 33rd Massachusetts managed to penetrate the Rebel positions while the 55th Ohio, 73rd Ohio, and 136th New York held fast against two Confederate counterattacks prompting Wood to credit them with preventing a "disaster." Joseph A. Sladen of the 33rd Massachusetts received the Medal of Honor for voluntarily leaving his non-combat assignment as a headquarters clerk to ride to the threatened flank and inspire the troops to repulse the enemy attack. Meanwhile, Col. James Robinson's brigade of former XI Corps regiments—82nd Illinois, 61st Ohio, and 143rd New York—were credited with saving the flank of Maj. Gen. David Stanley's division of the IV Corps when it was in jeopardy of being turned and rolled up. In his report on the campaign, Maj. Gen. Alpheus Williams asserted, with reference to the amalgamation of the XI an XII Corps into the new XX Corps, that "the brave and efficient conduct of Robinson's brigade in this affair served to create a strong confidence and good-will between troops recently brought together from different corps in a new organization, a feeling closely cemented by the subsequent events and occurrences of the campaign."[12]

On yet another part of the field, Buschbeck's 33rd New Jersey, 134th New York and 73rd Pennsylvania forced the defenders of Capt. Max van den Corput's Confederate battery to abandon their guns that were then dragged into Union lines later that night. The division leader, Gen. Daniel Butterfield, singled out the Ohio regiment for its gallantry, while the Jersey men gained praise for "handsomely" repelling a Rebel counterattack.[13] Later in the war, William Magee from the New Jersey regiment was awarded the Medal of Honor for being among the first to reach an enemy battery during a charge, then using the captured battery horses to haul the two captured guns into Union lines.

11 *OR* 38, pt. 2, 115; Conklin, *Crescent and Star*, 166; Cosgrove, *134th New York*, 137-41; Dunkelman and Winey, *Hardtack Regiment*, 103-09.

12 *OR* 38, pt. 2, 28; Benjaminson, "Regiment of Immigrants," 138.

13 Sladen Family Papers, USMHI; Underwood, *33rd Massachusetts*, 208-09; *Annual Report of the Adjutant General of the State of Wisconsin*, 406; Hurst, *Seventy-Third Ohio*, 121; Conklin, *Crescent and Star*, 175-76; *OR* 38, pt. 2, 263.

At Pine Knob on June 15, Buschbeck's brigade, now under Col. Patrick H. Jones of the 154th New York since Buschbeck had mustered out with his 27th Pennsylvania at the end of their term of service, received plaudits from Geary for conducting "their advance with skill and gallantry." Two days later the 26th Wisconsin skirmished with the rear guard of Gen. Patrick Cleburne's veteran Confederate division near Muddy Creek. A spirited charge broke the Rebel defenses with Jacob Baldes of Company B capturing a prized Confederate battle flag. Moving further south, at Kenesaw Mountain the Wisconsin regiment again broke the Rebel lines, capturing a breastwork in a determined assault. On June 22 at Kolb's Farm accurate fire from Capt. William Wheeler's 13th New York Independent Battery helped to defeat a determined Rebel attack, but at the cost of the brave captain's life.[14]

Frustrated with Gen. Joseph E. Johnston's defensive tactics and continuing retreats toward Atlanta, Pres. Jefferson Davis replaced him in command of the forces opposing Sherman with Gen. John Bell Hood on July 17. It was a gamble for Davis and the Confederacy that all-but guaranteed the Southern army would turn and fight. By July 20, the XX Corps and Gen. John Newton's division of the Fourth Corps were across Peach Tree Creek. Sensing an opportunity to crush the Northern army while its various units were separated by the stream, Hood ordered a major assault by the corps of Gens. Alexander P. Stewart and William J. Hardee. The unexpected attack drove back some of the Union forces and threatened to unhinge the entire left flank. Gen. George Maney's division of Hardee's corps smashed into a gap that developed between Newton's and Geary's divisions, a tactical advantage that offered the possibility of breaking through the line and inflicting a sharp defeat on Sherman's army. Into the widening gap rushed Wood's brigade led by the fierce counterattack of the 26th Wisconsin. The 55th and 73rd Ohio and 136th New York arrived in quick order, assisted by the 20th Connecticut. The reinforcements halted the Confederate advance and drove it back. Particularly mauled was Gen. Winfield Scott Featherston's Mississippi brigade. Led by the 33rd Mississippi, the brigade descended down a slope onto the exposed position of the Wisconsin regiment, only to be met there with a devastating fire. Brigade commander Wood recounted that "Cooly and deliberately the men poured into their [the Confederate] line a well-directed, withering, and destructive fire, which covered the ground with dead and wounded." The fire decimated the Rebels. Capt. John Fuchs captured the battle flag of the 33rd Mississippi while the

14 Karsten diary, June 17, 1864; *OR* 38, pt. 2, 22, 129, 465; *Annual Report of the Adjutant General of the State of Wisconsin*, 406; Conklin, *Crescent and Star*, 187.

regiment scooped up six officers swords, some forty prisoners, and what they described as the "flag of the Confederacy."[15]

Col. Wood called it "a brilliant feat of arms. We encountered the enemy in superior numbers in the open field. We met his offensive attack with an offensive return; his charge with a countercharge. The victory was complete and decisive. . . . Where all behaved well, it may be regarded as invidious to call attention to individuals, yet it seems to me that I cannot discharge my whole duty in this report without pointing out for especial commendation the conduct of the 26th Wisconsin Volunteer Infantry, and its brave and able commander. The position of this regiment in the line was such that the brunt of the attack on this brigade fell upon it. The brave, skillful and determinate manner in which it met this attack, rolled back the onset, pressed forward in a counter charge and drove back the enemy, could not be excelled by the troops in this or any other army, and is worthy of the highest commendation and praise. It is to be hoped that such conduct will be held up as an example for others, and will meet the appropriate reward."[16]

The Badgers were not the only ones who earned combat laurels that day. Canadian-born Dennis Buckley of the 136th New York received the Medal of Honor for capturing the colors of the 31st Mississippi, while William H. Williams of the 82nd Ohio was also recognized with a Medal of Honor for volunteering to advance between the lines to observe enemy movements and aid a wounded comrade. The stand of Wood's former XI Corps brigade relieved the pressure on Newton's embattled division, allowing that unit to rally and hold its otherwise shaky position. So effective was the brigade's steady fire that every Confederate regimental commander that it faced, save one, was either killed or wounded, and Featherston's brigade reported that the "severe fire" cut down 616 of its 1,230 effectives, a staggering loss of fifty percent of its effective strength.[17]

"With drums beating and colors flying," reported Col. George Mindil of the 33rd New Jersey, a former XI Corps regiment, "the Second Brigade, Second Division, XX Corps, at about 6:30 p.m. [September 2], was the first organization to enter the works

15 Pula, *Sigel Regiment*, 256-61; Evans, *Confederate Military History*, 212; *OR* 38, pt. 2, 442, 466; Winkler, *Letters*, 151; *Annual Report of the Adjutant General of the State of Wisconsin*, 407; Love, *Wisconsin in the War*, 728-29; *Kenosha News*, June 20, 1914.

16 *OR* 38, pt. 2, 442-43.

17 Love, *Wisconsin in the War*, 728; Bruce, *History of Milwaukee*, 800 (the latter places the loss at 6 killed and 39 wounded); Underwood, *Three Years' Service*, 226; Evans, *Confederate Military History*, XI, 212.

and city of Atlanta."[18] Following the city's fall, Sherman turned his army east for the march through Georgia to the sea at Savannah, destroying railroads, factories, government stores, and other resources supporting the Southern war effort. The move was designed to accomplish three goals: it would destroy much of the economic infrastructure of the Southern war effort, strike a blow at Southern morale, and place Sherman in position to move north through the Carolinas to cooperate with Gen. Grant's forces in destroying the Army of Northern Virginia. The XX Corps performed well during the march, spending most of its time tearing up rails, burning railroad ties, and destroying anything that might be of use to the Confederacy. By Christmas, Savannah was in Union hands.

With the capitulation of Savannah, Sherman turned north into South Carolina with the XX Corps heading directly toward Columbia. Aside from the tremendous damage done to the Confederate economic infrastructure supporting the war effort, Sherman's movement forced the outnumbered Confederates to retire north and west. The corps arrived near Columbia on February 16, then continued northward through Cheraw into North Carolina. Once again led by Gen. Joseph E. Johnston, the Rebels turned to make a stand at Averasboro on March 15. Led by Brig. Gen. William Cogswell, the 33rd Massachusetts, 136th New York, 55th Ohio, 73rd Ohio, and 26th Wisconsin moved forward to the relief of the hard-pressed Federal advance. After about an hour, the Federals advanced further, taking possession of "a slight line of breastworks" before moving on to seize a "stronger line of works" some distance from the first. Throughout the day Cogswell's men steadily pushed the Confederates back capturing "three pieces of artillery and two hundred prisoners."[19] Unable to hold their lines, the Rebels retreated during the night.

Two days later Johnston attempted another stand at Bentonville. Once again Cogswell's regiments were in the middle of the fight, and once again they proved their mettle by pushing back a major Confederate assault that threatened the XIV Corps. Outflanked and in danger of being pressed back, the call for help reached Cogswell's men at the head of the XX Corps advance. In fact, the Federal line had been broken and the Fourteenth Corps was in imminent danger of being driven from the field. Cogswell's brigade pushed into the threatened gap. Smashing into the right flank and rear of the attacking Confederate force, it shattered the attack, drove it back, cut off a portion of the Confederate troops and took scores of prisoners and the colors of the

18 Conklin, *Crescent and Star*, 204.

19 Love, *Wisconsin in the War*, 962; *Annual Report of the Adjutant General of the State of Wisconsin*, 409; *OR* 47, pt. 1, 824-25; Winkler, *Letters*, 202-03.

26th Tennessee. Johnston's attack failed. According to Nathaniel Hughes, historian of the Battle of Bentonville, "Some consider Cogswell's role the most important of all" in restoring the Union lines and bringing about the victory. "Cogswell's timely and powerful attack," Hughes concluded, "after 'coming on the field with tired troops,' had saved [the Fourteenth Corps], restored the Union line, and broken the Confederate attack. The initiative passed. It was a remarkable, if not decisive performance."[20] These, of course, were troops from the original Eleventh Corps. And they, as much as anyone, deserved the credit for the successful campaigns in Tennessee, Georgia and through the Carolinas to the eventual surrender of Johnston's army on April 26, 1865.

Of the approximately 3,500 regiments that Frederick H. Dyer lists in his *A Compendium of the War of the Rebellion* as serving in the Union armies during the conflict, the 26th Wisconsin ranked fifth in the percentage of its men who were killed in action or mortally wounded at 17.2 percent. Brig. Gen. William Cogswell, the brigade commander in the Carolinas, labeled the 26th Wisconsin "one of the finest military organizations in the service."[21]

Among the other units of the XI Corps that ranked high on this list were the 73rd Ohio (13.4 percent), 82nd Ohio (10.6 percent), and 55th Ohio (10.2 percent). William F. Fox's classic *Regimental Losses in the American Civil War 1861-1865*, listed six of the former XI Corps regiments among his "300 Fighting Regiments"—82nd Illinois, 25th Ohio, 55th Ohio, 73rd Ohio, 82nd Ohio, and 26th Wisconsin. Fox listed 26 XI Corps units that lost over 100 dead during the war. Ten lost over 200 with the 73rd Ohio topping the list with 321. In total, at least 5,356 men wearing the crescent emblem lost their lives defending the United States and eliminating the stain of slavery.[22]

☽ ☽ ☽

Andrew Johnson, the new president of the United States, along with thousands of dignitaries and spectators, lined the streets of Washington, D.C., to witness the victorious Army of the Potomac pass in review on May 23, 1865. The following day was reserved for the 65,000 veterans of Sherman's campaigns in Georgia and the Carolinas. The admiring throng loved what they saw and applauded and often broke into patriotic song as the "western" troops wound their way through the capital's

20 *OR* 47, pt. 1., 144, 826, 834; Bradley, "Last Stand in the Carolinas," 62; Hughes, *Bentonville*, 116, 118-19.

21 *Annual Report of the Adjutant General of the State of Wisconsin*, 410.

22 Fox, *Regimental Losses*, 8, 10 13, 318, 328, 331-32, 371, 399.

The XX Corps approaching near the Treasury Building on Pennsylvania Avenue during the Grand Review. *Library of Congress*

streets. Corp. John Langhans of the 154th New York thoroughly enjoyed the experience. It was, he later wrote to his brother, "a grate time I wish you could have seen us that day, there were a good maney people in the city. The sidewalks, trees and housetops on the street through which we marched were crowded full, the people gave us a hearty wellcome as we past through the street, such spatting of hands such waveing of handkerchifs and such cheering as they made I never heard before[.] the Ladies had prepared all kinds of flours which they gave to us as we past them." In his letter home, Langhans reflected on his journey through the war, explaining that when he left his home "it looked rather dark, but things look better now, since then we have made a greate circle in the United States and have seen many a hard day or night, but still I have seen lots of good times. . . . I would not have missed this chance for 1,000 doll[ars]."

Corp. John Langhans, 154th New York. His great-great grandson, Mark Dunkelman, became the regiment's historian and creator of the famous mural on the Gettysburg battlefield.
Dunkelman and Winey Collection, St. Bonaventure University

Like Langhans, for most of those who marched under the XI Corps crescent and survived, their wartime experience was the defining event of their lives.[23]

But now the war was over. The bloody fields and deprivations of Chancellorsville, Gettysburg, Wauhatchie, Chattanooga, the Atlanta Campaign, the March to the Sea, and the Carolinas were now behind them. It was time for the Boys in Blue to go home.

☽ ☽ ☽

The end of the war did not come soon enough for some. Among the diarists and correspondents whose works are quoted in this book, several did not survive to enjoy the satisfaction of final victory. Captured at Gettysburg, Adam Muenzenberger was confined to Belle Isle prison in Richmond where he died in December 1863 never seeing his beloved Barbara again. Sherman's campaign to Atlanta was fatal to three others. Ernst Damkoehler was wounded and captured at Reseca, Georgia, on May 15, 1864. He died of disease in Andersonville prison on June 26. He is buried in Grave 2522 in the Wisconsin Section of the National Cemetery at Americus, Georgia. Sergt. Karl Wickesberg was also wounded at Resaca and died the following day. He is buried in grave 570, Section K, in the National Cemetery at Chattanooga, Tennessee. Capt. William Wheeler, who fought so bravely at Gettysburg, met his end near Marietta, Georgia, in June of 1864 leading the 13th New York Independent Battery.

23 Letter, Langhans to brother, May 28 and June 9, 1865, from Dunkelman and Winey Collection at St. Bonaventure University.

Most of those who survived found their way home to resume their lives as best they could. Some went on to prominence, but the vast majority led relatively ordinary and quiet lives. Luther Mesnard rose from the ranks to major, served in the occupation of South Carolina, then returned home to Ohio where he became the surveyor of Huron County. He died in February 1903. Friedrich Kappelmann went home to Illinois to work as a barber, became active in veterans' affairs, and served two terms as supervisor of Evanston Township. He passed away in January 1911. Surgeon Henry Van Aernam resumed life in upstate New York where he was elected to the U.S. House of Representatives as a Republican and served a term as Commissioner of Pensions under President Grant. When he died in June 1894 the GAR post in Ellicottville was named in his honor. Some veterans even made a living from their Civil War experience. Lt. Karl Doerflinger, his ankle shattered at Chancellorsville, established the Doerflinger Artifical Limb Company to serve fellow amputees. He died in November 1911.[24]

Severely wounded at Dug Gap, Georgia, William Levey suffered through the amputation of his lower left leg before finally returning to Schoharie County, New York, where he married and earned a living as a laborer until his death in 1921. Capt. Friedrich Otto von Fritsch mustered out with the 68th New York to become a partner in a brokerage and commission merchant business in New York City. A member of the Military Order of the Loyal Legion, von Fritschh attempted to enlist once again when the Spanish-American War broke out, but was rejected because of his age. He died in 1909.[25]

Capt. Friedrich Irsch, whose stubbornness at Gettysburg was rewarded with a Medal of Honor, proved just as pugnacious in captivity as he had been on the battlefield. He escaped from Libby Prison but was recaptured after three days, confined to a subterranean cell for about three weeks, and singled out for repeated punishment including "close confinement and other methods of torture." Transferred to a prison in Macon, Georgia, his refusal to comply with prison rules led to his being "bucked and gagged and kept in this position until he fainted away and was supposed to be dead." Moved to a prison in Charleston he was exposed on the bare earth in all weather conditions, contracting acute rheumatism. Following the war he owned a prosperous business, but suffered from recurring rheumatism and other disabilities

24 Mesnard, http://www.findagrave.com/cgi-bin/fg.cgi?page=gr&GRid=56848486; Reinhart, *Yankee Dutchmen*, 199; Dunkelman and Winey, *Hardtack Regiment*, 189-90; *National New Education*, Vol. 1, No. 2, 29-30; Watrous, *Memoirs of Milwaukee County*, II, 50-52.

25 Levey, *Memoir*, xiv-xvi; Butts, *Gallant Captain*, 143.

due to his wartime privations, often requiring crutches or a cane to walk. He died in New York City in August 1906.[26]

Adj. Theodore A. Dodge survived the amputation of his lower right leg at Gettysburg to accept a post in the War Department, retiring to Boston in 1870 with the rank of major. He became a noted author on military affairs whose works included *The Campaign of Chancellorsville* (1881) and a multi-volume series on the *History of the Art of War.* The voluminous journal he kept during his service with the Army of the Potomac was published posthumously in 2001. He passed away in Paris, France, in October 1909.[27]

Adj. Albert Wallber was confined in Richmond's notorious Libby Prison. On February 9, 1864, he was one of 109 Union prisoners to escape through a makeshift tunnel. His feet badly frozen, his body emaciated, suffering from exposure, he reached Union lines after five grueling days. Following the war he wrote his memoirs, co-authored with Capt. Bernhard Domschcke a description of life in Confederate prisons titled "Erinnerungen: 20 Monate in Gefangenschaft," participated actively in veterans affairs, and spoke before many patriotic gatherings. He became vice president of the a manufacturing firm in Wisconsin, and was an active member of the Milwaukee *Turnverein*, the *Deutsche Gesellschaft*, Robert Chivas Post No. 2, G.A.R., and the German English Academy which he served as president. He died in Milwaukee in December 1911.[28]

Major Owen Rice who pleaded that preparations be made before the flank attack at Chancellorsville was severely wounded in the arm during the fight. He mustered out with the 153rd Pennsylvania on July 28, 1863, returning home to be elected to the Pennsylvania State House of Representatives. Later he took several engineering positions on Midwestern railroads. A member of the Grand Army of the Republic and the Military Order of the Loyal Legion, he passed away in April 1892. Col. Edward S. Salomon was elected Cook County Clerk in Chicago a year after the war ended. President U. S. Grant appointed him governor of the Washington Territory in 1870 after which he retired to San Francisco to practice law. An active member of the Grand Army of the Republic and the Military Order of the Loyal Legion, he died in July 1913.[29]

26 Francis Irsch Pension Record, NARA; House of Representatives, 51st Congress, 1st Session, Report No. 2284.

27 Dodge, http://en.wikipedia.org/wiki/Theodore_Ayrault_Dodge.

28 Legler, 276; Chivas Post, 141; *Soldiers' and Citizens' Album*, 593.

29 Weaver, *Owen Rice*; Reinhart, *Yankee Dutchmen*, 196.

Frederick C. Winkler rose to lieutenant colonel and received brevet promotions to the ranks of colonel and brigadier general in recognition of his services. Following the war he resumed the practice of law, and served as president of the Milwaukee County Bar Association and Wisconsin State Bar Association, and vice president of the American Bar Association. A zealous Republican, he was a delegate to the Republican National Conventions in 1880 and 1894, a member of the Wisconsin State Assembly in 1872, championed civil service reform, and served as a member of the Milwaukee City Board of School Commissioners in 1878-1880. An activist in veterans affairs, he was a member of the Grand Army of the Republic and gained election as Commander of the Wisconsin Commandery of the Military Order of the Loyal Legion of the United States. Vice president of the Milwaukee Art Association, he served as Trustee of the Northwestern Mutual Life Insurance Company for thirty-two years. He died in Los Angeles in March 1921.[30]

Hubert Dilger continued to gain praise during the Atlanta campaign, eventually being breveted lieutenant colonel. Following the war he served as Adjutant General for the State of Illinois before purchasing a farm in the Shenandoah Valley near Front Royal, Virginia, where he died in May 1911. Michael Wiedrich resigned his commission as captain to accept the lieutenant colonelcy of the 15th New York Heavy Artillery that was converted to infantry to participate in Grant's campaign against Petersburg. He was wounded slightly at Globe Tavern in August 1864 and seriously at Five Forks on April 1, 1865. Breveted colonel for "gallant and meritorious service in the battles on the Weldon Railroad," he returned to Buffalo after the war to work for the Germania Fire Insurance Company. He served two terms as the city's Receiver of Taxes, and four years as Assessor of Internal Revenue. Prominent in Republican politics and veterans affairs, he died in Buffalo in March 1899.[31]

Theodore A. Meysenburg joined the staff of Gen. Franz Sigel in Virginia serving at New Market and the defense of Maryland Heights. Following the war he returned to his home in St. Louis to become a successful iron manufacturer, an active member of the Grand Army of the Republic and the Military Order of the Loyal Legion, a supporter of the Public Library, and one of the founders of the St. Louis Museum of Fine Arts. He passed away in March 1901. Thomas Ward Osborn became inspector

30 Winkler, *Letters*, 218; Lamers, "Hero in Blue," 27; Watrous, *Memoirs of Milwaukee County*, 18-19; King, *"Frederick C. Winkler, Distinguished Soldier and Citizen,"* 96; quote from "Obituary," *Wisconsin Magazine of History*, Vol. IV, 460-61; *Milwaukee Sentinel*, March 23, 1921, 1 and March 24, 1921, 14.

31 Dilger pension file, NARA; Wiedrich, http://www.ohio.edu/people/lowery/dil.htm; http://www.findagrave.com/cgi-bin/fg.cgi?page=sh&GRid=49469124.

general when Howard assumed command of the Army of the Tennessee. Following the war he served as an assistant commissioner in the Freedman's Bureau in Florida where he also practiced law, participated as a Republican in the state constitutional convention, and gained election to the state senate. When Florida was readmitted to the Union he served in the U.S. Senate. Appointed U. S. commissioner to the Centennial Exposition in Philadelphia, he then retired to New York City where he died in December 1898.[32]

Charles Howard was appointed lieutenant colonel and assistant inspector general of his brother's Fourth Corps under Sherman. When Savannah surrendered in December 1864 he was selected to carry the formal dispatches announcing the city's capture to President Lincoln. In April 1865 he accepted appointment as colonel of the 128th U. S. Colored Infantry, a position he held until 1866. After a brief stint as chief of staff for the Reconstruction government in South Carolina, Georgia and Florida he joined his brother again as assistant commissioner of the Freedman's Bureau for the District of Columbia. Moving to Illinois, he served as western secretary for the American Missionary Association in Chicago where he supervised the establishment of missionary schools for Indians in the northwest and the Chinese in California. In later life he became the western editor and business manager for the *National Tribune*, the leading veterans newspaper of the day. He died a brevet brigadier general in January 1908.[33]

Among the XI Corps brigade commanders, Charles Coster and George von Amsberg were each superseded following their brief command at Gettysburg. Coster resigned before the end of the year to accept appointment as provost marshal for the New York State Board of Enrollment. Following the war he served as a Federal pension agent in New York City where he was active in veterans' affairs. He died in the city in December 1888. Von Amsberg managed a hotel in Hoboken, New Jersey, passing away in November 1876. Hector Tyndale resigned due to ill health in August 1864 but was brevetted major general the following March. He returned to Philadelphia where he operated a porcelain business becoming expert enough to be

32 Cox, *Old and New St. Louis*, 343-44; *In Memoriam. Theodore August Meysenburg*; www.Findagrave.com/cgi-bin/fg.cgi?page=gr&GRid=38891020; Osborn, http://bioguide.Congress.gov/scripts/biodisplay.pl?index=O000109.

33 *Memorials of Deceased Companions of the Commandery of the State of Illinois*, II, 475-78.

appointed a judge during the Centennial Exhibition. He died in the city in March 1880.[34]

Despite distinguished service, Adolphus Buschbeck was never promoted to brigadier general, even by brevet. He mustered out with his regiment in 1864, settling in Philadelphia where he taught at the Episcopal Academy. In 1883 he traveled to Europe seeking a cure for deteriorating health, but died in Florence, Italy. With the consolidation of the XI and XII Corps, Orland Smith was returned to regimental command but resigned rather than accept the demotion. He received a brevet promotion to brigadier general in March 1865. Returning to his former career, he became vice president and president of three different Midwestern railroads. He passed away in Chicago in October 1903. Nathaniel McLean was also superseded in command of his brigade, then shipped west into a desk job as provost marshal in the Department of Ohio. He later led a brigade in the Twenty-third Corps during the Atlanta Campaign. Following the war he practiced law in Cincinnati, but later moved to Minnesota and then New York, establishing Episcopal churches in both places. He died in Bellport, New York, in January 1905.[35]

Friedrich Hecker resigned when he lost his brigade in the consolidation of the corps. He settled on his farm in Summerville, Illinois, where he took an active part in the 1864 presidential campaign, championing the short-lived liberal effort to replace Lincoln with John C. Frémont. Following the election he continued involvement in liberal Republican politics and German American affairs, visiting Germany following its unification in the early 1870s. He died in Summerville in March 1881. Wlodzimierz Krzyzanowski was assigned to command of a brigade in the Defenses of the Nashville & Chattanooga Railroad in the Department of the Cumberland. He was brevetted brigadier general in March 1865. After the war he served as a U.S. treasury agent for the District of Georgia and Florida, followed by similar appointments in Louisiana and the Washington Territory. Retiring, he settled in San Francisco where he owned a tavern frequented by Union army veterans and Polish immigrants, but his business fell victim to the financial recession of the mid-1870s. Appointed treasury agent in Panama, he ended his career in New York City where he died in January 1887. He is buried in Arlington National Cemetery.[36]

34 "Funeral of Col. Charles R. Coster," *New York Times*, Dec. 27, 1888, 8; Tyndale, http://en.wikipedia.org/wiki/Hector_Tyndale.

35 Smith obituary, *New York Times*. Oct. 4, 1903; McLean, http://en.wikipedia.org/wiki/Nathaniel_McLean.

36 Hecker, http://en.wikipedia.org/wiki/Friedrich_Hecker; Pula, *For Liberty and Justice.*

Leopold von Gilsa commanded a brigade in the Tenth Corps and the garrison on Folly Island, South Carolina. When his original regiment, the 41st New York, left for New York City to muster out in June 1864 von Gilsa remained in the service without a command until he mustered out in December 1865, never having been promoted to brigadier general despite his long and faithful service. He died in New York City in March 1870. Alexander Schimmelfenning served in the Tenth Corps on Folly Island, commanded the District of Charleston, and accepted that city's capitulation in February of 1865. While in South Carolina he contracted malaria and a serious form of tuberculosis. Following the war he visited the mineral spring in Wernersville, Pennsylvania, hoping for a cure, but died there in September of 1865.[37]

After recovering from his serious wound at Gettysburg, Francis Barlow returned to the field in April 1864 in command of a division in the Second Corps during Grant's Overland Campaign. Heavily engaged in the fighting, he was awarded a brevet promotion to major general for his actions at Spotsylvania. He resigned from the army in November 1865 to become a U.S. Marshal, New York State Secretary of State, and later New York State Attorney General where he prosecuted the political machine led by William "Boss" Tweed. Returning to the practice of law, he was a founder of the American Bar Association. He died of Bright's disease in New York City in January 1896.

Adelbert Ames commanded a division in the Tenth Corps and later transferred to the Twenty-fourth Corps where he led the successful assault on Fort Fisher, North Carolina, in January 1865. After the war he commanded the Fourth Military District including Arkansas and Mississippi during the Reconstruction. In this position he supported the extension of legal and political rights to former slaves. The Reconstruction legislature elected him U.S. Senator from Mississippi (1870-74), a position he left when elected governor of Mississippi which he held until the end of the Reconstruction. After leaving public office he managed flour mills in Minnesota, New York and Massachusetts. He was one of the original companions of the Military Order of the Loyal Legion. When the Spanish-American War began, Ames was appointed brigadier general and participated in the invasion of Cuba. He died in Florida at the age of 97 in 1933 as the last surviving general officer of the Civil War.

After leaving the XI Corps in 1863, Julius Stahel went on to command the cavalry attached to the Department of the Susquehanna and later a cavalry division under Franz Sigel in the Shenandoah Valley in 1864 where he was seriously wounded at

37 "Funeral of Colonel von Gilsa," *New York Times*, Mar. 4, 1870; Kaufmann, *Die Deutschen*, 549; Zucker, *Forty-Eighters*, 337.

Piedmont and awarded the Medal of Honor for gallantry. Following the war he served as United States Consul in Yokohama and Osaka in Japan and Consul General in Shanghai, China. Because of deteriorating health he returned to New York where he worked for the Equitable Life Insurance Company. He died in New York City in December 1912 and is buried in Arlington National Cemetery.[38]

Charles Devens participated in Grant's Overland Campaign and commanded a division in the Twenty-Fourth Corps during the Siege of Petersburg. His troops were the first to enter Richmond. Following the war he commanded the Military District of Charleston, South Carolina, for a year before returning to civilian life. He served in judicial positions in Massachusetts including the state Supreme Court (1873-77) before being named Attorney General of the United States by Pres. Rutherford B. Hayes (1877-81). Active in veterans affairs, he was a companion of the Military Order of the Loyal Legion and was elected Commander-in-Chief of the Grand Army of the Republic (1873-75). He died in Boston in 1891.

Following his resignation over demotion to brigade command, Adolf von Steinwehr earned a living as a geographer and cartographer, serving for a time as a professor at Yale University. Among his many contributions to these fields, he authored *A School Geography: Embracing Mathematical, Physical, and Political Descriptions of the Earth* (1870), co-authored *Primary Geography* (1870) and *An Elementary Treatise on Physical Geography* (1873), and edited *The Centennial Gazetteer of the United States* (1874). He died in Buffalo, New York, in February 1877.

During the summer of 1865 Carl Schurz toured the South at the behest of Pres. Andrew Johnson, writing a lengthy report on the conditions he found along with his recommendations. Returning to civilian life, he served as editor in chief of the *Detroit Post*, then moved to St. Louis to edit the *Westliche Post.* The attraction of politics lured him into the 1868 campaign from which he emerged as U.S. Senator from Missouri. Gaining a reputation for his advocacy of fiscal responsibility, integrity, and opposition to imperialism, he clashed with Pres. Grant over several issues that led him to form the Liberal Republican faction that backed Horace Greeley against Grant in the 1872 election. He supported Rutherford B. Hayes in the 1876 election. Rewarded with appointment as Secretary of the Interior (1877-81), he championed civil service reform, attacked corruption in the Office of Indian Affairs, and supported the conservation of forests and other natural resources. After leaving office he continued to be active in politics, served as president of the Hamburg American Steamship Company, president of the National Civil Service Reform League, and wrote editorials

38 Stahel, https://en.wikipedia.org/wiki/Julius_Stahel.

for *Harper's Weekly*. He published a biography of Henry Clay, essays on Abraham Lincoln and Charles Sumner, and his own three-volume *Reminiscences*. He died in New York City in May 1906.

After leaving the XI Corps, Franz Sigel was assigned to command the Military District of West Virginia where he was defeated at the Battle of New Market and was relieved of command. Following the war he served as an editor for newspapers in Baltimore and New York, becoming collector of internal revenue in the latter city in 1871 and in 1877 the city pension agent. He died in 1902 and is buried in Woodlawn Cemetery in New York.

Oliver Otis Howard led the Fourth Corps in Sherman's campaign against Atlanta and the Army of the Tennessee during the march to the sea and the campaign in the Carolinas. Following the war he was appointed head of the Freedman's Bureau where he fought to provide former slaves with opportunities for education and social programs to provide them with food, medical care, legal assistance, political rights, and other forms of support. His efforts on behalf of the Freedmen led to the naming of a college in Washington, D.C., Howard University in his honor. In 1874 he assumed command of the Department of the Columbia in the Washington Territory where he participated in a series of wars against the indigenous peoples, notably the Nez Perce under Chief Joseph. He later served as superintendent of the U.S. Military Academy (1881-82) and in various department commands until his retirement in 1894. He died in Vermont in October 1909.

☽ ☽ ☽

"You bid me speak for you. What language shall I borrow that can hold the meaning of this hour? How translate into mortal tongue the power and glory of immortal deeds?" So began Gen. Joshua Lawrence Chamberlain in an address given at Delmonico's in New York City on July 5, 1869. The occasion was the first annual reunion of the Society of the Army of the Potomac. Organized at a meeting in the 22nd Regiment Armory building in the same city on February 22 of that year, those in attendance at the July 5-6 event elected Gen. Philip Sheridan as their first president.[39]

Each corps in the army was entitled to elect a vice president, the initial XI Corps honor going to Oliver Otis Howard, while Gen. John Geary was appointed to represent the XI Corps on the society's executive committee. Since Geary did not serve

39 Minutes of the Society of the Army of the Potomac, Feb. 22, 1896, Library of Congress; Minutes of the Society of the Army of the Potomac, First Annual Meeting, Library of Congress.

in the XI Corps, this is probably a good indication of the sparse participation of veterans of that organization. Judging from the minutes of its earliest meetings, there was particularly scant participation by the German element of the corps in the society. The members at the second annual meeting selected Gen. Adelbert Ames as the XI Corps vice president with Gen. Adin Underwood on the executive committee. Ironically, given Ames's stated dislike of Germans, the local German Sangerbund performed at the meeting where he was installed.[40]

The society's third annual meeting likewise had its moment of incongruity when Gen. Stewart L. Woodford was elected vice president and Capt. J. D. Bothwell a member of the executive committee. In his acceptance remarks Woodford, who had only served in the XI Corps for a brief six months, insensitively alluded in negative terms to the conduct of the corps at Chancellorsville. He went on to say that it behaved well at Gettysburg, but the positive comments appeared merely to be laying the groundwork for praising Hooker when he alluded to Lookout Mountain only by stating that "Fighting Joe Hooker wiped out Chancellorsville, and wrote his name forever on the granite peaks of the mountain." It was not until the fourth annual meeting that a positive statement was recorded about the fighting quality of the XI Corps, and then it was made by a visiting member of the Society of the Army of the Cumberland who praised the service of the XI and XII Corps during the Tennessee campaigns.[41]

Only with the fifth meeting did a German name appear prominently when Gen. Adolf von Steinwehr gained appointment to the executive committee, to be followed in that position by Adolphus Buschbeck and then Capt. Adolph F. Vogelbach. Still, it appears that few of the thousands who served in the XI Corps chose to participate in these reunions. In 1882 there were 963 people listed in the Society of the Army of the Potomac annual program, yet only 27 of these were from the XI Corps, and of these only six were German. Indeed, in most years through the end of the 1890s there was no report form the XI Corps entered into the society's annual report. Only gradually does this appear to have changed despite the fact that an Eleventh Army Corps Association came into being in 1869. Its early presidents were Oliver Otis Howard (1869), Adelbert Ames (1870), Stewart L. Woodford (1871-72), Adelbert Ames (1873), Adin B. Underwood (1874-75), Charles Devens (1876-78), Carl Schurz (1879), Henry W. Slocum (1880), Adin B. Underwood (1881-82), Emil Frey (1883), Oliver Otis Howard

40 Minutes of the Society of the Army of the Potomac, Second Annual Meeting, Library of Congress.

41 Minutes of the Society of the Army of the Potomac, Third and Fourth Annual Meetings, Library of Congress.

(1884), James C. Robinson (1885), Edward S. Salomon (1886), Henry Root (1887-88), and Oliver Otis Howard (1889).[42] It was not until 1879 when Carl Schurz gained election that a German name appears. He was joined by Emil Frey and Edward S. Salomon, both from the 82nd Illinois, as the only Germans on the list.

Howard commented on the meager participation by the XI Corps veterans in the affairs of the Society of the Army of the Potomac when he addressed his former comrades-in-arms at the corps association's meeting in Washington, D. C. on December 15, 1892. "It is also most proper and right that here and at this time our Corps should take its position in the Grand Old Army of the Potomac and fill in the space left for it and open our lips too long sealed and raise our voices in the recital of the part we took and speak of our deeds of valor in the great and bloody drama," he challenged them. "It is a duty we must discharge; we owe it to the dead and the brave men who still survive." He continued by reminding them that at Gettysburg "our only object being to delay the progress of the enemy until our other Corps came up, history will show that we did our part well and nobly. We fought overwhelming numbers in our front, well knowing that our right flank was enveloped from the start. We did check the advance of the enemy and caused him to exercise greater caution and wait the concentration of his troops." Then he went on to recall how the men had continued the fight even after the old XI Corps was no longer. "The Corps participated in all the battles of the Atlanta Campaign, and never lost a foot of ground, and were among the first to enter Atlanta. . . . In conclusion, Comrades, I trust that this meeting will bear abundant fruit, that our Association will grow until it embraces every worthy living member of our Corps, and let me urge upon those here, to devote a little time and give some thought and work to the end that the dark clouds which have obscured the fair fame of our Corps may be rolled aside by the pure air of truth, so that we be enabled to hand down its record untarnished and resplendent with the glory of its heroic deeds. This duty we owe to the living, and also to the dead who sealed their devotion with their lives."[43]

Over the years a few XI Corps veterans heeded his call, but not nearly as many as those of the other corps. Some thought participation would help to rectify the stereotype, many chose to avoid the occasion fearing the recalling bad memories. Far fewer of those of German heritage chose to associate with their former tormenters.

42 Minutes of the Society of the Army of the Potomac, Fifth, Sixth and Seventh Annual Meetings, Library of Congress; *Society of the Army of the Potomac. Report of the Thirteenth Annual Re-Union; Society of the Army of the Potomac. Twenty-first Annual Reunion.*

43 Howard address to XI Corps Association, Dec. 15, 1892, Washington, D.C., Library of Congress.

☽ ☽ ☽

It was a typically hot, humid August day in Virginia. Sometime, perhaps in the morning, perhaps the afternoon, the postman arrived at a small farm near Front Royal, scaled the stairs and knocked on the door. Inside, an elderly man arose gingerly, his aged body straining under the weight of time. Once young and strong, his face was now weathered, creased with wrinkles, his former thick dark hair now a thinning light gray. It had been a full generation since he led men into battle. Now, in the twilight of his life, he slowly opened the door, greeting the letter carrier as he accepted the correspondence. It was from the War Department in Washington. Puzzled, he undid the wrapping, his eyes slowly focusing on the words that met his curious gaze. "Distinguished Gallantry"—"Medal of Honor"—"Chancellorsville"—no doubt he read them more than once. The government of the United States was awarding him its highest military decoration. What Hubert Dilger's thoughts were at that moment we do not know, but perhaps his mind drifted back more than thirty years to the time when he and his fellow soldiers were the last hope of preserving the nation that now honored him.[44]

The letter asked him to acknowledge receipt. After a momentary thought, no doubt with great emotion he wrote: "I have the honor to acknowledge the receipt of the Medal of Honor. It is highly gratifying to me, as an old professional soldier, to have my services . . . even after a lapse of thirty years, at last officially appreciated and thus handsomely rewarded."[45]

It is my hope that this history will, after the passage of a century and a half, at last bring to the officers and men of the XI Corps the recognition that has thus far been denied them despite their many sacrifices for their country.

44 Kurtz, "Dilger's Battery," 41; Hubert Dilger Pension File, Department of the Interior, document dated July 2, 1909, NARA; War Department to Dilger, Aug. 17, 1893.

45 Dilger to War Department, Aug. 19, 1893; Kurtz, "Dilger's Battery," 41.

Appendix A

Returns of the Army of the Potomac, June 30, 1863[1]

IN THE FOLLOWING TABLE, THERE is an important distinction to be made between "Present" and "Present Equipped." The former includes cooks, commissaries, hospital stewards, medical staff, musicians, quartermasters, and other non-combatants. The latter is a more accurate reflection of the actual strength of the various units because it includes "only those who were actually available for line of battle at the date of the regimental reports."[2] It also breaks down the aggregate figures by infantry, cavalry, and artillery. This is useful information in determining the relative strength of the different commands.

O - Officers; M - Men; A - Aggregate Present; G - Guns (Artillery Pieces)

	PRESENT			**PRESENT EQUIPPED**						
				INFANTRY		**CAVALRY**		**ARTILLERY**		
COMMAND	**O**	**M**	**A**	**O**	**M**	**O**	**M**	**O**	**M**	**G**
Headquarters	50	....	50	....	....	....	....	....	....	....
Provost Guard	84	1,445	1,529	....	....	....	....	....	....	....
Engineer Bde.	40	906	946	....	....	....	....	....	....	....
Guards and Orderlies	2	47	49	....	....	....	....	....	....	....
Signal Corps	6	....	6	....	....	....	....	....	....	....
I Corps	759	9,596	10,355	687	8,716	....	....	21	598	28
II Corps	968	12,088	13,056	927	11,436	3	79	14	537	24
III Corps	831	11,799	12,630	796	10,451	....	....	19	658	30

1 *OR* 28, pt. 1, 151.

2 New York Monuments Commission, *Final Report on the Battlefield at Gettysburg* (Albany: J. B. Lyon Company, 1900), I, 102.

	PRESENT			PRESENT EQUIPPED						
				INFANTRY		CAVALRY		ARTILLERY		
COMMAND	**O**	**M**	**A**	**O**	**M**	**O**	**M**	**O**	**M**	**G**
V Corps	837	12,374	13,211	797	11,157	....	....	8	547	26
VI Corps	1,031	14,679	15,710	986	13,530	5	119	33	1,006	48
XI Corps	603	9,973	10,576	549	8,648	6	46	15	629	26
XII Corps	541	8,056	8,597	521	7,672	....	....	12	384	20
Cavalry Corps	773	14,200	14,973	....	....	....	....	....	....	50
Artillery Reserve	104	2,464	2,568	23	312	....	....	72	2,139	110
TOTAL	**6,629**	**97,627**	**104,256**	**5,575**	**71,610**	**14**	**316**	**2,261**	**4,469**	**252**

Appendix B

Union Casualties at Gettysburg[1]

O - Officers A - Aggregate
M - Enlisted Men C/M - Captured/Missing

	Killed		Wounded		C/M		Aggregate
COMMAND	**O**	**M**	**O**	**M**	**O**	**M**	**A**
Headquarters	....	....	2	2	....	....	4
I Corps	42	624	262	2,969	83	2,079	6,059
II Corps	66	731	270	2,924	18	365	4,374
III Corps	50	543	251	2,778	14	575	4,211
V Corps	28	337	129	1,482	1	210	2,187
VI Corps	2	25	14	171	....	30	242
XI Corps	33	336	120	1,802	62	1,448	3,801
XII Corps	18	186	43	769	2	64	1,082
Cavalry Corps	5	86	39	315	8	399	852
Artillery Reserve	2	41	15	172	....	12	242
TOTAL	*246*	*2,909*	*1,145*	*13,384*	*188*	*5,182*	*23,054*

1 *OR* 27, pt. 1, 188.

XI Corps Casualties at Gettysburg[2]

O - Officers A - Aggregate
M - Enlisted Men C/M - Captured/Missing

	Killed		**Wounded**		**C/M**		**Aggregate**
COMMAND	**O**	**M**	**O**	**M**	**O**	**M**	**A**
Headquarters Staff	....	....	1	....	....	....	1
1st Indiana Cavalry, Co I & K	....	....	....	....	....	3	3
1st Division							
Staff	1	....	....	....	....	....	1
1st Brigade, 1st Division							
41st New York	1	14	8	50	....	2	75
54th New York	...	7	2	45	4	44	102
68th New York	1	7	4	59	2	65	138
153rd Pennsylvania	1	22	7	135	....	46	211
Brigade Total	*4*	*50*	*21*	*289*	*6*	*157*	*527*
2nd Brigade, 1st Division							
17th Connecticut	2	18	4	77	2	94	197
25th Ohio	1	8	5	95	3	72	184
75th Ohio	2	14	7	67	4	92	186

2 *OR* 27, pt. 1, 183-84.

	Killed		Wounded		C/M		Aggregate
COMMAND	**O**	**M**	**O**	**M**	**O**	**M**	**A**
107th Ohio	....	23	8	103	....	77	211
Brigade Total	*5*	*63*	*24*	*342*	*9*	*335*	*778*
1st Division Total	**9**	**113**	**46**	**631**	**15**	**492**	**1,306**
2nd Division							
Staff	....	....	1	....	....	....	1
1st Brigade, 2nd Division							
134th New York	1	41	4	147	2	57	252
154th New York	....	1	1	20	9	169	200
27th Pennsylvania	2	4	3	26	1	75	111
73rd Pennsylvania	....	7	....	27	....	....	34
Brigade Total	*3*	*53*	*8*	*220*	*12*	*301*	*597*
2nd Brigade, 2nd Division							
33rd Massachusetts	....	7	....	38	....	....	45
136th New York	....	17	1	88	1	2	109
55th Ohio	....	6	1	30	1	11	49
73rd Ohio	....	21	3	117	....	4	145
Brigade Total	....	*51*	*5*	*273*	*2*	*17*	*348*
2nd Division Total	**3**	**104**	**14**	**493**	**14**	**318**	**946**

	Killed		Wounded		C/M		Aggregate
COMMAND	**O**	**M**	**O**	**M**	**O**	**M**	**A**
3rd Division							
Staff	....	....	....	....	....	....	....
1st Brigade, 3rd Division							
82nd Illinois	....	4	1	18	4	85	112
45th New York	....	11	1	34	14	164	224
157th New York	4	23	8	158	6	108	307
61st Ohio	2	4	6	30	2	10	54
74th Pennsylvania	2	8	4	36	2	58	110
Brigade Total	*8*	*50*	*20*	*276*	*28*	*425*	*807*
2nd Brigade, 3rd Division							
58th New York	1	1	2	13	...	3	20
119th New York	2	9	4	66	1	58	140
82nd Ohio	4	13	14	71	2	77	181
75th Pennsylvania	3	16	5	84	...	3	111
26th Wisconsin	2	24	11	118	2	60	217
Brigade Total	*12*	*63*	*36*	*352*	*5*	*201*	*669*
3rd Division Total	**20**	**113**	**56**	**628**	**33**	**626**	**1,476**
Artillery Brigade							
I, 1st New York Light	.....	3	2	8	....	....	13
13th New York Indep.	....	....	....	8	....	3	11
I, 1st Ohio Light	....	....	....	13	....	....	13
K, 1st Ohio Light	....	2	1	10	....	2	15

	Killed		Wounded		C/M		Aggregate
COMMAND	**O**	**M**	**O**	**M**	**O**	**M**	**A**
G, 4th U. S. Light	1	1	....	11	....	4	17
Artillery Total	**1**	**6**	**3**	**50**	**....**	**9**	**69**
Corps Total	**33**	**336**	**120**	**1,802**	**62**	**1,448**	**3,801**

Appendix C

XI Corps Order of Battle at Chattanooga

Maj. Gen. Oliver Otis Howard

Headquarters Guard—8th New York, Independent Company, Capt. Anton Bruhn

Second Division—Brig. Gen. Adolph von Steinwehr

First Brigade—Col. Adolphus Buschbeck

27th Pennsylvania, Maj. Peter A. McAloon; Capt. August Riedt
33rd New Jersey, Col. Geroge W. Mindil
73rd Pennsylvania, Lt. Col. Jospeh B. Taft; Capt. Daniel F. Kelley
134th New York, Col. Alan H. Jackson
154th New York, Col. Patrick H. Jones

Second Brigade—Col. Orland Smith

33rd Massachusetts, Lt. Col. Godfrey Rider, Jr.
55th Ohio, Col. Charles B. Gambee
73rd Ohio, Maj. Samuel H. Hurst
136th New York, Col. James Wood

Third Division—Maj. Gen. Carl Schurz

First Brigade—Brig. Gen. Hector Tyndale

45th New York, Maj. Charles Koch
61st Ohio, Col. Stephen J. McGroarty
82nd Ohio. Lt. Col. David Thomson
101st Illinois, Col. Charles H. Fox
143rd New York, Col. Horace Boughton

Second Brigade—Col. Wlodzimierz B. Krzyzanowski

26th Wisconsin, Maj. Frederick C. Winkler
58th New York, Capt. Michael Esembaux
119th New York, Col. John T. Lockman
141st New York, Col. William K. Logie

Third Brigade—Col. Friedrich Hecker

68th New York, Lt. Col. Albert von Steinhausen
75th Pennsylvania, Maj. August Ledig
80th Illinois, Capt. James Neville
82nd Illinois, Lt. Col. Edward S. Salomon

Artillery—Maj. Thomas W. Osborn

13th Independent New York Light, Capt. William Wheeler
Battery I, 1st New York Light, Capt. Michael Wiedrich
Battery I, 1st Ohio Light, Capt. Hubert Dilger
Battery K, 1st Ohio Light, Lt. Nicholas Sahm
Battery G, 4th United States Light, Lt. Christopher F. Merkle

Appendix D

Medals of Honor Awarded to Soldiers Who Served in the XI Corps

Name	Engagement	Comment
Ames, Adelbert	First Bull Run	Prior to service in XI Corps. With 5th U.S. Light Artillery.
Buckley, Dennis	Peach Tree Creek	136th New York. Captured colors of 31st Mississippi.
Dilger, Hubert	Chancellorsville	Battery I, 1st Ohio Light Artillery. Fought guns in rear guard and last man to retreat.
Enderlin, Richard	Gettysburg	73rd Ohio. Voluntarily joined front line and rescued a wounded comrade under fire.
Finkenbiner, Henry S.	Dingel's Mill	107th Ohio. Crossed burning bridge under artillery fire to determine enemy positions.
Howard, Oliver Otis	Fair Oaks	Prior to service in XI Corps. Led 61st New York in charge and severely wounded twice in right arm necessitating amputation.
Irsch, Francis [Friedrich]	Gettysburg	45th New York. Capturing enemy prisoners and holding a portion of town against heavy odds.
Magee, William	Murfreesboro	33rd New Jersey. Among the first to enter an enemy battery, captured two guns, and used battery horses to drag them to Union lines.
McKay, Charles W.	Dug Gap	154th New York. Voluntarily rescued wounded comrade under enemy fire.

Name	Engagement	Comment
Morley, Delano	McDowell	82nd Ohio. Prior to service in XI Corps. Captured two enemy sharpshooters under fire, alone and with an empty musket.
Sladen, Joseph A.	Resaca	33rd Massachusetts. Voluntarily moved to front line to inspire troops to repel critical enemy attack.
Stacey, Charles	Gettysburg	55th Ohio. Voluntarily took position in advance of skirmish line under heavy fire to ascertain location of enemy sharpshooters.
Stahel, Julius		For actions while commanding a cavalry division at Piedmont in 1864 after his service with the XI Corps.
Toffey, John J.	Chattanooga	33rd New Jersey. Though excused for illness, led a storming party in assault on Missionary Ridge where he was wounded and permanently disabled.
Welch, Stephen	Dug Gap	154th New York. Voluntarily rescued wounded comrade under enemy fire.
Williams, William H.	Peach Tree Creek	82nd Ohio. Voluntarily went beyond the front line to observe the enemy and also to aid a wounded comrade.

Bibliography

Abbreviations

GNMP–Archives, Gettysburg National Military Park, Gettysburg, Pennsylvania.
LC–Library of Congress.
MCHS–Milwaukee County Historical Society.
MHMA–Missouri History Museum Archives, St. Louis.
NYSMA–New York State Department of Military and Naval Affairs.
NARA–National Archives and Records Administration.
NYSA–New York State Archives
OHS–Ohio Historical Society, Columbus, Ohio.
USMHI–United States Military History Institute, Carlisle, Pennsylvania.

Archival Sources

Allen, S. S. Letter to family, May 20, 1863, Battery I, 1st Ohio Light Artillery, GNMP.
Arnold, Joseph. Papers, 26th Wisconsin. Oshkosh Historical Museum, Oshkosh, Wisconsin.
Army of the Potomac Society. Minutes, Library of Congress.
Barlow, Francis C. Papers, Massachusetts Historical Society, Boston.
Barned, Numa. Papers in the Schoff Civil War Collection, William L. Clements Library, University of Michigan. 73rd Pennsylvania Infantry.
Barnett, James. Papers (Ms 675), Cincinnati Newspaper Clippings, Cincinnati Historical Society.
Betty, Edward. Papers (Ms fxB565), Cincinnati Newspaper Clippings, Cincinnati Historical Society.
Biographical File, State Historical Society of Wisconsin, Madison, Wisconsin.
Bornemann, Charles [Carl] S. Bornemann. Diary, 41st New York Infantry, Civil War Miscellaneous Collection, USAMHI.
Boynton, Jonathan. "Reminiscences of Jonathan W. W. Boynton, 157th New York Infantry," handwritten manuscript, Civil War Miscellaneous Collection, USMHI.
Braütigam, Friedrich August. Letters, 82nd Illinois Infantry, U.S. Army Military History Institute, Carlisle Barracks.
Bromley, Robert. Diary, 55th Ohio, OHS.
Brooks, William E. Collection, Library of Congress.
Brown, Elon Francis. Diary, 2nd Wisconsin, Wisconsin Historical Society, Microfilm 512 P82-2498, pages 53-54.
Buek, Charles. Account of Chancellorsville, 41st New York, Civil War Miscellaneous Collection, USMHI.

Burch, Newell. Diary, 154th New York, Wisconsin Historical Society.
Campbell, Alexander. Diary, sergeant, 73rd Ohio, VFM 234, OHS.
Chapin, Willard S. Papers, 136th New York, Lewis Leigh Collection, USMHI.
Civil War Organizations Returns, Record of the Adjutant General's Office, Record Group 92, National Archives, Washington, D. C.
Conklin, George W. Manuscript, "History of the 134th N.Y.," GNMP.
Currier, Charles A., "Recollections of Service with the Fortieth Massachusetts Infantry Volunteers," unpublished manuscript dated 1886, USAMHI.
Daily Log of 11th Corps, April 1, 1863 to April 9, 1864, Schoff Civil War Collection, William L. Clements Library, University of Michigan.
Damkoehler, Ernst. Letters, 26th Wisconsin. Library of Congress. Edited by W. L. Damkoehler. Translated by Martin Boehme, Ralph Bojar and Carl Endres.
Davis, Leadner E. Letters, Battery M, 1st New York Light Artillery. Civil War Miscellaneous Collection, USMHI.
Defoy, William B. Letters, 73rd Ohio Infantry, OHS.
Descriptive Book, Robert Chivas Post No. 2, Grand Army of the Republic. Milwaukee County Historical Society.
Dodge, Theodore A. Diary, 119th New York, microfilm, LC.
Doubleday, Gen. Abner. Letter to M. O'Donnell, February 26, 1891, Northwest Corner CW Roundtable, USMHI.
Early, Jubal. Papers, Virginia Historical Society.
Eaton, Samuel W. Diary, Co. B, 57th North Carolina, GNMP.
Edes, Edward L. Letters, Massachusetts Historical Society, Boston.
Estabrook, Charles A. Correspondence, State Historical Society of Wisconsin.
Evans, Thomas. Diary, 25th Ohio, VFM 2506, OHS.
Ewell, Richard S. Papers, Tennessee State Library and Archives.
Flory, John. Diary, 107th Ohio, C. D. W. Nelson Collection, USMHI.
Fox, George Benson. Papers, 75th Ohio, MS755, Cincinnati Historical Society.
Frank, Jacob J. Diary, 41st New York, Library of Congress.
Frazier, John W. "Reply of the Philadelphia Brigade to the Foolish and Absurd Narrative of Lieutenant Frank A. Haskell...." Unpublished MOLLUS Papers, Box 41, USMHI.
Fritsch, Friedrich Otto Baron von. "'A Modern Soldier of Fortune.' The Diary of Baron von Fritsch. A German by Birth, but in Principles a Citizen of the World.' Unpublished manuscript dated May, 1903, Library of Congress. 68th New York Infantry.
Gardner, Isaac. Diary, Battery I, 1st Ohio Light Artillery, Kenneth M. Kepf Collection, USMHI.
——. Letters, Gregory A. Coco Collection, USMHI.
Gill, Nathan Atwood. Papers, 33rd Massachusetts, Civil War Misc Collection, USMHI.
Gillis, Joseph. Letters, 82nd Ohio, in the possession of Joseph H. Gillis.
Graefe, Karl August. Letter, 26th Wisconsin. File SC 2058, State Historical Society of Wisconsin.
Hamlin, Augustus C. Hamlin Family Papers, Raymond H. Fogler Library, University of Maine.
Hall, Daniel. Letters, O.O. Howard Collection, OHS.
Henny, Henry. "The Faithful Diary of An Unterrified Patriot," 55th Ohio, USAMHI.
Hively, Augustus. Diary, 61st Ohio. USAMHI. Published version appeared under the title *A Civil War Diary February 1864-February 1865* (Pittsburgh, PA: 1982).
Hoenig, George. Diary, 26th Wisconsin. Translated from the original Old German script by Dieter and Erika Schirmer of Germany.
Hooker, Joseph. Miscellaneous Correspondence, Jay Luvaas Collection, USMHI.
Horstmann, Augustus. Adjutant, 45th New York. Account of the Battle of Gettysburg, GNMP.
Houghton, William. Letters, Bentley Historical Library, University of Michigan.

Howard, Charles H. Letters, brother and aide-de-camp to Gen. O.O. Howard. Letters, William E. Brooks Collection, LC.

Howard, Oliver Otis. Letter to M. S. O'Donnell, March 9, 1891, Northwest Corner CW Roundtable, USMHI.

——. "Report on the Operations of the 11th Corps from June 29th to July 25th exclusive of the Battle of Gettysburg," William L. Clements Library, University of Michigan.

——. Papers, Bowdoin College, Brunswick, Maine.

——. Papers, Ohio Historical Society.

——. Papers, Schoff Civil War Collection, William L. Clements Library, University of Michigan.

Howard, Rowland Bailey. Papers, Bowdoin College, Brunswick, Maine.

Howe, Alva W. Letters, 55th Ohio Infantry, Ohio Historical Society.

Howland, Thomas S. Letters, 33rd Massachusetts, Massachusetts Historical Society, Boston.

Hubbard, Robert. Letters, Surgeon, 17th Connecticut Infantry, USAMHI.

Hübschmann, Franz. Papers, Surgeon, 26th Wisconsin. In Robert Wild Papers, Box 3, Milwaukee County Historical Society.

Hughey, William Fletcher. Diary, 73rd Ohio, in the possession of Steve Braun.

Hutchinson, Ephraim M. Papers, 82nd Ohio and 61st Ohio, Civil War Times Illustrated Collection, USMHI.

Jacobs, William H. Colonel, 26th Wisconsin. Papers, Milwaukee County Historical Society.

Jones, George W. 2nd Lieutenant and Adjutant, 26th Wisconsin. Diary, Washington County Historical Society, West Bend, Wisconsin.

Kappelman, Friedrich P. Papers, 82nd Illinois. Civil War Times Illustrated Collection, USAMHI.

Karsten, Karl M. 2nd Lieutenant, Company F, 26th Wisconsin. Diary, microfilm copy in the State Historical Society of Wisconsin, Microfilm 251.

Keeler, Alonzo. Diary, 55th Ohio Infantry, Civil War Miscellaneous Collection, USAMHI.

Kuechenmeister, Franz. Papers, 26th Wisconsin, courtesy of Erv Seeger.

Kummer, John U. Letters, 82nd Ohio. Lewis Leigh Collection. USAMHI.

Lackner, Francis "Franz." Major, 26th Wisconsin. Diary, Milwaukee County Historical Society.

——. "Toward a History of the Twenty-Sixth," unpublished manuscript written in the summer of 1865, in the possession of Alexander G. Morehouse. Lackner said that this was later published in the *Milwaukee Herald.*

——. "Twenty-Sixth Wisconsin Volunteer Infantry," unpublished manuscript dated June 18, 1911, in the possession of Alexander G. Morehouse.

Langhans, John. Letters, 154th New York. Mark H. Dunkelman and Michael J. Winey Collection at St. Bonaventure University.

Ley, Hubert. Letter to the New York Monuments Commission, September 8, 1896, Grand Army of the Republic File, Department of New York Records, Box 25, Folder 19, 45th New York , New York State Archives.

Loefstroem, John Henry. Papers, 74th Pennsylvania Infantry, USAMHI.

Maluski, Aleksander. *Pamietniczek A. Maluskiego Wychodzcy z 1831 roku 1831-1881* (Paris, France, February 1, 1881), 58th New York, Institut Polonais Paris.

Markham, Philo A. "Sketch of the Life & Army Service of P. A. Markham," 154th New York Infantry, U.S. Army Military History Institute, Carlisle Barracks.

Mesnard, Luther B. Reminiscences, manuscript, 55th Ohio and 25th Ohio, Civil War Miscellaneous Collection, USMHI.

Metcalf, George. "Reminiscence," 136th New York, Gregory Coco Collection, USMHI.

Meysenburg, Theodore Augustus. Journals, Missouri History Museum Archives, St. Louis, A1039.

——. Order Book, Assistant Adjutant General, Eleventh Corps, New-York Historical Society.

Miller, Thaddeus K. Letters, 61st Ohio Infantry, Ohio Historical Society, VFM 2657.

Mills, Charles J. Letters, officer, 2nd Massachusetts Infantry, Harrisburg Civil War Roundtable, Gregory Coco Collection, USAMHI.

Milwaukee Turners Foundation, Inc. Miscellaneous File Folders. Milwaukee, Wisconsin.

Mitchell, William D. W. Letters, captain, 82nd Ohio, in the possession of Stanley R. Burleson.

Muenzenberger, Adam. Acting Sergeant, Company C, 26th Regiment Wisconsin Volunteers, letters, October 1862 to November, 1863. Translated by Clara M. Lamers and William M. Lamers, 1933. Courtesy of William M. Lamers.

Murdoch, James R. Papers (Ms fxM974), Cincinnati Newspaper Clippings, Cincinnati Historical Society.

154th New York Volunteer Infantry, the Mark H. Dunkelman and Michael J. Winey Collection at St. Bonaventure University.

Osborn, Thomas Ward. Papers, Colgate University, Hamilton, N.Y.

Osgood, Vriling. Diary, Co. H, 136th NY, Box B-16, GNMP.

Patterson, William H. Diary, 1st Pennsylvania Light Artillery, Battery F, Harrisburg Civil War Roundtable Collection, USAMHI.

Paynton, William W. "From Virginia to Gettysburg and Back," 17th Connecticut, manuscript, GNMP.

Porter, Isaac N. Letters, 154th New York, Civil War Miscellaneous Collection, USMHI.

Potts, Lt. Joseph H. Letters, 75th Ohio, Ohio Historical Society.

Preiser, Emil. Prayerbook, 27th Pennsylvania File, GNMP.

Robinson, Col. James S. Papers, 82nd Ohio, Ohio Historical Society.

Ross, A. W. Letters, 73rd Ohio, Ohio Historical Society.

Roth, Wilhelm. Letters, 74th Pennsylvania, U.S. Army Military History Institute, Carlisle Barracks.

Salomon, Edward S. "Gettysburg," Gettysburg National Military Park.

Sanford, Addison. Papers, 82nd Ohio. VFM 2451, Ohio Historical Society.

Schlumpf, Leonhard. Diary, 45th New York, Civil War Times Illustrated Collection, USMHI.

Schlund, Max. Diary, 82nd Illinois, courtesy of Clay Feeter.

Schurz, Carl. Papers and diary for 1862, Box 175, Library of Congress.

"Seventeenth Regiment," *The Connecticut War Record*, Vol. I, No. 2, in Unpublished MOLLUS Papers, Box No. 41, USAMHI.

Seymour, William J. Diary, captain and A.A.G., Hays' Louisiana Infantry Brigade. Harrisburg Civil War Roundtable, Gregory A. Coco Collection, Carlisle Barracks.

Sigel, Franz. Letterbook, 1862-1865, Library of Congress.

——. "Memoranda" book, New-York Historical Society.

____. Papers, New-York Historical Society.

Sladen, Joseph A. Papers, 33rd Massachusetts and aide-de-camp to Gen. O.O. Howard. Sladen Family Papers, USAMHI.

Smith, Horace. Diary, 154th New York, Wisconsin Historical Society.

Smith, Thomas C. H. Papers. Ohio Historical Society.

Smrcek, Frank. 26th Wisconsin. Diary, http://www.russscott.com/~rscott/26thwis/frsmrcek.htm. The original is in the possession of Peggy Keck.

Society of the Army of the Potomac. Minutes of Meetings. Library of Congress.

Southerton, William B. "What We Did There," unpublished memoirs as told to Marie W. Higgins, dated 1935, 75th Ohio, VFM 3177, Ohio Historical Society.

Spindler, Henry. Letters, 55th Ohio Infantry, Ohio Historical Society.

Sprengling, Andrew. Papers, 26th Wisconsin, Milwaukee County Historical Society, Milwaukee, Wisconsin.

Stahel, Julius. Papers, Levetarak Orszagas Kospontja, Hungary. Copies in Library of Congress.

Stotz, Jacob. Veterans survey document, Grand Army of the Republic, Department of New York Records, Box 25, Folder 19, 45th New York, New York State Archives.

Thomson, David. Papers, 82nd Ohio Infantry, courtesy of Ms. Mary A. Geiger.

Van Aernam, Henry. Papers, 154th New York, chief surgeon for 2nd Division, Eleventh Corps, USMHI.

Vanderhoef, James W. Letters, 45th New York, Brooklyn Collection, Brooklyn Public Library.

Warren, William. Diary, 17th Connecticut, Bridgeport Historical Society, Bridgeport, Connecticut.

Wells, Marlow D. Letter to father, 157th New York, New York State Division of Military and Naval Affairs: Military History.

Wickesberg, Karl [Charles]. Letters, Sergeant, 26th Wisconsin, courtesy of Mr. Alfred Wickesberg, Milwaukee, Wisconsin.

Wiedrich, Michael. Papers, Buffalo and Erie County Historical Soceity.

Wild, Robert. Papers, Milwaukee County Historical Society.

Winkler, Frederick C. Papers, 26th Wisconsin Infantry, Milwaukee County Historical Society, Box 1.

——. "Winkler's Reminiscences of Frank Haskell," unpublished manuscript in the University of Wisconsin-Milwaukee Library, n.d.

Printed Primary Sources

Adjutant General's Office, State of Connecticut. *Catalogue of Connecticut Volunteer Organizations (Infantry, Cavalry and Artillery) in the Service of the United States 1861-1865, with Additional Enlistments, Casualties, and Brief Summaries Showing the Operations and Service of the Several Regiments and Batteries.* Hartford: Brown & Gross, 1869.

Adjutant General's Office, State of Connecticut. *Seventeenth Annual Reunion of the 17th Regiment C.V.I. Held at Fairfield, Conn., August 28th, 1883.* Bridgeport, CT: Standard Association, 1884.

Adjutant General's Office, State of Connecticut. *17th Connecticut Volunteers at Gettysburg, June 30th, and July 1st, 2nd and 3rd, 1884.* Bridgeport, CT: The Standard Association, 1884.

Adjutant General's Office, State of Illinois. *Report of the Adjutant General of the State of Illinois.* Springfield: Phillips, 1901. Vol. 5, 100-124.

Alexander, Edward P. *Military Memoirs of a Confederate* (Bloomington: Indiana University Press, 1962).

Ames, Blanche Ames. *Adelbert Ames General Senator Governor 1835-1933* (London: Macdonald, 1964).

Annual Report of the Adjutant General of Ohio, 1863 (Columbus: The State, 1864).

Annual Report of the Adjutant General of the State of Wisconsin with Reports from the Quartermaster General and Surgeon General, for the Year Ending December 30th, 1865 (Madison: William J. Park & Co., 1866).

Applegate, John Stilwell. *Reminiscences and Letters of George Arrowsmith of New Jersey, late Lieutenant-Colonel of the One Hundred and Fifty-Seventh Regiment, New York State Volunteers.* (Red Bank, NJ: John H. Cook, 1893).

Arnold, Joseph. "Belle Island," in Bernhard Domschcke, *Twenty Months in Captivity, Memoirs of a Union Officer in Confederate Prison* (Associated University Presses, 1987), 135-37. The author was 1st lieutenant, Company E, 26th Wisconsin.

Asch, S. A. "The First Day at Gettysburg," *Confederate Veteran*, XXXVIII, No. 10 (October 1930).

Atkinson, John. *The Story of Lookout Mountain and Missionary Ridge* (Detroit: Winn and Hammond, Printers, 1893).

Barlow, Albert Rowe. "A Defense of the Eleventh Corps," *National Tribune*, January 15, 1885.

——. *Company G: A Record of the Services of One Company of the 157th N.Y. Vols. in the War of the Rebellion, from Sept. 19, 1862 to July 10, 1865, Including the Roster of the Company.* (Syracuse: A. W. Hall, 1899).

Barthel, Thomas. *Abner Doubleday: A Civil War Biography* (Jefferson, DC: McFarland & Company, Inc., 2010).

Becker, Carl M. and Ritchie Thomas, eds. *Hearth and Knapsack: The Ladley Letters, 1857-1880* (Athens, OH: Ohio University Press, 1988).

Benjaminson, Eric. "A Regiment of Immigrants: The 82nd Illinois Volunteer Infantry and the Letters of Captain Rudolph Mueller," *Journal of the Illinois State Historical Society*, Vol. 94, No. 2 (Summer 2001), 137-80.

Biddle, Chapman. *The First Day of the Battle of Gettysburg* (Philadelphia: J. B. Lippincott & Co., 1880).

Blair, William Alan, ed. *A Politician Goes to War: The Civil War Letters of John White Geary* (University Park, PA: The Pennsylvania State University Press, 1995).

Blood, Caleb. *Makng the Circle of the Confederacy* (Chicago, IL: n.p., 1916). He was in the 33rd Massachusetts Volunteer Infantry.

Böhm, Christian. Address at the dedication of the monument of the 45th New York at Gettysburg, printed in German in William F. Fox, ed., *New York at Gettysburg* (Albany: J. B. Lyon Company, 1900), I, 375-77.

Boies, Andrew J. *Record of the Thirty-third Massachusetts Volunteer Infantry, from Aug. 1862 to Aug. 1865* (Fitchburg: Sentinel Printing Co., 1880).

Breshears, Guy. *Loyal Till Death: A Diary of the 13th New York Artillery* (Bowie, MD: Heritage Books, Inc., 2003).

Bryant, Edwin E. "The Battle of Gettysburg," *MOLLUS-Wisconsin*, II (1896).

Ceremonies and Addresses at the Dedication of a Monument by the 119th Regiment, N. Y. State Vols. at Gettysburg, July 3, 1888 (Boston: Wright & Potter Printing, 1889).

Civil War Papers Read Before the Commandery of the States of Massachusetts: Military Order of the Loyal Legion of the United States (Boston: For the Commandery, 1900).

Cooke, Sidney G. "The First Day at Gettysburg," *Papers Read Before the Kansas Commandery of the Military Order of the Loyal Legion of the United States* (Kansas City, KS: Franklin Hudson Publishing Company, 1906), Vol. I, 277-89.

Crumb, Herb and Katherine Dhalle, *No Middle Ground: Thomas Ward Osborn's Letters from the Field (1862-1864)* (Hamilton, NY: Edmonston Publishing, Inc., 1993).

Culp, Edward C. *The 25th Ohio Veteran Volunteer Infantry in the War for the Union* (Topeka, KS: George W. Crane, 1885).

——. "Reminiscences of the Great Fight by a Participant," *National Tribune*, March 19, 1885.

Dineen, John. "Credit to Whom Credit is Due: The 33d Mass. Puts in a Claim for the Repulse of the Louisiana Division," *National Tribune*, January 28, 1909.

Dodge, Theodore A. *Addresses and Reviews* (Boston: Henry S. Dunn, 1898).

——. "Gettysburg Campaign, The," *The United Service*, Philadephia, XIII, (1885).

——. "Left Wounded on the Field," *Putnam's Magazine*, NS IV (New York 1869), 317-326.

——. "Was Either the Better Soldier," *Century Magazine*, XL (1890), 144-48.

Domschcke, Bernhard. *Twenty Months in Captivity, Memoirs of a Union Officer in Confederate Prison* (London: Associated University Presses, 1987). Edited and translated by Frederic Trautmann. Author was captain, Company H, 26th Wisconsin.

Doubleday, Abner. *Chancellorsville and Gettysburg* (New York: Charles Scribner's Sons, 1882).

Early, Jubal A. *Autobiographical Sketch and Narrative of the War Between the States* (Philadelphia: J. B. Lippincott, 1912).

Fenton, R. E. *Fifth Annual Report of the Chief of the Bureau of Military Statistics, with Appendices* (Albany: C. Van Benthuysen & Sons' Steam Printing House, 1868), 362-71.

Fischer, Louis. "The 11th Corps at Gettysburg," *National Tribune*, December 12, 1869.

Fox, William F., ed. *Final Report on the Battlefield of Gettysburg* (Albany: J. B. Lyon Company Printers, 1900, 1902), 3 Volumes. Report of the New York Monuments Commission for the Battlefields of Gettysburg and Chattanooga.

Frazier, John W. "Reply of the Philadelphia Brigade to the Foolish and Absurd Narrative of Lieutenant Frank A. Haskell," unpublished manuscript, MOLLUS Papers, Box 41, USMHI.

Frueauff, John. Letter to Col. Samuel Yohe, *Rebllion Record*, Vol. 6, 589-90. He was Acting Assistant Inspector General on Gen. Devens' staff, XI Corps.

Frey, Emil. "My American Experience," *North American Review*, CLVIII (February 1894), 129-139.

Fullerton, Joseph S. "The Army of the Cumberland at Chattanooga," *Battles and Leaders*, III.

Gordon, John B. *Reminiscences of the Civil War* (Baton Rouge, LA: Louisiana State University Press, 1993).

Goss, Warren Lee. *The Soldier's Story of His Captivity at Andersonville, Belle Isle, and Other Rebel Prisons* (Boston: I. N. Richardson & Co., 1871).

Grant, Ulysses S. "Chattanooga," *Retreat from Gettysburg: Battles and Leaders of the Civil War*, (New York: Castle Books, 1956), 679-711.

——. *Personal Memoirs of U. S. Grant* (New York: Dover Publications, Inc.,1995).

Green, John P. "The Movement of the 11th and 12th Army Corps From the Potomac to the Tennessee," *Military Essays and Recollections of the Pennsylvania Commandery*, MOLLUS, Michael A. Cavanaugh, complr. (Wilmington, NC: Broadfoot Publishing Co., 1995), Vol. I, 107-22.

Greene, Albert R. "From Bridgeport to Ringgold by Way of Lookout Mountain: The Lookout Mountain-Chattanooga Tennessee Civil War Campaign of the 3rd Brigade commanded by General George Sears Greene Fall 1863," MOLLUS-Rhode Island (Providence: Published by the Rhode Island Soldiers and Sailors Historical Society, 1890), Vol. 6.

Gross, Jacob. 82nd Illinois, *Illinois Monuments at Gettysburg* (Springfield, IL: H. W. Rokker, State Printer and Binder, 1892).

Halstead, Edward P. "Incidents of the First Day at Gettysburg," *Retreat from Gettysburg: Battles and Leaders of the Civil War* (New York: Castle Books, 1956).

——. *The First Day of the Battle of Gettysburg* (Washington, DC: Judd & Detweiler, 1887).

——. "The First Day of the Battle of Gettysburg," *Individual Papers, Military Order of the Loyal Legion of the United States* (Washington, DC: District of Columbia Commandery, 1887), Vol. 1, 3-10.

Hancock, Winfield S. "Gettysburg: A Reply to General Howard," in Peter Cozzens, ed., *Battles and Leaders of the Civil War* (Urbana: University of Illinois Press, 2002), Vol. 5, 348-64.

Hand, J. W. "A Graphic Account of the Battle by a Eleventh Corps Captain," *National Tribune*, July 24, 1890.

History of the 134th Regiment, N.Y.S. Vol., Also a Sketch of Prison Life (Schenectady: J. J. Marlett, n.d.).

Hitz, Louise W., ed. *The Letters of Frederick C. Winkler* (n.p.: Privately Printed, 1963).

Hooker, Joseph. "Report on the Battle of Wauhatchie," *Rebellion Record*, VII.

Howard, Charles H. "First Day at Gettysburg," *The Gettysburg Papers*. Press of Morningside Bookshop, 1978, 310-336.

——. "The First Day at Gettysburg," *MOLLUS-Illinois*, IV, 238-264.

Howard, Oliver Otis. *Autobiography of Oliver Otis Howard* (New York: The Baker & Taylor Company, 1907), 2 vols.

——. "Gen'l O. O. Howard's Reminiscences of the War of the Rebellion," *National Tribune*, November 20, 1884.

——. "Gen'l O. O. Howard's Reminiscences of the War of the Rebellion," *National Tribune*, December 18, 1884.

——. "Gen'l O. O. Howard's Reminiscences of the War of the Rebellion," *National Tribune*, January 1, 1885.

——. "Gen'l O. O. Howard's Reminiscences of the War of the Rebellion," *National Tribune*, January 15, 1885.

——. "Gen'l O. O. Howard's Reminiscences of the War of the Rebellion," *National Tribune*, January 29, 1885.

——. "Grant at Chattanooga," in Peter Cozzens, ed., *Battles and Leaders of the Civil War* (Urbana and Chicago: University of Illinois Press, 2004), Vol. 6, 375-379.

——. "O. O. Howard's Commencement Address at Syracuse University," *The Gettysburg Magazine*, Vol. 11 (July 1994), 71-79.

——. "The Campaign and Battle of Gettysburg," *Atlantic Monthly*, 13 (July 8, 1876).

——. "The Campaign and Battle of Gettysburg," in Peter Cozzens, ed., *Battles and Leaders of the Civil War* (Urbana: University of Illinois Press, 2002), Vol. 5, 314-348.

Howard, William F., ed. *The Civil War Memoir of William T. Levey* (Manchester Center, VT: Northshire Press, 2008).

Huber, A. H. "The 33d Mass. And 'Stevens's Knoll' at Gettysburg," *National Tribune*, March 11, 1909.

Hunt, Henry J. "The Second Day at Gettysburg," *Battles and Leaders*, III.

Hurst, Samuel H. *Journal-History of the Seventy-Third Ohio Volunteer Infantry* (Chillicothe, OH: Privately Printed, 1866).

Illinois in the War for the Union: A Comprehensive and Succinct History (Springfield and Chicago: Publishing House of H. W. Rokker, 1887).

Illinois Monuments at Gettysburg (Springfield, IL: H. W. Rokker, State Printer and Binder, 1892).

Jewett, Leonidas M. "The Boys in Blue at Missionary Ridge," *MOLLUS-Ohio* (Cincinnati: Monfort, 1908), Vol. VI, 89-94.

——. "From Stafford Heights to Gettysburg in 1863," *MOLLUS-Ohio* (Cincinnati: Robert Clarke, 1903), Vol. V, 213-22.

Jones, Terry L., ed. *The Civil War Memoirs of Captain William J. Seymour: Reminiscences of a Louisiana Tiger* (Baton Rouge: Louisiana State University Press, 1991).

Kamphoefer, Walter D., and Wolfgang Helbich, eds., Susan Carter Vogel, trans., *Germans in the Civil War: The Letters They Wrote Home* (Chapel Hill: University of North Carolina Press, 2006).

Keifer, William R. *History of the One Hundred Fifty Third Regiment Pennsylvania Volunteer Infantry* (Easton: Press of the Chemical Publishing Co., 1905).

Kelly, Andrew W. *History of the 134th Regiment, N.Y.S. Vol.* (Schenectady: J. J. Marlett Star Office, n.d.).

Krzyzanowski, Wlodzimierz. *Wspomnienia z Pobytu w Ameryce Podczas Wojny* (Chicago: Polish Museum of America, 1963).

Ladd, David L. and Audrey J., eds. *The Bachelder Papers: Gettysburg in Their Own Words* (Dayton, OH: Morningside House, Inc., 1994), 3 Vols.

——. *John Bachelder's History of the Battle of Gettysburg* (Dayton, OH: Morningside, 1997).

Le Duc, William G. *Recollections of a Civil War Quartermaster. The Autobiography of William G. Le Duc* (St. Paul, MN: The North Central Publishing Company, 1963).

Lee, Alfred E. "The Battle of Gettysburg," *Report of the Ohio Gettysburg Memorial Commission (1888)*, 95-142.

——. *The Battle of Gettysburg* (Columbus, OH: A. H. Smythe, 1888).

——. "The Eleventh Corps. The Disadvantages Under Which it Fought at Gettysburg," *Weekly Press* (Philadelphia), XXIX, January 26, 1887, 1.

——. "Campaigning in the Mountain Department," *Magazine of American History*, Vol. XV (1885), 391-96, 483-91, 590-95.

——. "Reminiscences of the Gettysburg Battle," *Lippincott Magazine*, Volume 6 (1883), 54-60.

Levey, William T. *The Blue and the Gray, a Sketch of Soldier Life in Camp and Field in the Army of the Civil War* (Schenectady: Roy Burton Myers, 1904).

Livermore, Thomas L. *Memoir of Theodore Ayrault Dodge* (Boston: Massachusetts Historical Society, 1909).

Longstreet, James. *From Manassas to Appomattox* (Bloomington: Indiana University Press, 1960).

Marcus, Edward, ed. *A New Canaan Private in the Civil War. Letters of Justus M. Silliman, 17th Connecticut Volunteers* (New Canaan, CT: New Canaan historical Society, 1984).

McKay, Charles W. "Three Years or During the War with the Crescent and Star," *National Tribune* Scrap Book (Washington, n.d.), II, 121-60.

McLean, James L., Jr., and Judy W. McLean, complrs. *Gettysburg Sources Volume 1* (Baltimore, MD: Butternut and Blue, 1986).

——. *Gettysburg Sources Volume 2* (Baltimore, MD: Butternut and Blue, 1987).

——. *Gettysburg Sources Volume 3* (Baltimore, MD: Butternut and Blue, 1990).

McNeil, Betty Ann. *Charity Afire: Daughters of Charity Civil War Nurses. Maryland, 1862-1865* (Emmitsburg, MD: Daughters of Charity of Saint Vincent de Paul, 2011).

——. *Charity Afire: Daughters of Charity Civil War Nurses. Pennsylvania, 1862-1865* (Emmitsburg, MD: Daughters of Charity of Saint Vincent de Paul, 2011).

——. *Dear Masters: Daughters of Charity of Saint Vincent de Paul, Civil War Nurses: Extracts from Accounts by Sister Nurses* (Emmitsburg, MD: Daughters of Charity of Saint Vincent de Paul, 2011.

Meade, George Gordon. *With Meade at Gettysburg* (Philadelphia: Military Order of the Loyal Legion of the United States, 1930).

Meier, Heinz K. *Memoirs of a Swiss Officer in the American Civil War* (Bern and Frankfurt am Main: Herbert Lang, 1972).

Meline, Mary M. and Edward F. X. McSweeney, *The Story of the Mountain. Mount St. Mary's College and Seminary Emmitsburg, Maryland* (Emmitsburg, MD: The Daily Chronicle, 1911), Volume II.

Mesnard, Luther B, "The Rise and Survival of Private Mesnard," *Civil War Times Illustrated*, Part I (January 1986), 18-25, and Part II (February 1986), 10-17, 44-45.

Meysenburg, Theodore A. "Reminiscences of Chancellorsville," *War Papers and Personal Reminiscences, 1861-1865. Read Before the Commandery of the State of Missouri, Military Order of the Loyal Legion of the United States* (St. Louis: Becktold & Co., 1892), I, 295-307.

Mitchell, Robert Dale and Robert Hoffsommer. "The Rise and Survival of Private Mesnard—Part I," *Civil War Times Illustrated*, Vol. XXIV, no. 9 (January 1986), 18-25.

——. "The Rise and Survival of Private Mesnard Part II," *Civil War Times Illustrated*, Vol. XXIV, no. 10 (February 1986), 10-17, 44-45.

Monfort, E. R. "The First Division, Eleventh Corps at Chancellorsville," *G. A. R. War Papers: Papers Read Before Fred C. Jones Post, No. 401, Department of Ohio, G. A. R.*(Cincinnati: Fred C. Jones Post, No. 401, 1891), Vol. I, 60-75.

Nachtigall, Herrmann. *Geschichte des 75sten Regiments, Pa. Vols.* (Philadelphia: C. B. Kretschman, 1886).

Nevins, Allan, ed. *A Diary of Battle: The Personal Journals of Colonel Charles S. Wainwright 1861-1865* (New York: Harcourt, Brace & World, Inc., 1962).

New York Monuments Commission, *Final Report on the Battlefield at Gettysburg* (Albany: J. B. Lyon Company, 1900), 3 Vols.

Nichols, G. W. *A Soldier's Story of His Regiment* (Kennesaw, GA: Continental Book Company, 1961).

Noble, William H. "The Seventeenth Connecticut Volunteer Infantry. The Fairfield County Regiment," from http://home.att.net/~DogSgt/history1.html.

Nussbaum, Frederick "Louisiana Tigers and the 107th Ohio," *National Tribune*, July 15, 1909.

Osborn, Hartwell. "The Eleventh Corps in East Tennessee," *MOLLUS-Illinois* (Chicago: Cozzens & Beaton Company, 1907), IV, 348-78.

——. *Trials and Triumphs: The Record of the Fifty-Fifth Ohio Volunteer Infantry* (Chicago: A.C. McClurg & Co., 1904).

Osborn, Thomas W. "Annals of the War/Chapters of Unwritten History/The Artillery at Gettysburg/An Account of the Operations at Cemetery Hill/General Howard's Position/The Work of the Batteries Described by an Artillery Chief," *Weekly Times* (Philadelphia), May 31, 1879.

——. "The Artillery at Gettysburg," *Philadelphia Weekly Times*, May 31, 1879.

Paris, Comte de, O. O. Howard, Henry W. Slocum, and Abner Doubleday, "Gettysburg Thirty Years After," *North American Review*, CCCCXI (February 1891), 129-47.

Pennsylvania at Gettysburg Ceremonies at the Dedication of the Monuments Erected by the Commonwealth of Pennsylvania to Major General George G. Meade Major General Winfield S. Hancock Major General John F. Reynolds and to Mark the Positions of the Pennsylvania Commands Engaged in the Battle (Harrisburg: W. S. Ray, State Printer, 1904), Vol. 1.

Pratt, Calvin E. *Oration at the Re-union of the Army of the Potomac, Baltimore, Md., May 6th, 1885* (Baltimore: n.p., 1885).

Priest, John Michael, ed., *John T. McMahon's Diary of the 136th New York 1861-1864* (Shippensburg, PA: White Mane Publishing Company, Inc., 1993).

Quaife, Milo M., ed., *From the Cannon's Mouth: The Civil War Letters of General Alpheus S. Williams* (Detroit: Wayne State University Press and The Detroit Historical Society, 1959).

Rappolt, Hedwig, ed., transl., *An American Apprenticeship: The Letters of Emil Frey 1860-1865* (New York: Peter Lang, 1986).

Raum, Green B. "Hazen's Night Expedition to Brown's Ferry," *Military Essays and Recollections: Papers Read Before the Commandery of the State of Illinois, Military Order of the Loyal Legion of the United States* (Chicago: Published by the Commandery, 1907), Vol. IV, 276-83.

——. "The Forgotten Fight on Tunnell Hill," Peter Cozzens, ed., *Battles and Leaders of the Civil War* (Urbana and Chicago: University of Illinois Press, 2002), Vol. V, 466-80.

Reinhart, Joseph R. *Yankee Dutchmen under Fire: Civil War Letters from the 82nd Illinois Infantry* (Kent, OH: Kent State University Press, 2013).

Report of the Joint Committee on the Conduct of the War, at the Second Session Thirty-eighth Congress (Washington, DC: Government Printing Office, 1865).

Report of the Ohio Gettysburg Memorial Commission (Columbus: Nitschke Bros., 1887).

Report on the New York Monuments at Chattanooga and Proceedings of Dedication of the Central Historical Memorial or Peace Monument on Lookout Mountain (Albany: J. B. Lyon Company, Printers, 1928).

Rich, Earle. *Cape Cod Echoes.* (Olreans, MA: Salt Meadow Publishers, 1973).

Ryder, John J. *Reminiscences of Three Years' Service in the Civil War by a Cape Cod Boy* (New Bedford, MA: Reynolds Printing, 1928).

Salomon, Edward Selig. "Gettysburg," *MOLLUS-California* (San Francisco: Shannon-Conmy Print Co., 1913).

Schurz, Carl. "The Battle of Gettysburg," *McClure's Magazine*, 29 (July 1907), 272-85.

——. *The Reminiscences of Carl Schurz* (New York: The McClure Co., 1907-1908), 3 vols.

Schwinge, Heinz D. and Karl E. Sundstrom, transl. and eds. *History of the 75th Regiment, Pa. Vols.* (North Riverside, IL: Privately Printed, 1987).

Scott, James K. P. *The Lost History of Gettysburg: The Story of the Battles of Gettysburg* (New York: ibooks, distributed by Simon and Schuster, 2002).

Seventeenth Annual Reunion of the 17th Regiment Connecticut Volunteer Infantry Held at Fairfield, Conn., August 28th 1883 (Bridgeport: n.p., 1884).

17th Connecticut Volunteers at Gettysburg (Bridgeport, CT: The Standard Association, Printers, 1884).

"Seventeenth Regiment," *The Connecticut War Record* (New Haven, CT: Peck, White & Peck, 1863-65), Vol. I, No. 2.

"Seventeenth Regiment," Unpublished MOLLUS Papers, Box 2, No. 41, USMHI.

Seventeenth Regiment Connecticut Volunteer Infantry in the War of the Rebellion, 1862-1865 (Hartford: Press of the Case, Lockwood & Brainard Co., 1889).

Seventy-third Regiment Pennsylvania Volunteers at Gettysburg (Pennsylvania?: n.p., 1889).

Sickles, Daniel E., D[avid] M. Gregg, John Newton, and Daniel Butterfield, "Further Recollections of Gettysburg," *North American Review*, CCCCXII (March 1891), 257-86.

Sickles, Daniel E., John Newton and Daniel Butterfield, "Further Recollections of Gettysburg," in Peter Cozzens, ed., *Battles and Leaders of the Civil War* (Urbana and Chicago: University of Illinois Press, 2004), Vol. 6, 253-272.

Simmers, William, and Paul Bachschmid, *The Volunteer's Manual; or, Ten Months with the 153d Penn'a Volunteers* (Easton, PA: D. Neiman, Printer, 1863).

Sketches of War History, 1861-1865: Papers Read Before the Ohio Commandery of the Military Order of the Loyal Legion of the United States (Cincinnati: Published by the Commandery, R. Clark, 1888).

Smith, Jacob. *Camps and Campaigns of the 107th Regiment Ohio Volunteer Infantry 1862-1865* (Navarre, OH: Indian River Graphics, 2000).

Smith, Lucian A. "Recollections of Gettysburg," *War Papers Read Before the Michigan Commandery of the Military Order of the Loyal Legion of the United States* (Detroit: Published by the Comandery, 1898), Vol. 2, 297-308.

Society of the Army of the Potomac, Record of Proceedings at Reunions, 1st to 37th (New York: Various Publishers, 1870-1907).

Society of the Army of the Potomac. Report of the Nineteenth Annual Re-Union at Gettysburg, Pennsylvania, July 1st, 2d, & 3d, 1888 (New York: MacGowan & Slipper, 1888).

Society of the Army of the Potomac. Report of the Thirteenth Annual Re-Union, at Detroit, Michigan, June 14 & 15, 1882 (New York: MacGowan & Slipper, Printers, 1882).

Society of the Army of the Potomac. Report of the Thirty-Sixth Annual Re-Union at Manassas, VA May Tenth and Eleventh Nineteen Hundred and Five (New York: MacGowan & Slipper, Printers, 1890).

Society of the Army of the Potomac. Sixteenth Annual Reunion Held in the City of Baltimore May 7th & 8th 1885, Report of Proceedings (New York: Macgowan & Slipper, Printers, 1885).

Society of the Army of the Potomac. Twenty-first Annual Reunion Held at Portland, Me. July 3rd & 4th, 1890, Report of Proceedings (New York: Macgowan & Slipper, Printers, 1890).

Soldiers' and Citizens' Album of Biographical Record Containing Personal Sketches of Army Men and Citizens Prominent in Loyalty to the Union (Chicago: Grand Army Publishing Co., 1890).

Souder, Edmund A. *Leaves from the Battle-field of Gettysburg* (Philadelphia: Caxton Press, 1864).

Southard, Edwin. "Graphic Description of What a Veteran Saw on the First Day," *National Tribune*, August 19, 1897.

"Squad of the 17th Conn. First Learned of Lee's Retreat at Gettysburg," *National Tribune*, October 8, 1896. It was signed "A Veteran" from New Canaan, Conn. It may have been written by Justus M. Silliman.

Steinwehr, Adolph von. "Report on the Battle of Wauhatchie," *Rebellion Record*, III.

Styple, William B., *Generals in Bronze: Interviewing the Commanders of the Civil War* (Kearny, NJ: Belle Grove Publishing Company, 2005).

——. *Writing & Fighting the Civil War: Soldier Letters from the Battlefront* (Kearny, NJ: Belle Grove Pub. Co., 2000).

Sweetland, A. F. "Repulsing the 'Tigers' at the Cemetery, Gettysburg, July 2, 1863," *National Tribune*, October 21, 1909.

——. "Some Criticisms of Comrade McConnell's Account," *National Tribune*, November 2, 1916.

Thayer, George A. "Gettysburg as We Men on the Right Saw It," *MOLLUS-Ohio* (Cincinnati: H.C. Sherick & Co., 1886).

Underwood, Adin B. *Three Years' Service of the Thirty-Third Mass. Infantry Regiment 1862-1865* (Boston: A. Williams & Co., Publisher, 1881).

——. *The Three Years' Service of the 33rd Massachusetts Infantry* (Huntington, WV: Blue Acorn Press, 1993).

Wallace, Frederick Stephen. *The Sixty-First Ohio Volunteers, 1861-1865* (Marysville, OH: T. Mullen, 1902).

Wallber, Albert. "From Gettysburg to Libby Prison," in *War Papers Read Before the Commandery of the State of Wisconsin, Military Order of the Loyal Legion of the United States*. (Milwaukee: Burdick & Allen, 1914, Vol. IV, 191-200).

——. "The Escape from the Libby," in Bernhard Domschcke, *Twenty Months in Captivity, Memoirs of a Union Officer in Confederate Prison* (Associated University Presses, 1987), pp. 125-34.

War of the Rebellion: A Compilation of the Official Records of the Union and Confederate Armies (Washington: Government Printing Office, 1891).

Warner, George H. *Military Records of Schoharie County Veterans of Four Wars* (Albany: Weed, Parsons & Company, 1891).

Warren, George L. "Exceptions to Gen. John C. Robinson's Statements," *National Tribune*, July 21, 1887.

Wasson, Stanley P., ed. "Civil War Letters of Darwin Cody," *The Ohio Historical Quarterly*, Vol. 68 (1959), 371-407.

White, Gregory C. *"The Most Bloody and Cruel Drama": A History of the 31st Gerogia Volunteer Infantry, Lawton-Gordon-Evans Brigade, Army of Northern Virginia, Confederate States of America, 1861-1865* (Baltimore: Butternut & Blue, 1997).

Whittier, Edward N. "The Left Attack (Ewell's) Gettysburg," *Campaigns in Virginia, Maryland and Pennsylvania 1862-1863* (Boston: Papers of the Military Historical Society of Massachusetts, 1903, Vol. III), 315-50.

Wickesberg, Charles. *Letters of Sergeant Charles Wickesberg* (Milwaukee: Alfred Wickesberg, 1961). Transl. by Ingeborg Wolferstetter, historical notes by Donald A. Woods.

Winkler, Frederick C. *Letters of Frederick C. Winkler 1862 to 1865* (Milwaukee: William K. Winkler, 1963). Edited by William K. Winkler.

Secondary Sources

NOTE: Although some of the following sources were authored by participants in the various events they describe, I have listed them as secondary sources if they include significant material which the author could not possibly have personally observed. For example, while H. S. Huidekoper was a participant in the Battle of Gettysburg, his book on the first day clearly is based on research beyond his own specific observations on that day.

A Brief History of the 54th Regiment N. Y. Vet. Vol. Infantry (Hiram Barney Rifles) (New York: A. H. Kellogg, 1888).

Allers, Ken, Jr., *The Fog of Gettysburg: The Myths and Mysteries of the Battle* (Naperville, IL: Cumberland House Publishing, 2008).

Ames, Blanche Ames. *Adelbert Ames General Senator Governor 1835-1933* (London: Macdonald, 1964).

Archer, John M. *"The Hour Was One of Horror": East Cemetery Hill at Gettysburg* (Gettysburg: Thomas Publications, 1997).

Arrington, Benjamin T. *The Medal of Honor at Gettysburg* (Gettysburg: Thomas Publications, 1996).

Barnett, Bert. "If Ever Men Stayed By Their Guns": Leadership in the 1st and 11th Corps Artillery on the First Day of the Battle of Gettysburg," *I Ordered No Man to go When I Would Not go Myself: Leadership in the Campaign and Battle of Gettysburg* (Gettysburg: Gettysburg National Military Park, 2002), 81-100.

Barnett, Louise. *Acts Ungentlemanly: The Army's Notorious Incest Trial* (New York: Hill and Wang, 2000).

Bates, Samuel P. *History of Pennsylvania Volunteers 1861-5* (Harrisburg: B. Singerly, 1869).

——. *Martial Deeds of Philadelphia* (Philadelphia: T. H. Davis & Co., 1875).

Baumgartner, Richard A. *Buckeye Blood. Ohio at Gettysburg* (Huntington, WV: Blue Acorn Press, 2003).

Beale, James. *Tabulated Roster of the Army of the Potomac at Gettysburg, Penna, July 1, 2, 3, 1863* (Philadelphia: James Beale, 1888).

——. *The Statements of Time on July 1 at Gettysburg Pa. 1863* (Philadelphia: James Beale Printer, 1897), 48, 69-72.

Beecham, R. K. *Gettysburg: The Pivotol Battle of the Civil War* (Chicago: A. C. McClurg, 1911).

Bellah, James Warner. *Soldiers' Battle. Gettysburg* (New York: David McKay Company, Inc., 1962).

Benjaminson, Eric. "A Regiment of Immigrants: The 82nd Illinois Volunteer Infantry and the Letters of Captain Rudolph Mueller," *Journal of the Illinois State Historical Society*, Vol. 94, no. 2 (2001), 137-80.

Beveridge, John I. *Illinois Monuments at Gettysburg* (Springfield: H. W. Rokker, 1892).

Beyer, W. F., and O. F. Keydel, eds. *Deeds of Valor* (Detroit: Perrien-Keydel Co., 1906).

Bicheno, Hugh. *Gettysburg* (London: Cassell & Co., 2001).

Biddle, Chapman. *The First Day of the Battle of Gettysburg* (Philadelphia: J.B. Lippincott & Co., 1880).

Bishop, Ethan F. *The Gettysburg Battlefield: The Union Regimental Commanders Who Were Casualties in the Battle* (Westminster, MD: Heritage Books, 2008).

Boatner, Mark Mayo. *The Civil War Dictionary* (New York: David McKay Co., 1961).

Bowden, Scott, and Bill Ward, *Last Chance for Victory: Robert E. Lee and the Gettysburg Campaign* (Cambridge, MA: Da Capo Press, 2001).

Bowers, John. *Chickamauga & Chattanooga: The Battles that Doomed the Confederacy* (New York: HarperCollins Publishers, 1994).

Bracy, Isabel. *157th New York Volunteer (Infantry) Regiment 1862-1865 Madison and Cortland Counties, New York* (Interlaken, NY: Heart of the Lakes Publishing, 1991).

Bradley, Mark L. "Last Stand in the Carolinas: The Battle of Bentonville, March 19-21, 1865," *Blue & Gray Magazine*, XIII, No. 2 (December 1995), 9-22, 56-69.

Brady, James P. *Hurrah for the Artillery! Knap's Independent Battery "E," Pennsylvania Light Artillery* (Gettysburg, PA: Thomas Publications, 1992).

Brown, Andrew. *Geology and the Gettysburg Campaign* (n.p.: 1963).

Browne, Edward C., Jr. "Maj. Thomas Osborn's Artillery Line on July 3, 1863," *Gettysburg Magazine*, Vol. 41 (July 2009), 88-105.

Busey, John W. *These Honored Dead: The Union Casualties at Gettysburg* (Hightstown, NJ: Longstreet House, 1996).

Busey, John and David Martin. *Regimental Strengths at Gettysburg* (Hightstown, NJ: Longstreet House, 2005).

Butts, Joseph Tyler. *A Gallant Captain of the Civil War* (New York: F. Tennyson Neely, 1902).

Callihan, David. "'The Men of Battery 'I' Fought Splendidly": Captain Michael Wiedrich's Company I, First New York Light Artillery at Gettysburg," *The Gettysburg Magazine*, Vol. 33 (July 2005), 82-88.

Cameron, Bill. "The Signal Corps at Gettysburg," *The Gettysburg Magazine*, No. 3 (July 1990), 9-15.

Cameron, James L. "How Far On Oak Ridge? An Examination of the Planned Deployment of the Eleventh Corps, July 1, 1863," *The Gettysburg Magazine*, 27 (2002), 29-38.

Carpenter, John A. "General O. O. Howard at Gettysburg," *Civil War History*, IX, No. 3 (September 1963), 261-276.

Carroon, Robert G. *From Freeman's Ford to Bentonville: The 61st Ohio Volunteer Infantry* (Shippensburg, PA: Burd Street Press, 1998).

Ceremonies and Addresses at the Dedication of a Monument by the 119th Regiment, N. Y. State Vols. at Gettysburg, July 3, 1888 (Boston: Wright & Potter Printing, 1889).

Cheeks, Robert C. "Failure on the Heights," *America's Civil War*, 42-49.

Cist, Henry M. *The Army of the Cumberland* (Wilmington, NC: Broadfoot, 1989).

Clark, Robert Denning. "From Union Army Volunteer to President of Switzerland," *Civil War Times Illustrated*, April, 1963.

Coco, Gregory A. *On the Bloodstained Field* (Gettysburg, PA: Thomas Publications, 1987).

——. *On the Bloodstained Field II* (Gettysburg, PA: Thomas Publications, 1989)

Coddington, E. B. *The Gettysburg Campaign: A Study in Command* (New York: Charles Scrbiner's Sons, 1968).

Cole, Philip M. *Civil War Artillery at Gettysburg: Organization, Equipment, Ammunition, and Tactics* (Cambridge, MA: Da Capo Press, 2002).

Comte de Paris, *History of the Civil War in America* (Philadelphia: Porter and Coates, 1883), III.

Conklin, George W. "The Long March to Stevens Run: The 134th New York Volunteer Infantry at Gettysburg," *Gettysburg Magazine*, Vol. 21 (July 1999), 45-56.

——. *Under the Crescent and Star: The 134th New York Volunteer Infantry in the Civil War* (Port Reading, NJ: Axworthy Publishing, 1999).

Cooksey, Paul Clark. "Forcing the Issue: Brig. Gen. Henry Hunt at Gettysburg on July 3, 1863," *Gettysburg Magazine*, Vol. 30 (January 2004), 77-88.

——. "The Union Artillery at Gettysburg on July 3," *Gettysburg Magazine*, Vol. 28 (January 2008), 72-90.

Cosgrove, Charles S. *A History of the 134th New York Volunteer Infantry Regiment in the American Civil War 1862-1865: Long Night's Journey into Day* (Lewiston, NY: Edwin Mellen Press, 1997).

Cowell, A. T. *Tactics at Gettysburg, as Described by Participants in the Battle* (Gaithersburg, MD: Olde Soldier Books, Inc., 1987).

Cox, John D. *Culp's Hill: The Attack and Defense of the Union Left Flank July 2, 1863* (Cambridge, MA: Da Capo Press, 2003).

Cozzens, Peter. *The Shipwreck of Their Hopes: The Battles for Chattanooga* (Urbana: University of Illinois Press, 1994).

Creighton, Margaret S. *The Colors of Courage: Gettysburg's Forgotten History. Immigrants, Women, and African Americans in the Civil War's Defining Battle* (New York: Basic Books, 2005).

Croffut, William Augustus. *The Military and Civil History of Connecticut During the War of 1861-65: Comprising a Detailed Account of the Various Regiments and Batteries, through March, Encampment, Bivouac, and Battle: Also Instances of Distinguished Personal Gallantry, and Biographical Sketches of Many Heroic Soldiers: Together With a Record of the Patriotic Action of Citizens at Home, and of the Liberal Support Furnished by the State in Its Executive and Legislative Departments* (New York: Ledyard Bill, 1868).

——. and John M. Morris. *The Military and Civil History of Connecticut During the War of 1861-65* (New York: Ledyard Bill, 1868).

Crumb, Herb S. *The Eleventh Corps Artillery at Gettysburg: The Papers of Major Thomas Ward Osborn Chief of Artillery* (Hamilton, NY: Edmonston Publishing, Inc., 1991).

Cubbison, Douglas R. "Midnight Engagement: Geary's White Star Division at Wauhatchie, Tennessee, October 28-29, 1863," *Civil War Regiments*, Vol. 3, no. 2 (1993), 70-101.

Davis, Burke. *Sherman's March* (New York: Random House, 1980).

Dempsey, Stuart. "'The Heaviest Skirmishing I Have Ever Witnessed': The Fight for 'Smith's Ridge,'" *Blue & Gray Magazine*, XXV:3 (Fall 2008), 44-53.

"Die tapferen unseres 'deutschen' regiments, 1862-1912; goldene jubelfeier der 26er freiwilligen von Wisconsin," *Germania*, August 21, 1912.

Diembach, Andrew. "An Incident at Cemetery Hill," *Blue & Gray*, 2 (July 1983), 21-22.

Dluger, Marc A. "Fighting for the Cause: The 82nd Illinois Volunteer Infantry at the Battle of Gettysburg" (Chicago: Roosevelt University, MA Thesis, 2003).

Downey, Fairfax. *The Guns at Gettysburg* (New York: David McKay Co., 1958).

Dreese, Michael. *Never Desert the Old Flag! 50 Stories of Union Battle Flags and Color-bearers at Gettysburg* (Gettysburg: Thomas Publications, 2002).

Dunkelman, Mark H. "Additional Notes on the 154th New York at Gettysburg," *Gettysburg Magazine*, 29 (July 2003), 71-85.

——. *Brothers One and All: Esprit de Corps in a Civil War Regiment* (Baton Rouge: Louisiana State University Press, 2004).

——. "East Meets West," *North & South*, Vol. 10, No. 1 (May 2007), 48-56.

——. *Gettysburg's Unknown Soldier: The Life, Death, and Celebrity of Amos Humiston* (Westport, CT: Praeger, 1999), 181-82.

——. "Hartack and Sauerkraut Stew: Ethnic Tensions in the 154th New York Volunteers, Eleventh Corps, during the Civil War," *Yearbook of German-American Studies*, Vol. 36 (2001), 69-90.

——. "'We Were Compelled to Cut Our Way Through Them, and in Doing so Our Losses Were Heavy:' Gettysburg Casualties of the 154th New York Volunteers," *Gettysburg Magazine*, 18 (January 1998), 34-56.

——, and Michael J. Winey, *The Hardtack Regiment: An Illustrated History of the 154th Regiment, New York State Infantry Volunteers* (Rutherford, NJ: Fairleigh Dickinson University press, 1981).

——, and Michael J. Winey, "The Hardtack Regiment in the Brickyard Fight," *Gettysburg Magazine*, 8 (January 1993), 16-30.

——, and Michael J. Winey, "The Hunt for Sergeant Humiston," *Civil War Times Illustrated*, XXI:1 (March 1982), 28-31.

Dyer, Frederick H. *A Compendium of the War of the Rebellion* (New York: Thomas Yoseloff, 1959), 3 vols.

Eddy, Thomas Mears. *The Patriotism of Illinois: A Record of the Civil War and Military History of the State in the War for the Union, with a History of the Campaigns in Which Illinois Soldiers Have Been Conspicuous, Sketches of Distinguished Officers, the Roll of the Illustrious Officers, the Roll of the Illustrious Dead, Movements of the Sanitary and Christian Commissions* (Chicago: Clarke & Co., 1865-66), 2 Vols.

Elmore, Thomas L. "Torrid Heat and Blinding Rain: A Meteorological and Astronomical Chronology of the Gettysburg Campaign," *The Gettysburg Magazine*, Vol. 13 (July 1995), 7-19.

Esposito, Vincent J. *The West Point Atlas of American Wars* (New York: Frederick A. Praeger, 1959).

Estabrook. Charles E., ed. *Wisconsin Losses in the Civil War* (Madison: Democrat Printing Company, 1915).

Fanton, Ben. "Battle on the Brickyard Wall," *Civil War Times Illustrated*, XXXIII, No. 4 (September/October, 1994), 34-39.

Fazio, John C. "The Barlow-Gordon Controversy: Rest in Peace," *The Gettysburg Magazine*, 41 (July 2009), 33-54.

Fox, Charles K. *Gettysburg* (New York: A. S. Barner & Co., 1969).

Fox, William F. *New York at Gettysburg* (Albany: J. B. Lyon, 1900).

——. *Regimental Losses in the American Civil War 1861-1865* (Albany: Albany Publishing Company, 1898).

Furqueron, James R. "Point Blank Business," *North & South*, Vol. 5, no. 6 (November 2002), 22-42.

Gambone, A. M. *Hancock at Gettysburg . . . and Beyond* (Baltimore: Butternut and Blue, 1997).

Gannon, James P. *Irish Rebels Confederate Tigers: The 6th Louisiana Volunteers, 1861-1865* (Campbell, CA: Savas Publishing Company, 1998).

——. "The 6th Louisiana Infantry at Gettysburg," *The Gettysburg Magazine*, 21 (July 1999), 88-99.

Gottfried, Bradley M. *Brigades of Gettysburg* (Cambridge, MA: Da Capo Press, 2002).

——. *The Maps of Gettysburg: An Atlas of the Gettysburg Campaign, June 3-July 13, 1863* (New York: Savas Beatie, 2007).

Graham, Martin. *Ohioans at Gettysburg: Ohio Regiments at Gettysburg and How Their Veterans Remembered Their Sacrifice* (n.p.: Martin Graham, 2008).

Greene, A. Wilson. "From Chancellorsville to Cemetery Hill: O. O. Howard and Eleventh Corps Leadership," in Gary Gallagher, ed., *The First Day at Gettysburg: Essays on Confederate and Union Leadership* (Kent, OH: Kent State University Press, 1992), 57-91.

Hamblen, Charles P. *Connecticut Yankees at Gettysburg* (Kent, OH: Kent State University Press, 1993).

Hanna, William F. "A Gettysburg Myth Exploded: The Barlow-Gordon Incident," *Civil War Times Illustrated*, No. 24 (May 1985), 42-47.

Hartwig, D. Scott, "The 11th Army Corps on July 1, 1863—The Unlucky 11th," *The Gettysburg Magazine*, No. 2 (January, 1990), 33-49.

Hassler, Warren W., Jr. *Crisis at the Crossroads: The First Day at Gettysburg* (Gettysburg: Stan Clark Military Books, 1970).

Havens, L. C. *Historical Sketch of the 136th New York Infantry, 1862-1865* (Dalton, NY: Dalton Burts Printing Service, 1934).

Haviland, Richard H. *Splendid Gallantry: The Union Army's XI Corps' German-American Volunteers—Chancellorsville, Gettysburg, Sherman's March* (Charleston, SC: BookSurge, 2006).

Himmer, Robert. "July 1, 1863: George Gordon Meade's Lost Afternoon Re-Examined," *North & South*, Vol. 9, no. 1 (March 2006), 52-64.

Hoke, Jacob. *The Great Invasion of 1863* (Dayton, OH: W. J. S. Huey Publications, 1887).

Hughes, Nathaniel C. *Bentonville: the Final Battle of Sherman and Johnston* (Chapel Hill: University of North Carolina Press, 1996).

Huidekoper, H. S. *A Short Story of the First Day's Fight at Gettysburg* (Philadelphia: Bicking Print., 1906).

Hunt, Roger D. and Jack R. Brown, *Brevet Brigadier Generals in Blue* (Gaithersburg, MD: Olde Soldier Books, Inc., 1990).

Illinois in the War for the Union (Springfield: H. W. Rokker, 1887).

In Memoriam Francis Channing Barlow 1834-1896 (Albany, NY: J. B. Lyon, 1923).

Jones, Terry L. *Cemetery Hill: The Struggle for the High Ground, July 1-3, 1863* (Cambridge, MA: Da Capo Press, 2003).

——. *Lee's Tigers: The Louisiana Infantry in the Army of Northern Virginia* (Baton Rouge: Louisiana State University Press, 2002).

——. *The Civil War Memoirs of Captain William J. Seymour: Reminiscences of a Louisiana Tiger* (Baton Rouge: Louisiana State University Press, 1991).

——. "Twice Lost: The 8th Louisiana Volunteers' Battle Flag at Gettysburg," *Civil War Regiments*, Vol. 6, no. 3 (2009), 89-105.

Jorgensen, Jay. "Joseph W. Latimer: The 'Boy Major' at Gettysburg," *The Gettysburg Magazine*, 9 (July 1993), 29-34.

Katcher, Philip. *American Civil War Artillery, 1861-1865 (1): Field Artillery* (London: Osprey Military, 2001).

Kaufmann, Wilhelm. *Die Deutschen in amerikanischen bürgerkriege* (Munich and Berlin: R. Oldenbourg, 1911).

Keifer, Joseph Warren. *Civil War Regiments from Ohio* (Pensacola, FL: eBooksOnDisk.com, 2004).

Keneally, Thomas. *American Scoundrel: The Life of the Notorious Civil War General Dan Sickles* (New York: Anchor Books, 2003).

Kepf, Kenneth M. "Dilger's Battery at Gettysburg," *The Gettysburg Magazine*, Issue 4 (January 1991), 49-64.

King, Charles. "Frederick C. Winkler, Distinguished Soldier and Citizen," *Historical Messenger of the Milwaukee County Historical Society*, Vol. 23, No. 3 (September, 19167), 89-98.

Klein, Maury. "The Knoxville Campaign," *Civil War Times Illustrated*, Vol. X, no. 6 (October 1971), 4-10, 40-42.

Klement, Frank L. *Wisconsin and the Civil War* (Madison: The State Historical Society of Wisconsin, 1963).

Knoche, Carl H. "Dr. Franz Huebschmann's Political Career," *Historical Messenger of the Milwaukee County Historical Society*, Vol. 28, No. 4 (Winter 1972), 114-31.

Korn, B. C. "The Civil War Drafts in Milwaukee," *Historical Messenger of the Milwaukee County Historical Society*, September 1961, 7-12.

Korn, Bertram W. *American Jewry and the Civil War* (Philadelphia: Jewish Publication Society of America, 1961).

Krolick, Marshall D. "The Union Command: Decisions That Shaped the Battle," *Blue & Gray Magazine*, Vol. V, no. 2, 10-20, 23-55.

Kross, Gary. "The XI Corps at Gettysburg July 1, 1863," *Blue & Gray Magazine*, Vol. XIX, no. 2 (December 2001), 6-24, 48-51.

Kurtz, Henry I. "Dilger's Battery the Best Artillery Unit in the Federal Army? Here's Its Record," *Civil War Times Illustrated*, 1 (November 1962), 38-41.

Ladd, David L. and Audrey J. Ladd, *John Bachelder's History of the Battle of Gettysburg* (Dayton, OH: Morningside, 1997), 3 vols.

Lamers, William M. "A Humble Soldier Dies in Libby Prison," *Lore*, Vol. 11, No. 2 (Spring 1961), 68-72.

Lash, Gary G. *The Gibraltar Brigade on East Cemetery Hill* (Baltimore: Butternut and Blue, 1995).

Law, Sister Loyola, ed. *Annals of the Civil War*, 3 vols. (unpublished ms 1904).

——. "Hero in Blue," *Lore*, Vol. 10, No 1 (Winter 1959), 26-28.

Lovenstein, Lochard H. *In Lieu of A Draft: A History of the 153rd Pennsylvania Volunteer Regiment* (Bloomington, IN: AuthorHouse, 2012).

Livermore, Thomas Leonard. "Memoir of Theodore Ayrault Dodge," *Proceedings October, 1909—June, 1910* (Boston: Massachusetts Historical Society, 1910).

Lonn, Ella. *Foreigners in the Union Army and Navy* (Baton Rouge: Louisiana State University Press, 1951).

Love, William DeLoss. *Wisconsin in the War of the Rebellion; A History of all Regiments and Batteries the State Has Sent to the Field, and Deeds of Her Citizens, Governors and Other Military Officers, and State and National Legislators to Suppress the Rebellion* (Chicago: Church and Goodman, Publishers, 1866).

Lowery, Roland. *The Story of Battery I First Regiment Ohio Volunteer Light Artillery, 1861-1865* (Cincinnati: Published by the Author, 1971).

Luvaas, Jay, and Harold W. Nelson. *U.S. Army War College Guide to the Battle of Gettysburg* (Carlisle, PA: South Mountain Press, 1986).

Macaluso, Gregory J. *Morris, Orange and King William Artillery* (Lynchburg, VA: H. E. Howard, Inc., 1991).

Mahin, Dean B. *The Blessed Place of Freedom: Europeans in Civil War America* (Washington, DC: Brassey's, Inc., 2002).

Marszalek, John F. *Commander of All Lincoln's Armies: A Life of General Henry W. Halleck* (Cambridge, MA: Belknap Press of Harvard University Press, 2004).

Martin, David G. *Carl Bornemann's Regiment. The Forty-First New York Infantry* (DeKalb Regiment) in the Civil War (Highstown, NJ: Longstreet House, 1987).

——. *Gettysburg July 1* (Conshohocken, PA: Combined Books, 1995).

Martin, Samuel J. *The Road to Glory. Confederate General Richard S. Ewell* (Indianapolis: Guild Press of Indiana, Inc.).

McBride, Jerry. "Ethnic Groups and the Civil War" Box-30, GNMP.

McDonough, James Lee. *Chattanooga—A Death Grip on the Confederacy* (Knoxville: University of Tennessee Press, 1984).

Miers, Earl Schenck and Richard A. Brown, *Gettysburg* (New Brunswick: Rutgers University Press, 1948).

Mitchell, Robert Dale, and Robert Hoffsommer, "The Rise and Survival of Private Mesnard—Part II," *Civil War Times Illustrated*, Vol. XXIV, no. 10 (February 1986).

Moore, Allison. *The Louisiana Tigers* (Baton Rouge: Ortlieb Press, 1961).

Murray, R. L. *A Perfect Storm of Lead: George Sears Greene's New York Brigade in Defense of Culp's Hill* (Wolcott, NY: Benedum Books, 2000).

——. "The 157th New York Volunteers at Gettysburg," *The Gettysburg Magazine*, 40 (January 2009), 29-41.

Naisawald, L. Van Loan. *Grape and Canister: The Story of the Field Artillery of the Army of the Potomac* (New York: Oxford University Press, 1960).

Niven, John. *Connecticut for the Union: The Role of the State in the Civil War* (New Haven: Yale University Press, 1965).

Nofi, Albert A. *The Gettysburg Campaign June-July 1863* (Conshohocken, PA: Combined Books, 1986).

Nye, Wilbur S. "Lieutenant General Richard S. Ewell in the Gettysburg Campaign," paper presented at the Fifth Annual Civil War Study Group, Gettysburg College, July 26, 1962.

Öfele, Martin W. *True Sons of the Republic: European Immigrants in the Union Army* (Westport, CT: Praeger, 2008).

Ohio Memorials at Gettysburg (Baltimore, MD: Butternut and Blue, 1998), reprint of *Report of the Gettysburg Memorial Commission* (Columbus, OH: Nitschke Bros., 1887).

Osten, Walter. "Dr. Francis Huebschmann: The Cultured Pioneer and Framer of Our State Constitution," *The Milwaukee Turner*, IV, No. 2 (February 1943).

Pennsylvania at Gettysburg (Harrisburg: William Stanley Ray, 1919).

Pfanz, Donald. *Richard S. Ewell, a Soldier's Life* (Chapel Hill: University of North Carolina Press, 1998).

Pfanz, Harry W. *Gettysburg: Culp's Hill & Cemetery Hill* (Chapel Hill: University of North Carolina Press, 1993).

——. *Gettysburg: The First Day* (Chapel Hill, NC: University of North Carolina Press, 2001).

——. *Gettysburg: The Second Day* (Chapel Hill: University of North Carolina Press, 1987).

Phisterer, Frederick. *New York in the War of the Rebellion, 1861-1865* (Albany: Weed, 1890), 5 vols.

Pickenpaugh, Roger. *Rescue by Rail: Troop Transfer and the Civil War in the West 1863* (Lincoln: University of Nebraska Press, 1998).

Pohlsander, Hans A. "Adolph von Steinwehr: A Neglected Civil War General," *The Report 45. A Journal of German-American History*, XLV, 2004, 81-99.

Popchock, Barry. "German-born Artillerist Hubert Dilger Was as Tough as His Nickname 'Leatherbreeches' Implied," *America's Civil War*, 1 (January 1989), 10, 62-63.

Powles, James M. "New Jersey's Western Warriors," *America's Civil War*, September 2001, 46-52.

Pula, James S. "'Bullets Thick as Hail': The 26th Wisconsin Volunteer Infantry at Gettysburg," *Gettysburg Magazine*, 23 (January 2000), 76-87.

——. "Fighting for Time: Carl Schurz on the First Day at Gettysburg," *Gettysburg Magazine*, 35 (July 2006), 26-35.

——. *For Liberty and Justice: The Life and Times of Wladimir Krzyzanowski* (Chicago: Polish American Congress Charitable Foundation, 1978).

——. *For Liberty and Justice: A Biography of Brigadier General Wlodzimierz B. Krzyzanowski, 1824-1887* (Utica, NY: Ethnic Heritage Studies Center, Utica College, 2008).

——. "The Fifth German Rifles at Gettysburg," *Gettysburg Magazine*, 37 (July 2007). 50-70.

——. *The History of a German-Polish Civil War Brigade* (San Francisco: R & E Research, 1976).

——. "The Sigel Regiment," *German-American Studies*, Vol. 8 (1974), 27-52.

——. *The Sigel Regiment: A History of the 26th Wisconsin Volunteer Infantry, 1862-1865* (Campbell, CA: Savas Woodbury Publishers, 1997).

Quiner, E. B. *The Military History of Wisconsin: A Record of the Civil and Military Patriotism of the State, in the War for the Union* (Chicago: Clarke & Co., Publishers, 1866).

Rattermann, H. A. "Adolph von Steinwehr," *Der deutsche Pionier*, Vol. 9 (1877), 17-29, 160-66.

Raus, Edmund J., Jr. *A Generation on the March—The Union Army at Gettysburg* (Lynchburg, VA: H. E. Howard, Inc., 1987).

Reid, Whitelaw. *Ohio in the War: Her Statesmen, Her Generals, and Soldiers* (Cincinnati: Moore, Wilstack & Baldwin, 1868), 2 Vols.

Remington, Cyrus Kingsbury. *A Record of Battery I, First N.Y. Light Artillery Vols.: Otherwise Known as Wiedrich's Battery, during the War of the Rebellion, 1861-65* (Buffalo: Press of the Courier Co., 1891).

Rich, Earle. *Cape Cod Echoes* (Orleans, MA: Salt Meadow Publishers, 1973).

Rollins, Richard. *"The Damned Red Flags of the Rebellion": The Confederate Battle Flag at Gettysburg* (Redondo Beach, CA: Rank and File Publications, 1997).

Rosengarten, J. G. *The German Soldier in the Wars of the United States* (Philadelphia: Lippincott, 1886).

Sallee, Scott E. "Women's Memorial Dedicated at Gettysburg," *Blue & Gray Magazine*, Vol. XX, no. 2 (Holiday 2002), 31-32.

Sandburg, Carl. *Abraham Lincoln: The War Years* (New York: Harcourt, Brace & World, Inc., 1939), 4 vols.

Sauers, Richard A. *Advance the Colors! Pennsylvania Civil War Battle Flags* (Harrisburg: Capitol Preservation Commission, 1987), Vols. I and II.

Sauers, Richard A. and Peter Tomasak, *Ricketts' Battery: A History of Battery F, 1st Pennsylvania Light Artillery* (np: Luzerne National Bank, 2001).

Schafer, Joseph. *Carl Schurz Militant Liberal* (Madison: State Historical Society of Wisconsin, 1930).

Schlicher, J. J. "Bernhard Domschcke. I. A Life of Hardship," *Magazine of Wisconsin History*, March, 1946, 319-32.

——. "Bernhard Domschcke. II. The Editor and the Man," *Magazine of Wisconsin History*, June, 1946, 435-56.

Schultz, David. "Benner's Hill: What Value? Andrews' Artillery Battalion and the Heights East of Town," *The Gettysburg Magazine*, 44 (January 2011), 56-60, 68.

Sears, Stephen W. *Gettysburg* (Boston: Houghton Mifflin Company, 2003).

Sefton, James E. "Gettysburg: An Exercise in the Evaluation of Historical Evidence," *Military Affairs*, Vol. 28, no. 2 (Summer 1964), 64-72.

Sherrill, Lee W., Jr. *The 21st North Carolina Infantry: A Civil War History, with a Roster of Officers* (Jefferson, NC: McFarland Publishers, 2015).

Simonhoff, Harry. *Jewish Participants in the Civil War* (New York: Arco Publishing Co., Inc., 1963).

Spieß, Emil. *Illustrierte Geschichte der Schweiz* (Zürich, Switzerland: Benziger Verlag, 1961).

Stackpole, Edward J. *They Met at Gettysburg* (Harrisburg: Stackpole Books, 1996).

Stahl, Joseph. "Pvt. John Wright of the 61st Ohio," *The Gettysburg Magazine*, No. 38 (2008), 56-58.

Steele, Matthew F. *American Campaigns* (Washington: The Telegraph Press, 1909).

Stine, James H. *History of the Army of the Potomac* (Washington, DC: Gibson, 1893).

Styple, William B. *Generals in Bronze* (Kearny, NJ: Belle Grove Publishing Company. 2005).

Swinton, William. *Campaigns of the Army of the Potomac. A Critical History of Operations in Virginia, Maryland and Pennsylvania From the Commencement to the Close of the War, 1861-1865* (New York: Scribners, 1882).

Swisher, James K. "Brig. Gen. George Doles and His Georgia Brigade on July 1, 1863, Gettysburg, Pennsylvania," *The Gettysburg Magazine*, 27 (July 2002), 39-51.

Sword, Wiley. *Mountains Touched with Fire: Chattanooga Besieged, 1863* (New York: St. Martin's Press, 1995).

——. "Personal Battle Weapons of the Civil War: Defending Cemetery Hill: Two Massachusetts Captains Wield Their Personal Weapons Amid the Great Crisis," *The Gettysburg Magazine*, 19 (July 1998), 94-99.

Tagg, Larry. *The Generals of Gettysburg: The Leaders of America's Greatest Battle* (Campbell, CA: Savas Publishing Company, 1998).

Taylor, Frank H. *Philadelphia in the Civil War* (Philadelphia: The City, 1913).

Thomas, Henry W. *History of the Doles-Cook Brigade of Northern Virginia, C.S.A.; Containing Muster Roles of Each Company of the Fourth, Twelfth, Twenty-first and Forty-fourth Georgia Regiments, with a Short Sketch of the Services of Each Member, and a Complete History of Each Regiment, by One of its Own Members* (Atlanta: Franklin Publishing and Printing Co., 1903).

Tomasak, Pete. "An Encounter with Battery Hell," *The Gettysburg Magazine*, 12 (January 1995), 30-41.

Trefousse, Hans L. *Carl Schurz. A Biography* (Knoxville: University of Tennessee Press, 1982).

Tucker, Glenn. "The Battles for Chattanooga," *Civil War Times Illustrated*, Vol. X, no. 5 (August 1971), 3-45.

——. *High Tide at Gettysburg: The Campaign in Pennsylvania* (New York: Barnes & Noble Books, 2004).

Trudeau, Noah Andre. "Taking Aim at Cemetery Hill," *America's Civil War*, July 2001, 46-53.

Urban, Richard. "Absolutely Essential to Victory: Brig. Gen. George S. Greene's Brigade and the Fight for Culp's Hill," *The Gettysburg Magazine*, 40 (January 2009), 54-60.

Valuska, David L. and Christian B. Keller. *Damn Dutch: Pennsylvania Germans at Gettysburg* (Mechanicsburg, PA: Stackpole Books, 2004).

Van Horne, Thomas Budd. *History of the Army of the Cumberland: Its Organization, Campaigns, and Battles, Written at the Request of Major-General George H. Thomas Chiefly from His Private Military Journal and Official and Other Documents Furnished by Him* (Cincinnati: R. Clarke & Co., 1875).

Vanderslice, John M. *Gettysburg: Where and How the Regiments Fought, and the Troops They Encountered* (Philadelphia: J. B. Lippincott Co., 1897).

Wallace, Frederick Stephen. *The Sixty-First Ohio Volunteers, 1861-1865* (Marysville, OH: Theodore Mullen, 1902).

Weaver, Ethen Allen. *Owen Rice* (Christian, Scholar and Patriot). A Genealogical, Biographical and Historical Memoir (Germantown, PA: Privately Printed, 1911).

Welch, Richard F. "Encounter on Blocher's Knoll," *America's Civil War*, March 2004, 46-51.

——. *The Boy General: The Life and Careers of Francis Channing Barlow* (Kent & London: Kent State University Press, 2003).

Welsh, Jack D. *Medical Histories of Union Generals* (Kent, OH: Kent State University Press, 1996).

Wittke, Carl Frederick. *Refugees of Revolution: The German Forty-Eighters in America* (Philadelphia: University of Pennsylvania Press, 1952).

Woods, James A. "The 17th Connecticut and 41st New York: A Revisionist History of the Defense of East Cemetery Hill," *The Gettysburg Magazine*, 28 (January 2003), 87-97.

Yee, Gary. "Sharpshooting at Gettysburg," *The Gettysburg Magazine*, 39 (2008), 45-62.

Young, Jesse Bowman. *Battle of Gettysburg: A Comprehensive Narrative* (New York: Harper & Brothers Publishers, 1913).

Zinn, John G. *The Mutinous Regiment: The Thirty-third New Jersey in the Civil War* (Jefferson, NC: McFarland & Company, 2005).

Zucker, A. E. *The Forty-Eighters; Political Refugees of the German Revolution of 1848*. New York: Columbia University Press, 1950.

Index

James S. Pula is Professor of History at Purdue University Northwest. The author and editor of more than two dozen books on immigration history and the American Civil War, he is currently the editor-in-chief of *Gettysburg Magazine.*

Among his books on Civil War topics are: *For Liberty and Justice: A Biography of Brig. Gen. Wlodzimierz B. Krzyzanowski* (Ethnic Heritage Studies Series distributed by Syracuse University Press, 2008); *The Sigel Regiment: A History of the 26th Wisconsin Volunteer Infantry, 1862-1865* (Savas Publishers, 1998; Winner of the Gambrinus Prize in History from the Milwaukee County Historical Society); *With Courage and Honor: The Role of Oneida County in the Civil War* (Ethnic Heritage Studies Series distributed by Syracuse University Press, 2010); *The Memoirs of Ludwik Zychlinski* (Columbia University Press, East European Monographs, 1993); *The Memoirs of Wladimir Krzyzanowski* (R&E Research, 1978), and *Under the Crescent Moon with the XI Corps in the Civil War, vol. 1: From the Defenses of Washington to Chancellorsville, 1862-1863* (Savas Beatie, 2017).